CW00517901

# TOBACCO COAST

## Publisher's Note

Works published as part of the Maryland Paperback Bookshelf are, we like to think, books that have stood the test of time. They are classics of a kind, so we reprint them today as they appeared when first published many years ago. While some social attitudes have changed and knowledge of our surroundings has increased, we believe that the value of these books as literature, as history, and as timeless perspectives on our region remains undiminished.

*Also available in the series:*

*The Amiable Baltimoreans* by Francis F. Beirne
*The Bay* by Gilbert C. Klingel

*A tobacco wharf along the shores of the Chesapeake, c. 1750, by Elmo Jones, after Charles Grignion's engraving of Francis Hayman's cartouche on the Fry and Jefferson* Map of Virginia and Maryland, *London, 1751.*

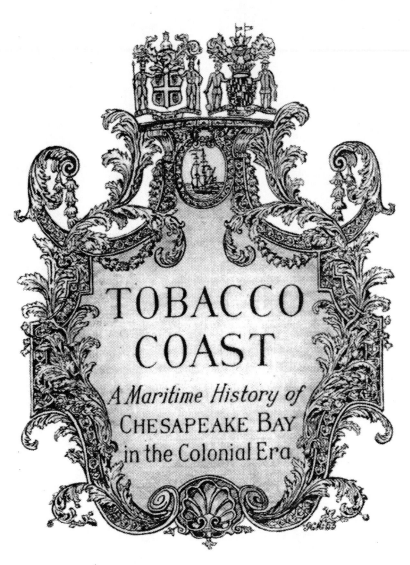

# TOBACCO COAST

*A Maritime History of*
CHESAPEAKE BAY
in the Colonial Era

*by* ARTHUR PIERCE MIDDLETON

The Johns Hopkins University Press
BALTIMORE AND LONDON
*and*
The Maryland State Archives

This book has been brought to publication with the generous assistance
of the Maryland State Archives.

Originally published by The Mariners' Museum,
Newport News, Virginia, in 1953
Foreword to the Maryland Paperback Bookshelf edition © 1984
by The Johns Hopkins University Press
All rights reserved
Printed in the United States of America

The Johns Hopkins University Press, Baltimore, Maryland 21218
The Johns Hopkins Press Ltd., London

*The paper in this book is acid-free and meets the guidelines for
permanence and durability of the Committee on Production Guidelines
for Book Longevity of the Council on Library Resources.*

Library of Congress Cataloging in Publication Data
Middleton, Arthur Pierce.
Tobacco coast.

(Maryland paperback bookshelf)
Reprint. Originally published: Newport News, Va.:
Mariners' Museum, c1953. With a new foreword.
Bibliography: p.
Includes index.
1. Chesapeake Bay Region (Md. and Va.)—History, Naval.
2. Shipping—Chesapeake Bay Region (Md. and Va.)—History.
3. Navigation—Chesapeake Bay Region (Md. and Va.)—
History.   4. Tobacco manufacture and trade—Chesapeake
Bay Region (Md. and Va.)—History.   5. Chesapeake Bay
Region (Md. and Va.)—Commerce.   I. Title.   II. Series.
F187.C5M5   1984   975.2   84-47962
ISBN 0-8018-2534-2 (pbk.: alk. paper)

TO

MY FATHER AND MOTHER

WHOSE FOREBEARS FOR TEN GENERATIONS

LIVED AND MOVED AND

HAD THEIR BEING

IN THE "DELIGHTSOME LANDS" THAT ENCOMPASS

THE GREAT BAY OF CHESAPEAKE

THERE is something so grave and solemn in History, that it necessarily affects the honest Reader with that awful Respect, which an impartial Historian always pays to Truth; for if the Writer keeps a strict Guard over his Passions, not suffering them to be any ways interested in the Facts and Circumstances which he is indispensably obliged to relate, though some few may wish that several Things had not been so openly exposed to public View; yet the impartial Reader will, doubtless, approve the Author's Candor, and make use of the Mirror set before him, to correct for the future, according to his own Judgment and Ability, the Errors of former Times.

Sir William Keith, *The History of the British Plantations in America*. Part I, *Containing the History of Virginia*. London, 1738. Page 2.

# Foreword

Arthur Pierce Middleton's *Tobacco Coast* is a classic. In it the mighty Chesapeake unfolds in a grand panorama. This is a story of the courage and ingenuity of the men and women who faced enormous odds in search of a better life in America. Sickness, failure, and death were often their reward. But the infant settlements on the banks of the Chesapeake Bay survived, and in time a unique society was born, grew, and prospered. There is drama here, skillfully told by a master of his craft. *Tobacco Coast* endures as a superb history of the Chesapeake Bay. It remains unsurpassed in scope, content, and style.

This is an economic history, and Pierce Middleton develops two themes that have powerfully influenced subsequent study of the Chesapeake Bay region. With a compelling command of primary sources, Middleton argues, first, that the Chesapeake Bay was the "principal factor in the development of Virginia and Maryland." The Bay and its hundreds of miles of navigable tributaries made adoption of the tobacco staple possible, eliminated the need for cities and towns, and perpetuated a social and cultural dependence on Great Britain. Second, Middleton argues that the Bay's physical dominance of the area created an "essential unity" of the colonies that shared its shores, despite the political decisions that created the separate colonies of Maryland and Virginia.

Two generations of historians have tested Middleton's seminal propositions in dozens of articles and theses. After thirty years' assessment, certain refinements and elaborations have been made. But Middleton's views on the overriding importance of the Chesapeake Bay in the region's development, and on the fundamental similarity of the economic structure of Maryland and Virginia, remain unchallenged.

While this is a milestone in the economic history of the Chesapeake Bay region, more often than not the reader turns to *Tobacco Coast* for the details of everyday life that cram its pages. Middleton's knowledge of the lives of the mariners, merchants, and planters who sailed to and settled in the Chesapeake Bay country is nearly encyclopedic. Ship construction and navigation techniques, import and export regulations, pirates and privateers, and the trade to Europe, Africa, and the West Indies are only a few of the diverse but interrelated topics covered.

Described as "monumental" when it was published in 1953, *Tobacco Coast* has been an indispensable source of information and inspiration for over three decades, and in fact it is probably better appreciated today than when it first appeared. The trend in the study of Chesapeake history since the 1960s has been toward microeconomic analysis—concentrated examination of carefully defined populations in relatively confined geographic areas. In comparison, Middleton's *Tobacco Coast* is grand opera, with elaborate costuming, frequent changes of scenery, and a cast of thousands. It describes the setting, broad in scope and rich in detail, that provides the context necessary to fully appreciate more recent studies in Chesapeake history.

The single problem with Middleton's *Tobacco Coast* is that for years it has been out of print and virtually unobtainable. My own experience in searching for a copy illustrates the point. I decided to buy a copy of *Tobacco Coast* in 1973, shortly after I began my first job as a historian on the research staff of the Colonial Williamsburg Foundation in Williamsburg, Virginia. The book was still listed in *Books in Print* at the modest price of five dollars. I sent a check to the publisher and received a prompt but disheartening reply that the book had recently gone out of print. Surely I would now have to pay double its original price at a local bookstore!

Eight years later I possessed a substantial collection of both standard and uncommon titles in Chesapeake history, but a copy of *Tobacco Coast* still eluded me.

My conception of what was a reasonable price for the book

*Foreword*

had been redefined from five or ten dollars, to thirty or forty, then fifty or sixty. Since my wife was in the rare book field, I had access to hundreds of catalogs for rare and out-of-print books each year. *Tobacco Coast* appeared infrequently, however, and when a decent copy did turn up it was always gone by the time I called the dealer.

But one spring day in 1981, while on vacation in Williamsburg, I stopped in at my favorite rare book store in town. Scanning the shelves my eyes riveted on the elusive but familiar thick brown spine with gold lettering. It was an immaculate copy of *Tobacco Coast*, but the book's fine condition suggested the necessity of shortening the vacation to meet its asking price. But the penciled number inside the front cover was affordable— mismarked according to the shop manager—and at long last Middleton's *Tobacco Coast* was mine! My euphoria at finding the book, in the town where my search for it had begun eight years before, was heightened later in the day when on a Williamsburg street I happened upon fellow vacationers from Annapolis, Dr. and Mrs. Arthur Pierce Middleton.

This recounting of my own quest for a copy of *Tobacco Coast* is not intended as justification for the reprinting that follows. Reprinting the book is intended to do more than satisfy the passions of bibliophiles. *Tobacco Coast* is, quite simply, a very good book with enduring value. Middleton brought together a commanding knowledge of the subject with a felicitous writing style. The result is a book that is not only full of valuable information and insights, but also one that is eminently readable by both the specialist and the generalist.

The very high price commanded by *Tobacco Coast* in the out-of-print book market (a recent catalogue headlined a "RARE APPEARANCE OF MIDDLETON'S TOBACCO COAST" at $85) is a testament to the book's lasting importance. The Maryland State Archives and the Maryland Hall of Records Commission, with support from the Maryland Heritage Committee, are therefore pleased to join the Johns Hopkins University Press in sponsoring

## Foreword

this reprinting of *Tobacco Coast*. Not only will the book be available once more at a reasonable price, but collectors should benefit as well. I spent so many years searching for *Tobacco Coast*, and ultimately found such a pristine copy, that I have steadfastly refused to remove it from its place in the glass-doored bookcase reserved for my choicest acquisitions. Now even I can again enjoy surveying with the author the lives of the stalwart adventurers who braved the Atlantic crossing and the history of the distinctive society they created in the land that was to become the Tobacco Coast.

Gregory A. Stiverson
*Maryland State Archives*

*4 July 1984*

# Foreword to the First Edition

THE reader is entitled at the outset to know the sad truth that I have never found the expression "Tobacco Coast" in any colonial document pertaining to the Chesapeake country. Yet I like to think that English tobacco merchants sitting over their steaming bowls of coffee and puffing churchwarden pipes in the Virginia and Maryland Coffee House, near the Royal Exchange, London, referred informally to their commercial activities along the Tobacco Coast, much as the merchants trading to Africa spoke of the Grain Coast, Ivory Coast, Gold Coast, and Slave Coast to designate areas along the Gulf of Guinea from Sierra Leone to Nigeria in accordance with their principal exports to Europe.

But whether it was used in the eighteenth century or not, the expression is admirably adapted to my purposes. It epitomizes Great Britain's mercantile interest in the Cheasapeake colonies and places emphasis on the maritime rather than the territorial aspect of colonial Virginia and Maryland, and on the commercial rather than the agricultural aspect of the history of tobacco.

Just as a condemned criminal used to be permitted to speak to the crowd gathered to watch him hang, so, by ancient custom, an author is allowed to state his purpose and define the scope of his work before the reviewers pull the trap and leave him dangling at the end of a rope. And I mean to avail myself of the opportunity to speak before anyone cuts the ground out from under me.

My purpose is to deal with every aspect of the maritime history of colonial Virginia and Maryland and thereby to show how Chesapeake Bay and its many tributaries profoundly influenced the historical development of those colonies by providing a natural system of waterways that facilitated rapid settlement, made possible the large-scale production of tobacco, rendered seaports unnecessary below the fall line, and presented Virginia and Maryland with problems of internal transportation and of naval defense quite unlike those of other British American colonies. As a by-product, the study reveals the fact—often neglected by historians —that the Chesapeake Bay country, despite its division into two colonies, remained a single economic and physiographic unit.

Chronologically, this study is concerned with the period when a mature and normal colonial relationship existed between the tobacco colonies and the Mother Country. Consequently, I have dealt lightly with the early seventeenth century, and avoided the events after 1763 that are a function of revolt against rather than conformity to the British imperial system—I refer to such things as the non-importation agreements. Occasional references to earlier or later events have been made for illustrative purposes, but my chief emphasis is on the middle period, roughly from the Restoration of Charles II in 1660 to the Treaty of Paris in 1763.

Lastly, I do not claim literary merit for this work. My reason for allowing it to be published at all in its present state is simply that I have been persuaded that its contents, rather than its form, are of immediate value and use to others who are interested in the subject. An active life affords me little leisure to tinker with the manuscript. Under the circumstances, to withhold it from the public indefinitely in order to lavish time and thought on the style strikes me as being a form of pride ill-becoming one of my cloth. So I offer it to the public for what it is worth, with no illusions on my part as to its literary quality, in the hope that it will interest others in the history of Chesapeake Bay and revive in both Virginians and Marylanders a love of salt water and a just pride in their own maritime traditions.

o     o     o

It is with pleasure that I take this opportunity to acknowledge my debt to others. First, to Samuel Eliot Morison, and in particular to his stimulating *Maritime History of Massachusetts,* I owe the inspiration for this work which began as a doctoral dissertation at Harvard under Professor Morison. Secondly, to Colonial Williamsburg I am indebted for a fellowship for the year 1940-41 and a research associateship 1942-46, interrupted by three and a half years of service in the United States Coast Guard, and to the Institute of Early American History and Culture, Williamsburg, Virginia, for the post of research associate 1946-48.

Among the persons who have given me help and advice are the late Dr. Hunter D. Farish, my predecessor as Director of Research for Colonial Williamsburg; Professor Emeritus Thomas J. Wertenbaker of Princeton who justly ranks as the Dean of Virginia historians; Lieutenant Commander Marion V. Brewington, USNR (Ret.), of Cambridge, Maryland, foremost of Chesapeake maritime historians; and Drs. Carl Bridenbaugh and Lester J. Cappon, my former colleagues in the Institute of Early American History.

For assistance in finding material in the course of my research, I am indebted to Dr. Earl G. Swem, Librarian Emeritus, to Mr. John Jennings, formerly in charge of rare books and manuscripts, and to Mrs. Rose Belk, of the Library of the College of William and Mary; to Miss C. W. Evans, Librarian Emeritus of the Mariners' Museum, Newport News, Virginia; to the Rev. Clayton Torrence and Mrs. J. A. Johnston of the Virginia Historical Society; to Dr. St. George Leakin Sioussat, Dr. Grace Gardner Griffin, and Mr. Burton W. Adkinson of the Library of Congress; to Mr. Thomas M. Pitkin, formerly Superintendent of the Colonial National Historical Park, Yorktown, Virginia; to Dr. Morris L. Radoff, Archivist, and Miss Elizabeth Meade, formerly Assistant Archivist, of the Hall of Records, Annapolis; to Dr. Raphael Semmes and Miss Florence J. Kennedy of the Maryland Historical Society; to Mr. Robert C. Hill of the manuscript division of the New York Public Library; and to the staffs of the Virginia and Maryland State Libraries.

I wish also to acknowledge the courtesy of Dr. Douglass Adair, editor of the *William and Mary Quarterly,* in granting permission to reprint Chapter Ten which appeared as an article in the

## Foreword to the First Edition

*Quarterly* in April, 1946; of the Maryland Historical Society, in granting permission to reproduce the cartouche of their Walter Hoxton chart, as adapted to the title-page design; and of Mr. Walter Muir Whitehill and Mr. Alexander Crosby Brown, editors of *The American Neptune*, in extending valuable help and encouragement.

Lastly, I wish to commend the Mariners' Museum, and in particular Mr. George Carrington Mason, its editor of publications, for undertaking to edit and publish this study. And I wish to thank my colleagues in the Research Department, Mrs. Rutherfoord Goodwin, Miss Mary Stephenson, and Miss Fanona Knox for their co-operation and help.

A.P.M.

*Epiphanytide, 1951*

# Contents

# Illustrations

# *Part I*

## SEA AND BAY

## CHAPTER ONE

# Ocean Passage

"IN the Name of the Father son and holy Ghost . . . Amen," wrote William Fitzhugh of Stafford County, Virginia, in 1700, "being by GOD's grace bound for England and knowing the frailty and Uncertainty of Man's life . . . [I] do now Ordain, Constitute and Appoint this my last will and Testament."[1] And well he might draw up his will in preparation for a voyage to the Mother Country, for the Atlantic Ocean in the seventeenth and eighteenth centuries was a formidable body of water, accorded more respect by those who would cross it than is the case today. Life at best was uncertain, and the chances of safe arrival at one's destination were none too good.

In view of the apprehension that haunted the minds of persons about to embark on a transatlantic voyage, it is not surprising that there were no gaiety, no confetti and no paper streamers. Gravity and seriousness marked the departure of a vessel. Thomas Chalkley, about to sail from Gravesend for Maryland in 1699, observed that the passengers and their relatives took solemn leave of each other, "as never expecting to see each other any more in this world."[2]

The most terrifying part of crossing the Atlantic was the danger from the frequent storms that raged at sea, especially off Cape Hatteras. Christopher Newport's little fleet experienced a "vehement tempest" off the American coast, and so did Leonard Calvert's *Ark* and *Dove*. Father Andrew White, who came in the *Ark,* wrote about the clouds that gathered in a "fearefull manner, terrible to the beholders." Even before the storm struck, it seemed to him that "all the Sprights and witches of Maryland" were in battle array against the ship. At the height of the gale a violent squall split the mainsail, after which the crew bound up the helm and left the vessel to the mercy of the wind and waves, "till God were pleased to take pittie upon her."[3]

3

Another Jesuit, Father Fitzherbert, bound to Maryland, ran into a "fearful storm" a little west of the Azores. Shattered by the violent waves, the vessel sprang a dangerous leak. As the hold filled with water, the crew and passengers sweated at the great pump in ceaseless labor, day and night. According to the reverend father, the storm continued for the space of two months, giving rise to the belief that it was the product, not of natural causes, but of the malevolence of witches. The frenzied ship's company eventually seized and slew a little old woman suspected of sorcery, then cast her body and possessions into the sea, but the winds did not "remit their violence, or the raging sea its threatenings."[4]

Storms at sea often carried away topgallantmasts, topmasts, and yards, ripped sails, broke rudders, started timbers, and sprung masts. Such accidents generally diminished the speed of vessels, lengthened their passage, and added to the cost of the voyage if refitting became necessary. Completely disabled vessels sailing alone faced serious peril at the mercy of the waves until they could sight another ship, attract its attention, and secure assistance. The ship *Josiah* in 1700 met with a storm off the Azores that carried away the mainmast, sprung the foremast, and broke the crossjack yard. After "rowling upon the Sea" for about two weeks, she was fortunate enough to sight the ship *Bristol Merchant,* which lent her a spare topmast. Stepping this in place of her mainmast and using her own topgallantmast for a topmast, the *Josiah* completed her passage to the Chesapeake.[5]

Similarly, a merchant vessel on an eastward passage in 1759 broke its tiller. Sighting seven ships lying-to, the disabled vessel succeeded in attracting the attention of one of them, a man-of-war, which offered to provide materials for a makeshift tiller, but the sea ran so high that sixty-six hours elapsed before the warship's carpenter could be sent aboard. Meanwhile the merchantman suffered further damage from the heavy sea, which carried away the port rails, the binnacle, and the top of the companionway, split and started the stringers,[6] planeshear,[7] and upper strake of the quickwork,[8] broke the caboose[9] to pieces, washed the sailors' sea chests overboard, and smashed the longboat.[10]

Other vessels disabled at sea were less fortunate in securing assistance. In many cases they foundered and left no trace behind them, or the people on board perished for want of provisions, leaving battered derelicts subsequently sighted by other vessels too late to render effective assistance. The ill-fated ship *Delaware* sailed from Gravesend March 21, 1749, bound for Philadelphia, and encountered a violent storm at sea which opened her seams. Pumping continuously from April 10 until May 21, the crew failed to control the leak. When sighted and offered help by the snow *Brazil* of Whitehaven, bound for Maryland, the crew of the *Delaware*, being "all jaded," unanimously agreed to abandon ship and so left her sinking.[11]

Storms at sea occasionally caused such pitching and rolling that the cargo or ballast shifted, laying the unhappy vessel on her beam ends. In such extremities the vessels were usually righted by cutting away the mainmast. As masters resorted to such drastic expedients only after all else had failed, upon reaching port they invariably swore out statements supported by the depositions of their mates, boatswains, and one or more sailors, before a provincial or county justice, setting forth the circumstances. Then they carried these statements to the secretary of the colony, if in Virginia, or to the deputy notary public, if in Maryland, who, at their request, issued the customary "solemn protest" against wind and waves, thereby absolving the captains from the implication that the loss of masts and rigging, the cost of refitting, and the damage sustained by the cargo were due to their negligence or carelessness.

Masters followed the same procedure whenever a vessel was damaged in its timbers, rigging, furniture, or cargo, or even suspected of being damaged. The schooner *Charming Polly* of Barbados struck a "Great Sea and hard Gale of Wind" while bound for Maryland with a cargo of rum. Trying the pump and finding that the water smelt strong, a mariner tasted it and found that it was rum, several hogsheads having been stove by the rolling of the schooner. Upon reaching Annapolis, the master swore out a deposition before a provincial justice, carried it to John Brice, the Deputy Notary Public of Maryland, and received from him a protest against "Wind and Sea," relieving the captain of all responsibility.[12] The ship *Chester* of Bristol, loaded with bale goods for Maryland, met with bad weather in her passage in 1749. Heaving-to under a reefed mainsail, the vessel rode out the storm without losing any masts or spars. But she suffered such a battering that upon reaching port the mate and a mariner deposed that they had "great Suspicion" that the cargo sustained injury from the great quantities of water that had come into the ship. In consequence, the notary public issued an instrument of protest against wind and sea, relieving the crew of responsibility for damage even before it was ascertained that there was any.[13]

In addition to imperilling ships and damaging cargo, storms at sea made the passengers extremely uncomfortable. Apart from frightening such landlubbers to the marrow, storms forced them to spend days and even weeks huddled together in crowded, evil-smelling quarters while the vessel tossed about like a cork upon the waves. When vessels sprang serious leaks, passengers sometimes had to stand their turn at the pumps day and night. Even without this indignity their lot was hard enough. Cooking was impossible in rough weather and many voyagers were too seasick to eat even the simple fare that was put before them. In 1708, Ebenezer Cook summed up the discomforts of a stormy passage to the Chesapeake in these words:[14]

> Freighted with Fools, from *Plymouth* sound,
> To *Mary-Land* our Ship was bound,
> Where we arrived in dreadful Pain,
> Shock'd by the Terrours of the Main;
> For full Three Months, our wavering Boat,
> Did thro' the surley Ocean float,
> And furious Storms and threat'ning Blasts,
> Both tore our Sails and sprung our Masts.

6

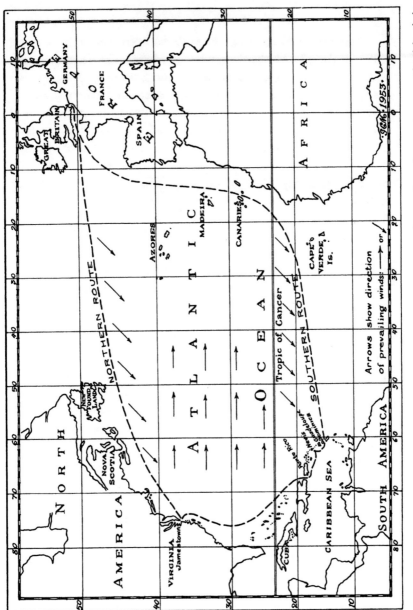

*Map showing the southern and northern routes across the Atlantic in the colonial period (from drawing by George Carrington Mason).*

## Ocean Passage

There were two routes or passages between England and the Chesapeake, the southern and the northern. The former, used extensively in the first half of the seventeenth century, was gradually superseded by the shorter, more convenient northern passage after 1650. For want of information about a better route to the New World, English navigators for a hundred and fifty years after the discovery of America followed the course Columbus had taken to the West Indies, and from these islands made their way northward as best they could by coasting. The usual procedure involved sailing southward from England, clearing Cape Finisterre. Off the coast of Portugal in the spring and summer the mariner picked up the favorable northerly winds that blew with sufficient regularity to warrant their being known as the "Portuguese trades." These carried him as far as the Canaries, where he caught the northeast trades. From the Canaries to the West Indies, some three thousand miles, favorable winds might be had, provided the mariner kept well below the Tropic of Cancer. Between the twentieth and thirtieth parallels of latitude was an era of variable winds interspersed with calms, known as the "Horse Latitudes," because, as the early navigators discovered, the confused sea, muggy heat, and the rolling and pitching of becalmed vessels proved fatal to horses and cattle. Below the twentieth parallel, however, the favorable northeast trades rendered the passage fast and comfortable.[15]

After watering and victualling his vessel in the West Indies, the mariner headed north. Off the Florida coast he entered the Gulf Stream and continued in it until he cleared Cape Hatteras. As a rule this was the most dangerous part of the southern passage to Virginia. The warm waters of the Gulf Stream here met the cold waters of the north with the result that the sea was choppy and the weather thick.[16] Off Hatteras, Virginiamen frequently ran into severe storms, notoriously sudden and furious. Fleets were separated, topmasts and yards carried away, mainmasts sprung, and seams opened. Some vessels, badly damaged by storms, limped back to the West Indies to refit before venturing around Cape Hatteras a second time. Others, blown far off their course, found it expedient to sail with the westerlies, which prevail above the thirtieth parallel,[17] back to the Azores or even to England, to begin the passage anew. More fortunate ships, after heaving-to for the duration of the tempest and escaping serious damage, resumed their course along the coast until they reached the thirty-seventh parallel, on which Cape Henry lies. Even then their troubles did not end: they had to jog off and on the coast until they were fortunate enough to fetch an easterly wind in order to run between the Virginia Capes and stand into Chesapeake Bay. With prevailing westerly winds, vessels waited for many days virtually within sight of their destination. The ship *Bristow* of London reached the Capes after a fairly favorable passage, only to spend nearly twelve weeks within forty or fifty leagues of the Virginia coast before an easterly wind made it possible for the vessel to enter the Bay.[18]

Early in the seventeenth century navigators began to appreciate the advantages of the northern passage, which approximates the great circle track between England and the American coast. It was shorter, it avoided the perilous waters off Hatteras, and it lay entirely within the Temperate Zone, thus minimizing discomfort and disease on shipboard. Bartholomew Gosnold took this route on his voyage to America in 1602, Martin Pring did so in 1603, and Samuel Argall in 1609, but it did not supplant the southern passage for several decades. Christopher Newport's fleet came by way of the West Indies to settle Jamestown even though Gosnold was second in command, and Leonard Calvert's *Ark* and *Dove* came by the same route to settle St. Mary's in 1634.

Including the delay in the Downs and the dallying in the West Indies, the passage of the *Sarah Constant, Goodspeed,* and *Discovery* lasted over four months, as they sailed from Blackwall on December 20, 1606, and sighted the Virginia Capes on April 26, 1607.[19] The passage of the *Ark* and *Dove,* including their sojourn at Barbados and St. Kitts, took three months. By the end

9

of the seventeenth century, when the northern passage had super-seded the southern, seven or eight weeks constituted the normal length of time for a passage to the Chesapeake in good weather, but bad weather often prolonged it considerably. The *Bristow,* already mentioned, made the passage in five months, the delay resulting from adverse winds off the Virginia Capes. On the other hand, William Byrd I in 1688 crossed from Land's End to Cape Henry in twenty-eight days. Exceptional even in summer, this short passage is the more remarkable because it occurred in winter when storms and thick weather usually delayed vessels and when the westerlies were generally strong. But Byrd wrote that despite the season of the year, he had "none but Halcyon days."[20]

No less fortunate than his father, William Byrd II made a winter passage in 1720 that proved to be the most agreeable crossing he ever experienced. He wrote the Earl of Orrery that "in about a week we got into a pleasant Lattitude betwixt 30 and 40, where we found the Air as mild as it is with you in April; in that fine Clymate we sail'd about a thousand leagues till we got to the west of Bermudas, having all the while the finest weather in the World."[21] The normal winter passage, in addition to being cold and rough, was often prolonged by bad weather to twelve or fourteen weeks.

Vessels from London bound outward to the American colonies dropped down the Thames with an ebb current and anchored at Dover, at Cowes, or in the Downs,[22] where they awaited favorable winds. Adverse ones, especially in winter, sometimes delayed their departure for weeks. Newport's fleet rode at anchor for a fortnight until "unprosperous winds" turned favorable, and the *Virginia Gazette* in 1739 reported that "by the late Contrary Winds, no less than 126 outbound Vessels, besides Coasters, are detained from pursuing their intended Voyages, viz. 63 in the Downs, 41 at Cowes, and 22 at Dover."[23] On the other hand, Thomas Chalkley aboard the ship *Josiah* in 1697 waited in the Downs but four days before catching a fair wind.[24]

The return crossing to England, because of the Gulf Stream and the prevailing westerlies, enjoyed the reputation of being much easier and shorter than the Virginia passage. Gosnold, who took seven weeks to reach the American coast in 1602, returned to England in thirty-two days. In favorable weather the eastward passage from the Chesapeake to England commonly required no more than six or seven weeks. A crossing from Virginia to Dover in 1743 was so rough that everything was washed off the decks and the vessel scudded under a reefed mainsail for four days and nights, yet the passage took only seven weeks and two days.[25]

Most remarkable of recorded passages was that of the Maryland sloop *Endeavour,* which sailed from Annapolis on December 13, 1747, bound for the West Indies. A week or two out of her home port she encountered "exceeding hard Gales of Wind" which carried away all her masts, boats and rigging. Completely disabled, she tossed about in the Atlantic for six months, eventually being carried by the Gulf Stream to the Isle of Tirie in the Hebrides. Her owner, William Govane, had given her up for lost when an unexpected report from Edinburgh, dated June 21, 1748, told of the safe arrival of the *Endeavour* and described the famishing crew as being "quite thin, and all as grey as Rats."[26]

Conditions on shipboard during the seventeenth century were generally appalling. Dozens and even hundreds of passengers were crowded into small, dark, ill-ventilated cabins for weeks at a time. In addition to the discomfort of rough seas they had to put up with poor food and minimum sanitary facilities. In many instances the ships were filthy and rat-infested. Under these circumstances it is not surprising that disease was rampant and mortality frightful. Bradford in his *Plymouth Plantation* told of a vessel bound for Virginia that lost one hundred and thirty of its hundred and eighty passengers.[27] An early voyager to Virginia wrote home describing his experience on shipboard: "betwixt decks," he said, "there can hardly a man fetch his breath by reason there arisith such a funke in the night that it causes putrifaction of blood and breedeth disease much like the plague."[28]

Quite early, observant persons realized that the filthy condition of the vessels caused much of the disease on shipboard. When strict precautions were taken to keep a ship clean and to time its arrival in Virginia with late autumn, sickness rarely appeared among the passengers. William Capps, who came to Virginia with Sir Thomas Gates and Sir George Somers, wrote the deputy treasurer of the Virginia Company in 1623 that, although they came in the summer, after fifteen weeks at sea they had not lost a man. The reason was that swabbers carefully cleaned the orlop, and every passenger daily brought up his bed to air in the shrouds during fair weather. Meanwhile, quartermasters swabbed the cabins with vinegar, which "cast such a savour of sharpness to the stomach that it bred health."[29]

By 1636 Governor John West informed the Lords Commissioners for Plantations that mortality on shipboard was high only when the merchants crowded passengers aboard in numbers beyond the capacity of the quarters. He called this the merchants' crime, because overcrowded ships "carry with them almost a general mortality."[30] These conditions continued during the second half of the seventeenth century, for Lord Culpeper, referring to his passage to Virginia in 1680, mentioned that the fleet was full of death, scurvy, and calenture or jail fever.[31]

In the eighteenth century when the northern passage had superseded the southern, conditions on shipboard greatly improved. Passengers rarely died except aboard convict and slave ships. A crowded vessel, however, continued to be dangerous, especially in the tropics. When a colonial expedition against St. Augustine was being considered in 1740, William Byrd II wrote Admiral Sir Charles Wager that he feared the troops would suffer greatly from jail fever "by being stow'd so thick on bord," and concluded that this "joyn'd with a Hot Clymate, and bad season of the year, will certainly kill more of them than the Spaniards." Instead, Byrd urged that the expedition be undertaken solely by naval forces, because sailors, accustomed to the sea and to all kinds of hardships, would have a "Spirit and a Vigour beyond any Land-men in those Hot Countrys."[32]

The transportation of convicts was an unsavory affair. A few British merchants, under contract with the government, undertook to transport to America all the felons that the prisons delivered to them for that purpose. Many of the convicts taken from Newgate, Old Bailey, and the other prisons of London were infected with jail fever and other diseases contracted in crowded and unsanitary jails before embarking for Virginia and Maryland. Like slaves, they were brought over in large numbers, often several hundred in a ship, and were thrown together for so long a period that disease spread rapidly. Governor Sharpe of Maryland asserted in 1767 that some vessels brought twice the number they should have carried, the contractors being neither anxious themselves about the consequences to the convicts "nor very solicitous whether or no the crowding too great a number of the poor wretches into small compass may not be the means of destroying some of them."[33] Convict ships generally lost a few on each passage. The *Patapsco Merchant* bound from London to Annapolis in 1729 lost ten of her ninety-five convicts. On a second crossing the same year she lost twenty-eight out of one hundred and fifty. The *Forward* galley in 1730 delivered seventy-seven alive, but buried thirty-two at sea. The ship *St. George* reached Annapolis in 1748 with one hundred and sixteen, having lost three in her passage from London.[34]

Sometimes passengers on such ships contracted disease from the convicts and died at sea. The *Virginia Gazette* in 1737 reported the arrival of a convict ship in the Potomac which had sailed from London with two passengers, Captain Augustine Washington and Captain Hugh French. "The Former," the report continued, "is arrived in Health but the latter dy'd at Sea and tis said of Gaol Distemper which he got on Board."[35]

Conditions on slaving vessels were even worse. The Negroes, fresh from the African jungles, proved less able to bear the hardship of close confinement in large numbers than the convicts from English prisons. The masters and crews of slaving ships often suffered ill health, partly from the ravages of the Guinea climate and partly from contracting disease from the slaves. A Swiss visitor to Virginia in 1702 told of a slaver that arrived from Guinea having lost one hundred of its two hundred and thirty Negroes. Half the crew died also, and the others were sickly and "yellow in their faces." Guinea was such an unhealthful country, he was informed, that it often happened that ships had to be left there because the captain and all the mariners died of sickness. "Negro fever," the common illness contracted by the crews of vessels in the African slave trade, made food taste bad to them and its long duration emaciated them extremely.[36]

Because of the heat of the Virginia summer, in the early days it was important to time correctly one's arrival in Virginia. Bruce asserted that it was dangerous to reach the colony before the late autumn when the frosts had killed the germs of the ague.[37] If ships arrived during the summer, the mortality was likely to be high among captains and crews as well as among passengers. In the summer of 1635 no fewer than fifteen masters, out of thirty-six who had never before visited the Chesapeake, sickened and died. Bruce declared that this mortality exceeded that on the African coast. A Dutch visitor to Virginia in the 1630's reported that unseasoned people died like cats and dogs in June, July, and August.[38]

Although attributed at the time to the supposed unwholesomeness of the Virginia climate, these diseases commonly began during the ocean passage. On arrival in James River the ships discharged dozens of disease-ridden wretches upon the infant settlement, a fact which partly explains the frightful epidemics and dreadful mortality that characterized early Jamestown, although much of this was due to malaria, typhoid, and dysentery, spread by swamp mosquitoes and bad drinking water in conjunction with faulty sanitation.

Eventually the communication of disease by ships became so serious that the colonial authorities took steps to arrest it. The Norfolk Council from time to time established a quarantine for that town, then the principal Chesapeake port for West Indian trade. In 1744 it ordered some sailors infected with smallpox to withdraw from their ships or remove to the country. In 1746 the Council set aside a certain place as "infirmary or reception house" for mariners from an infected vessel, warning all shipmasters at their peril not to land any infected person within the borough.[39] In 1766 the Maryland Assembly passed a quarantine act "to oblige infected ships, and other vessels coming into this Province to perform quarantine."[40] The reason given was that imported servants and German passengers had spread disease contracted during their close confinement on shipboard. This law not only required masters of vessels to swear that "neither the small-pox, jail-fever, flux or any other such dangerous infectious distemper is, or hath been on board," but also required two credible persons to make oath to that effect.[41]

As the Maryland quarantine act seriously affected the convict trade, the principal importers, Sedgely and Company, vigorously protested against this law. Upon Lord Baltimore's refusal to veto the law, they carried it to the King for disallowance. The Crown refused to interfere, and the act remained on the statute books for the rest of the colonial period. Apparently it was not without a salutary effect, for Governor Sharpe wrote that before Sedgely and Company dared appeal to the Crown, they furnished their ships with ventilators, as they should have done long before, and another concern, Stewart and Campbell, made theirs airy by opening a range of ports on each side between decks. Improvements of this kind made it possible for them to keep their ships healthful, even though they carried as many as a hundred and fifty convicts at a time.[42]

Even when vessels were not overcrowded, life on shipboard was not altogether agreeable, particularly in the days when Englishmen were hearty eaters. Ship's provisions consisted largely of bread, ship's biscuit, salt meat, peas, and cheese—all of which kept well. In the "roast-beef age" of English history, food of this

A nocturnal, a kind of astrolabe used in finding the latitude at night (replica made in England for The Mariners' Museum from original in the British Museum).

kind seemed poor indeed, and its tastelessness and lack of variety led passengers to rely on drink even more heavily at sea than on land. The unbalanced diet of seafarers on voyages of three or four months took its toll. When the Rabelaisian George Alsop reached Maryland in 1658, he wrote home, "I am got ashoar with much ado, and it is very well that it is as it is, for if I had stayed a little longer, I had certainly been a Creature of the Water, for I had hardly flesh enough to carry me to Land." He readily admitted that the ship provided him with everything within reason, adding "But oh the great bowls of Pease-porridge that appeared in sight every day about the hour of twelve, ingulfed the senses of my Appetite so, with the restringent quality of the Salt Beef, upon the internal Inhabitants of my belly, that a *Galenist* for some dayes after my arrival, with his Bag-pipes of Physical operations, could hardly make my Puddings dance in any methodical order."[43]

Food was usually distributed at noon, the hour being announced by ringing a bell. Specific quantities of food were allotted to each mess of six or eight, into which groups the passengers and crew had been divided. One vessel late in the seventeenth century gave seven pounds of bread a week to each person over six years old. Other provisions issued daily, included pork, beef, lard, flour, peas, water, and beer. A mess of eight received four pounds of pork and a quantity of peas five days a week, and four pounds of beef and peas or a pudding on the other two days.[44] A mess of five got four pounds of biscuit, a quart of beer, two quarts of water, a large dish of peas, and six pounds of beef or pork daily. Occasionally two pounds of flour and half a pound of pork lard replaced the meat, in which case the passengers made a thick paste, flavored it with grape juice, and cooked it in a linen sack, calling the result a pudding.[45]

In addition to being simple and monotonous, food on shipboard was often of very poor quality and in bad condition. Because biscuit and salt meat kept well, vessels sometimes carried them for years until the meat was putrid and the biscuit full of worms. Owners and charterers of vessels occasionally purchased spoilt provisions in order to save money. When George Fisher crossed from London to Yorktown on the ship *Berry,* he found the food inedible because the charterer had victualled the ship with damaged provisions from a man-of-war which had been in the West Indies a long time.[46] More commonly, the food became bad simply through carelessness. Meat was inadequately salted and water allowed to acquire a foul taste. Ship's biscuit and bread, carelessly stored, suffered the ravages of rats and worms. The heat of the Virginia summer or of the tropics frequently spoilt flour and meat. On his outward passage, Michel discovered not only that the meat and water tasted bad, but also that the bread had been badly damaged by mice. He found the food on his return passage even worse; the biscuit was so full of worms that the smallest particle could not be broken off without finding them in it.[47]

Although vessels supplied passengers with food, fastidious travellers occasionally brought aboard their own supplies so that they might fare better than would otherwise have been the case. A Mrs. Browne, crossing from London to Virginia in 1754-55 with her brother, a maid, and a Negro servant named Pompey, recorded in her journal that she obtained stores for their voyage at Gravesend late in November. On January 16, 1755, she discovered that thirty gallons of brandy in her "sea Store" had leaked out of the cask in the hold, a loss so serious that "poor Pompy the Negroe allmost turned white on the thought of it." Several days later a live sheep, two pigs, eight turkeys, and six ducks belonging to one of the passengers were lost overboard.[48]

Passengers occasionally augmented their food supply by fishing at sea. Michel told how the crew of the ship *Indian King* while waiting for a favorable wind off the Virginia Capes fished with a large hook baited with four pounds of meat, eventually catching a hundred-pound fish "which caused great joy and rejoicing." On his return passage to England, while five hundred leagues from land, the ship's company amused themselves by fishing for the many dolphins that played about the vessel. Some fished with baited hooks; others used seven-foot harpoons with five hook-like points.[49] Mrs. Browne told of cooking a twenty-inch flying fish caught at sea, which everyone declared "eat like a young Sturgeon."[50]

Life at sea in colonial days differed from the easy and comfortable existence on modern luxury liners in many ways, but in none more strikingly than in the absence of leisure. The passengers in olden days were not waited on, hand and foot. Like the crew they worked hard, taking care of their own supplies, making bunks, airing bedding, washing linen, and preparing food. Mrs. Browne noted in her journal that one of her shipmates, Mrs. Barbut, arose early and made a "sea Pye," the first she ever made. On another occasion she recorded that Mrs. Barbut spent four hours making a cake, and baked it six hours in a rusty pudding pan, notwithstanding which "it eat like a Pancake." A few days later Mrs. Browne killed a pig and was hard at work making "Black Puddings."[51]

The galley or caboose where food was cooked on shipboard was a room or deckhouse containing an open hearth usually built of brick, but occasionally made of iron, either on deck or in the forecastle with a smoke pipe through a deck scuttle. In smaller, less pretentious vessels an ordinary cask, barrel or hogshead, cut in two and half filled with sand served as a cookstove. As they were generally on deck, these hearths could not be used in a heavy sea or during high winds. In stormy weather when no food was cooked, passengers and crew went for days and even weeks with nothing to eat but bread and cheese. Cabooses were sometimes broken to pieces or washed overboard, and a stove had to be improvised. This was attempted on a rough crossing in the seventeenth century by the passengers aboard the *Virginia Merchant*. Weary of cold food, they sawed a cask in two and tried to parch peas and boil salt meat over a makeshift hearth, but the scheme failed, as the rough sea threw the cask topsy-turvy "to the great defeat of emptly stomachs."[52]

Gales occasionally drove ships off their course, thereby prolonging passages beyond expectation and causing a dearth of provisions. The *Virginia Merchant,* already mentioned, experienced just such a calamity. A passenger who survived the ordeal wrote that

Women and children made dismal cries and grievous complaints. The infinite number of rats that all the voyage had been our plague, we now were glad to make our prey to feed on; and as they were insnared and taken, a well grown rat was sold for sixteen shillings as a market rate. Nay, before the voyage did end, a woman great with child offered twenty shillings for a rat, which the proprietor refusing, the woman died.[53]

With good weather and a short passage, however, travellers fared well at sea, particularly if they sat at the captain's table. From an early time this was a much sought-after privilege. Michel in 1701 found that while the cost of passage to Virginia amounted to five or six pounds and from Virginia to London about half as much, it cost ten pounds for the journey outward and six pounds for the return passage, over and above the transportation fare, to dine at the captain's table. The difference in quality and variety of food, however, was commensurate with the difference in cost. As the ship *Nassau* carried forty-five pigs, one calf, three sheep, more than twenty turkeys, fourteen geese, and more than a hundred chickens in order to supply the captain's table with fresh meat daily, Michel concluded that "Englishmen pay much attention to good eating and drinking, but especially to meat."[54]

On a passage from London to Maryland the ship *Elizabeth* in 1747 had nine passengers at the table of Captain John Ker. Some idea of the variety and abundance of food served may be had from the itemized account presented to them at the end of the voyage. Amounting to £67 18s. 5d., it included sixteen gallons of rum, 324 bottles of beer, twenty-four gallons of wine, and forty-eight bottles of cider, besides a hundred and forty pounds

*Hadley quadrant, c. 1750, at The Mariners' Museum.*

of bacon, pickled tongues, two kegs of soused tripe, six hogs, three sheep, fourteen ducks, and eight dozen fowls, as well as lemons, cheese, butter, coffee, tea, sugar, rice, anchovies, mustard, vinegar, and oil.[55]

Shipboard routine was sometimes interrupted by a pleasant social event. When ships sailed in company and the weather was moderate, visiting between ships provided a common diversion. Otherwise, the captain occasionally invited one or more passengers to dine with him, or a passenger who had brought his own food asked another to join him for a meal. Mrs. Browne, accepting an invitation from a fellow-passenger, the director of the hospital supplies intended for Braddock's army, had ham, fowls, and a pudding for dinner. Later she received a present of a quarter of pork from the cabin mess, and on Mrs. Barbut's birthday had the captain's mess to dine "on Ham, a Turkey and Fowls and for Drink French wine and Bristol Beer."[56]

As the large quantities of liquor suggest, time was often passed in friendly conviviality. One Sunday aboard the ship *London,* the morning prayer had to be postponed until the afternoon, the "Parson being indisposed by drinking too much Grog the Night before." When the ship reached Hampton Roads, four officers came on board and drank fifteen bottles of port, after which, as might have been expected, they were "all in the Cabbin drunk."[57]

Thrown together in small quarters for long periods of time, passengers sometimes got into violent disputes. Mr. Cherrington, a particularly quarrelsome man aboard the ship *London,* frequently became involved in what Mrs. Browne recorded in her journal as "a Squall." On one occasion a Mr. Bass made some allusions to Miss David, "a friendly fair" of Cherrington, who, being hasty-tempered, demanded an explanation. Bass made one, "but not in the Lady's favour," and in the course of it many "Ill natured Truths" were said, whereupon the furious Cherrington forbade Bass to enter the cabin they shared. Quite naturally Bass protested that he had as much right to the cabin as Cherrington. The latter went off in a huff, not being able to bear "the Insolence of the little fellow." On another occasion a quarrel occurred between Cherrington and Captain Browne over the loss of some water gruel. A week later when the pigs, turkeys, and ducks were lost overboard a heated argument took place between the suspicious Cherrington and Mrs. Browne's brother, in which Cherrington said it was "not clear to him why so many of his should die and not one of ours."[58]

When there was a death at sea, the body was usually placed in a sack weighted with stones and consigned to the deep with little or no ceremony. When passengers of consequence died, the master sometimes saw fit to order a coffin made. Michel records this was done on the death of an English lady who had been guilty of some indiscretion for which her family was sending her to the colonies. Since she was of distinguished family and great wealth the captain ordered a coffin made in which holes were bored and stones placed to make it sink readily. When a captain died, the ceremony was more elaborate, particularly if his ship were sailing in a fleet. Captain West of the ship *Bristol* died en route from the Chesapeake to England in convoy. In accordance with custom, his ship lowered her colors to half-mast and fired two guns, a minute apart. The next day when his body was consigned to the sea all colors in the convoy were half-masted. Then each captain who knew him fired a salute of four guns, a minute apart, which the acting master of the *Bristol* returned by discharging all his guns slowly in rotation.[59]

The monotony of a passage was sometimes broken by a brush with privateers or pirates, which caused great excitement and provided the passengers with a new subject for conversation. In 1702, the *Nassau* at daybreak sighted a suspicious vessel clearly trying to overtake her. Since the overtaking vessel appeared to be a better sailer than the *Nassau,* the master ordered all hands piped on deck and a defense prepared. They loaded cannons and muskets, distributed cutlasses and pikes, strengthened the masts with chains, and made a breastwork of sailors' hammocks and beds against small arms on the quarterdeck. They locked the women in the hold and made ready forty bottles of rum "to fill the people with courage." The expected attack did not occur; the *Nassau* kept her distance and lost sight of the pursuing vessel during the following night.[60]

Another precaution usually taken by a vessel in danger of capture was the disposal of all mail. At the outbreak of Queen Anne's War the French secured information concerning the state of the English colonies through the capture of merchantmen carrying letters from private persons in America to English correspondents. To prevent a repetition of this, the Board of Trade instructed colonial governors to urge all merchants and planters to be very cautious in giving any account by letters of the "Publick State and condition" of their respective colonies and to order all masters to whom official communications were entrusted to put such letters into a bag with a sufficient weight to sink the same immediately in case of imminent danger from the enemy. The authorities also requested merchants to give similar instructions to masters in order to prevent advices concerning the sailing of ships from falling into the hands of privateers and pirates.[61]

The problem of maintaining overseas communication in wartime became so serious that in 1704 a number of merchants trading to the Chesapeake, the middle colonies, and New England petitioned the Lord High Treasurer to establish packet boats from London to New York under the direction of the Post Office. They recommended that these packets carry nothing but mail and passengers, and sail regularly so that warships might be sent out to meet them off the coast and convoy them to port; but since the authorities failed to settle the question as to who would bear the cost of operating these vessels, nothing came of the proposal so far as the Chesapeake was concerned.[62] In 1707 when the British government considered a proposal to extend the West Indian packetboat system to the continental colonies, especially

Virginia and Maryland, those who favored the plan pointed out that the Chesapeake colonies were capable of great improvement by trade and that "the settling of a fixed correspondence and conveniency of passengers" would contribute largely to that end. They further maintained that news was the life of trade and that timely news the previous year would have saved many ships in the tobacco trade that were lost for want of it. Considering regularity and frequency of sailing quite as essential as speed, they proposed that the West Indian packets sail every month and the continental ones eight times a year. Under no circumstances were they to be detained more than a week and not even that long except upon the most urgent grounds.[63] As the authorities rejected the proposal, the Chesapeake colonies never enjoyed the advantages of a packet system.

Navigation in the seventeenth and eighteenth centuries was a relatively simple matter. The navigator required no other equipment than a compass, sandglasses, a lead line, a chip and log line, "sea cards" (charts), solar declination tables, and one of the several instruments for measuring altitudes in celestial observations. In addition, he might also have a nocturnal (a kind of astrolabe) for telling time at night and a spyglass for identifying landmarks as he approached shore.

Navigation at sea involved ascertaining latitude by celestial observation and estimating position by dead reckoning. The latter, by far the more important of the two, consisted of plotting the track of a vessel by computing the difference of latitude and the departure ("easting" or "westing") of the vessel for every course and distance sailed or by laying off on a chart the direction and distance, a procedure known as "pricking the card." The navigator carefully recorded the various compass courses in a logbook together with the estimated distance found by casting the chip log periodically, usually every two hours day and night.

According to an early description, the chip log was a "little board in triangle shape," weighted with lead at the lower edge

*Navigator's sandglass, eighteenth century, at The Mariners' Museum.*

and attached to a line in such a way as to remain "perpendicular and almost immovable in one place in the water."[64] A mariner cast the log astern and, as the "mark knot" went over the taffrail, turned a sandglass of approximately half a minute. The line attached to the log was payed out—"veered handsomely," as a sailor would have said—until the last grain of sand passed through the neck of the glass, when the observer made fast the line and marked it. The log line was a light rope knotted at intervals of 47 feet 3 inches, which distance is to the 6,080 feet of a nautical mile as 28 seconds is to the 3,600 seconds of an hour. The "half a minute" of the sandglass was then really only 28 seconds. In this way, the number of knots run out in 28 seconds gave the ship's speed in nautical miles per hour, i.e., in knots, and this multiplied by two gave the distance run since the last previous casting of the log, two hours earlier. The observer then recorded this distance in the logbook, later using it in his dead reckoning.[65] This was a crude, inaccurate method—sometimes the navigator was as much as fifty leagues off in his position by dead reckoning on a single Atlantic crossing—but it was the only practicable means of estimating longitude at sea in the days before Harrison's chronometer and the time sight. The other method, lunar distances, was impracticable at sea before the establishment of the *Nautical Almanac* by Nevil Maskelyne in 1766, and even afterward was an awkward method involving tedious computation with many opportunities for error. John Harrison's successful fourth chronometer was made public in 1763, and the time-sight method was devised soon afterwards.

Latitude on the other hand was easily found by means of a noon sight or an altitude of Polaris at night. At the vernal and autumnal equinoxes (March 21 and September 23) each year, when the sun is on the equinoctial circle, the altitude of the sun subtracted from 90° yields the latitude of the observer. At other times of the year the navigator allowed for the sun's declination or angular distance north or south of the equinoctial line. He found the value of this correction for the day of observation in tables of solar declination, available in Western Europe since the late Middle Ages. By adding the solar declination to the sun's altitude at noon when the sun was south of the equinoctial and by subtracting it when the sun was north of the equinoctial, the navigator corrected for the perennial alternation of the sun between winter and summer solstices.

Sidereal observation was even simpler. As the elevation of the celestial pole is axiomatically equivalent to the observer's latitude and as Polaris nearly coincides with the north celestial pole, the navigator merely determined the altitude of Polaris. This yielded his latitude without calculation and without lapse of time. If clouds obscured the Pole Star or if it had no clear-cut horizon beneath it, sidereal observations could be made on any other circumpolar star—any star that never sets—provided latitude were changing slowly or not at all. The observer measured the altitude of a star at upper and lower transit of the meridian— that is, at its highest and lowest point in the heavens—a procedure that required a twelve-hour wait. The mean of these two observations yielded the latitude of the observer.[66] This method, beside involving two sights and a long wait, was impracticable except in the winter months or in very high latitudes when stars were visible for twelve hours at a time.

Perhaps because of the conservatism for which seafaring men are justly celebrated, early navigational instruments persisted in use long after they had been improved upon and rendered obsolete by new inventions and technical improvements, a surprisingly large number of which were made by landsmen rather than by mariners. The astrolabe and cross-staff, known since ancient times, were still in use at sea in the seventeenth century although greatly improved upon by the English navigator, John Davis, late in the sixteenth century. Captain John Smith included an "astrolabe quadrant" and a "crosse staffe" in his list of recommended nautical instruments in 1626.

The astrolabe was a disc with a scale of degrees on the periphery and with a movable arm pivoted to its center. Suspending the disc vertically in the plane of his meridian, the navigator sighted the celestial body by orienting the arm until a ray from the body passed through the aperture at the upper end of the arm and fell upon a plate at the lower end. The zenith distance (co-altitude) of the body was read where the arm intersected the peripheral scale of the disc.

The cross-staff employed two crossed staffs which together with the observer's lines of sight to the horizon and the celestial body formed two right triangles. As two of the sides were of measurable length, the angles were ascertainable by trigonometric principles. The cross-staff involved "looking two ways at once" but it had an advantage over the astrolabe in that it required only one observer instead of two or three.

The simple quadrant, a primitive instrument, continued in use from the time of Columbus until well into the eighteenth century. It was the fourth part of a disc with a periphery graduated in units of arc from 0° to 90°, made to be freely suspended from a ring, and provided with a plumb bob. The instrument was suspended vertically in the plane of the meridian and tilted within that plane until the index edge was parallel to the rays from the body observed. When this parallelism was achieved, the peripheral graduation cut by the plumb line yielded the body's zenith distance.

When the boundary between Virginia and North Carolina was surveyed in 1710-11 the surveying party employed this type of instrument, for a member of the group mentioned that one of the quadrants was not "fast in the ring" and by moving it one way or the other it made a difference of about five minutes of arc in the reading. The party carried four quadrants and took simultaneous noon sights. The instruments often differed by 6' or 7' and on one occasion by as much as 32'. Another of their four instruments, described as a "sea-quadrant," had a radius of two feet three inches, well graduated to two minutes of arc, and a "good plumb and fine thread."[67]

Davis's instrument, the back-staff, represented a great advance over its predecessors. The observer stood with his back to the sun and simultaneously sighted the horizon and the shadow of a vane fastened to the arc of least radius.[68] Notwithstanding its unflattering nicknames, "jackass quadrant" and "hog yoke," mariners considered it the most accurate navigational instrument of the day and continued to use it until the second half of the eighteenth century, long after it had been improved upon.

The double-reflecting octant, invented independently by John Hadley in London and Thomas Godfrey in Philadelphia and made public in 1731, was a great advance over Davis's quadrant and still survives in a modified form as our modern marine sextant.[69] The novel feature of Hadley's quadrant, as it was usually called, was the use of mirrors to superimpose the image of the celestial body upon the horizon, thus facilitating the operation and increasing the accuracy of solar and sidereal observations. The arc of Hadley's quadrant was an eighth part of a circle (45°) and therefore was technically an octant. But the double-reflection principle made possible the measuring of angles up to 90°, for which reason it was called a quadrant at the time of its invention. In the interests of practical navigation the instrument was modified by Captain Campbell in 1757 when the arc was enlarged to a sixth part of a circle (60°). Thereafter it became known as a sextant.

In spite of its marked superiority, Hadley's quadrant was slow to replace its predecessor. Although William Allason of Virginia had a Hadley's quadrant as early as 1756, Thomas Fleming of Annapolis and Neil Jameson of Norfolk continued to supply vessels with Davis's quadrants during the 1750's and 1760's.[70] Similarly, the cross-staff, an inferior and much more primitive instrument, continued to be employed until the middle of the eighteenth century and its use to be taught in colonial schools.[71]

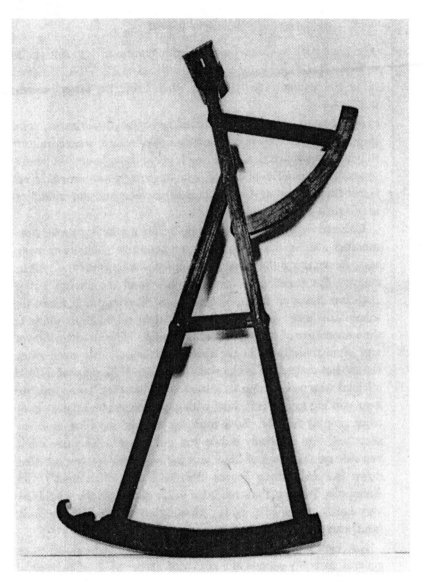

*Davis quadrant or back-staff, 1780, at The Mariners' Museum.*

The cross-staff was sometimes called a "fore-staff," to distinguish it from Davis's quadrant, called a "back-staff." The observer using the former faced the sun; when using the latter, he had his back to it.

The remaining paraphernalia of the colonial navigator, compasses and binnacles, sandglasses ranging from a quarter-minute to two hours, charts, lead lines, log lines, and spyglasses, frequently appear in inventories of estates, in invoices for goods ordered from Great Britain, and in the papers of shipowners and ship chandlers in Virginia and Maryland.[72]

Colonial dependence upon shipping for marketing staple commodities abroad, for importation of necessary goods from overseas, for securing the latest news and fashions from the mother country, for travel, and for protection from the enemy, lent a maritime flavor to life in Virginia and Maryland and made the inhabitants more acutely aware than their descendants today of the importance of the sea and of navigation. This maritime flavor was often manifested in the speech of the colonists, even when the subject-matter did not pertain to the sea. William Byrd II told a friend who was wooing an attractive widow that "sometimes we hear you are sailing into Port with a prosperous Gale, just ready to let go your Anchor. Soon after, we are told the wind took you short and had spitefully blown you out to sea again; one while you ride on the wings of hope and the next Post you are tumbled down like an aspiring Icarus into the Gulph of despair."[73] In Annapolis, William Faris recorded in his diary that the wind blew very hard, "upset Miss Kittey Fleming on the Stad House Hill, [and] carryed away all her top rigging."[74]

Knowledge of navigation and astronomy enjoyed a much more general currency among the educated classes of the Chesapeake colonies in the eighteenth century than they do today.[75] The practical application of astronomy to navigation and surveying, together with its traditional place in the educational system inherited from the Middle Ages, made it an essential part of the education of a gentleman, and not merely a technical subject for the expert. In consequence, colonial schools usually possessed celestial and terrestrial globes and advertised courses in surveying, navigation, and the use of globes. On the Eastern Shore of Maryland, Charles Peale, father of Charles Willson Peale, taught navigation as well as Greek, Latin, arithmetic, and merchants' accounts at the Kent County School, which claimed to have the largest and most accurate pair of globes in America. At Upper Marlboro, Prince George's County, Maryland, Peter Robinson advertised classes in navigation, "either in Plain, Mercator, or Circular Sailing," cosmography, astronomy, as well as the description and use of "Sea Charts, Maps, Quadrants, Fore-Staffs, Nocturnal, Protractor, Scales, . . . Globes, and other Mathematical Instruments."[76]

Familiarity with navigation was so common in colonial days that when the boundary line was surveyed between Virginia and North Carolina in 1710-11, there was no difficulty in finding gentlemen capable of doing it. The Virginia commissioners, Philip Ludwell and Nathaniel Harrison, later joined by Harry Beverley, needed no technical experts; they proved quite able to take and work latitude sights, and they owned their own instruments. Upon their return to Williamsburg, the commissioners gave a public demonstration of their methods before an audience at the Governor's House gathered "to see the manner of our taking an observation." One spectator, Mr. LeFeavour, professor of mathematics at the College of William and Mary, seemed to be of the opinion that "our way is more exact than is taken at sea."[77]

In view of the widespread interest in maritime affairs, it is not surprising that when Virginians and Marylanders travelled at sea they took a keen interest in navigation. When Ben Galloway sailed to England to attend school in 1764, the captain of the ship wrote Samuel Galloway, Ben's father, that the boy took naturally to navigation, knew all the lines on the quarterdeck, and quickly learned the compass and how to work an observation.[78] Similarily, when St. George Tucker sailed home to Bermuda on a vacation from the College of William and Mary in 1773, he took an intelligent interest in navigation, discussed the effect of the "Gulph Stream" upon their dead reckoning, observed the captain taking a noon sight with his quadrant, and watched him "working his Observation with a bit of Chalk upon the Rail of the Quarter Deck."[79]

As the westbound vessel approached the American continental shelf, the mariner often detected the aroma of the pine trees as much as sixty leagues off shore. Then he saw signs of land in the water, bits of organic matter, plants, logs, and branches. Land birds were observed skimming the crests of the waves, and the sea changed color from the deep blue of mid-ocean to off-shore green.[80] Weary of their long and tedious voyage, the passengers restlessly awaited the happy moment when they would reach their destination and once more set foot on land. Being particularly anxious to strike the coast at the thirty-seventh parallel, upon which lay the channel between Cape Henry and Middle Ground Shoal, the navigator made careful observations of latitude, dead reckoning not being sufficiently reliable. Having taken a noon sight on the day he expected to make a landfall, the mariner might safely stand into Chesapeake Bay even after dark, but he considered it advisable to sound continually to verify his position.

The continental shelf near the entrance to the Bay is a uniform and gradual slope. Bottom was usually found in eighty or ninety fathoms at a distance of forty or fifty leagues off shore. The regularity of the slope enabled an experienced master to estimate his distance off land by the depth of the water, and the nature of the bottom provided a further means of checking his latitude, by sampling it with a lead line. At the parallel where the Chesapeake joins the Atlantic, it consists of mud mixed with sand and small oyster shells as far out as the soundings; above Cape Charles and below Cape Henry the bottom is composed of hard sand, somewhat reddish in color. If the mariner's lead (having been "armed" or greased with tallow) brought up the former, he might be certain that his latitude was 37° N and that the Capes of Virginia lay dead ahead. This fortunate circumstance, greatly appreciated by colonial navigators, led Robert Beverley to declare that "a bolder and safer Coast is not known in the Universe," and Sir William Berkeley to boast that "fewer ships miscarry going to *Virginia,* than to any Port at that distance in the world."[81]

When the bottom was found, a wave of relief swept through the ship's company. The lead and tallow that provided the unmistakable evidence of the proximity of the Virginia Capes were, according to custom, cut off and fastened to the mizzenmast and the number of fathoms inscribed under it with chalk. If the wind continued fair and visibility good, Cape Henry would be sighted the next day or two. Everyone on board, excited at the prospect of landing, strained his eyes to be the first to catch sight of the welcome foreland, and as soon as the ship made landfall, the cry of "Land, land!" arose. Crew and passengers alike rejoiced, thanked God for their preservation from the perils of the deep, and bestowed a bottle of whiskey upon the man who first espied the cape.[82]

As early as 1720 the governor of Virginia suggested that a lighthouse be built on Cape Henry to enable incoming ships to enter the Chesapeake at night with safety, but the suggestion was not carried out on this occasion because of opposition of British merchants to the duty on shipping necessary to provide funds for the project. Several other unsuccessful attempts were made during the next half-century. Finally, in 1772 both Virginia and Maryland, with the previous assent of the British Board of Trade, passed the necessary legislation. Work began on the lighthouse in 1774, continued until interrupted by the Revolution, and was resumed in 1791. The lighthouse was not completed until 1792. So it was that Chesapeake Bay, with a greater volume of shipping than any other region of continental America in the eighteenth

*Eighteenth-century compass card (from Hitchins and May, FROM LODESTONE TO GYRO-COMPASS).*

century, was the last important region to be provided with the benefits of so useful an aid to navigation, or, as Governor Gooch called it, a "noted landmark to guide the doubting mariner."[83]

In the absence of a lighthouse, the mariner dared to stand into the Bay regardless of the hour and visibility only if he were experienced in sailing those waters and certain of his latitude. More commonly mariners did not do so unless there remained enough hours of daylight to clear the Capes and come to anchor in Lynnhaven Roads before dark. Otherwise, the vessel wore and jogged off and on the cost during the night, keeping well out beyond the fifty-fathom sounding. In the early hours of daylight the next morning, she stood into the Chesapeake and perhaps came to anchor in Hampton Roads or the mouth of York River that afternoon, to the immeasurable joy and relief of the passengers.

## CHAPTER TWO

# The Great Bay of Chesapeake

ONCE safely past the Virginia Capes and the dangerous Middle Ground Shoal that lies between them, the mariner had before him the great Bay of Chesapeake, a vast inland sea thrusting its deep estuaries and long tidal reaches far into the wooded coastal plain. Here in this delightful country, interlaced with innumerable rivers, the seed of the British Empire (and ultimately of the United States) was successfully planted in 1607, and here was the physiographical habitat in which it flourished more luxuriantly than the Virginia Council dared hope in 1609 when it prayed God "so to nourish this graine of seed, that it may spread till all the people of the earth admire the greatnesse, and seek the shades and fruite thereof."[1]

It is not surprising to anyone who knows the Bay country that the Chesapeake captured the imagination of Europeans in the seventeenth and eighteenth centuries. It was called the "Noblest Bay in the Universe," in which the whole navies of Great Britain, France, and the Netherlands might simultaneously ride at anchor. When it came to the number of rivers and creeks, the intricacy of the drainage pattern led one to compare "the many Rivers, Creeks, and Rivulets of Water . . . to veins in humane Bodies."[2] A seventeenth-century visitor thought that "no Country in the World can be more curiously watered," and predicted that the Chesapeake tidewater would eventually become "like the *Netherlands,* the richest place in all America."[3] By the eighteenth century the extent of the Bay and its commercial advantages had become so celebrated that even writers who never came to America devoted their best rhetoric to extolling the Chesapeake. In his *History of America,* Robertson spoke of the Bay as "that grand reservoir, into which are poured all the vast rivers, which . . .

open the interior parts of the country to navigation, and render a commercial intercourse more extensive and commodious than in any other region of the globe."[4]

Chesapeake Bay lies roughly north and south, extending from slightly below 37°N to a little above 39° 30' N in latitude, and from 75° 30' W to 77° 30' W in longitude. It is one hundred and ninety-five miles in length and curves so slightly that the mariner's course up the channel as far as Swan Point, one hundred and sixty-one miles from the Capes, varies no more than two points of the compass. The width of the Bay varies from about twenty-two miles at its widest part to between three and ten miles at the upper part. The distance between the Capes, its only natural connection with the sea, is about twelve miles. Its depth varies considerably: the deepest point is one hundred and fifty-six feet and the shallowest part of the channel, near the head of the Bay, about nineteen feet.

Impressive though it is, the Bay is overshadowed by the many deep-water estuaries that flow into it and by their rivers and creeks. The Chesapeake has forty-eight principal tributaries, some of them navigable for upwards of a hundred miles, and these in turn have a hundred and two branches, some of them navigable for more than fifty miles. In all, the hundred and fifty rivers, creeks, and branches in the Chesapeake region make a navigable distance within the Virginia Capes of 1,750 miles, but this figure does not accurately reflect the length of the shore-line, which is extremely indented on the Eastern Shore. The total shore-line of the Bay and the tidewater portions of its tributaries has been estimated at 4,612 miles. The surface area of the waters of the Chesapeake is about 3,237 square miles and the drainage area 64,900 square miles, or approximately the combined area of the six New England states.[5]

The Chesapeake's tributaries, no less than the Bay itself, excited the admiration of colonial visitors. The Reverend Andrew Burnaby said that the Bay "receives into its bosom at least twenty great rivers" and as many smaller ones. And Sir William Berkeley boasted that these rivers would "securely harbour twenty Thousand Ships at once." On the western shore of Virginia were four large rivers of such safe navigation and such noble and majestic appearance, "as cannot be exceeded, perhaps, in the whole known world."[6] The southernmost of them, James River, extending inland to the fall line, a distance of a hundred and sixty miles from Cape Henry, was navigable by the largest ships for about a hundred miles and by vessels of a hundred and forty tons to within five miles of the falls at Richmond.[7]

The York River was straight and deep for about forty miles above its mouth and, like the lower James, suitable for the largest vessels. Above West Point the river branched into two, the Pamunkey and the Mattaponi, each of which "including the windings and meanders" was accessible to small vessels for seventy miles and to large ones for about twenty.[8] The Rappahannock was navigable to the falls at Fredericksburg, one hundred miles from the Bay. The largest ships went as high as Port Royal, seventy miles above its mouth, and vessels of sixty or seventy tons as high as Fredericksburg.[9] The Potomac River, the largest of the tributaries of the Chesapeake and "one of the finest rivers in North America," was a hundred and forty miles from its mouth to the falls, about ten miles above Georgetown. It was accessible for a hundred and ten miles for "a ship of almost any Burthen," and nearly to the falls for smaller vessels.[10]

In addition to the Potomac, only one bank of which belonged to Virginia while the river itself and its other shore lay in Maryland, there are twelve other rivers on Maryland's western shore, some of them navigable for many miles. The Patuxent, although generally rather narrow except in its lower courses, is extremely deep. In colonial days it admitted ships of three hundred tons for about thirty miles and smaller vessels for twenty miles farther.[11] Above the Patuxent is a series of smaller rivers: West River, Rhode River, South River, the Severn, and the Magothy. Of these, the

Severn was navigable for about ten miles and the others for about five miles each. Then comes the Patapsco, accessible for about fifteen miles. Above it is a series of short, broad rivers too shallow for large vessels except at their mouths: Back River, Middle River, the Gunpowder, and the Bush. At the head of the Bay is the majestic but almost unnavigable Susquehanna, which was navigable in its lower course for only about five miles.[12]

Coming down the Eastern Shore, one finds an intricate pattern of interlacing rivers and necks, complicated by innumerable islands. For the most part these rivers afforded passage for large ships only in their lower courses but admitted smaller vessels, especially schooners and sloops, for sometimes as much as fifty miles above their mouths.[13] The Chester River had a mudbank that carried no more than thirteen feet just below Chestertown, about twenty miles from its mouth.[14] For vessels of small draft, however, it was navigable for another ten miles. The Choptank and Miles Rivers being fairly deep gave admittance to large ships for at least twenty miles and to small craft much farther. The Nanticoke and Wicomico had channels of fourteen feet in their lower courses, and the Annemessex, Menokin River, and Monie Bay admitted vessels of eight or nine foot draft; but the Pocomoke, having "the least water of any," was navigable only for Bay craft and very small vessels.[15] The Eastern Shore of Virginia, which lies below the Pocomoke, has no rivers, and its creeks though fairly deep were closed to larger ships by shoals at their mouths. Only four of the creeks admitted vessels as large as seventy or eighty tons.[16]

The influence of geographic factors upon the historical development of a region is nowhere more clearly seen than in the colonial history of the Chesapeake tidewater. The presence of the Bay profoundly affected the history of Virginia and Maryland by providing an unsurpassed network of natural waterways. This in turn opened 10,000 square miles of hinterland to immediate settlement and made possible the adoption of tobacco as a staple. These factors account for the rapid growth of the Chesapeake

41

country in population, wealth, and preëminence among the American continental colonies. Had there been no Chesapeake Bay, it is certain that Virginia and Maryland would have increased in population and wealth at a much slower rate. Moreover, it is probable that they would not have become a great tobacco-producing area.

The problem of conveying thousands of hogsheads (averaging nearly half a ton apiece) many miles through densely wooded country to a distant seaport would have been insuperable, not only because of the difficuty of road building, but because tobacco was too delicate to be rolled as much as twenty miles overland without suffering damage and loss of value.[17] Hence the enthusiasm of the colonists for their "well watered" country where "Planters can deliver their Commodities at their own Back doors,"[18] an enthusiasm reflected in Dr. Charles Carroll's observation that but for the convenient water carriage, "it would be impracticable or at least very Expensive to Carry on the making of Tobacco."[19]

The production of tobacco on a world-market scale by colonial Virginia and Maryland was not primarily due to the fertility of the soil—it may be successfully grown in many other areas of the eastern United States and the center of production has now shifted away from the Chesapeake tidewater—but to the unusually extensive transportation facilities provided by Chesapeake Bay and its tributaries.

This extraordinary system of waterways—the glory of the Chesapeake country—is the product of normal geologic process. As the glacial sheets retreated to the north at the end of the Pleistocene, or Great Ice Age, the Chesapeake area emerged, rising perhaps a thousand feet above sea level. The rejuvenated streams of the region carved a series of valleys in the coastal plain, eroding away the softer deposits and leaving the resistant beds standing as watersheds between the valleys. The prehistoric Susquehanna excavated the valley now occupied by Chesapeake

Bay and into it flowed the fresh-water streams that drained the valleys of the present James, York, Rappahannock, and Potomac. The Susquehanna at that time discharged its waters into the ocean between what are now the Virginia Capes.

In the post-Pleistocene era, many thousands of years before the coming of Christopher Newport and his fleet, this entire area began to sink. The principal valley, in its lower course, eventually became to low that the sea engulfed its mouth. The subsidence continued gradually, and in time the sea thrust its flood tides half-way up the valley and into the lower portions of the valleys of the principal tributaries. At this point in the transition, the river was still a steadily-flowing stream of fresh water in its upper courses, but in its lower reaches it had become a salt-water estuary, accessible to the flux and reflux of the tides. In due course the gradual process reached the stage where it is today. Now the tides of the ocean, pushing their way two hundred miles inland, are stopped only by the great elevation of the adjacent piedmont plateau. The beds of resistant deposits that formed the water-sheds of the post-Pleistocene valleys, upon submergence became the long, interfluvial points of land—called "necks"—so characteristic of the region today.

The water is salty at the Capes and in the lower parts of the Bay, becoming brackish further up, and fresh at the head of the Bay and in the upper courses of the rivers. The creeks and those portions of the rivers that are fresh are known in the Chesapeake region as "freshes." Oysters and crabs, requiring a relatively high degree of salt concentration, seldom advance very far up the rivers into the brackish waters, but certain varieties of fish, notably herring, are attracted to the head of the rivers and into the freshes to spawn. Even more significant is the fact that seagoing vessels may sail directly into fresh water, thus protecting themselves from barnacles and the destructive shipworm.

*Teredo navalis,* called the "worm" in colonial days, caused considerable damage to wooden vessels in the days before metal

43

sheathing came into general use. Beverley describes the method of attack: "In the Month of *June* Annually, there rise up in the Salts, vast Beds of Seedling-Worms, which enter the Ships, Sloops, or Boats where-ever they find the Coat of Pitch, Tar, or Lime worn off the Timber; and by degrees eat the Plank into Cells like those of an Honey-comb." The worms were a menace from their rise in June until the first great rains after the middle of July. Then they disappeared until the next summer.

The colonists employed four methods of protecting vessels from the worm. One consisted in coating the bottom with pitch, tar, lime, or tallow, for, as Beverley informs us, "the Worms never fasten nor enter, but where the Timber is naked." Another involved anchoring a vessel "in the Strength of the Tide," where the worms were apt to be carried by, before they could attach themselves to the ship's timbers. A third called for heaving down a vessel immediately after the "Worm-Season" and burning and breaming the bottom, for the teredos "are but just stuck into the Plank, and have not buried themselves in it, so that the least Fire in the World destroys them entirely." The fourth and easiest means of prevention was to run the vessel up the rivers into the freshes during the five or six weeks when the worms were active, "for they never bite, nor do any Damage in fresh Water, or where it is not very salt."[20]

The formation of the Chesapeake is such that vessels of any size could easily avoid or kill the worm by running up to the freshes. This tremendous advantage was frequently advanced as one of the principal merits of the Bay. Sir William Berkeley proudly declared that in Virginia "Ships of three hundred tuns sail near two hundred miles, and anchor in the fresh waters; and by this means are not troubled with those Worms which endamage ships, both in the Western Islands of *America,* and in the *Mediterranean sea.*"[21] Chesapeake merchants commonly dispatched vessels of their British correspondents up to the head of the Bay or the upper waters of the rivers during the summer months. Vessels

44

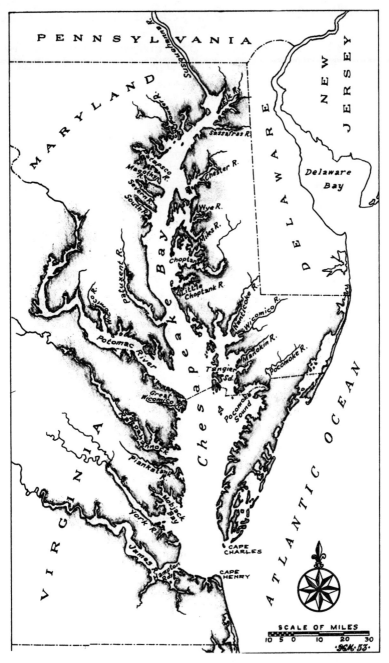

*Map of Chesapeake Bay, showing tributaries
(from drawing by George Carrington Mason).*

ready to be launched in June or July remained on the stocks until well along in September to avoid unnecessary exposure to the worm,[22] and those planters who lived on the upper waters carefully mentioned that fact in correspondence with British merchants, so important was it to shipowners. George Washington, urging Robert Cary and Company of London to send an annual ship to Piscataway Creek—just opposite Mount Vernon—recommended it as a good anchorage safe from the winds and "out of the way of the Worm which is very hurtful to shipping a little lower down."[23]

Vessels were sometimes protected from the worm by sheathing their bottoms with a thin layer of boards, usually pine. The worms might enter the sheathing, but would not transfer from one board to another, hence the ship's timbers remained unscathed. Notwithstanding all precautions, damage to vessels by worms eating their timbers remained a common feature of the maritime history of Virginia and Maryland. Heaving down and breaming a vessel proved too troublesome, and in many cases the pitching or sheathing was carelessly done. Moreover, for reasons of trade or stowage, shipmasters frequently delayed running their vessels up into the freshes until too late, with the result that they sustained considerable damage. When a schooner from Guadeloupe put into Annapolis to clear for home and to stop a leak, several masters and ship carpenters examined the vessel and pronounced her "insufficient to perform her Voyage, her Bottom, Stem, Stern Posts, and Rudder being eaten quite through."[24]

As the part of the coastal plain in which Chesapeake Bay is situated has no exposed rock formations,[25] vessels were not endangered by reefs nor were pilots "affrighted with dangerous Rocks,"[26] but the Chesapeake is encumbered with numerous shoals that are a hindrance to navigation. The constant washing of the shores by the ebb and flow of the tides and by the occasional tempest-driven waves erodes them away, depositing sand and gravel in offshore bars. In addition, the Chesapeake is dotted with islands, and into its waters project long, narrow points of land. These are continuously eroding into mere spits of sand or perhaps into a succession of islands with shoal water between them. The remaining points, more rounded than formerly, are often accompanied by a long, sandy shoal under the greenish water, pointing an accusing finger at the aggressive Bay. Islands are growing smaller: adjacent to each is an area of shallow water —of lighter hue than the deeper channel water—which clearly marks the extent of the island's former dominion over the surrounding waters. According to tradition, Sharpe's Island and Tilghman's Island were formerly so near each other that one of the colonial governors of Maryland rode on horseback across the narrows that separated them. Now some three miles of open water intervene.[27] Doubtless the long chain of islands that separates Tangier Sound from the Bay proper was once a peninsula. Now several dozen islets survive the buffeting of the waves and a large area of shoal water reveals this peninsula's former extent. Various islands within the Bay, such as Smith's Island, Bloodsworth Island, and Tangier, are even now being broken into smaller units.

The passage of time will also bring about further reduction of long points of land like Windmill Point at the mouth of the Rappahannock. It may be washed away to a spit and then to a shoal, or it may be detached from the mainland and divided into several little islands, like the point that formerly separated Honga River from the Bay. If one cares to look far enough into the future, perhaps the ceaseless action of the waves will one day convert the indented eastern shore line of Chesapeake Bay into a straight one, as it has already done on the western shore from Herring Bay to the mouth of the Patuxent.

o    o    o

An important geologic and physiographic feature of the Chesapeake region is that the rivers of the western short rise in the piedmont plateau and empty into a tidal bay in the tidewater.

47

Thus they flow across two geologic formations, the former an elevated region composed of older rock, and the latter a low-lying region of soft, alluvial deposits. The line of demarcation between these two regions, although sometimes visible as an escarpment, is usually not apparent to the untrained eye. Above it the rivers are swift-flowing streams of fresh water fed by mountain brooks, and drain a large area of upland country. Being at a greater elevation than the sea, the piedmont streams are not accessible to the ocean tides. Below the line of demarcation, as has been explained, the rivers are drowned-valleys or estuaries, giving admittance to the tides of the sea and varying in saline concentration according to their distance from the Atlantic.

The junction between the two regions, choked with rapids or falls where the swift piedmont waters cascade into the tidewater estuaries, is known as the fall line. If this occurs at a point where the piedmont boundary is marked by a natural escarpment, a cataract results; if it occurs at a point where no escarpment exists, the erosive action of the swift-flowing water carries away the soft topsoils at the edge of the piedmont plateau, exposing the igneous rocks beneath, and a series of rapids results. In either case it is known as a "falls."

If one were to draw a line on a map of the Chesapeake Bay region connecting the falls of all of the western-shore rivers from the Susquehanna to the James, the resultant would be the so-called fall line, the approximate boundary between piedmont and tidewater. What is more important from the maritime point of view, this line would represent the limit of navigation into the hinterland. As long as the process of settlement of Virginia and Maryland did not cross the fall line and the individual plantations carved out of the wilderness were accessible to ocean-borne commerce, each planter could ship his tobacco and receive goods from England at his own landing, or at least near his own plantation, and the need for ports and towns did not exist. This was generally the case in the tobacco colonies during the seventeenth century.[28]

As late as the beginning of the last quarter of the century there existed not a single incorporated town in Virginia and Maryland and only two villages of any size, Jamestown and St. Mary's. As soon as the capital of its colony was removed from each of them, these two villages fell almost immediately into decay, and half a century later were as dead as Troy or Herculaneum.

In the course of the eighteenth century, as the process of settlement in the Bay region crossed the fall line, large areas in the piedmont were adapted to agricultural production. These new areas grew tobacco, wheat, corn, and flour for export and required a great variety of European and West India goods for their own consumption. Living above the heads of navigation, the inhabitants were obliged to convey their exports overland or in small boats down to the fall line, in order to load them aboard vessels bound for other parts of the Chesapeake or for places overseas. Similarily, their imports could be carried no further than the falls, where they had to be unloaded for overland transportation to their destination. Consequently, warehouses, ordinaries, and stores for the handling of these goods sprang up at the falls of each of the western-shore rivers. Around these nuclei grew towns, the size and importance of which depended upon the nature and extent of the hinterland they served, its products, and the navigational facilities. At the fall line there arose such towns as Baltimore on the Patapsco, Upper Marlboro on the Patuxent, Georgetown and Alexandria on the Potomac, Fredericksburg and Falmouth on the Rappahannock, Richmond on the James, and Petersburg on the Appomattox.

Although the fall-line towns became the most important urban group in the Chesapeake region during the eighteenth century, there were several towns of considerable consequence that were not situated on the fall line, notably Norfolk, Annapolis, Williamsburg, and Chestertown. Their importance was the result of special circumstances. Norfolk, the leading port and commercial center of the Chesapeake until overtaken by Baltimore in the 1770's, was adjacent to a hinterland rich in lumber, naval stores, and livestock as well as tobacco, wheat, and corn. Besides its excellent facilities for shipbuilding, Norfolk had a thriving class of merchants, developed a large ship-chandlery business, almost monopolized the West India trade of the lower Chesapeake, and became the principal entrepôt for the upper part of North Carolina, whose own inlets and rivers were too treacherous and shallow to admit large vessels.[29] Williamsburg and Annapolis were important because they were the seats of the colonial governments, administrative offices, provincial courts, the College of William and Mary, and King William's School. During the "public times" when the assembly met, these little capitals were frequented by a concourse of well-to-do planters, their families and retinues, who sustained a number of tavern keepers, shopkeepers, craftsmen, and merchants. Unlike her sister city of Williamsburg, Annapolis was a port on navigable water and, in addition to the former's reasons for existing, had shipyards, ship carpenters, ropewalks, blockmakers, sailmakers, and ship chandlers. The maritime activities of Norfolk, Annapolis, and Chestertown are treated at greater length in Chapter Seven.

A more numerous, though less important, group were the river towns, small communities like Cabin Point, Yorktown, Urbanna, Port Royal, Aquia, Dumfries, and Occoquan in Virginia, and Port Tobacco, Piscataway, Bladensburg, Londontown, Joppa, and Charlestown in Maryland, which are the principal but by no means the only river towns of the Chesapeake. Although in some cases founded earlier, these towns flourished in the half century before the Revolution. Their prosperity was bound up with the warehouses set up under the tobacco inspection acts of 1730 in Virginia and 1747 in Maryland, and with the stores established and operated by the resident factors of British merchants.

Situated on navigable creeks, the river towns served the adjacent areas as commercial centers much as the fall-line towns served the piedmont region, although on a smaller scale. As the tobacco trade passed more and more out of the hands of London consignment merchants into those of British outport merchants who preferred to buy the commodity outright, many planters sold their crops to resident factors and drew against their balance at local river-town stores. Since it was necessary to supply the planters with everything they wanted in order to keep their custom, the factors imported West India as well as European products. Thus the river towns became centers for the sale of imported goods as well as for the sale of tobacco, corn, wheat, lumber, iron, and naval stores for export.

After the Revolution the conditions that favored the river towns changed. The older tidewater lands had become exhausted, causing the upper Bay region to abandon tobacco for corn, wheat, and flour, and the center of tobacco production to shift from the lower Bay region to the piedmont. Moreover, soil erosion rapidly silted up creeks on which river towns were situated, cutting off their navigational facilities. The Revolution itself removed two of the main economic buttresses of these towns, the warehouse inspection acts and the British factorage system. Some disappeared altogether and are but memories today; others decayed but continued to exist as sleepy little villages with grass growing in their once-busy streets and with dilapidated remains of fine mansions, taverns, assembly rooms, and wharves. What was left of their former trade was drawn into the orbit of the fast-growing city of Baltimore, soon to become the "Queen of the Chesapeake."[30]

o   o   o

The climate of the Chesapeake colonies was regarded as favorable, although too hot in the summer months for the unacclimatized Englishman. In all accounts of colonial days Virginia and Maryland were considered well placed as far as latitude is concerned. Captain John Smith declared that the Chesapeake country "may have the prerogative over the most pleasant places knowne" and thought that "heaven and earth never agreed better to frame a place for man's habitation." In later years Governor Gooch found the region comparable with some of the finest countries in the world.[31]

As to heat and cold, Smith reported that "the Sommer is hot as in *Spaine*; the Winter cold as in France or England," adding that "coole Breeses asswage the vehemency of the heat" in summer.[32] Nonetheless, the early settlers suffered considerably from the heat of the Virginia summer. As early as 1649 some Virginians made a practice of withdrawing to the hills at the upper part of the Chesapeake in order to escape the extreme heat and to preserve uninterrupted good health. Years later Lord Howard of Effingham wrote King Charles II from Jamestown that he intended to retreat from the "almost indispensable sickness of this place in the dog days."[33] Jonathan Boucher, shortly after he came to the Chesapeake, told a friend in England that the heat of Virginia "fevers the Blood and sets all the animal Spirits in an Uprore," as a result of which the colonists think and act "tumultuously and all in a flutter, and are Strangers to that cool Steadiness" which Englishmen justly pride themselves upon.[34]

The climate, however, was not quite so bad as Boucher pictured it. The period of extreme heat generally lasted but thirty or forty days, and even during this time it was often relieved by cool breezes. Although William Byrd's English bride suffered from the heat at first, shortly after her arrival she began "to be seasoned to the Heat, and to think more favourably of our Clymate," comforting herself with the thought that a warm sun is necessary to ripen the fine fruit, and so paid herself "with the Pleasure of one Sense, for the Inconvenience that attends the other." Byrd, writing to Lord Orrery, assured him that there were about three months that "impatient People" called warm, yet there were not ten days in the whole summer that he would complain of, and they happen when "the Breazes fail us and it is a dead Calme." Aside from the three hot summer months, Byrd extolled the Chesapeake's climate as most charmingly delightfull, with a fine Air and a Serene Sky that keeps us in Good Health and Good Humour. Spleen and vapours are as absolute Rarities here as a Winter's Sun, or a Publick Spirit in England. A man may eat Beef, be as lazy as Captain Hardy, or even marry in this Clymate, without having the least Inclination to hang himself . . . Your Lordship will allow it to be a fair Commendation of a Country that it reconciles a Man to himself, and makes him suffer the weight of his misfortunes with the same tranquility that he bears with his own Frailtys.[35]

The direction of the wind, then as now, largely determined the weather of the Chesapeake region. The north and northwest winds prevailed during the short winter season, the former accompanied by snow, the latter by clear, crisp weather and freezing temperatures. At this time of year snow was occasionally quite deep, although it seldom lay for more than a few days. The ice in the Bay and rivers, however, sometimes lasted several weeks. The south and southeast winds were invariably warm even in midwinter, and in summer they brought sultry weather attended by hazy, humid atmosphere. The southwest wind, frequently accompanied by gusts, hail, rain, squalls, and electrical storms, caused great apprehension. When the wind was from this quarter the cautious mariner made for a safe anchorage or else prepared to battle the elements. Many a stout vessel "fetched up" on the shoals and islands of the Chesapeake during a southwest gale.[36]

The most characteristic feature of Chesapeake weather was the variableness of its winds, and consequently of its temperature. In the winter of 1672-73 George Fox, while in Maryland, recorded that in the midst of cold weather, "the Wind turning into the South, it grew so hot, that we could hardly bear the Heat; and the next Day and Night, the Wind chopping back into the North, we could hardly endure the Cold." In the eighteenth century, Burnaby, after describing the excellence of Chesapeake climate, added, "the only complaint that a person can reasonably make, is, of the very sudden changes to which the weather is liable, for this being intirely regulated by the winds, is exceedingly variable." "It is no uncommon thing," he went on to say, "for the thermometer to fall many degrees in a very few hours; and after a warm day, to have such severe cold, as to freeze over a river a mile broad in one night's time."[37]

The ice that choked up the rivers and creeks during the short, cold winters proved a great hindrance to navigation. It closed tributaries and the upper parts of the Bay to incoming vessels, it held fast and sometimes cracked the ribs of vessels that were ready to sail, and the floes took a heavy toll of boats and smaller vessels, occasionally driving even the largest ships aground. During the winter of 1732-33, one of the most severe in Chesapeake history, a man anxious to sail for London had to wait at Annapolis until March before any ship could "stir out," because of the ice that lay in all the rivers of Maryland.[38]

The winter of 1746-47, another severe one, also interrupted the normal commercial activities of the Chesapeake. There was so much ice in the Bay that communication with the Eastern Shore was cut off, and the Maryland *Gazette* announced that "the Severity of the Season has put a Stop to all our Navigation." A few months later a factor on the Eastern Shore wrote that "Trade seems to be quite sunk—We have had the severest Winter that can be remembered. The Creeks and Rivers have been frozen up for 7 Weeks together, the Bay was almost covered over with Ice for some small time."[39]

Instances of vessels being damaged and even destroyed by ice frequently appear in colonial records. The snow *Susanna* of Glasgow, a vessel of 160 tons, was "overset and Sunk" by ice in the Potomac near Nanjemoy and her lading of 213 hogsheads of tobacco lost or damaged. The sloop *Sea Flower* of Boston was driven up and down the Bay by ice for five days, and on the sixth day grounded in two and a half feet of water on Thomas Point with the result that she "thumped very hard upon the Sand as she lay Exposed to the Bay and Waves," and sustained damage to her cargo of Fayal wine.[40]

In addition to ice, the mariners of the Chesapeake had to contend with the peril of squalls and storms in the Bay. On his voyage of discovery in 1608 Smith experienced several sudden and violent squalls. The first, accompanied by rain, thunder, and lightning, transformed the Bay into the "unmercifull raging" of "ocean-like water." The second carried away the foremast of his little vessel and kicked up "mightie waves" that threatened to overturn the boat.[41] When Governor Leonard Calvert dispatched a military expedition from St. Mary's to reduce Kent Island in the winter of 1637-38, storms lengthened the passage of the little armada to a week, although the distance was but sixty miles.[42] In later years adverse weather was accepted by the assemblies of Virginia and Maryland as a valid excuse for the absence or tardiness of burgesses and delegates from the Eastern Shore and for delay on the part of sheriffs in returning writs.[43]

Occasionally the Chesapeake area suffered really bad storms. The worst was the great "Hurry-Cane" of August, 1667. Hailstones as large as turkey eggs pelted the countryside, destroying the fruit, beating down the grass, and killing cattle. Then came a heavy and prolonged rainfall which ruined almost all the grain and tobacco. The hurricane itself, which lasted twenty-four hours, began at northeast, gradually backed into the north, and finally to southeast. This raging fury was attended by heavy rain that caused unprecedented floods in the upper waters of the rivers and raised the water even in the lower estuaries to a destructive height. Fields were inundated, crops torn to shreds, houses and barns carried away, and even the largest vessels washed up on the beach. Philip Ludwell estimated that some ten thousand houses were ruined in Virginia alone. Other contemporary estimates put the destruction of crops at from two-thirds to four-fifths.[44]

Fortunately this dreadful experience was never repeated in the Chesapeake colonies. It seems to have been a West India hurricane that in moving northward failed to recurve and go eastward from Cape Hatteras. From time to time, however, storms of less violence took their toll of shipping, frequently driving vessels aground on shoals and points. The sloop *Benedict* tried to ride out a stiff northwest wind off Bodkin Point in 1745. With two anchors ahead she parted her cables and drove over the Bay to Swan Point where she grounded. The sea ran so high that the master and crew abandoned her and waded ashore to save their lives. The sloop *Oxford,* riding out a gale in Choptank River in 1749, pitched so violently "as to be near foundring." She started her knightheads and windlass-bitts and suffered damage to her cargo of 56 hogsheads of tobacco.[45]

The Capes of Virginia and the dangerous Middle Ground Shoal between them were the scene of frequent wrecks. A London ship grounded on Cape Charles in a fresh northwest wind in 1729, the master and crew barely escaping with their lives. A Glasgow ship, the *Success,* was driven by a violent storm in 1746 from her anchorage at the mouth of York River clear over to the Middle Ground "with 3 Anchors ahead," and a sudden storm in 1761 overtook the schooner *Good Intent* of North Carolina just after she stood into the Chesapeake, and drove her over the Middle Ground where "the Seas broke very high."[46]

A more serious storm attended by torrents of rain in 1769 leveled houses and crops, spoilt tobacco, blew down trees, blocked roads, and destroyed mills. Four ships in the York River were driven aground; another ship, lately arrived from London, successfully rode out the storm only by cutting away both main and mizzenmasts. All the smaller vessels grounded: one sank at Gloucester Point, another went ashore, and a third was stove to pieces. Moreover, the top of a wharf at Yorktown was carried away, and a schooner ran her bowsprit into a nearby storehouse. Perhaps the most destructive storm since 1667, it was called "a most dreadful hurricane" by the *Virginia Gazette.*[47]

Electrical storms, also unusually violent by Old-World standards, from an early time attracted the attention of settlers and visitors. Clayton wrote the Royal Society in 1688 that they often destroyed chimneys and killed people, and while at Jamestown he saw lightning split the mast of a vessel.[48] When large ships were struck, serious damage sometimes resulted; at other times the bolt ran harmlessly down the mast, across the deck, and into the water. The ship *Expedition,* riding in Patuxent River in 1745, ready to sail for England with a full cargo of tobacco, had her mast split by lightning during a severe electrical storm in which a house was struck, several people burnt, and cattle killed. This misfortune obliged her master to unload a good part of her cargo in order to refit her and caused great delay in her dispatch.[49] A delay of this kind in wartime might be very serious. A ship that missed convoy had to remain in the Chesapeake for another year or risk capture by the enemy that lurked off the Capes. In time of peace a delay might mean that a ship would miss the peak of the market in England, thereby depriving the owners of the crop of their profit that year.

Another seasonal phenomenon was the spring freshet. These floods were caused by heavy spring rainfall and by the melting of snow in the piedmont and mountains where the rivers of the western shore took their rise. Although troublesome, most freshets caused little comment. Occasionally they were unusually destructive. William Byrd I wrote that on April 26 and 27, 1685, when "a mighty fresh" came down James River, the water rose three feet higher than ever before, carried away all the fences, and ruined all his tobacco plants. Before passing its peak a few days later, it flooded the ground floor of his dwelling house, Belvidere, in the heart of the present site of Richmond.[50]

Another unusually bad freshet occurred in James River in 1724. John Custis wrote that "wee had such a violent flood of rain and prodigious gust of wind that the like I do believe never happened since the universall deluge," adding that it destroyed most of the tobacco in the region, wrecked some houses, and drove several vessels ashore. In 1738 the Rappahannock River suffered a severe freshet, "occasion'd," as the *Virginia Gazette* reported, "by excessive hasty Rains." Considerable damage resulted, especially to the public warehouse at Falmouth where the water rose within a few inches of the roof and entirely spoilt the forty or fifty hogsheads of tobacco that were lodged there. Again in 1752 the upper parts of Virginia, the Rappahannock and Potomac basins, experienced what was regarded as the greatest freshet known for many years. On this occasion the *Virginia Gazette* reported that the water rose in many places "near Thirty Feet perpendicular" causing considerable damage to the land adjoining the rivers and destroying many houses, bridges and tobacco barns.[51]

As a result of the rapid settlement and deforestation of the piedmont upcountry during the eighteenth century, freshets became progressively more destructive, reaching their culmination in 1771, with the worst flood in Chesapeake history. News of it first reached Williamsburg in a letter from Richmond reporting that "the greatest Fresh in James River ever known," at least twenty feet higher than in 1766, had either carried away or submerged the warehouses at Westham and Shockoe, the former containing three hundred and the latter about three thousand hogsheads of tobacco. The many trees driven down by the rapidity of the current imperilled even the largest ships, driving them from their moorings and carrying several ashore, besides overturning small boats and thus drowning a number of mariners.

The next issue of the *Gazette* carried a full account of the unexampled destruction. The flood ruined many acres of fertile soil. One tract of land worth £10,000 was reduced in value to as many hundreds. Farrar's Island, never before affected by freshets, had eighty acres of fine land rendered useless, "the Soil being gone, and in its Stead ten or twelve Feet deep of Sand, upon which a layer of Stones, as if paved." In some places hills of sand deposited by the flood stopped up channels and altered their courses. A ship at Warwick sounded at the height of the freshet and found that it exceeded the common tides by more than forty feet. In Richmond an observer noted that the time from "the first perceivable Rise of the River at that Place was about Sixty Hours and the Water sometimes rose at the Rapid Rate of sixteen Inches an Hour."[52]

This freshet also affected the Rappahannock, causing even more damage there than the great freshet of 1738. Colonel Richard Bland wrote that "Impetuous Torrents rushed from the mountains with such astonishing Rapidity that nothing could withstand their mighty Force." The flood rose so high that large numbers of hogsheads floated out of the warehouses, Falmouth losing nine hundred and Dixon's three hundred. In addition, much salt and other goods washed away, and several vessels were driven from their moorings. In all, the colony lost about six thousand hogsheads of tobacco and sustained damage to the extent of £2,000,000 sterling, according to contemporary estimates.[53] Little wonder, then that the *Gazette,* in summing up the destruction, declared the freshet of 1771 to be an "almost general Calamity!"

It must not be supposed, however, that life along the Chesapeake was in constant turmoil. Hurricanes, storms, and freshets were uncommon occurrences, rarely as destructive as the exceptional ones just described. Except for the normal succession of the seasons accompanied by varying phases of agricultural activity, life was serene and uneventful, and the violence of nature was seldom manifested. Despite a few unpleasant aspects such as the heat of summer, the abundance of mosquitos, and an occasional storm, the colonists generally considered the country to be, as Smith put it, "a faire Bay, compassed but at the mouth with fruitfull and delightsome land."[54]

o   o   o

The New World cast a spell over the minds of seventeenth- and eighteenth-century Europeans. It was a vast hemisphere hitherto unoccupied by Christian people; a land of tremendous distances, impenetrable forests, gigantic trees, and lush vegetation;

a land of rich and surprising variety, untold natural resources, and limitless potentialities. To the Englishman of Shakespeare's day it seemed that this paradise had been reserved by Providence since the beginning of time as the theatre for the empire of the latter ages! The primeval aspect of the country, with its forests of tall trees, created the impression of great antiquity and reminded the visitor of the probable appearance of Europe in ancient days. One English traveller, impressed by the thickly-wooded shores of the Chesapeake, remarked on their "Reverend Gloom," thought they "seemed the Retreat of some antient Druids," and felt "a kind of Reverence for so awful a Scene, really much calculated for a Sear of Superstitious Rites and Ceremonies." He reflected that in prehistoric times "the now despoiled and desart Regions of Achaia, and the Territories of Italy, Gaul, and Britain, bore just such an aspect."[55] The same idea was expressed in a poem of 1612, called "London's Lotterie," calculated to induce people to buy tickets in the Virginia Company's lottery.[56] In consequence, the names America and Virginia became clothed with romantic associations for Englishmen of that day and news was eagerly sought from the plantation on the Chesapeake.

The early settlers, ravished by the first sight of it, considered the "whole Continent of Virginia" to be a place "beautified by God, with all the ornaments of nature, and enriched by his earthly treasures."[57] Being aware of the audience they had in England, the early explorers were not slow to send back glowing accounts to astound the Old World with the wonders of the New. The oaks, Smith reported, were so tall and straight that "they will beare two foot and a halfe square of good timber for 20 yards long." Of the cypresses he said there were some eighteen feet in circumference at the base and "50, 60, or 80 foot without a branch."[58] Other accounts substantiate these, and even as late as 1765 a Scottish visitor travelling in Virginia remarked on the great number of tulip trees "not less than twenty feet round, and Ninety high."[59]

Equally impressive were the numerous waterfowl that frequented the Chesapeake and fed upon the wild celery and other
aquatic plants that grew there in such profusion. Smith and two
companions in a small boat off Kecoughtan brought down 148
waterfowl with three shots. About the middle of the seventeenth-
century Robert Evelyn, describing a flock of ducks he had seen
in flight near the head of the Bay, estimated it to be a mile square
and seven miles long. Alsop, in his breezy fashion, stated that
waterfowl "arrive in millionous multitudes" in Maryland about
the middle of September and take their "winged farewell" about
the middle of March, "but while they do remain, and beleaguer
the borders of the shoar with their winged Dragoons, several of
them are summoned by a Writ of Fieri facias, to answer their
presumptuous contempt upon a Spit."[60]

The most striking account of the large numbers of waterfowl
appears in the journal of Danckaerts and Sluyters in 1680, who
found the water so black with ducks that it resembled "a mass of
filth or turf." When the ducks took flight there was a "rushing
and vibration" of the air like a great storm coming through the
trees or like the rumbling of distant thunder. Wild geese were
also abundant. The same two Labadists recorded that, as they
pushed their way in a small canoe into a creek, the geese rose
in such enormous numbers that the noise made by their wings
sounded like a whirlwind or storm.[61] Although these early accounts seem almost fantastic, there is good reason to believe that
conditions in the Chesapeake made it an unsurpassed natural feed-
ing-ground for waterfowl. The bows and arrows of the Indians
were too short-ranged and inaccurate seriously to reduce the
enormous numbers of fowl, which propagated free from any
effective hostile influence until the coming of the white man.

Other creatures of the New World also intrigued the early
settlers, the flocks of four or five hundred turkeys (some weighing
fifty pounds), the foot-long bullfrogs whose deep bellowing resembled that of an ox, and the numerous turtles that sunned

*A portion of Thornton and Fisher's chart of* VIRGINIA, MARYLAND, PENSILVANIA, EAST AND WEST JARSEY, *London, 1706, showing lower part of Chesapeake Bay.*

themselves on the riverbanks and swam with their heads out of water. Occasionally a sea turtle found its way into the Chesapeake—a ninety-pound one was caught with a hook and line off the mouth of Chester River in 1753[62]—but the more common variety was the terrapin, a creature that abounds in the salt marshes of the Eastern Shore. Today considered the choicest variety by the gourmet, the diamond-back terrapin was so common in the eighteenth century that it is said to have been an annoyance to fishermen. In 1797 the Maryland Assembly, in order to protect slaves from being forced to eat terrapin too often, passed a law forbidding slaveholders to feed it to them oftener than once a week.[63] This delicacy is now so rare that a five-inch diamond-back terrapin brings four dollars, and an ordinary portion of stew made from its meat—even in a Maryland restaurant —costs at least three and a half dollars.[64]

Swarming with every sort of fauna, the Chesapeake country received an enthusiastic tribute from an eighteenth-century settler who reported that "Nothing less than a Whole Volume could give a Catalogue of the rareties of this New World."[65] The Swiss visitor, Michel, pronounced the country to be a "real zoological garden,"[66] and Alsop in his grandiloquent style declared that

he who out of curiosity desires to see the Landskip of the Creation drawn to the Life, or to read Natures universal Herbal without book, may with the Opticks of a discreet discerning, view *Mary-Land* drest in her green and fragrant Mantle of the Spring. Neither do I think there is any place under the Heavenly altitude, or that had footing or room upon the circular Globe of this world, that can parallel this fertile and pleasant piece of ground in its multiplicity, or rather Natures extravagancy of a super abounding plenty.[67]

Most impressive of all, from the maritime point of view, were the variety, abundance, and size of fish that thrived in the warm waters of Chesapeake Bay. The Reverend Alexander Whitaker reported that the sea fish came into the rivers of Virginia in

March, remaining until the end of September: first the herring, then shad, and finally rockfish. Trout, bass, and flounders entered before the others had gone. Then came multitudes of great sturgeons. He also mentioned having caught pike, carp, eels, perch, crawfish, and terrapin,[68] and the Jesuit Father White spoke of whales, porpoises, mullets, soles, plaice, and mackerel.[69] Sheepshead and alewives were also numerous, the former, according to an early account, having received its name because a broth made of its flesh tasted like mutton broth, and according to another, "from the resemblance the eye of it bears with the eye of a Sheep."[70] Oldmixon in 1708 mentioned the stingray as peculiar to the Chesapeake, and told of certain other curious fish, such as the "Coney-Fish" (a fresh-water fish like an eel, usually called burbot), the catfish, a fish "in the form of a Dragon," and the "Toad-Fish" which when taken out of water swells until it is "like to burst."[71]

The great plenty of fish in Virginia and Maryland particularly appealed to the fancy of Englishmen. Oldmixon thought the "prodigious Plenty" of them hardly credible to a European. "Some of the Stories that have been told," he admitted, "are certainly romantick, and are rejected as fictitious, such as Shoals of Fishes, swimming with their Heads above Water, and to be taken by Hand, loading a Canoe with Fish in the open Sea by one *Indian* in half an Hour," yet he insisted that no other rivers in the world were better stored than those of the Chesapeake country.[72] Just before the Revolution Dr. Robert Honyman while travelling on the Eastern Shore found a large number of fish in a shallow run from a milldam—so many, in fact, that "they were obliged in many places to swim slanting on their sides" and that he could have caught a good number of fine fish with his hands "without the water coming over my shoes." The fish were yellow perch (*Perca americana* or *flavescens*) and Honyman was told that they were equally plentiful in the other runs and millponds of the region, that "the Hogs were the principal devourers of them and that they fattened them mightily."[73]

64

As in the case of the trees and flocks of wildfowl, the enormous size of the fish amazed the early settlers. Shad were commonly a yard long, sturgeon varied from three to twelve feet, and drumfish often six.[74]

The three aquatic animals that particularly attracted the attention of European visitors were the stingray, the sea nettle, and the porpoise. The first was mentioned by Smith, whose experience with a stingray near the mouth of the Rappahannock River is well known. When stung by one, his thigh swelled and smarted so painfully that he thought himself dying, and gave instructions to his men for the disposal of his body. Upon his recovery, Smith bestowed the name Stingray upon the nearest point of land—the southern lip of the mouth of the Rappahannock—and Stingray point retains the name until this day.[75]

In 1688 the Reverend John Clayton described sea nettles, or jellyfish, as little things "like a Jelly, or Starch that is made with a cast of Blue in it; they Swim like a small Sheeps Bladder above the Water—downwards there are long fibrous strings, some whereof I have found near half a Yard long." One day when his ship was becalmed off the Virginia Capes, Clayton induced a mariner to scoop up several sea nettles in a bucket of water so that he might observe them at close range. The sailors, in a "sportful" mood, rubbed the creatures on one another's hands and faces, and where they touched "it would make it look very Red, and . . . smart worse than a Nettle."[76]

A century later Nicholas Cresswell described "a Fish called a Portugeeze Man of War," nine inches across and sixteen feet long, as a "bladder upon the water, always swimming upon the top," transparent in color, with a body "like a bunch of red worsted."[77] These creatures caused a great deal of suffering in the Chesapeake, generally of too minor a nature to find its way into the annals of history: fishermen, oystermen, mariners, and bathers frequently felt the sting of the picric acid in the streamers of jellyfish. On one occasion, however, the *Maryland Gazette* car-

ried the news item that in 1750 an Annapolis laborer fell overboard from a small boat in Rappahannock River, became entangled "in a great number of Sea nettles," and was drowned.[78]

Visitors seldom failed to mention the porpoises of the Chesapeake. Michel wrote that these "fish" were found in great numbers and grew so large that "by their leaps, especially when the
weather changes, they make a great noise and often cause anxiety
for the small boats or canoes." While swimming one day, he was
warned by a colonist of the danger from porpoises.[79] An English
traveller in 1736 lost his baggage and was cast into the Bay when
his punt was overturned by wantoning porpoises, one of which
"stupid Hogs came souse against one Side of the Punt."[80]

As the Chesapeake is invariably associated with the oyster, it
is interesting that this was the first food seen by Christopher
Newport upon landing in Virginia. Percy's *Discourse* relates that
on April 27, 1607, an exploring party came upon a fire in which
the Indians "had been newly roasting Oysters." The Englishmen
tasted the oysters and described them as being "very large and
delicious."[81] Like the primeval trees and native fish, Chesapeake
oysters were remarkable for their gigantic size, and like the fish
and waterfowl, for their extraordinary abundance. The warm
waters of the Bay, continually supplied with organic sediment
washed down by the freshets from the rich piedmont lands and
the fertile topsoil of the tidewater, provided generous nourishment
for the oysters that abounded in them. Huge clusters of oysters
in the lower courses of the principal estuaries were exposed like
reefs at low tide. Michel, writing that the abundance of oysters
was incredible, told of his experience in York River, when the
sloop which was to land him at King's Creek grounded on an
oyster bed, and had to wait two hours for the flood tide to
get free.[82]

As for their size, Strachey reported in 1610 that he saw oysters
thirteen inches long in Virginia, and Michel, nearly a century
later, found them four times as large as English oysters, so that he

66

cut them in two before putting them in his mouth. Oldmixon stated in 1708 that some of them were as big as a horse's hoof, and early in the nineteenth century a visitor described them as varying in size from one to seven inches in length and being "in the shape of a negro child's foot."[83]

Oddly enough, notwithstanding Percy's praise of the delicacy of their taste, oysters were not highly esteemed by seventeenth-century Virginians and Marylanders, who considered it a hardship when circumstances forced them to rely upon oysters as their principal source of food. During the "starving time" at Jamestown, a number of colonists repaired to the oyster banks in the lower James and subsisted for nine weeks on nothing but oysters and a pint of Indian corn apiece per week. In Maryland, the Kent Islanders took to eating oysters only when they were faced with starvation. Indians, it seems, had a more discriminating palate than our ancestors![84]

The process of oystering, still familiar to those who sail the waters of the Chesapeake, was graphically described in 1702 by the observant Michel. All that was needed was a boat and a pair of wooden tongs. Of the latter he said: "below they are wide, tipped with iron." At the time of the ebb the oystermen rowed out to the beds and reached down with their long tongs, which they pinch tightly together and then "pull or tear up that which has been seized."[85]

Only a few years later, in 1705, the Reverend Francis Makemie, in making a plea to Virginians and Marylanders to build towns in their colonies, suggested that the "vast plenty of oysters" would provide a beneficial trade both with the towns and with foreign parts. The Chesapeake, he thought, had "the best Oysters for Pickling and Transportation, if Carefully and skillfully Managed."[86] This was the first time that an oyster trade or the feasibility of preserving oysters was suggested. Makemie's proposal fell through, but by the middle of the century oystering had become a regular vocation rather than a part-time occupation. In

1752 Benjamin Bryan, a tavern keeper in Williamsburg, advertised for "a Sober Person, who hath been us'd to the Employment of an Oysterman on York River," intending to pay him to supply his tavern with oysters,[87] and in 1760 George Washington had trouble with an oysterman who tied his boat up at Mount Vernon landing, offended the fastidious colonel by his "disorderly behaviour," and had to be ordered away in a most peremptory manner. By 1779 there were oyster merchants who advertised their wares in the *Virginia Gazette*, offering to supply oysters in considerable quantity at their landings, either open or in shells.[88]

Methods of preserving oysters remained a subject of discussion down to the end of the colonial period. Landon Carter of Sabine Hall recorded in his diary in January, 1770, after his annual three-day house party, that "the oysters lasted till the third day of the feast, which, to be sure, proves that the methods of keeping them is good, although much disputed by others." Because of the prevailing skepticism about preserving them, the prejudice against eating oysters in the summer months became established in colonial days. Those who lived near the source of supply, however, ignored the prejudice. Carter ordered eight bushels of oysters in July, 1776, and served them in every known form: "raw, stewed, caked in fritters and pickled."[89]

In addition to providing food for the colonists, oysters supplied them with shells that were used as flux for iron smelting, and for making roads, garden paths, and mortar for bricks. In 1751 Carter Burwell, while engaged in building Carter's Grove, a fine mansion on the James south of Williamsburg, advertised for oyster shells for building purposes, offering three shillings a hogshead "for any Quantity that can be delivered at his Landing."[90]

The natural plenty of oysters was so great that there was no need to cultivate them in colonial days, yet a gentleman on the Eastern Shore of Maryland appears to have done so as a hobby. He did not make it his whole business—his "Schemes were of a much higher nature than for anything that can be pickt out of the mud." But happening to hear of a person famous for raising mushrooms, a sudden thought entered his mind, "why may not a man become famous for raising Oysters, since a little care and management may make the relish of the one equal to the Flavour of the other?"[91] This example of cultivation of oysters by a "Connoisseur of that Turn" on the Eastern Shore in 1753 stands alone in the colonial history of Chesapeake Bay. The oystering industry, as we know it, began in the nineteenth century.

The crab, like the oyster, was remarkable for its size and abundance. One variety in early colonial days grew to be at least a foot long and six inches wide, providing a meal for four men,[92] but as a gastronomic delicacy, the crab suffered an even more ignominious reception than the oyster. Quite unappreciated in the seventeenth century, it was slow to gain headway in the eighteenth century against the conservatism of English eating habits. Oldmixon mentioned them in 1708, Fithian referred to them in 1774, William Byrd III fancied them and, late in the century, the inhabitants of the Bay region came to acquire a taste for them. Jedidiah Morse wrote in his American Universal Geography in 1796 that the Chesapeake was "remarkable for the excellency of its crabs."[93]

## CHAPTER THREE

# Shoals and Shallows

THE maritime flavor which the many tidal estuaries gave to life in the Chesapeake tidewater forcefully manifested itself in colonial travel conditions. Early in the seventeenth century the governor of Virginia told King James I that the inhabitants of the colony required boats and canoes for their "sudden transport" across creeks and rivers. Near the end of the colonial period, William Eddis wrote that one could not travel any considerable distance in Maryland without crossing rivers "wider than the Thames at Woolwich." Such rivers, of course, were too wide to bridge. Consequently, transportation in the Chesapeake country was dependent upon a series of ferries on both sides of the Bay. Tidewater roads often did little more than connect one ferry with another. Travel was a constant alternation between riding a few miles—perhaps a dozen—overland and ferrying over a broad creek or river. Before the middle of the eighteenth century the colonial traveller going from Williamsburg to Annapolis, a distance of about one hundred and twenty miles as the crow flies, had to cross no fewer than a dozen ferries.[1]

Chesapeake travel required two kinds of ferry: one that crossed a narrow river or creek in well-protected waters, and another that crossed a wide expanse of water like the Bay itself or the lower courses of the great rivers, where a sudden squall might raise a rough sea. The boats used for the two kinds were very different. The former were described as "a kind of flat-bottomed lighter or *scow*" with "upright sides of about two feet six inches or three feet, and sloped up at each end so as to ride over the waves." Drawing very little water, they could come close to shore, and the lowering of a gangplank or apron allowed horses and men to pass directly from the ferry to dry land. On some occasions, however, there is mention of a causeway or wharf to facilitate landing.[2]

Sometimes as much as thirty feet long and eight feet wide, these ferries carried from three to six horses besides passengers. The ferrymen rowed, poled, or pulled the boat across the river by means of a rope. Rope ferries slid along a fixed line, the propulsion being accomplished by means of a notched heaver, and the ferryboat was thus "walked" across the stream. A contract for a ferry in Baltimore County specified a rope four and a half inches in circumference.[3]

In 1703 Thomas Chalkley crossed a river eight miles broad in a curious kind of ferry that was nothing more than two canoes tied together. The eight men and seven horses in the party were all transported at once. The horses were obliged to stand with the forefeet in one canoe and their hind legs in the other.[4]

The gusts and squalls so characteristic of the region, particularly when the wind is from the southwest, made ferrying dangerous even where the rivers and creeks were narrow. When Chalkley crossed in the two canoes tied together, the wind suddenly rose while they were in midstream, and the water ran so high that the waves split one of the canoes, obliging the passengers to bail continuously with their hats to keep the frail craft afloat. On another occasion, while crossing the Potomac at Piscataway where the river is less than a mile wide, a ferryboat was struck by a violent squall that made the horses lose their footing and caused apprehension on the part of the passengers. The brother of the Reverend Hugh Jones was drowned while crossing the Chickahominy ferry, and on another occasion the *Virginia Gazette* regretfully announced that Francis Russworm of Nansemond County, "who played such a sweet Fiddle," was drowned in crossing over a ferry in 1773.[5]

Because of their frailty, ferryboats of this sort were of no use on the broad estuaries, the lower courses of the great rivers, or on the Bay itself. Such waters required a more seaworthy vessel propelled by other means than poling or pulling ropes. Usually rigged as sloops or schooners and occasionally decked, the vessels used for this purpose were generally called "passage boats" or "packet sloops." They were often trim craft of good construction.[6] Fithian found the Rock Hall ferries, which crossed from Annapolis to the Eastern Shore, well built and strongly manned.[7]

One of the sailing ferries operated by Samuel Middleton of Annapolis was described as a "neat sailing Boat, 20 Feet Keel, rigged Schooner Fashion, deck'd to her Stern Sheets, and neatly painted Green." A packet sloop in Virginia, "built entirely for the purpose," had "the largest and best cabin of any boat in the colony,"[8] but they were not all so commodious. A passenger from Annapolis to Kent Island said that the ferry was an open boat, and a traveller aboard a Rock Hall sailing ferry slept in "one of the men's holes they call beds," and had nothing to eat but salt beef and hard biscuit. Some idea of the size of sailing ferries can be had from the fact that the schooner *Peggy* of Hampton carried ten persons to Annapolis in 1746, and one of the Kent Island ferries rescued twelve sailors from an overturned longboat in the middle of Chesapeake Bay, the same year.[9]

As early as 1729 John Carman at Bohemia Landing, at the head of Chesapeake Bay, advertised a sailing ferry that would transport passengers and goods to any part of the Virginia and Maryland tidewater—a kind of water taxi rather than a ferry with a specified destination. He also maintained horses and carts to convey goods overland from Delaware Bay to the headwaters of the Chesapeake. In 1736 a sailing ferry was in operation between the Eastern Shore of Virginia and Yorktown, Norfolk, Gloucester, Jamestown, and other ports. This ferryboat, described as a "Chaloupe," was apparently a deep-draft vessel, as it anchored beyond a shoal a mile off the Eastern Shore and carried the passengers ashore in a small punt. In 1746 at least two sailing ferries regularly ran between Annapolis and Kent Island, one operated by Ashbury Sutton, the Annapolis shipbuilder, and the other by Elizabeth Wilson. By 1753 another ferry had joined the Kent Island competition.[10]

## Shoals and Shallows

In 1761 the residents of Annapolis discussed the proposal to run a decked packet boat weekly between that city and Oxford on the Eastern Shore. Persons subscribing thirty shillings a year toward its maintenance were to enjoy free passage, although they had to provide their own food.[11] In 1765 a regular passage boat plied between Norfolk and Hampton, and four years later a packet sloop was in regular service between Norfolk and Williamsburg. At the end of the colonial period the most important of Chesapeake sailing ferries was the Rock Hall ferry, which made a passage of over twenty-five miles up the Bay from Annapolis. It had the advantage over the older Kent Island route of cutting off no less than thirty miles of land travel between Annapolis and Philadelphia. This became the principal route to the north, esteemed preferable to the other two—the Western Shore route and the Kent Island route—whenever the wind was favorable.[12]

The sailing ferries of the Bay, like the rope-hauled ferries of the rivers and creeks, occasionally made rough passages. The ferryboat *Kent,* belonging to James Hutchings of Kent Island, was overturned by a "Sudden Flaw of Wind" in 1760, but the passengers were saved by the heroic action of the skipper, who swam ashore to procure a boat "to fetch the others off." When Fithian crossed in the Rock Hall ferry in 1774, he recorded in his journal that he was very seasick for the first time in his life. The most uncomfortable passage of all was that of Dr. Robert Honyman, who crossed from Annapolis to Rock Hall in 1775 in a decked, schooner-rigged ferry. Towards evening a strong breeze sprang up; after dark, the ferry missed port, beat up and down for some hours, and grounded several times. It was a bitter cold night, and no food was available except "sailor's salt beef and hardtack." Moreover, the bunk into which he crawled was too hard and uncomfortable for sleeping.[13]

However, it was not always cold and rough on the Chesapeake. On fine spring and summer days, with fluffy white clouds scudding across the blue sky, and with schools of porpoises diving as

73

the cutwater plowed the waves, crossing the Bay in a sailing ferry proved to be a delightful experience. One English traveller who crossed from the Eastern Shore to Yorktown in 1736 was quite carried away by the beauty of it all, which, as he said, "plung'd us into an admiring Extasy." Being in the middle of the lower Bay about noon on one of those days when the Bay wore a mirror-like surface, he was entranced by the "golden Rays of the Sun darting thro' the Gloom of the surrounding Woods, and reflected upon the translucent Face of the watry Plain." He became lyrical over "the infinity of Sloops and Barks that appeared everywhere around, the fine Vista's up York and James Rivers . . . the prodigious Flights of Wild Fowl, that darken'd the Air . . . the Dolphins and Porpoises wantoning on every Side, and a long, long View of wide Ocean." Years later, even the critical William Eddis was obliged to admit, while sailing from Yorktown to Annapolis, that "a gentle breeze wafts us pleasantly on our course; the day is splendid, and the interesting and magnificent objects which continually strike the eyes, infinitely exceed the utmost powers of description."[14]

From the early days ferries were licensed in Virginia. In 1640 Henry Hawley received a patent under the seal of the colony authorizing him to keep a ferry on Hampton River and giving him a life monopoly in return for limiting his fee to a penny for carrying across a passenger.[15] The next year, and again in 1643, the Virginia Assembly passed an act creating free ferries to be maintained by means of a levy in each county. As this attempt to establish public carriers proved premature, the assembly repealed the acts in 1647. The levies worked a hardship upon the "poore people scarce makeing Use of the said Ferryes." Thereafter county courts established ferries as they saw fit and prescribed rates and conditions, but were forbidden to charge the county for their maintenance.

In 1673 another fruitless attempt was made to establish free ferries, when the assembly announced its intention of doing so, and called upon the county officials to recommend the most convenient places for such service.[16] Bruce found that during the years following the act's passage the wages of ferrymen varied between eight hundred and two thousand pounds of tobacco a year. By 1696, however, ferrymen were being allowed to charge fees—indicating the failure of the system established in 1673. At Bermuda Hundred the fee for a man and horse was 1s. and for a foot passenger, 6d. At Jamestown where the river was wider, the rate was 3s. 6d. for a man and horse and 1s. for a pedestrian. In Lancaster County foot passengers paid as much as 2s. 6d.[17]

In 1702 the Virginia Assembly passed an act that reduced ferries to an orderly system and established by law all rates for ferriage. This act also set forth the duties and privileges of ferrymen. They were obliged to serve from sunrise to sunset, and were subject to penalties if they sought to charge more than the fixed rates. On the other hand, they were exempt from the public levies and from all public service such as the muster of the militia, clearing highways, and impressment. Moreover, they were protected in their monopoly by a fine of five pounds imposed on unlicensed persons who presumed to set passengers over a river or creek where there was a licensed ferry, unless the passengers were going to church. Half the fine went to the informer, and half to the injured ferryman.

For the rest of the colonial period the principles laid down in the act of 1702 remained the basis of the Virginia ferriage system. It was re-enacted in 1705 and made perpetual in 1713.[18] After that there was a series of acts establishing new ferries and altering rates of the existing ones. Before 1720 rates were prescribed for men and horses. By that year, however, carriages and wagons had begun to appear on the scene, and the act of 1720 provided that four-wheeled vehicles be charged at the rate of six horses and two-wheeled vehicles at the rate of four horses.[19]

The various acts concerning ferries tended to reduce the previous rates rather than to increase them, probably as a result of the increasing volume of traffic. In 1734 the rates for coaches and wagons were reduced by a third or more, a four-wheeled vehicle to be charged the same as four horses, and a two-wheeled one the same as two horses, a reduction of one-half.[20]

The ferriage system in Maryland differed from that of Virginia in two ways: Maryland was more successful in establishing free ferries, and, unlike Virginia, did not license, grant monopolies to, or fix the rates of privately operated ferries. By about 1720 a system of free public carriers existed in the province side by side with private boats charging fees. The sailing ferries of the Bay and most of the ferries on the Potomac and certain other rivers were private, while on many of the smaller rivers, especially in the upper part of the Bay, free ferries supported by county levies flourished. The wages of the public ferrymen varied considerably. The Patapsco ferryman in 1719 received only five hundred pounds of tobacco, while in 1723 he received seven thousand pounds of tobacco. In other cases, annual wages of from three thousand to eight thousand pounds were customary.[21]

There was considerable variety in the details of the contract between the county courts and the public ferrymen. Sometimes special requirements or exemptions were included, for example that only a certain number of horses must be carried, that a certain number of men must be in attendance, that wheat and other produce must be transported, or that only passengers and horses need be carried. Sometimes the public ferries were free to all comers; sometimes only the residents of the county that supported them enjoyed free passage. But Gould believes that, in general, the public ferries were free to all, otherwise there would have been numerous complaints about rates.[22]

On several occasions in the eighteenth century Lord Baltimore sought to obtain control over the ferries of Maryland with a view to augmenting the proprietary revenues. He derived his claim from the Maryland Charter of 1632 which specified that the Lord Proprietor was to enjoy all the rights and privileges in his American palatinate that the Bishop of Durham exercised in County Durham, and among these was the licensing of ferries. Repeated attempts to enforce his claim were made by the Lord Proprietor in the years 1723-41, and in the former year he referred to ferry licenses as an established privilege in his instructions to his agent. In 1731 a statement of the proprietary revenues included an item of £13 10s. sterling from this source. Growing bolder, the proprietor sought to stop the county courts from contracting with public ferrymen concerning rates and assessing the amount upon the inhabitants of the county, a practice which Lord Baltimore called "an Invasion of our Right," and an injury to the people without any law to warrant it.[23]

This precipitated a struggle between the county courts and the agents of Lord Baltimore. At the November court of Baltimore County in 1733, Daniel Dulany claimed the sole right of establishing ferries for the Lord Proprietor and threatening with prosecution all ferrymen who neglected to obtain a license from the proprietary agent. The county court, however, formally denied the claim and wrote Governor Ogle informing him of their decision.

Despite the popular protest, as the decision of the Baltimore County Court proved to be, the proprietary agent began a series of suits against recalcitrant ferrymen who refused to buy licenses. The program seems to have been remarkably effective, for in 1741 the lower house of the assembly complained that "Persons Traveling the King's High-Ways . . . are stopt and hindered in their Journeys . . . by means of the Restraint laid on the several Ferries . . . by his Lordship's Agents . . . by terrifying the People with vexatious Law Suits and heavy Fines." The House adopted by a vote of thirty-six to three a long resolution aimed at this proprietary prerogative. The protest was so vigorous that the elderly Lord Baltimore immediately dropped the attempt and let the claim lapse.[24]

In 1752, however, the new proprietor renewed the attempt, but with no more success than attended the efforts of his predecessor. Governor Sharpe wrote in 1755 that "our Ferries are kept by Order of County Courts," and the ferrymen paid in tobacco levied by the justices of the county, or else they are privately operated by persons who "demand of Passengers what they please and passengers must pay their Demand or be refused conveyance." Although convinced that regulation of ferries was imperative, Sharpe predicted that the people of Maryland would never vest the proprietor with the right and power of granting licenses and that Lord Baltimore would never assent to a regulating bill passed by the assembly. This deadlock explains the laissez-faire policy of Maryland.[25]

Among those ferries that were operated by private persons, free from government regulation, great competition existed. When, as often happened, several ferries crossed the same river only a mile or two apart, there was keen rivalry between them. One of the most vigorous of these contests took place on Potomac River. In 1745-47 six ferries over that river carried on a verbal battle in the *Maryland Gazette*. Richard Harrison and Robert Dade, who kept rival ferries at Nanjemoy, both advertised "a good Boat and Hands" and "constant Attendance." One operated from his house, the other from the Nanjemoy post office. Charles Jones, keeper of the Lower Cedar Point ferry, stressed good boats, skilful hands, "good Usage," and above all else, the fact that his ferry was "by 18 or 20 Miles the nearest Way to *Williamsburg*."[26] Henry Thompson, on the other hand, expressed his determination to continue his ferry notwithstanding the malicious rumor to the contrary spread by "some evil-minded, spiteful Persons in order to prevent me getting Custom to my Ferry." Thompson also stressed the excellency of his boats, saying that in addition to "a very good Boat, with able Hands," and "a fine Yaul in order to set those over, who do not incline to go with their Horses," he was then building a very commodious ferryboat, large enough to carry six horses. The keeper of the Clifton ferry, in Fairfax County, pointed out that although the distance from Annapolis to Williams-

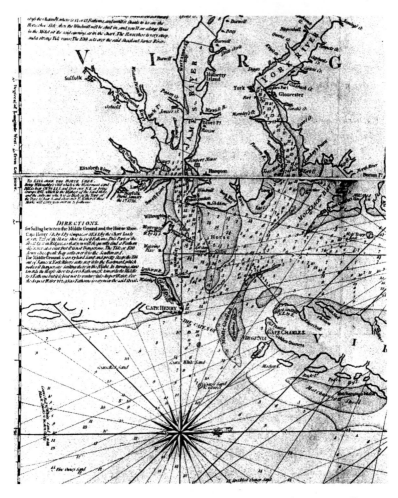

*A portion of Anthony Smith's* NEW AND ACCURATE CHART OF THE BAY OF CHESAPEAKE, *London, 1794, showing the Capes, Hampton Roads, etc. First edition appeared in 1776.*

burg was "something greater" than by other routes, yet "as the great River Potomack is so narrow at this Place, and passable almost in all Weather, it may justly be accounted the readiest way."[27]

The lengths to which ferrymen would go to obtain custom may be seen in the advertisement of George Dent, who kept a ferry in Charles County about two miles above Thompson's ferry. His passengers, he said, "avoided a Creek that lies in the usual Way to *Thompson's Ferry,* dangerous to Strangers: And Marks are set up at convenient Places on the Road from *Port-Tobacco,* for the Direction of those that incline to pass over the said Ferry." Another ferryman, Richard Mackubbin, who kept a ferry on South River above Londontown, advertised that it provided a shorter and easier route between Queen Anne and Annapolis than the Londontown ferry.[28]

Similarly, the sailing ferries between Annapolis and the Eastern Shore vigorously competed with one another. In 1746 Sutton's ferry to Kent Island charged 10s. for a man and horse, 7s. 6d. for a single passenger, and 10s. for two passengers. At the same time, Elizabeth Wilson operated her deceased husband's ferry from Broad Creek on Kent Island to Annapolis. In 1753 James Hutchings of Cow Pen Point, Kent Island, began a ferry to Annapolis, charging 12s. 6. for a man and horse, 7s. 6d. for a single man, and 5s. per passenger if more than one. In 1762 Samuel Middleton of Annapolis was operating a Kent Island ferry, charging 12s. 6d. for a man and horse.[29]

Ferries were often kept by persons who had other vocations as well. William Brown, who kept the Londontown ferry on South River, also carried on the "Business of Joyner and Cabinet Maker." Ashbury Sutton was a shipbuilder in Annapolis, and Samuel Middleton was the jovial host of one of the most frequented taverns in Annapolis. In several instances, women kept ferries, particularly Elizabeth Wilson in Maryland and Jane Claiborne in Virginia.[30] A number of other ferrymen also operated taverns. Advertisements frequently offered "good Beds, Liquors, and Provender for Horses," as well as "good Boats and skilful Hands." As this was an important source of revenue for ferrymen, some who kept free ferries found it worth their while as tavern-keepers to advertise them in the colonial newspapers.

The absence of regulation of ferries in Maryland was not so disastrous as might be supposed. As long as there was competition, the standard of performance remained high and the rates low. In general, ferriage in Maryland was no more costly than in Virginia. Now and again, however, the lack of regulation led to great injustice. When the freshet of 1752 broke down milldams and carried away the bridge over the Patuxent near Upper Marlboro, several unscrupulous persons owning boats took advantage of the necessity of travellers by charging them the outrageous sum of two shillings for setting them over the river although it was so narrow that "a Man may toss a Maul over." They even had the effrontery to charge the same rate for ferrying the carrier of His Majesty's mail from Williamsburg.[31]

Other complaints about colonial ferries were also common. Sometimes they had to do with the ferryman, sometimes with the delays ferrying caused travellers. An accusation was made in Cecil County that the county ferry over Elk River "hath of Late been kept by Negroes whose Master being for the most part absent" have been "very Negligent in Discharging their Duty." When Dr. Honyman crossed from Annapolis to Rock Hall in a sailing ferry, he found the vessel navigated by "two young lads, and but indifferent sailors," and the food and accommodations poor. Complaints about delay were even more frequent. The heavy scows that served as river ferries were slow and cumbersome. If only one were in operation and the ferryman happened to be on the other side of the river, the traveller had to build a fire in order to make "a Smoak" to attract the ferryman's attention. Then two complete crossings were necessary before the impatient traveller was enabled to continue his journey. Even without the indifference and incompetence of ferrymen—and those shortcomings were common—numerous ferries necessarily slowed down one's journey considerably. Eddis, writing in 1769, said that "though every proper method is adopted for expedition yet such a number of considerable waters unavoidably occasion great delays."[32]

All contemporary comments were not in criticism of the ferries of the Chesapeake country. At least one British writer, Lord Adam Gordon, had nothing but praise for them. He wrote in 1765 that "the Ferries, which would retard in another Country, rather accelerate" travel in Virginia, and the ferrymen "assist . . . all Strangers with their Equipages in so easy and kind a manner, as must deeply touch a person of any feeling."[33]

o    o    o

The mouths of many of the rivers flowing into the Chesapeake, though broad, are partially obstructed by sandbars and mudbanks, and the Bay itself, though free from reefs, has certain rather inconveniently-placed shoals, like the Middle Ground, the Horseshoe and Wolf Trap. Together with many long points, sandspits, and islands which abound in certain parts of the Bay, these shoals render the navigation of the Chesapeake somewhat precarious for mariners not familiar with its waters.

In the days before lighthouses and buoys, the mariner was obliged to know the bottom intimately—a familiarity which came only from long experience and which, contrary to the proverb, bred respect rather than contempt. The position of shoals and spits, discovered by sounding, was remembered by a series of compass bearings taken on prominent landmarks. By a combination of these soundings and bearings, the mariner, in clear weather at least, could thread his way between the underwater obstructions and find channels, however tortuous, with no other instruments than a lead line and compass.

The sailing directions for the Capes compiled by Lieutenant Inglis of H.M.S. *Sultana* in 1772 directed the incoming mariner bound to Hampton Roads to verify his latitude by sounding, the channel or fairway carrying nine to twelve fathoms. When up with Willoughby Point, the navigator, according to Inglis, "cannot fail of seeing the Mark tree bearing W½N." Similarly, he instructed incoming vessels to look for Selden's house (at Buckroe), telling them they might expect nine or ten fathoms when it bore NW by N at a distance of two and a half miles.[34]

An example of the use of landmarks as ranges is to be found in Anthony Smith's sailing directions for entering James River. "Point Comfort," he declared in 1776, "is Chiefly covered with Woods, but there are Two Places on it where no Trees grow; which make it appear like Two Islands. The Leading Mark is a Windmill over the Middle of the Northernmost opening, which will carry you by the Shoal of Willoughby's Point, in 7 or 8 Fathoms." Smith warned the navigator not to "Stand to the Northward" beyond the point where it shoals to ten fathoms on the Horseshoe side. There, he continued, "The Windmill will be shut in, and you'll see a large House in the Midst of the said Opening."[35]

Between 1590 and 1776 no fewer than two hundred and forty-seven maps pertaining to the Chesapeake country were published. Most of these were copies, varying in scale and exactitude, of the John Smith map of 1612, the Augustine Herrman map of 1673, or the Fry and Jefferson map of 1751, and were largely unconcerned with hydrography.[36] Hence after more than a century of settlement, the needs of the mariner were as yet unmet.

In response to royal instructions to the governor, the Virginia Council in 1731 took steps to prepare a map of the colony based on accurate surveys and a hydrographic chart of the soundings of the coast, Bay, and rivers. The work was interrupted two years later when Horace Walpole, then Auditor-general of the Plantations, objected to the payment of an annual salary of £150 to Councillor John Robinson, the director of the project in Virginia, and to the estimated cost of £5,000.[37]

Nothing further was done officially until 1763 when the Board of Trade recommended to the Privy Council that a general survey of all the colonies be made on a scale of one mile to an inch with important channels and harbors on a scale of four inches to the mile. For the purpose of determining latitude and longitude by astronomical observation, the surveying party required a cutter, two whaleboats, and one large longboat, besides £200 worth of instruments—astronomical and Hadley's marine quadrants, theodolites, telescopes, compasses, a pair of seventeen-inch globes, and "Shelton's Clock or Time piece for Astronomical Observations."[38] As the estimated cost over a five-year period was £3,700, the proposal, like the earlier one, fell through, and the mapping and charting of the colonies was left to private initiative.

Some of the seventeenth-century maps, such as that of Augustine Herrman, contained a few soundings, indicating channels and the more important shoals near the mouth of the Bay, but the earliest surviving mariner's chart is Thornton and Fisher's chart of Virginia, Maryland, Pennsylvania, and New Jersey. This chart, based largely upon Herrman's map but with more attention to hydrography, was made about 1695 and published in *The English Pilot* of 1706.[39] It was on a small scale—about nine nautical miles to an inch. Although reissued in nine subsequent editions of *The English Pilot* before the Revolution, it was probably of no more than limited use in actual navigation.

The first large-scale mariner's chart of Chesapeake Bay, complete with soundings and sailing directions and sufficiently detailed for actual navigation, was that of Captain Walter Hoxton in 1735,[40] an extraordinary piece of work that was perhaps the best hydrographic chart of any part of colonial America of that day. Not having the opportunity to survey all the tributaries of the Chesapeake, Hoxton incorporated data "borrow'd from the Old Map" with his own findings in order to make his work as complete as possible. Whether or not the map he referred to was the Thornton and Fisher chart is not known.

84

The outline of the land is sketchily done. Compass roses and variation for 1732 and 1733 are given. Soundings are in fathoms except at the head of the Bay, where they are in feet. A latitude but no longitude scale is shown. Except for the Potomac, Patapsco, Northeast, and Chester rivers, only the mouths of the tributaries of Chesapeake Bay appear, and in the case of the Chester River no soundings are indicated. Sailing directions are included for navigating between Middle Ground and Horseshoe Shoals, for entering James River, for sailing from Love Point (on Kent Island) into Patapsco River, and there is an extensive account of the Gulf Stream with an "Attempt towards Assertaining" its limits, course, and strength.

As a result of observations made during his twenty-three voyages to Maryland, Hoxton concluded that "the said Current always runs nearly in the same part or space of the Ocean," a fact which he rightly considered to be "very useful to those who have occasion to Sail in it." In order to enable the northbound mariner to stay in the current and the southbound one to avoid it, Hoxton gave the difference of longitude between Cape Henry and the eastern and western limits of the Gulf Stream for intervals of thirty minutes of latitude from 35° N to 37° 30′ N inclusive and the breadth of the current in longitude for each of those latitudes.

To enable the mariner approaching the Virginia Capes to estimate his distance off land by soundings, Hoxton included the following table:

Lat. 36° 28′ N  Distance from the Land  20      Leagues is 45 Fathoms
Lat. 36° 40′ N  Distance from the Land  20      Leagues is 32 Fathoms
Lat. 36° 52′ N  Distance from the Land  20      Leagues is 80 Fathoms
Lat. 36° 55′ N  Distance from the Land  18½ Leagues is 35 Fathoms
Lat. 37° 08′ N  Dist. from Cape Henry  26½ Leagues is 30 Fathoms

In order to fill out the lower right-hand corner of his map, Hoxton inserted a large-scale chart of Herring Bay with sailing directions and soundings in feet. As this bay was unimportant, its inclusion can only be explained by the supposition that Hoxton had family or business relations with Samuel Chew, whose house and plantation were situated on Herring Bay. The only connection of this kind that has been found is that Walter Smith (1715-1743) of Calvert County, stepson of Hyde Hoxton, the brother of the cartographer, married Elizabeth Chew about the time of—or shortly after—the publication of the chart. This union, like many others in colonial days, may have grown out of friendship begun and sustained by commercial relations between two families.

Captain Walter Hoxton, son of another Captain Walter Hoxton of London who had business relations with—and may have been a partner of—John and Samuel Hyde and Company, merchants, of London, was master of several vessels operated by that concern in the Maryland trade for at least eight years prior to the publication of the chart.[41] Apparently he was not well educated, because the spelling on his chart was even more eccentric than was justified by the variable practice of educated men of the day, but in maritime affairs he was a man of outstanding ability, careful, observant, and skilful in his profession. To his qualifications in this respect his chart bears abundant witness.

His brother, Hyde Hoxton, settled in Maryland and by marrying Susanna Brooke, daughter of Clement Brooke and granddaughter of Major Nicholas Sewell, became allied with some of the most powerful families in the province. Hyde Hoxton's son, Walter, a nephew and namesake of the cartographer and through his mother a first cousin of Charles Carroll of Carrollton, was the "Cousin Watty" who attended the Collège de St. Omer in French Flanders with the "Signer" during the years 1750 to 1753.[42]

Undoubtedly a boon to the masters in the Chesapeake trade—particularly to those of British vessels—the Hoxton chart represented in convenient graphic form information that would fill many pages of sailing directions. It was a short-cut to knowledge of the Bay that would otherwise have taken a mariner years to acquire. Running through several editions, it was used so much that the four surviving copies are in extremely poor condition.[43] However, it had the disadvantage of not including the important western shore rivers—the James, York, Rappahannock, and Patuxent. The need was filled in 1776 by the appearance of *A New and Accurate Chart of the Bay of Chesapeake*—one of the most beautiful products of American colonial cartography—which claimed to be based on "Several Draughts made by the most Experienced Navigators, Chiefly from those of Anthony Smith, Pilot of St. Mary's."[44]

Actually, this new chart was based very largely upon Hoxton's work. It has the same appearance—cliffs and headlands are represented in the same way—and in a majority of cases in the Bay itself Hoxton's soundings are reproduced. Smith gave the same information about the Gulf Stream, the same table of distance off shore by soundings and latitude, and the same sailing directions for Middle Ground and Horseshoe Shoals, for entering James River, and for sailing from Love Point into Patapsco River. Most remarkable of all, he included the same insert of Herring Bay with landmarks, soundings, sailing directions, and variation just as they were forty years before.

On the other hand, the Anthony Smith chart was a great improvement over its predecessor in that it was more handsomely drawn and engraved, provided a longitude as well as a latitude scale, showed more soundings around the Middle Ground, Horseshoe Shoal, and Hampton Roads, and extended the hydrography to include most of the western-shore and some of the Eastern-Shore rivers. It includes Norfolk, the Elizabeth and Nansemond Rivers, the James as far as Jamestown, the York to West Point (with soundings only as high as Yorktown), the Piankatank (with no soundings), the Rappahannock to a little below Fredericksburg (with no soundings), the Patuxent to Lyon's Creek, and the Elk, Bohemia, and Sassafras Rivers; soundings are provided for the Chester, Miles, and Choptank Rivers, and for Tangier and Pocomoke Sounds. In particular, the Potomac River was greatly

*Beach Scene (from an oil painting by Ludolf Backhuysen, 1631-1708, in* Chefs-d'oeuvre Old Sea Paintings, *London, 1928).*

elaborated by means of new soundings, more landmarks, tidal observations, indication of ferries, a table of distances, and sailing directions. Consequently, Smith's work was widely used by British vessels trading to the Chesapeake after the Revolution, and ran through several editions.[45] Unfortunately, we know little of its author except that he was a pilot of St. Mary's.[46]

o   o   o

Experienced masters who knew the bottom of the Chesapeake found little difficulty in negotiating a passage along winding channels between shoals and spits. To be sure, they occasionally miscalculated and grounded on a sand bar, but in calm weather little harm was done. If the flood tide failed to float the vessel, the master procured small craft and transferred enough of the cargo into them to accomplish the desired result. The inexperienced master, however, even if provided with sailing directions and charts, was not too sure of himself. To one not familiar with the Bay, one point is often indistinguishable from another and the sailing directions of the time depended upon the correct identification of landmarks for the purpose of taking bearings. Just how a master who never before entered the Chesapeake might be expected to recognize the "Mark tree" or "Selden's house" in Lieutenant Inglis' sailing directions is not very clear. Too much depended upon the navigator being thoroughly at home in the Chesapeake and knowing its waters like the palm of his hand. For this reason, professional pilots made their appearance in the Bay within a few decades of the first settlement.

One of the earliest of them, John Rablie (or Rablay), who served as a pilot on the Eastern Shore of Maryland as early as 1644, was apparently inexperienced in his profession. While piloting a ship belonging to a merchant named Henry Brooke, Rablie "brought his ship aground and carried her beyond the port"—the two unforgivable sins of a pilot. Brooke refused to pay him what he asked for pilotage and for attendance upon him with his hands and shallop. Rablie, carrying the case into court, sued Brooke for 4,130 pounds of tobacco. The defendant produced a witness to testify to the plaintiff's ineptitude as a pilot, but the court found for the latter, although awarding a much smaller compensation than requested, only 750 pounds of tobacco.[47]

In 1660 several masters trading to Virginia complained of the absence of pilots to steer their vessels up James River and of the lack of beacons or buoys to mark dangerous shoals. To meet the situation, the assembly passed an act in 1661 which created the office of Chief Pilot of James River, named the first incumbent, and fixed the amount of pilotage and beaconage fees. In return for rather generous recompense, the Chief Pilot was required to establish and maintain "good and sufficient beacons in all necessary places from Willoughbies Shole . . . to James Cittie," and to replace within fifteen days all beacons which for any reason might be removed. The first occupant of the office, Captain William Oewin, was authorized by the act to collect five pounds sterling for piloting vessels of greater burden than eighty tons, and to take two pounds from all vessels declining his services. In addition, all vessels riding in Hampton Roads had to pay him one pound ten shillings. In the case of ships not piloted by him, the fee reimbursed him for placing and maintaining beacons.[48]

Captain Chichester succeeded Oewin, and was in turn succeeded by his son, William Chichester, who, in petitioning Governor Nicholson in 1691 to continue his commission, set forth that his father for many years had been "the sole pylott of James River, Commissionated thereto" by the governor. William Chichester also revealed that he had made "itt his only business, care, and livelyhood," and offered to instruct others who might succeed him on his death.[49]

By 1702 James River had two pilots, John Lowry and Israel Vaulx; York River one, William Seyers; Rappahannock two, Garrett Minor and James Jones; while the Potomac and the Eastern Shore had none. In the same year Lowry, one of the two "commissionated" pilots in James River, petitioned the Virginia Council to protect him against the unauthorized competition of one John Pattison. Lowry pointed out that he and his family occupied a plantation near the mouth of the James and owned a boat, whereas the upstart, Pattison, "a single person, having no settled abode, boat nor hands" except a vessel he had borrowed, "doth take upon him to pilot ships in the River." The petitioner also prayed that if the governor should constitute more pilots than those formerly appointed, he might have his turn, as was usual in England.[50]

With John Lowry's petition began the movement that eventually gave a monopoly to commissioned pilots in Virginia, bringing the system of that colony into rough conformity with that of Great Britain. In 1720 a more vigorous demand for protection from unlicensed competitors was made by two pilots, James Bannister and William Loyall, who complained that "divers persons entirely ignorant of the Rivers" had presumed to serve as pilots.[51] As a result of this and other similar complaints, Virginia continued and extended the policy, begun in 1661, of maintaining a rigid system of licensing. As the safety of many vessels depended upon the professional skill and integrity of the pilots, they were regarded as public officials. Therefore, the assembly felt obliged to define their duties and privileges.

By an act passed in 1755,[52] which gave clear enunciation to the system, the power of appointing pilots was vested, as formerly, in the governor. A new feature consisted of the nomination of a board by the governor for each district of the colony, to examine all applicants. If the candidate passed the examination, the board certified the same to the governor, whereupon his excellency granted the applicant a certificate known as a "branch." This use of the name "branch" is an interesting example of the transference of English nomenclature to the colonies, since a "branch" originally was a certificate granted by the brethren of Trinity House to pilots who had passed an examination testing their competence. The term does not appear to have been used in Maryland.

The act of 1755 specified the duties of a pilot: he was required to keep a good watch for vessels, he was obliged to answer calls, and he was responsible for the results of his own negligence or carelessness. If he failed to go aboard a ship that signalled him, the district board might conduct an investigation, and unless he could plead sickness or some other lawful cause—of which there were very few—he might be suspended by the governor. If sued and convicted "by due course of law" for negligence or carelessness, the pilot was not only liable for damages, but also forever incapacitated for his former office.

The act also established an elaborate schedule of pilotage rates and provided penalties for pilots who collected, or attempted to collect fees in excess of the ordinary ones. The rate from Cape Henry to Hampton Roads amounted to £1 Virginia currency; to Yorktown £2; to Urbanna £3; and to Smith's Point, at the mouth of the Potomac, £5. With one exception, all the other rates, instead of being fixed sums, varied with the draft of the vessel in feet. For example, pilotage from Hampton Roads to Norfolk was 1s. 8d. per foot, and from Hampton Roads to Jamestown 4s. 6d. per foot. These rates applied only to ships, snows, and brigantines; for schooners and sloops the charges were two-thirds as much.

In return for duties and obligations, the pilot obtained certain privileges, for in addition to the fees which he might collect, he enjoyed exemption from the muster of the militia. Moreover, he received protection in his monopoly through fines imposed on unauthorized persons who piloted vessels. The act of 1755 levied a fine of £10 for the first offense, £20 for the second, and £40 for each subsequent one upon any unlicensed person who "shall presume to take upon himself to conduct or pilot any ship or vessel" in Virginia waters. An exception was made in the case of a person assisting a vessel in distress provided he delivered her up to the first licensed pilot who offered his services. Such a person was exempted from the fine and allowed by a subsequent act of 1762 to ask and receive half the statutory fees.[53] Another privilege of the utmost importance was granted by the act of 1755 through the requirement that every vessel entering the Bay must take the first pilot who offered his services or else pay him half pilotage to the first port. Although free to decline pilot services thereafter, vessels sailing without one, but following a vessel with a pilot, had to pay half fees.

The act of 1755 named certain points above which an incoming vessel need not take a pilot. A master of a ship bound to James River could decline the services of a pilot who failed to present himself below Willoughby Point; if to York River, below Egg Island; if to Rappahannock, Gwynn's Island; and if to Potomac, Smith's Point. The act of 1762 substituted for these provisions a general requirement that no vessel need take a pilot who failed to offer his services below Horseshoe Shoal.

Masters of vessels entering Chesapeake Bay before 1755 occasionally declined offers of pilotage—sometimes because of genuine familiarity with the Bay, sometimes because of parsimony. By piloting the vessel himself, the master could charge the usual pilotage against the vessel and pocket the money. This false economy on occasion led to catastrophe. When a pilot came alongside the ship *Berry* of London as she entered the Virginia Capes at dawn on August 2, 1750, the captain ignored the offer of his services. Taking advantage of a fine, fresh gale the *Berry* with all sails "set and full" soon left the pilot boat a good way astern. After a while the water began to shoal alarmingly. Soon the lead line found bottom in only three fathoms. A passenger named Mr. Sweeney, who had lived in Virginia, assured the captain that he was running on Willoughby Point Spit. The captain, being "superior to caution," was confident that he had cleared it. When the water shoaled to a point that was dangerous, the ship's company became terribly alarmed. At length even the captain was moved and in utmost terror and confusion backed all sails and looked imploringly astern for help. Notwithstanding his rebuff,

93

the pilot good-naturedly waved his hat to indicate that the *Berry* should bear off to the northward. By doing so she just cleared the spit, narrowly escaping shipwreck in sight of her destination.[54]

The provision obliging ships to take the first pilot that appeared as they entered the Bay prevented their exposure to unnecessary danger as a result of the avarice of their masters. It also prevented pilots from competing with one another, whereby the more proficient ones or those willing to serve at reduced rates would have the advantage over the others. As a result, it stimulated them to build faster pilot boats, each pilot aspiring to be the first to reach the side of an incoming ship. A specific type of vessel soon evolved for use as pilot boats—fast, weatherly boats, doubtless on the mold of the already developing clipper-schooner.

The act of 1762, which renewed and amended the act of 1755, withdrew from the governor the power of appointing local boards for examining pilots, transferring it to the county courts of the maritime region. Each board, consisting of three men, was entitled to a fee of twenty shillings for examining applicants and empowered to grant pilot's branches—a right which under the act of 1755 had resided in the governor. Each pilot, or firm of pilots,[55] had to keep "one sufficient pilot boat, rigged and provided according to the usual manner, of eighteen feet keel at the least," or forfeit fifty pounds. The act also established a new schedule of rates which added certain landings on the upper James and increased pilotage on the Potomac.[56]

The surviving bills and receipts for pilotage reveal that vessels frequently employed pilots to conduct them in and out of the Bay—by the Middle Ground, Horseshoe Shoal, to such places as Hampton Roads, Norfolk, Yorktown, Urbanna, and Smith's Point—but relatively seldom to guide them up and down the rivers. Although the first pilot to reach the side of an incoming ship had a virtual monopoly and could charge fees to the full extent of the law, no vessel was obliged to retain the services of a pilot beyond the first port within the Capes. Seasoned masters of many years' experience in the tobacco trade knew the Virginia rivers as well as they knew the Bristol Channel or the Firth of Clyde, and in consequence, the demand for river pilots was relatively small.[57]

Incoming vessels desiring the services of a pilot and finding no pilot boat signalled in one of several ways. One was to hoist certain flags, such as an ensign and a jack. Another and more common practice, especially in the rivers, was to discharge a cannon.[58]

The story of pilotage in Maryland is quite different. The proprietary authorities claimed the sole right of regulating pilots, just as they claimed the sole right of regulating ferries, and then neglected to use it. Meanwhile, by virtue of that claim, the assembly of the province was prevented by the Lord Proprietor from legislating on the subject. Consequently, nothing was accomplished and pilots, like ferrymen, were left unregulated in Maryland throughout the colonial period. In response to instructions from Lord Baltimore in 1743, Henry Ward, the proprietary agent, made a half-hearted attempt to force pilots to apply for licenses, in the hope of reducing the practice of Maryland to an orderly system like that of Virginia.[59] Although some pilots requested and received licenses, the system came to nothing because the Lord Proprietor neglected to prosecute unauthorized pilots or to establish fixed rates. As a result, anyone who chose could serve as a pilot in Maryland waters and charge what the traffic would bear.[60]

Another attempt in 1754 to revive the licensing system also failed hopelessly.[61] Thereafter the idea of regulating Maryland pilots was permanently abandoned. But although no limit was placed on pilotage fees and no regulation imposed on those who served as pilots, the rates charged were kept within reason by competition. On the whole they were about the same as those in Virginia.[62]

o     o     o

95

The waters of the Chesapeake and its tributaries as far inland as the fall line are accessible to ocean tides. In consequence, mariners had to contend with tidal currents as well as winds, shoals, and narrow channels. Fortunately, the tides in the Bay are much less than those at other places along the Atlantic coast. When the tidal current begins to flood, water flows into the Chesapeake between the Virginia Capes, but the distance between the Capes is so small in proportion to the surface area of the Bay that before a very large volume of water can flow into the Chesapeake, the sea current slackens and begins to ebb. Meanwhile, the relatively small volume of water that has passed between the Capes spreads itself over the large area of the Bay and rivers. This explains why the rise of the tide in the Chesapeake is so small. Upon the ebbing of the tide, the current sets eastward between the Capes, but before a very considerable quantity of water can flow through such a relatively narrow mouth, the sea tide turns again and the current begins to flood.

The mean tidal range, 2.8 feet at Cape Henry, decreases gradually as one sails up the Bay or into the mouths of the rivers. As one continues up the rivers, however, the tidal range increases slightly, reaching its maximum at the fall line.[63] In view of the fact that the rise of the tide is caused by the volume of water carried into the Bay between the Capes and up the rivers from the Bay by tidal currents, it seems surprising that the range is greater at the heads of the rivers than at their mouths. The reason is that the volume of water carried by the flood current is confined as it advances up the rivers by an increasingly narrow river bed, so that as the banks contract and the depth diminishes, the level of the water rises higher than it would in the open sea. Furthermore, the backing-up of the river current by the tide is more pronounced, for the same reason.

Being relatively small, Chesapeake tides are affected by the direction of the wind. Oldmixon wrote that the tides of the Bay were "scarce discernable" when the wind holds from the northwest, but at other times they "flow as they do in England." When the wind is southerly, however, the tides in the upper Bay are abnormally high. In 1754 a violent storm from the southeast "swell'd the Tide" at Annapolis to a height never before known by the oldest inhabitant. The water at the town dock rose fourteen or fifteen inches higher than the normal tide of twenty-four inches.[64]

There is a curious phenomenon in the rivers of the Chesapeake country known as half-tides, currents which at certain times run on either side of and opposite to the main current in the channel. After the current begins to flood in the channel, minor currents continue to ebb for several hours near the river banks. When the current begins to ebb in the channel and for several hours after the half-tide is in flood. The explanation is that the many tidal creeks and branches of the rivers continue to fill with water and do not have high tide until several hours after high water in the channel. When the channel current begins to ebb, these tidal tributaries continue to flood. In other words, there is a time-lag between the maximum rise and fall of the tide in the channel and in the tidal estuaries of the tributaries. This difference creates minor tidal currents on either side of and setting contrary to the main tidal current in the channel. The extent of the time difference depends upon the area and length of the tributary tidal reaches, and upon the width of the main channel and its proximity to one bank or the other. In rivers like the James and Potomac that have considerable tributaries, the half-tides in many places are relatively strong and often set for as long as two hours after the turn of the current in the channel.

Mariners of the Chesapeake were quick to perceive this phenomenon and to take advantage of the favorable currents it provided when the channel current was adverse. As early as 1688 an account of the half-tides of the Chesapeake was written by the Reverend John Clayton to the Royal Society. After describing the half-tides and attempting to explain them, Clayton observed that they were a great advantage to the boats passing up and down the rivers.[65]

However, tidal currents were not always helpful to mariners. Off the Virginia coast there is a tidal phenomenon that was dangerous in colonial days. It is called "rotary tides" and consists of a current that sets in one direction for a few hours, then slackens and sets in another direction. In due course, the current after setting in various directions, moving counter-clockwise around the compass, returns to its original direction. Clayton noticed this peculiarity of the tide on his voyage to Virginia in 1688 and even attempted to measure the velocity of the current. While becalmed one day off the coast of Virginia, the ship's company "hoisted out a Boat, and took one of the Scuttles that covered one of the Hatches of the Ship, tying thereto a great Weight, and a strong long Rope." Letting it sink to a considerable depth and fastening it to the boat, they provided themselves with a fixed point from which to take measurements. By means of a sandglass and log line they found that the current set eastward at the rate of a mile and a half an hour. By seriously upsetting the dead reckoning of vessels these rotary tides proved, as Clayton declared, "of mischievous Consequence," causing many ships to be lost. Being "before their Accounts," as a result of these tides, vessels "fall in with the Land before they are aware."[66]

o     o     o

As the forests of the coastal plain yielded to the clearings of ever-increasing numbers of settlers, soil erosion set in and caused the smaller rivers and creeks to silt up. Moreover, floating trees and branches, particularly at the time of the spring freshets, often became entangled and obstructed channels.[67] The practice of vessels dumping ballast overboard while at anchor in harbors further accelerated the process. The resulting hindrance to navigation concerned the provincial authorities from an early time and induced them to take steps to counteract it. In 1679 Virginia delegated to the maritime counties the power to "cleare the rivers from loggs and trees, which may annoy and endanger boates, and sloops." As little was done under the authority of this act, the Virginia Assembly in 1680 passed an act requiring the county courts annually to appoint and order the surveyors of the rivers to clear them, under penalty of a fine of five hundred pounds of tobacco for neglect of duty. To prevent the felling of trees into rivers and creeks, the act imposed a fine of five hundred pounds of tobacco for the first offense and a thousand for each subsequent one.[68]

In line with this program the Virginia Assembly in 1691 passed an act forbidding the discharge of stone, gravel, and other ballast overboard, and requiring shipmasters to have it carried ashore, under penalty of a fine of £10.[69] Maryland in 1692 and 1704 passed similar acts, making it illegal for vessels to unload or cast out any kind of ballast into harbors or creeks, and requiring it to be carried ashore and deposited above high-water mark under penalty of two thousand pounds of tobacco for each violation.[70] As the Maryland act of 1704 was technically defective, vessels commonly violated the law with impunity. To remedy the defect, the Maryland assembly in 1735 passed an act making it illegal to throw ballast overboard at night, strictly forbidding the discharge of it in the Bay above Cedar Point or in any river below the low-water mark, and fixing the penalty at £50 currency for each violation. This act apparently served its purpose, and it was renewed without alteration several times and eventually made perpetual. An additional act in 1753 specifically forbade ironworks on the Patapsco to dump dirt into the river, thereby obstructing the channel. Thereafter, vessels generally discharged in the lower Bay as soon as they entered the Capes, or else waited until they came to their moorings and then carried it ashore in small boats.[71] A low-lying point in West River, Maryland, called Chalk Point, is traditionally supposed to have been a favorite place for discharging chalk brought over as ballast from England.

Although the explanation of the name might appear apocryphal, there is definite evidence that Samuel Galloway of West River ordered Captain Tippell of his ship *Russell,* then in England, "please to put 50 Tons of Chalk on board her for ballast" and return to West River.[72]

Nothwithstanding all efforts on the part of the colonial governments, rivers and creeks continued to silt up, obstructing channels and isolating river towns that depended upon water carriage for their very existence. In 1738 the inhabitants of Beall Town, on the Eastern Branch of the Potomac, complained in a petition that the freshets had brought down trees that "Lodged in and Choak'd up the Channell" of the branch so that "Boats and other Craft Cannot be Brought up to Lade or Relade goods at the usuall Landing place." In this instance, as in many similar ones, the county authorities attended to the petition, but in a few cases—notably in connection with the upper Potomac, the Monocacy, and the Conococheague—the assembly took action.[73]

Not satisfied with the maintenance of existing channels, the inhabitants of the Chesapeake region occasionally became enthusiastic about plans for opening to navigation the upper reaches of some of their rivers. The Potomac and James, which in later years excited the ambitious dreams of the canal-builders, were by no means the principal objects of colonial schemes. Oddly enough, the opening up of the head waters of the Patuxent elicited more response than plans for the Potomac. In the early 1730's the inhabitants of Anne Arundel County and Prince George's County conceived a plan to open the Patuxent to navigation for some twenty miles above the town of Queen Anne, and in 1733 the Maryland Assembly passed an act empowering the residents of those two counties to raise funds for the purpose, and prohibiting the obstruction of the river by weirs and mills or by felling trees into it. Apparently the leading spirit behind the project was Richard Snowden of Montpelier, who sought to provide his Patuxent Iron Company with water-carriage. By 1736 the river must have been opened for small boats at least, for in that year the Patuxent Iron Company asked and received permission to build a towpath along the bank of the river.[74]

A quarter of a century later, the western branch of that river—on which Upper Marlboro is situated—was silting up at an alarming rate. In 1759 the second Patuxent scheme began. A lottery was drawn to provide money for the project of clearing the branch and building a town landing.[75] Meanwhile, the persons concerned with keeping open the reaches of the Patuxent above Queen Anne exercised their rights under the act of 1733 and a supplementary act of 1735, with great rigor but little success. The difficulties of combatting the natural tendency of the river to silt up were so great that Snowden and the others for whose benefit the project was given governmental encouragement failed to derive the advantage they expected. Moreover, the acts which the assembly passed to enable Snowden to undertake the project prohibited the inhabitants on the Patuxent for twenty miles above Queen Anne from building mills of any sort—a provision that caused loud complaints. In 1761 the injured persons petitioned the governor and assembly to repeal the acts on the grounds that the scheme was impracticable, and far from proving of advantage to Snowden or to any of the inhabitants along the river, was "a manifold Injury."[76]

With nearly two thousand miles of navigable waterways within the Virginia Capes, the failure of the plan to open up twenty miles of the headwaters of the Patuxent is not surprising. From an early time the colonists proved to be prolific in schemes for ambitious undertakings quite beyond their power to execute. In the seventeenth century a canal was envisioned to connect the upper Chesapeake with Delaware Bay and in the eighteenth William Byrd II proposed a canal through the Dismal Swamp.[77] There was serious talk of digging one around Great Falls on the Potomac[78] and another to connect the James and York Rivers at Williamsburg.[79] The two Patuxent schemes are interesting examples of the colonial propensity for planning elaborate improvements to facilitate navigation, a disposition recognized as early as 1663 by Sir William Berkeley, who said of the tobacco planters that they are like "those Architects, who can design excellent Buildings, but have not skill to square their Timber, or lay their Bricks, and for want of money to procure men for these labours, their models remaine onely in their imaginations or papers."[80]

# Part II

## COMMERCE

## CHAPTER FOUR

# The Tobacco Trade

ALTHOUGH tobacco, in King James' view, was "loathsome to the eye, hateful to the nose, harmful to the brain," and "dangerous to the lungs," it became the mainstay of Virginia and Maryland economy in the seventeenth and eighteenth centuries, and ever since has been popularly associated with the colonial history of the Chesapeake Bay country.[1]

Among the objectives of the Virginia Company in planting a colony on the shores of the Chesapeake was to secure a fruitful land from which England might import all necessary commodities she then had to buy from foreign countries, an objective that fitted in nicely with the theories of mercantilism, the prevailing economic philosophy of the day.[2] By supplying England with necessities she would otherwise have to import from abroad, the colony would help the mother country reduce her foreign imports and obtain a favorable balance of trade. With this in view, the Virginia Company urged the colonists to send home a great variety of products—lumber, naval stores, wine, skins, and fish, besides roots and herbs to be used medicinally or as dyestuffs.[3]

As none of these products could be cultivated on a large enough scale or commanded a sufficiently elastic market in England to make them suitable staples for Virginia, the colony languished during its early years. Eventually, as a result of experimentation, the Jamestown settlers stumbled upon a commodity that proved economically feasible. In 1612 a confirmed smoker, John Rolfe, found that tobacco would grow well in Virginia and sell profitably in England. Becoming the rage almost overnight, tobacco captivated the colonists' imaginations like precious metal during a gold rush. They planted it in every available clearing, including the fort and streets of Jamestown, and by 1619 Virginia, which three years before had sent eleven commodities to England, now sent nothing but tobacco and a little sassafras.[4]

Although the use of tobacco was fashionable among the wealthy young bloods of London, who willingly paid its weight in silver, Rolfe's discovery of a money-making product for the colony did not please the Virginia Company. Sharing King James' opinion of smoking and fearing that the "deceavable weed" which served neither for "necessity nor for ornament to the life of man" might prove to be a passing fancy, the Company vigorously resisted the colony's shift to a single staple.[5] Instead, the Company in 1618 began an ambitious program designed to place the colony on a more secure economic foundation by encouraging the production of food and a variety of commodities that England lacked, and by establishing a fishery and iron, glass, lumber, and shipbuilding industries.[6]

All these plans failed. Being unable after 1618 to attract enough new subscriptions to finance them, the Virginia Company relied on money raised by lotteries authorized under the charter of 1612. So much money was raised in this manner during the years 1619 and 1620 that Parliament received complaints that trade and industry were being demoralized as a result of popular excitement caused by lotteries. When the Privy Council in 1621 deprived the Virginia Company of its right to hold such lotteries, the Company lost its only source of revenue.[7] The final blow came on March 22, 1622, when the Virginia Indians attacked the outlying settlements of the colony and massacred between three and four hundred of Virginia's 1,240 inhabitants. Discouraged and in a precarious financial condition, the Virginia Company abandoned its schemes for diversification of agriculture and industry, and soon afterwards was dissolved by action of the Crown.[8]

Dominating Virginia economy after 1622, tobacco remained the staple of the Chesapeake colonies, and its phenomenal rise is one of the most remarkable aspects of our colonial history. Imports of colonial tobacco into England increased from 60,000 pounds in 1622 to 500,000 pounds in 1628 and 1,500,000 pounds in 1639. By the end of the seventeenth century tobacco production in Virginia and Maryland exceeded 20,000,000 pounds a year, and in 1775 it exceeded 100,000,000 pounds. In the latter year it represented over 75 per cent of the total value of commodities exported from the Chesapeake colonies and was worth about $4,000,000.[9]

Everything considered, tobacco proved an excellent staple for Virginia, particularly in the early years of the colony. It required less acreage than grain, therefore the cost of clearing the forests was less. It had a relatively small bulk as compared to grain, therefore the cost of freight to England was less. Moreover, it fetched better prices in proportion to weight than grain. As a result, Captain John Smith asserted, a man's labor in growing tobacco was worth fifty or sixty pounds a year, but in growing grain only ten pounds.[10] For another thing, the soil of Virginia proved suitable to its growth. It took the colonists some time to learn the best methods of cultivating and curing the plant, but when they had mastered them, the soil was sufficiently well-adapted to the requirements of tobacco to produce a sturdy crop of good quality. Finally, as we have seen, the natural waterways of the Chesapeake and its tributaries, by affording ocean-going ships easy access to plantations many miles inland, made possible the rapid and continued expansion of its production.

After the London authorities recovered from their initial dislike of it, tobacco proved to be a highly satisfactory staple from the English as well as the colonial point of view. Importation of the Virginia leaf enabled England to cut down her imports of Spanish tobacco—an important objective because England had an unfavorable balance of trade with Spain. Moreover, as Virginia and Maryland production reached large proportions, England received more than she could consume, and was thus enabled to export vast quantities of the colonial leaf to the European continent, thereby increasing the value of her exports. The most powerful argument of all, however, in winning the approval of the Crown, was the ever-increasing flow of money into the royal treasury as a result of duties on colonial tobacco.

At the time of the settlement of Virginia, the English government had had no experience with colonies. The authorities, to be sure, entertained certain general ideas about the place of a colony in the commercial system of England, but they left the formulation of the particular features of colonial policy and the details of colonial administration to be worked out from time to time as the occasion arose. As Virginia, the first English colony, developed more or less accidentally into one that produced a single staple which fitted nicely into the English commercial system, it was in connection with Virginia that the English government experimentally worked out the rudiments of its first colonial policy. When the experiment was completed, as it was by the middle of the seventeenth century, the English government extended to all its American possessions the colonial system that had been worked out largely in connection with the tobacco colonies.

Out of the welter of trial and error that characterized Virginia colonial administration during the early decades of the seventeenth century, there emerged certain basic principles destined to remain permanent features of the colonial system until the disruption of the first British Empire in the 1770's. The colony was considered to be outside the fiscal limits of the realm of England, therefore its exports to the mother country were subject to customs duties. The colony was required to export those of its commodities that England needed directly to the mother country and not to foreign countries. The colony, in return, was given a virtual monopoly of the home market, for after 1619 the cultivation of tobacco in England was forbidden, and after 1624 foreign ships were excluded from Virginia trade. The underlying motive of these two prohibitory acts was the same—the security of the royal revenue. Thus the fundamentals of the English colonial system as embodied in the Navigation Acts of 1650, 1660, 1663, and 1696 were worked out in connection with the tobacco colonies prior to 1640, and after a period of preoccupation with internal troubles, the English government elaborated and expanded the system to include the whole colonial empire.[11]

o o o

At an early date after Rolfe's successful experiment, the Virginia planters gave up indigenous types of tobacco and imported South American seed. Soon afterwards two distinct varieties emerged, called oronoco and sweetscented, distinguished by the thickness, texture, and shape of the leaf. Oronoco was bulkier and coarser than sweetscented, and had a sharper leaf "like a fox's ear;" the sweetscented leaf was rounder and had finer fibres.[12] Oronoco was stronger in flavor; sweetscented was mild. Planters grew the former all around the Bay, but particularly in Maryland and in the back country on all the rivers. Sweetscented, requiring a type of soil of limited distribution, was largely confined to the banks of the great rivers, the James, York, Rappahannock, and Potomac.[13] Oronoco, which probably originated in the vicinity of the South American river of that name, still survives today in the varieties called oronoco and Pryors and their numerous progeny. The origin and post-Revolutionary development of sweetscented, however, are shrouded in mystery. Although there is no certainty about it, some authorities hold that the Maryland tobacco of today is descended from the sweetscented of colonial days.[14]

At an early date oronoco developed sub-species. By the end of the seventeenth century we hear of "very fair and bright large Oronoko,"[15] and in the eighteenth of the "smaller sort of Browne aranoka."[16] In 1729 and 1741 oronoco was mentioned as though several sorts were known to exist.[17] As time went on, the planters came to distinguish other varieties, such as long-green, thick-joint, Brazil, lazy, shoestrings, and little Frederic. More commonly the planters spoke of the varieties as "Colonel Carter's sort," "John Cole's sort," or the sort of some other leading planter or crop master.[18]  Although there were several divergent species by the middle of the eighteenth century, for the purposes of inspection and trade all tobacco continued to be classified under the names of oronoco and sweetscented.[19]  As a result of the confusion caused by the increasing number of varieties, it became increasingly difficult for the inspectors to classify it.  Toward the end of the eighteenth century, therefore, almost all tobacco came to be classed as oronoco.[20]

Sweetscented, particularly that grown on the peninsula between the James and York Rivers, was considered the best in the world and was consumed largely in England.  As a result, it long brought a better price than oronoco, and down through 1724, when the market for it first fell off, a minister in a "sweetscented parish" could exchange his legal salary of 16,000 pounds of tobacco for half again as much cash as the minister in an "oronoco parish" could obtain for his.  Oronoco, on the other hand, was at first thought too strong for the Englishman of discriminating taste, although it was in great demand on the Continent, particularly in eastern and northern Europe, where smokers preferred it to sweetscented.  For that reason oronoco, although inferior by English standards, came to have a much wider market than sweetscented and, except in time of war when the Continental market was affected, was usually more profitable to planters than the more delicate sweetscented.[21]  Planters who specialized in sweetscented, not understanding why inferior tobacco brought greater net returns, considered the price differential unreasonable.  In 1735 a London merchant told John Carter that sweetscented would no longer sell at a high price and that the trade had so altered that "what formerly everyone was most forward to buy is now become a drugg."  He attributed the change in the position of sweetscented to the fact that "there is but little of this sort used in proportion to the whole Consumption, and the Tobacconists find among the common Tobacco . . . some as good as the most celebrated crops."  In any event, English tobacconists began to substitute the better grades of oronoco for sweetscented without complaint from their customers, and sweetscented began its long decline, ultimately disappearing from the records late in the eighteenth century.[22]

The annual routine of tobacco cultivation began in the spring, usually March or April, with the planting of the seeds.[23] Because of their small size—ten thousand may be accommodated in a teaspoon—they are not sown in the fields, but in specially-prepared seedbeds. The planter selected a site in the woods where the mould was virgin, cleared it, and burnt the timber and brush to enrich the soil and provide a layer of ashes in which the powdery seeds might be embedded. About May the tender plants appeared, and by June were sturdy enough to be transplanted to the fields, preferably freshly-cleared woodland.[24] Here the planter set them in little hillocks about three feet apart in parallel rows.[25] As the transplanting was done only in wet weather when the ground was soft, the wetness or dryness of the season at this time was of great concern to planters.[26]

Left alone, the tobacco plant would grow tall and produce many leaves of moderate size and thin texture. But the demand favored large leaves of full body. Therefore, when the desired number of leaves had appeared about a month after the plants had been set out, the plants were topped. This operation, frequently performed in the early days by the planter himself and later by a skilled servant or slave, was always regarded as a job for an expert. As the plant was topped by pressing it between the thumb and forefinger, the thumbnail serving as the cutting instrument, it was said that in the seventeenth century planters could be detected by means of the abnormal thickness and discoloration of their thumbnails.[27] After topping the tobacco, the planter, in order to keep the strength of the plant in the leaves, suckered it from time to time, an operation involving the removal of small shoots that sprang from the junction of each leaf with the stalk. Some planters also primed their plants, that is, removed the bottom leaves or lugs which were of low quality. Others did not do so, on the theory that it resulted in a serious loss of sap through bleeding. In addition to topping, suckering, and priming, plants were periodically weeded and wormed, the latter consisting of picking off and crushing the hornworms or grubs that fed upon the leaves.[28]

Reaching full growth about six weeks after being topped, the plants were between four and a half and seven feet tall.[29] When the leaves began to spot, thicken, and discolor, the plants were cut off at the base by means of a special tobacco knife and left in the fields to wilt. Then they were carried into specially-built tobacco barns or curing houses and suspended in such a way as to allow the air to circulate.[30] Sweetscented normally required about three weeks to cure; oronoco about six weeks. Thorough drying was important; otherwise the tobacco began to rot about three weeks after it had been packed in casks and proved worthless by the time it reached England.[31]

As the air-cured leaf was extremely brittle, the next step had to await moist weather. After a rainy day the stalks were taken down, bulked in piles, covered, and left a week or two to sweat, a process which humidified the leaf and made it pliable. Then the sweetscented was stripped by plucking the stem out of the leaf, thereafter being known as stemmed tobacco. Oronoco, which was seldom or never stripped, and sweetscented before undergoing that process were called leaf tobacco as distinguished from stemmed.[32]

In preparation for the final operation, that of prizing tobacco into hogsheads, the leaves were bound together in small bundles called hands and again bulked to keep them moist and pliable. Although hogsheads varied in size in Virginia and Maryland and at different periods, they were wooden casks about four feet tall and two and a half in diameter at the head. As soon as the weather was moist the prizing began. A barefoot laborer standing inside a cask laid the hands in smooth layers until the hogshead was full.

Then, by means of levers, weights, and screws, pressure was applied which forced the tobacco into a small space. More tobacco was put in, more pressure applied, until the hogshead was tightly packed. The head was inserted and secured, hoops put in place, and the hogshead weighed and marked with the owner's initials and personal device—the forerunner of the trade-mark. During the seventeenth century hogsheads weighed between 400 and 800 pounds, sweetscented being heavier than oronoco.[33] But in the course of the eighteenth century, as a result of an increase in the size of hogsheads and of the common practice of overprizing, hogsheads of sweetscented normally weighed between 950 and 1,400 pounds, and those of oronoco between 750 and 1,150 pounds.[34]

After the crop was prized, the casks were housed on the plantation until it was time to load them aboard tobacco ships anchored in the rivers, or, after the official inspection system had been established, transported by land or water to the nearest public warehouse. Where possible, planters transported their hogsheads by sloop or small craft called flats, because water carriage was easier, cheaper, and less damaging to the tobacco than overland transportation.[35] Sometimes, there being no choice, planters had to carry their hogsheads across country to the nearest navigable river or creek. This was done by rolling them on their sides along roads that were called and in some instances, where they have survived, are still called rolling roads. In order to protect the hogsheads, particularly when they had to be rolled a considerable distance, two large wooden hoops were affixed to each of them to absorb shocks and save wear and tear on the hogshead itself. But even this precaution was not always effective against the irregularities of colonial roads. Tobacco that was rolled ten or twenty miles generally sustained damage.[36] Horses were sometimes harnessed to the heavily-hooped hogsheads in the piedmont area, but this was uncommon in the tidewater, where they were rolled by hand. Late in the eighteenth century when wagons became more common they were sometimes used for carting hogsheads.[37] Although more or less continuous, the work of the plantation was not onerous. Work on the crop began before seedtime one year and extended beyond seedtime the next year, with no intervals of inactivity except during the late fall and winter when the frost made it impossible to strip or prize tobacco. The whole process of cultivation, including preparation of the seedbeds, planting, transplanting, topping, suckering, priming, frequent weeding and worming, cutting, bulking, curing, stripping, and prizing, consisted of at least thirty-six separate operations.[38] Tobacco required such detailed attention that a laborer seldom cultivated more than three or four acres containing ten thousand plants.[39] On the other hand, the work was not hard, except for hanging the tobacco to cure, and there was no physical hazard except when transplanting the seedlings in the wet fields in early summer.[40]

Although less strenuous than many other occupations, tobacco production was not without its anxieties and dangers. The planter always ran the risk of crop failure,[41] loss from improper curing and prizing,[42] or from shipwreck, pirates, and privateers,[43] and depression resulting from overproduction or the cutting off of the Continental market in time of war. Like other agricultural products, tobacco was greatly affected by the weather. A dry spell in the spring or fall delayed planting or stripping and prizing.[44] On the other hand, a wet spell—if sufficiently extreme—drowned the tobacco and ruined the crop by causing the leaves to spot.[45] In addition, the planter had to contend with the hazard of inept cooperage.

Plantation cooperage was seldom a professional performance; hogsheads were made by one or two servants or slaves on each of the larger plantations or by local carpenters rather as a matter of rural accommodation than as a profession.[46] The cost of a hogshead, 2s. 6d. currency plus 7½d. for the nails, amounted to half a crown sterling. As the tobacco exports of the Chesapeake colonies reached a hundred thousand hogsheads a year just prior to the Revolution, the value of cooperage in Virginia and Maryland was at least £12,500 sterling a year.

Contemporary records are full of references to hogsheads that fell apart, were shattered, or became stove in. In many cases this was the result of carelessness on the part of plantation coopers, but in others the fault lay with the planters for overprizing the casks, with the men who rolled them to the nearest landing, with the warehouse personnel, or with the mariners who stowed them in the holds of ships. As the charges for transportation, inspection, and freighting were based on the number of hogsheads, not on their weight, planters frequently succumbed to the temptation of packing too much tobacco into each cask.[47] In addition to sustaining damage by rolling over rough roads, hogsheads while being conveyed to warehouses by water were occasionally injured when flats overturned in an unexpected squall. Moreover, planters frequently complained of clumsy, careless mariners and of masters who forced hogsheads into place in the hold with levers which strained the casks.[48] Lastly, certain depredations that savor of theft customarily passed almost unnoticed by the long-suffering planters. While hogsheads awaited inspection at the public warehouses, every passer-by considered himself at liberty, according to the established custom, to help himself to a handful for chewing or smoking, by reaching into the cask through shattered headings or broken staves. During inspection the attendants often took some tobacco from the cask for their own use or to sell to sailors and unscrupulous traders. Tobacco rejected by the inspectors as inferior, which by law should have been burnt, was frequently pilfered by the warehouse attendants.[49]

At sea tobacco sometimes suffered from the weather, storms, leaks, and shrinkage. A dismasted ship that put into Antigua for repairs delivered a cargo of tobacco at London that the merchant said had lost most of its "Scents" as a result of the great heat in the West Indies.[50] On the other hand, tobacco on a ship that delayed its sailing until winter sustained damage from the cold, rough passage.[51] The master of a Maryland ship, after a rough winter passage in 1758, wrote from London that the tobacco "Suffered Very much . . . by the baddnes of the Weather," adding that some of the other vessels in the fleet had to throw a great part of their cargo overboard because it was so badly damaged as to be unsalable in England.[52] Old ships which were subject to leaks during the ocean passage were carefully avoided by shippers because water in the hold proved harmful to the cargo. Francis Jerdone told a Glasgow merchant in 1740 that "the advantage you have in getting old Ships for low freights does not near recompense the loss you Sustain when the Tobacco is damaged. The Shippers are always displeas'd and very often openly Swear that the Merchants are all cheats and pickpockets."[53] Then, as a result of natural causes, a hogshead of tobacco lost between 15 and 70 pounds of weight by shrinkage during the ocean passage, or between three and eight per cent.[54]

When properly cured and carefully prized, however, tobacco was remarkably resistant to deterioration. In 1757 a Captain Salisbury fished a hogshead out of the Atlantic that had been in the water so long it was covered with barnacles, yet of its 1,282 pounds, some five hundred pounds remained untouched by the water and were perfectly sound and good.[55] Similarly, in 1782 several shattered hogsheads from the shipwrecked brigantine *Maria* of Virginia washed up on the New Jersey coast and lay for several weeks where the tide constantly flowed over them. Although rotten on the outside and resembling heaps of manure, the tobacco was so well-prized that the center of each lump proved to be in good condition and fetched a good price.[56]

o     o     o

From an early time tobacco was marketed by consignment to a particular London or outport merchant who handled a planter's crop from the time it reached England until it was sold. The merchant received the bills of lading, ordered the cargo unloaded, paid the customs duty, carted the hogsheads to warehouses, sorted the leaf into several grades, and sold it in the market at the most advantageous price. From the time the crop left the Chesapeake until it was finally sold, it remained the property of the planter, being transported, unloaded, and stored at his risk. The consignment merchant merely served as an agent, receiving his remuneration in the form of a commission, usually two and a half or three per cent of the sale price.[57] After depositing the net proceeds of the sale of the tobacco to the planter's account, the merchant sent him a notification of his balance. Against this credit the planter drew from time to time by means of a short note called a bill of exchange, a forerunner of the modern check.

Frequently the planter directed the merchant not only to disburse money but also to make specific purchases, sending him long and detailed instructions that ran the gamut from nails, axes, cheap cloth, carpenters' tools, paper, ink, and other plantation supplies to special articles for the planter's own use, furniture, books, carriages, and clothing. As it was usually a year or eighteen months before they reached the Chesapeake country, the articles not infrequently fell short of expectation. The merchant did not follow instructions, or he exercised poor taste in selecting clothes and furniture; he was careless in packing goods to prevent breakage, or he sent inferior goods at prices appropriate to the finest. All things considered, this colonial mail-order business was anything but satisfactory.

Filling these orders for their colonial customers proved a great burden to the English merchants. Although they submitted to the indignity of running petty errands for the planters with an ill grace, they seldom failed to turn it to their financial advantage by charging a stiff commission for purchases and, in some instances, by advancing the price beyond what they paid for articles. On the other hand, the planters being optimistic about their crops generally ordered more goods than they could pay for in a given year.

When they received a statement of their account long after dispatching their crops to England, they often found themselves deeply in debt to the merchant.[58] By the end of Queen Anne's War (1713), most of the tobacco planters were in debt to English merchants.[59] To secure their interests the consignment merchants continued to extend credit to planters so they could continue to operate their plantations. In this way the debts annually grew, became permanent, and were handed down from father to son.

The relationship of debtor to creditor tended to reduce the planter to dependence upon the English merchant. The creditor had a right to expect—and was in a position to insist, if necessary —that the debtor continue to consign tobacco to him.[60] Once the planter fell into debt to a merchant, he was in his power and had to accept the results of the sale of his crop, however unsatisfactory. This naturally led to abuses, both accidental and intentional. When the planter was bound to the merchant through indebtedness, the latter was inclined to be not quite so careful in handling his tobacco or in purchasing his goods, and not quite so punctilious in honoring his bills of exchange as would otherwise have been the case. Planters often attributed damaged hogsheads, small returns for their crop, and disappointing supplies to the carelessness of the merchants. In a few cases merchants were unscrupulous enough deliberately to cheat planters by fraudulent sales of tobacco, by false statements of account, and by overcharging for goods ordered by them. The merchant's freedom from scrutiny afforded opportunity for fraud, and the realization that this was so led planters to be suspicious of English merchants and commonly accuse them of double-dealing.[61]

If a planter succeeded in keeping out of debt, however, the story was quite different. He was courted by the consignment merchants, who were ever solicitous about his health, family, and wishes. News and personal regards appeared in their business correspondence, gifts and tokens of esteem regularly accompanied letters.[62] The more prudent planters, realizing the importance of keeping out of debt, carefully avoided ordering more goods than their tobacco would cover. In order to keep a favorable balance with a consignment merchant, William Fitzhugh inserted in his orders the proviso "if my money will reach to itt, but rather leave some out than bring me a penny in Debt."[63] Similarly, when in debt to the London merchant Alderman Micajah Perry, William Byrd II sold land and slaves in a desperate attempt to extricate himself from the clutches of that "hungry magistrate," preferring to incommode himself rather than "continue in the Gripe of that userer."[64]

Another method of marketing tobacco, that became increasingly important in the eighteenth century, was to sell it outright in the colony either to a large planter or to an agent or factor of a British merchant. The planter, to be sure, got a lower price for his crop, but he was relieved of risk and delay in obtaining its proceeds. All things considered, he was often better off than the planter who became enmeshed in the consignment system with its many anxieties, petty irritations, and occasional disasters. The outright-purchase system was not so simple as it might appear at first sight. It was conducted by British merchants or firms of merchants who employed one or more factors permanently residing in the tobacco colonies. Sometimes given a salary,[65] sometimes allowed a share in the business,[66] factors usually settled in a strategic place either in a river town or at the head of a navigable river. They imported European goods from England and separately or in combination with their British employers engaged in the West India and wine trades, importing salt, sugar, rum, molasses, and wine. Also they invariably kept a "store" at which they retailed manufactured articles, wine, sugars, and slaves on credit or for tobacco, bills of exchange, wheat, corn, iron, or other commodities.

Tobacco was of course their main concern; the factors engaged in the West India and wine trades as a subsidiary activity. The smaller planters needed West India products, and in order to keep their custom the stores had to carry such goods.[67] Moreover, as planters occasionally paid for their imported articles in wheat and corn, the factors found the West Indies a profitable market for grain and a convenient source of coin and bills of exchange which were useful in the tobacco trade, both for purchases and for paying export duties.[68]

After the middle of the eighteenth century, when factors were numerous, competition between them became acute. In periods of price depression they had to maintain, or increase, the volume of their annual tobacco purchases yet keep down the cost in order to make a living. To obtain enough to load the ships consigned to them by their British employers, they frequently resorted to such tactics as encouraging planters to become indebted to them by freely extending credit,[69] or agreeing to buy tobacco "on the ground" for future delivery with a discount of between ten and twenty-five per cent for late deliveries.[70] To keep down the cost of tobacco, factors sometimes made regional agreements setting the price in advance, but they were seldom kept in good faith.[71] Another practice consisted of rating store goods in sterling and allowing accounts to be paid in currency at an increase of fifty or one hundred per cent, and in paper money at an increase of two hundred or three hundred per cent, thereby beguiling unwary planters into buying more high-priced goods than if they had been rated in currency.[72] Hence the factors could cover their overhead, the risk of a falling price for tobacco, and yet allow for a profit.

To keep down shipping costs, factors generally preferred to buy tobacco from the "best Planters," even at higher prices. In this way it could be purchased in quantity and usually proved of better quality, more expertly cured and prized, than tobacco of the smaller planters. Moreover, the convenient location of the large plantations on navigable rivers proved of great advantage. Buying in quantity all at one landing enabled factors to load ships quickly and cheaply, avoiding loss of time in sailing from river to river

*Curing and storage of tobacco (from Tatham, CULTURE AND COMMERCE OF TOBACCO, London, 1800. William Tatham came to Virginia as a tobacco merchant in 1769 and remained on James River until the Revolution).*

and additional cost of rolling and lightering hogsheads from several small, scattered, inland plantations.

As colonial export duties, handling charges, and freight were based on the number of hogsheads rather than on weight, the better grade, heavier hogsheads actually paid less in proportion to weight than the poorer, loosely-prized tobacco. This made it possible for factors to buy good tobacco at a higher price and yet keep down shipping costs. In 1745 a Maryland factor while paying only ten shillings per hundred pounds for tobacco in small quantities, willingly paid twelve shillings six pence for it in quantities of at least 3,000 pounds at one landing.[73]

Generally speaking, the larger planters did not sell their crops in the colony. On the contrary, they competed with the factors in buying tobacco from the smaller planters, and shipped it along with their own to England on consignment.[74] In order to enter the purchasing market they were obliged to import large quantities of European and West India goods and to keep a store.[75] Accordingly, they were obliged to own or charter vessels in the West India trade and to establish regular correspondence with Caribbean and British merchants. In return for tobacco sent to Great Britain on consignment, they imported goods for their stores as well as for their own use, and marked them up in price and extended credit, much as factors did, in order to obtain control of the smaller planters.[76] Thus emerged a group of powerful merchant-planters, peculiar to the tobacco colonies, who engaged in all the mercantile pursuits yet considered themselves primarily planters. Almost all of the great planters of colonial Virginia and Maryland, the Byrds, Carters, Carrolls, and Washingtons, who built up large estates within a lifetime, were merchants as well as planters.

In Chapter Eight the participation of the merchants of various British seaports is set forth in detail. It is necessary here merely to record a major shift that occurred between the seventeenth and eighteenth centuries. Early in the former, London assumed a leading role in Virginia and Maryland trade and since her merchants specialized in consignment they seldom employed resident factors in the colonies. Until about 1720 or a little later, the London merchants handled at least two-thirds of the tobacco imported into Great Britain.[77] Thereafter the outport merchants and the merchants of Scotland, to whom colonial trade was opened by the Act of Union in 1707, began to increase their activities by means of factors. As early as 1718 a London firm lamented the rise of the Scottish and outport competition.[78] By 1728 an authority on the tobacco trade asserted that many people in Virginia and more in Maryland that formerly consigned their tobacco to London "have (of late Years) declin'd Shipping, and Sold their Tobacco in the Country; which has given the Out-Ports a greater Weight in the Trade than they us'd to have, and subtracted . . . much from London."[79] The same year Micajah Perry and thirty-six other London merchants declared that very nearly one half of all colonial tobacco went to the outports.[80] This trend from consignment to outright purchase continued unabated throughout the rest of the colonial period. By the time of the Revolution three-fourths of the commodity was purchased in the colonies and only one-fourth sent on consignment.[81] Hence, by the middle of the eighteenth century Glasgow, Liverpool, and Bristol became great tobacco ports, thereby depriving London of the preëminent position she had enjoyed in the trade at the end of the previous century.

o      o      o

The tobacco trade, hedged about by rules and regulations and almost buried under the weight of financial impositions, proved a fruitful source of revenue both for the royal treasury and the colonial governments of Virginia and Maryland. From 1660, when English customs duties on colonial tobacco were two pence per pound, they rose to five pence in 1685, six pence and a third of a penny in 1703, seven pence and a third in 1748, and eight pence and a third in 1758, amounting at the end of the colonial period to from three to seven times the price of tobacco in the colonies.[82] In consequence, the trade was enormously valuable to the Crown and the tobacco colonies were considered as valuable to Great Britain as the fabulously wealthy Indies to Spain.[83] Between 1689 and 1775, the net annual income to the royal treasury rose from about £130,000 to £330,000.[84]

These duties would have been a great burden had it not been for the policy of granting substantial drawbacks upon reëxportation. From 1660 to 1723, all but a half penny per pound was refunded, and after 1723 the entire duty was refunded.[85] By the end of the seventeenth century about two-thirds of the tobacco imported into England was subsequently reëxported to foreign countries.[86] By 1750 the proportion reached seventy-five or eighty per cent, and by the Revolution nearly ninety per cent.[87] Thus, at the end of the colonial period, when the volume of trade approached 100,000,000 pounds a year, some 90,000,000 pounds paid no duty at all. The customs duties fell solely upon the 10,-000,000 pounds consumed in Great Britain, a burden which the merchants passed on to the consumers in the form of higher prices.

Another important concession to the trade was that the duties did not have to be paid in full upon entry. The subsidy of 1660, consisting of a penny per pound, was payable at any time within nine months of entry. In 1685 the government allowed importers to fix bond for three to six months for their "ease and comfort" for the entire duty. Later the time was extended to eighteen months. A rebate of ten per cent for duties paid in "ready money" and another of four per cent for waste and decayed tobacco encouraged early payment and allowed for losses from improper curing, rough handling, and leaky ships. The time limit for reëxportation, a generous allowance of one year, meant that the importer could offer his tobacco in the English market first and, if it did not sell, he could send it to the Continent without losing the advantage of the full drawback.[88]

In addition to paying considerable sums to the royal treasury, the tobacco trade provided the colonial governments of Virginia and Maryland with one of their principal sources of revenue. A duty of two shillings sterling levied on each hogshead of tobacco exported from those colonies yielded Virginia £3,000 a year in 1680 and £6,000 a year during the years 1758-1762.[89] The proceeds in Maryland rose from £2,500 a year at the turn of the century to about £3,000 per annum just prior to the Revolution.[90] There was also an export duty, called the "plantation duty," of one penny per pound levied on tobacco exported from Virginia or Maryland to any other British colony. The revenue from this duty amounted to very little because of inefficient administration and the fact that there was little intercolonial trade in tobacco. In 1691 it was officially reported as turning "to little or no account" because the collectors took half the receipts, the surveyor took a fourth, and the remaining quarter "is so loaded with charges of boats and sloops, men and horse . . . that it is almost eaten up."[91] After 1693, when the plantation duty of both Virginia and Maryland was granted by the Crown to the College of William and Mary, the college authorities made vigorous attempts to reduce the collection costs. But it never proved to be a valuable source of revenue. Negligence and indifference on the part of Virginia collectors and the occasional default of Maryland kept the revenue down.[92] In 1740 the college received only £200 from the duty.[93]

As the tobacco colonies increased in population their production of staple rose phenomenally. When the English market became glutted with the colonial product by about 1660, prices fell so low that the planters were scarcely able to subsist. Faced by poverty, many of them were driven to the expedient of shipping inferior leaves, lugs, slips, and even the "sweepings of their homes" in a desperate attempt to make up by quantity what they lost by low prices. The practice of exporting trash tobacco, so far from solving their problems, merely accentuated the evils of overproduction and added those of deterioration of quality.

## The Tobacco Trade

When the reputation of colonial tobacco began to decline, further reducing European demand for it, the seriousness of the situation impelled the colonial authorities to take corrective measures. During the next half century or more they tried to cope with the problem in three ways: reducing the amount of tobacco produced; regularizing the trade by fixing the size of the hogshead and prohibiting shipments of bulk tobacco; and improving the quality of the colonial staple by preventing the exportation of trash tobacco.

Attempts to reduce the volume of production centered at first in the statutory limitation of the number of leaves per plant, the number of plants per laborer, and restricting cultivation to certain dates—all of them impossible of enforcement. In a land of widely scattered plantations, of many small clearings separated by stretches of natural forest or by wide rivers and creeks, the law enforcement officials could not count the leaves on each plant or the plants on each plantation, or watch the date of each of the many operations that are involved in the production of tobacco. Therefore the authorities had no practicable means of enforcement other than relying upon information from informers to whom a part of the fine for infractions was assigned as a reward.

Little having been accomplished by the early attempts, more ambitious plans were made in 1663, 1666, and 1681 to solve the problem of overproduction by bringing about a general "stint" or total cessation of tobacco planting. These measures were easily enforced. After a specified date all tobacco growing was illegal and no ship could clear with a cargo of that commodity. But a new difficulty arose. As there were two tobacco colonies, a stint could not be undertaken without their coöperation, otherwise it would enrich one colony at the expense of the other. Moreover, a stint required the assent of the Crown, because any proposal designed to limit tobacco production would necessarily affect the royal revenue, and also the assent of Lord Baltimore, whose proprietary revenues were involved.

The proposed stint of 1663 was a partial one, providing for a cessation of planting after the twentieth of June. Maryland at once rejected it on the grounds that her season was three weeks later than that of southern Virginia and therefore she should be given twenty days after the date of Virginia's stint "to balance the difference of the climate."[94] The proposed stint of 1666, a thorough-going affair involving a total cessation for a year, was agreed to by the assemblies of Virginia and Maryland and also by the assembly of Carolina, a new colony that had just entered into tobacco production. But the plan fell through when Lord Baltimore vetoed the Maryland act.[95] Similarily, the proposed stint of 1681, suggested to the English authorities by the Virginia Assembly, came to nothing when the Commissioners of Customs rejected it.[96] In the first instance one colony disagreed with the other; in the second both colonies were in agreement, but the Lord Proprietor of Maryland vetoed the proposal; and in the third the royal government refused to allow a stint.

Only once in the colonial period was the production of tobacco substantially reduced—and that was by illegal means, an act of desperation committed in violation of the orders of King in Council and of the colonial Assembly. In 1682 when the fortunes of the planters reached their lowest ebb, plant-cutting riots broke out in Virginia in the counties of Gloucester, New Kent, Middlesex, and York, partly in protest against the Privy Council's action in disallowing the proposed stint of 1681, and partly in an attempt literally to strike at the obvious source of their troubles. Before the suppression of the insurrection, two-thirds of the tobacco in Gloucester and half that in New Kent had been destroyed and the crop for the year reduced by 10,000 hogsheads.[97] An improvement in the price of tobacco after 1682 alleviated the distress of the planters, and the plant-cutting frenzy was never repeated.[98]

In 1679 the Virginia Assembly made another attempt to reduce the volume of tobacco by excluding North Carolina's crops from

Virginia ports. Declaring that the Carolinians produced an inferior grade of the leaf, which when sent to England by way of Virginia greatly injured the reputation of Virginia tobacco, an act in that year forbade the importation of it into Virginia by sea. Although very harmful to North Carolina, which had no deepwater rivers or ports convenient to its tobacco region, this embargo remained in force, apparently without opposition by the London authorities, until 1726, by which time land routes had been established. A Virginia act in 1726 intended to remedy the defect of the act of 1679 prohibited importation by land as well as sea.

When the second act reached England, the surveyor general of customs took exception to it because the North Carolinians had "neither shipping of their own, nor ports to receive them," and because restraint of trade would force the inhabitants of that colony out of tobacco production, thereby lessening Crown revenue, and drive them into manufacturing, thereby lessening British exports.[99] Governor Gooch of Virginia argued in defense of the act that North Carolina tobacco was inferior, that it would not sell in England, and that it was all reëxported to the Continent thereby paying no duties to the Crown. Moreover, he pointed out that North Carolina had been under restraint for half a century "yet no such manufactures have as yet been sett up amongst them."[100] Siding with the Carolinians, the Board of Trade considered it highly unreasonable that any British subjects should be "debar'd from the liberty" of any ports in the Empire, and the Privy Council, acting on the Board's recommendation, disallowed the act in 1731.[101]

In another attempt to reduce volume, the Virginians were more successful. Early in the eighteenth century the practice of stripping sweetscented tobacco became increasingly popular. As the stems were unsalable, removing them before shipment reduced the quantity by a fourth, and saved that proportion of the cost of casks, packing, rolling, inspection, lighterage, freight, insurance, and duties.[102] As the practice grew, the British authorities became apprehensive about the royal revenue. Sweetscented, which alone was stripped, was largely consumed in Great Britain and therefore was the source of most of the revenue derived by the Crown from tobacco duties. In order to prevent the loss of a quarter of the revenue arising from sweetscented, Parliament in 1722 passed an act prohibiting the importation of stemmed tobacco.[103] As this aroused bitter opposition in the tobacco colonies, Governor Gooch of Virginia in a letter to the Duke of Newcastle in 1729 argued that as stemmed tobacco was better than leaf the demand would increase, Virginia would produce more sweetscented, and in the long run the Crown would obtain increased revenue if the act were repealed.[104] The same year John Randolph, the Clerk of the Virginia Council, was sent to London by the Virginia Assembly "to solicit the repeal" of the obnoxious act.[105] In this endeavor the persuasive Randolph (who later talked himself into a knighthood) was completely successful, and the assembly rewarded him with a gift of £1,000.[106]

Throughout the colonial period the size of the hogshead was a matter of considerable dispute between shipmasters and planters, between Virginia and Maryland, and between the colonists and the British government. As merchants in the Chesapeake trade built their ships to carry a specified number of hogsheads in the hold, it was imperative for purposes of stowage that the size of the hogshead be established by law. As most ships freighted in Maryland as well as Virginia and carried both sweetscented and oronoco, it was imperative that the hogshead in both colonies and for both kinds of tobacco be of the same size. Although both Virginia and Maryland passed acts prescribing the dimensions of the hogshead as early as 1658, strong economic motives for enlarging the cask prevented their enforcement.[107] Selling by the pound but bearing transportation and handling charges by the hogshead, tobacco yielded greater net returns in larger casks. Moreover, the Maryland oronoco planters thought they should

*a*

*b*

*c*

*d*

*Land and water transport of tobacco*
*(from Tatham, CULTURE AND COMMERCE OF TOBACCO).*

be allowed a larger hogshead than Virginia sweetscented planters because oronoco was bulkier and could not be as tightly prized, but the Virginians protested that the fault lay with the slovenly methods of prizing in Maryland and pointed out that as two-thirds of Virginia's tobacco was oronoco they were equally entitled to a large hogshead.[108]

During the latter part of the seventeenth century and early part of the eighteenth, the two colonies enacted a series of laws regulating the size of the hogshead, each colony trying to outdo the other. In 1692 Maryland increased the dimensions to 44 by 33 inches.[109] Three years later Virginia enlarged its hogshead to 48 by 30 inches.[110] In 1704 Maryland again increased it to 48 by 32 inches.[111] Finally, at the request of a group of merchants and shipowners the British authorities intervened. In 1708 Queen Anne disallowed the Maryland act of 1704 and instructed the governor to persuade the assembly to pass a new act making the hogshead conformable to the Virginia hogshead as specified in the act of 1695.[112] But the Maryland Assembly stubbornly held out for a larger hogshead.

When the Board of Trade reconsidered the question in 1711 it espoused the cause of uniformity, and upon its recommendation, the Privy Council again instructed the governor of Maryland to procure legislation reducing the Maryland hogshead to the size of the Virginia hogshead.[113] After a stubborn delay, Maryland grudgingly passed a gauge act that made the hogshead of that province the same size as that of Virginia.[114] But the triumph of uniformity was short-lived. When Maryland reverted to the proprietary government in 1715, one of the first legislative acts revised the gauge act of 1711, increasing the dimensions of the hogshead to 48 by 32 inches. By reënactment, the province continued this act until 1747 when the inspection law that prevailed for the rest of the colonial period went into effect, eventually bringing about genuine uniformity by creating the means for effective enforcement.[115]

In addition to striving for uniformity of size, the colonial governments endeavored to cope with the prevailing carelessness with which hogsheads were made. A Maryland act of 1692 required trees to be felled and sawed by the last day of April, and the lumber to be hewn and riven into staves before the last day of July. Half the number of hogsheads contracted for were to be completed by the tenth of October, and the remaining half by the tenth of December. The law required the finished cask to be in accordance with legal specifications as to length and diameter, and to weigh no more than 90 pounds.[116] The act provided penalties in the form of fines for violations, but in this case, as in in the case of the limitation of the number of leaves per plant or the plants per laborer, no effective means of enforcement existed. Consequently, before the warehouse-inspection system went into effect in Virginia in 1730 and Maryland in 1747, hogshead cooperage continued to be characterized by carelessness, haste, and lack of uniformity.

Another obstacle to regularizing the trade at the end of the seventeenth century was the exportation of large quantities of colonial tobacco in bulk, that is, in loose parcels rather than hogsheads. This practice was favored by small planters who had no facilities for prizing tobacco and whose remoteness from navigable waters made transportation of hogsheads difficult. Shipmasters preferred bulk because it could be easily loaded, admitting of stowage in irregular spaces too small to receive a hogshead, and because a ship could carry about 20 per cent more tobacco in bulk than in cask. English merchants, particularly those in the outports, favored bulk because it could be unloaded in the smaller English ports or in rivers where no wharves existed, because there were fewer handling charges and no delays in sorting and packing, and because it could be conveyed to the retail market more quickly, more easily, and more cheaply than tobacco in cask.

Most of all, smugglers favored bulk because it could easily be concealed aboard ship and because it could be unloaded in the smaller English ports where customs enforcement was lax. Even in the larger ports bulk tobacco could be smuggled ashore before the customs had been paid. Women and children came aboard ship before its official entry, bought tobacco "at the Mast," and carried it off in small parcels. Mariners also found means of carrying loose tobacco ashore in their ditty-bags and disposing of it illegally. When the customs inspectors observed a discrepancy between the weight of the tobacco landed at the custom-house wharf and the weight specified in the bill of lading and clearance papers, the masters blandly attributed it to shrinkage or to jettisoning spoilt tobacco at sea.[117]

As the proportion of tobacco shipped in bulk increased, the desirability of prohibiting it became a subject of debate. Between 1687 and 1698 a fierce struggle raged in England and the colonies between the rival factions, the large planters and London consignment merchants who opposed bulk, and the small planters and outport merchants who favored it. The opening shot was a petition laid before the Privy Council in 1687 by a group of London merchants requesting prohibition of bulk tobacco shipments.[118] Upon receiving favorable opinion from the commissioners of customs, King James II issued orders in council directing the governors of Virginia and Maryland to procure legislation to that effect.[119] But the small planters, who were in control of the lower houses of assembly in both colonies, refused to accede to the royal command.[120] Although their defiance escaped punishment because of the outbreak of the Glorious Revolution in 1688, the case was reopened in 1692 when a group of London merchants again petitioned the prohibition of bulk.[121] Influenced, perhaps, by the "Essay on Bulk Tobacco" which William Byrd II wrote to support the petition, the customs commissioners again reported favorably and the Lords of Trade instructed the governors of the tobacco colonies to procure the necessary legislation.[122] Still in control of the two lower houses, the small planters again refused to accede to the orders of the English government.

Finally, after considerable delay, Parliament intervened and passed an act in 1698 that prohibited the importation of bulk tobacco into England.[123]

Parliament's action ended the controversy over bulk tobacco, but not the shipping of it. After 1700 bulk was clandestinely shipped, either by smuggling it aboard ship and not declaring it or by binding staves around large parcels and calling them hogsheads. Rigid enforcement of the statute in England was prevented by the ease with which bulk could be unloaded in out-of-the-way places, and in the colonies by the configuration of the Chesapeake and absence of ports which made it virtually impossible for customs officers to watch each vessel load or to inspect every item in the hold of vessels already loaded.[124] In consequence, bulk shipments continued until the establishment of the warehouse-inspection system.

The problem of overproduction was bound up with that of deterioration of quality, because the volume of exports was swelled by the packing of lugs, suckers, slips, and other trash along with good tobacco. Consequently the colonial assemblies passed many laws limiting the number of leaves per plant, forbidding the growth of suckers and slips, and prohibiting the exportation of inferior leaves.[125] But these acts accomplished nothing. The seventeenth-century assemblies were financially unable to provide the necessary warehouses and inspectors for proper enforcement, and shrank from establishing a compulsory inspection system. Instead, they left the building of warehouses to private initiative and made inspection voluntary. As few persons willingly assumed the additional expense of having his tobacco inspected, the only means of enforcing the laws prohibiting trash tobacco involved the highly unsatisfactory system of relying upon informers and private lawsuits.[126]

The Virginia act of 1713 which established forty public warehouses and provided for inspection of tobacco by officials appointed by the governor represented a great step forward.[127]

## The Tobacco Trade

Although Governor Spotswood enthusiastically predicted that the act would eliminate trash, rescue colonial tobacco from the disesteem into which it had fallen, and lead to the recovery of the lost European market, the large planters opposed it on the grounds that the cost of transporting tobacco to warehouses and paying inspection fees was a great hardship and that Maryland tobacco would undersell theirs by 10 per cent.[128] The British merchants sided with the large planters, one of them complaining that the act cost him £300 a year in loss of time and additional seamen's wages, and that the inspectors mixed the hogsheads so that no one could be sure of receiving as good tobacco as he bought.[129] As a result of this and the estimated reduction of tobacco exports by an eighth, the British authorities intervened and disallowed the act by an order in council in 1717.[130]

A protracted depression in the 1720's accentuated suffering in the tobacco colonies and eventually led Virginia once again to establish an inspection system. This time, however, the governor previously prepared the way for British approval by persuading the London authorities that trash tobacco was largely handled by smugglers and therefore paid little duty, that unless something were done to relieve their distress many planters would turn to manufacturing, and that nothing except an inspection law could improve Virginia's staple.[131]

In 1730 Virginia passed the memorable inspection act that completely revolutionized tobacco regulation and became a permanent feature of the trade until the war for independence.[132] It established public warehouses, provided for the appointment of official inspectors, and required planters to transport every hogshead of tobacco in the colony to a warehouse for inspection. The inspectors, who received annual salaries and were obliged to refrain from engaging in trade, were empowered to break open each hogshead, remove and burn any trash, and issue tobacco notes to the owner specifying the weight and kind of tobacco. Forgery of tobacco notes, receipts, or stamps was made a felony.

In general, the warehouses were established on the lands of the great planters, perhaps to secure their support of the act.[133]

In Great Britain the act was received with mixed feelings: the merchants approving of it, but the customs commissioners opposing it.[134] The Board of Trade taking an intermediate position, urged the King to permit the act "to lye by probationary" until the effects of it might be seen.[135] In Virginia some opposition also developed when the most turbulent of the Northern Neck planters burnt four warehouses under the impression that British merchants would discontinue sending ships and supplies to the colony, but it soon died away when they found that the act had been well received by the merchants. Elsewhere in the colony the act operated smoothly.[136] In 1733 Governor Gooch assured the Duke of Newcastle that the colony enjoyed a happy prospect of a flourishing trade under the new act.[137] And by 1738 some Bristol merchants declared that but for the inspection system Virginia tobacco would not be worth carrying home.[138]

In Maryland the sequence of events was different. The depression in the 1720's impelled the assembly to enact laws prohibiting the exportation of trash, but their enforcement depended entirely upon oaths, fines, and informers, rather than compulsory inspection.[139] Eventually the low state of the trade won the small planters over to the idea of regulation, but led them to protect themselves by scaling down all fees and debts payable in tobacco in anticipation of the rise of price of their staple. This action alienated the large planters, lawyers, clergy of the established church, and proprietary officials, who succeeded in voting down every proposal for an effective inspection system.[140]

After 1730 the Marylanders gradually became sensible that the inspection system gave Virginia a great advantage over Maryland by raising the quality and reputation of its tobacco. In 1743 Daniel Dulany told Lord Baltimore that Maryland tobacco was in such "disreputation" that it would hardly defray the expense of freight to England, and that no improvement was possible without such a regulation "as will prevent the sending to Market Such trash as is unfit for any other use but Manure." He then pointed to the example of Virginia where the inspection system gave the planters a great advantage and would, he thought, "throw the Whole Trade in their hands" before long.[141] Meanwhile, conditions became so bad that the tobacco factors in Maryland set up their own inspection system and purchased no tobacco without carefully inspecting it beforehand, except in the case of planters whose crop had a good reputation.[142] By 1747 all opposition to an inspection law had vanished, and a compromise was reached concerning fees and debts. The same year the Assembly passed a law very much like that of Virginia, and the inspection system from that time until the Revolution remained a permanent feature of the trade in Maryland.[143]

In Virginia after 1730 and in Maryland after 1747, the conduct of the tobacco trade conformed to the pattern established by the inspection system. Public warehouses were erected at convenient points along navigable rivers in the tidewater and placed in the care of official inspectors who were nominated by the county courts in Virginia and by the parish vestries in Maryland, appointed by the governor, and paid an annual salary by the colony.[144] So soon as the planters cured and prized their crops, they had the hogsheads rolled down to the nearest landing, carried by sloop or flat to the most convenient warehouse, and delivered to the inspector.[145] The hogsheads were stored in a shed built for the purpose. Then, one by one they were brought out, broken open, and inspected. If any trash tobacco was found, it was condemned to be burnt. Then the hogshead was re-prized, nailed, and marked with a hot iron with the name of the warehouse, the tare, and the net weight of the tobacco.[146]

After inspection the planter received a certificate, called a "crop note," that listed his hogsheads by mark and number, recorded the gross, net, and tare of the tobacco, and specified whether it was sweetscented or oronoco, stemmed or leaf.[147] The

planter then, if he chose to consign his tobacco to a British merchant, arranged freight for his crop, turned the note over to the
shipmaster, who in turn presented it at the warehouse, received
the specified hogsheads, and proceeded to load them aboard ship
either at the warehouse wharf or by lighter to the anchorage of
his vessel. If the planter chose to sell his tobacco in the colony,
he delivered the crop note to the purchaser who, in turn, was at
liberty to present it at the warehouse for delivery or to sell it to
someone else.

If the planter turned in his tobacco loose, in bundles or hands,
he received a different kind of receipt, known as a "transfer note,"
which entitled the holder to a certain number of pounds of loose
tobacco drawn at random from the aggregate stock of transfer
tobacco.[148] Unlike the crop note, the transfer note did not entitle
the holder to the same tobacco that was delivered to the warehouse in return for the note, but merely to the same quantity,
kind, and grade.

Transfer tobacco was derived from several sources. It often
happened that after prizing his hogsheads, a planter had a
quantity left over insufficient to fill another hogshead. This excess
he usually delivered to the warehouse in bulk and received a
transfer note to cover it. The clergy, innkeepers, artisans, and
others whose main occupation was something other than tobacco
planting often tended a small patch in their spare time in order
to meet the various county and parish levies and to make purchases in the local stores—levies and retail prices usually being
in tobacco because of the scarcity of coin. These men carried their
small quantities of tobacco to the nearest warehouse and received
transfer notes that could either be sold or tendered in payment
of debts, fees, and taxes. In cases where hogsheads, upon inspection, were found to weigh less than 950 pounds net, the legal
minimum for crop tobacco, the contents were either returned to
the planter or added to the loose stockpile and transfer notes
issued. When portions of the tobacco in a hogshead were con-

Coll.° John Custis — To Charges on Fourteen Hogsheads of Tobacco received p. the Expedition Cha.° Friend Virginia

1743

| Old Subsidy of 14579 lb Tob.° p. lb. at 5 p. C.° deducted £ | 48.11.2 | | |
| New Subs. Add.' Duty & Subs. & Imposts p. lb. at 15 p. C.° deducted | 275.7.7 | 320.18.9 | |
| Freight at £ 8 p. Tonn | 28 | | |
| Country Dutys | 1.9 | | |
| Primage & Petty Charges | 1.5.0 | | |
| Entry inwards, Bonds & c. | 1.1 | | |
| Cooperage inward & outward | 1.0 | | |
| Cartage & Warehouse Room | 2.9 | | |
| Brokerage | 1.0 | | |
| Shiping Charges & Debenture &c. | 1.0 | | |
| Porterage wharfage & Lighterage | 1.1 | | |
| Postage of Letters | 5.6 | 44.13 | |
| To Commission on £497.4.5 | | 14.18.5 | |
| To Acco.t for Nett proceed | | 116.15.3 | |
| | | £497.4.5 | |

London y.e 10.th of April 1743
Errors Excepted

J. Hanbury

A typical tobacco sales account, 1743.

demned as inferior, the remainder was either repacked by the planter or, more commonly, put into the stockpile and the planter given a transfer note.

As transfer tobacco could not be exported—because the act of Parliament of 1698 prohibited the importation of bulk tobacco into England—the larger planters and tobacco factors frequently bought up transfer notes from the lesser planters, artisans, clergy, and innkeepers and, when they held notes calling for more than the minimum legal requirements, presented them at the warehouse. The tobacco they received from the stockpile of loose tobacco was then prized into hogsheads for which the inspectors issued the more desirable crop notes.[149]

An important feature of the warehouse system was that the crop and transfer notes were transferable and could circulate from hand to hand without endorsement. In this way they served as currency and greatly facilitated exchange at a time when coin was extremely scarce.[150] They also facilitated shipping. If a merchant came into possession of tobacco that was at several different warehouses, especially if the warehouses were on different rivers, he could exchange the notes for other tobacco lodged in more convenient warehouses. This helped to reduce the necessity of ships running into one river after another in order to collect their cargoes.[151]

In retrospect the warehouse system may be said to have been a great success. The occasional inconveniences resulting from poorly chosen inspectors, careless handling, and improper judging of the tobacco are completely overshadowed by the more conspicuous achievements of the system. It accomplished all the main objectives of the numerous seventeenth and early eighteenth-century acts designed to mend the condition of the staple, improve the quality of colonial tobacco, eliminate trash, and suppress bulk shipments, and it put an end to smuggling at the colonial end of the trade, facilitated exchange, and eased the burdens connected with freighting ships in many different rivers. Most of all, it went far toward providing the standardization that the tobacco trade required for its continued prosperity.

o    o    o

Before the middle of the seventeenth century the volume of tobacco production in Virginia and Maryland began to exceed the consumption in England. During the years before 1660, especially during the Commonwealth period when the Dutch enjoyed participation in Chesapeake trade, enough tobacco reached the Continent of Europe to prevent a serious glut on the English market. After 1660, however, when the English authorities began to enforce the navigation acts, a glut soon developed thereby causing a serious depression in the tobacco colonies. By 1681 the situation was so serious that dire predictions were made on all sides and Virginia and Maryland were thought to be on the verge of ruin. London alone was reported to have enough tobacco on hand to supply all England for five years, yet each succeeding crop in the colonies proved larger than its predecessor—a situation that Lord Culpeper, when governor of Virginia, summed up neatly by asserting that "Our thriving is our undoing."[152]

Fortunately, the impending disaster was averted by the gradual building up of the continental market for colonial tobacco. After 1660 all customs duties except a half penny per pound were refunded upon reëxportation of the colonial staple from England. By the end of the seventeenth century two-thirds of the Chesapeake crop was annually reëxported to the Baltic, Holland, France, Spain, Ireland, and other parts of Europe. The Dutch took considerable quantities of Virginia and Maryland tobacco and, serving as middlemen, supplied France and other Latin countries with it, and between the Peace of Ryswick in 1698 and the beginning of Queen Anne's War in 1702, English merchants developed a large direct trade with France, the Baltic, and Russia.[153]

From that time onward, during years of peace, the Chesapeake colonies supplied all Europe with tobacco and enjoyed a reason-

141

able degree of prosperity. But nearly half the years from 1689 to 1763 were years of war, and in time of war the reëxportation of colonial tobacco to the continent was interrupted. On these occasions the produce of the Chesapeake colonies glutted the British market, the low price produced a depression in the colonies, and home-grown tobacco captured the European market. During Queen Anne's War, 1702-13, the direct trade with France, Spain, Flanders, and the Baltic was lost.[154] The war stimulated tobacco production in Holland, Pomerania, Brandenburg, Hungary, and around Strasbourg and Frankfort. By 1706 Holland produced as much as 20,000,000 pounds a year.[155] The Dutch imported the best bright oronoco from England, mixed it with low grade Dutch and German tobacco, and supplied the continental market with the resulting mixture. In consequence, English merchants were unable to sell the poorer grades of oronoco at any price.

Meanwhile, the annual production of the Chesapeake colonies continued to increase. In 1706 Colonel Quary, a royal official in the colonies, reported to the Board of Trade that "Never was so great a quantity of tobacco come from the Plantations in one year, as is expected in England this summer, nor was there ever so dismall a prospect of a market."[156] Virginia and Maryland, he thought, were faced with ruin. And the next year the "greatest Fleet that ever went from the Tobacco Plantations," some three hundred ships, sailed to England, a fact which led Quary to declare that unless the merchants unanimously agree on the proper methods for reviving the foreign market, the trade would be ruined.[157]

To cope with the situation the English merchants did three things: (1) they petitioned Queen Anne to use her influence with Peter the Great to allow free importation of tobacco into the Czar's dominions by all English subjects and to order the immediate return of the tobacco cutters, rollers, and utensils sent to Russia by a small group of English merchants who in

1698 obtained a monopoly of trade there;[158] (2) they petitioned the House of Commons for permission to export colonial tobacco in Dutch or neutral vessels directly to France;[159] and (3) they proposed that since the Royal Navy consisted of 40,000 men of whom 30,000 smoked or chewed an average of one pound of tobacco a month apiece, making a total of 360,000 pounds a year, the pursers be restrained from buying foreign leaf and obliged to buy the colonial product.[160] The last two requests were acceded to by the government, but these expedients did little to alleviate the distress of the colonies. In 1713 the President and Council of Maryland lamented "the distressed circumstances of this poor Province" as a result of the extremely low price of oronoco, which they attributed to the loss of the continental market.[161]

After the end of Queen Anne's War conditions rapidly improved. By 1724 the Board of Trade reported to the King that the tobacco trade was flourishing and that the merchants and planters did not complain of the heavy duties on that commodity. The continental market had now been recaptured thanks to the peculiar quality of Virginia and Maryland oronoco which enjoyed a great demand in Europe, especially France.[162]

Tobacco was a monopoly in France, and a lucrative one both for the King and the Farmers General of the Revenue. Each year the French agent came to London and bought the entire quantity that his country was to consume in the coming year. By making their purchases through a single agent, the French eliminated competitive bidding and greatly affected the market. The only tobacco suitable for the French market was "Dull Leaf," a kind of oronoco grown along the James River and in several parts of Maryland. This kind was imported largely by the London consignment merchants. The bright oronoco, so much in demand in the Dutch market, was largely purchased outright in the colonies by factors of the outport merchants. The French and Dutch markets, therefore, were quite distinct. They consumed different kinds of tobacco and were supplied by different merchants, the former in London, the latter in the outports. This condition of the trade gave the French agent a great advantage over the London merchants. Being the most considerable buyer— in fact, almost the sole buyer—of dull leaf oronoco, he could control the price and, by his purchases, govern the market. As one London merchant put it, "he being but one, has a mighty Advantage over so many Sellers . . . so that it has not been what Price we pleased, but that Gentleman has set his own Price."[163]

In order to deal as a unified group with the French agent, the London merchants, twenty-nine firms in all led by Henry Darnall and John Falconer, formed an organization in 1728. The members met on the first Thursday of each month, and a board of managers met on the third Thursday. Once or twice a year they held a banquet "to beget a good Friendship and Harmony among the Merchants." They advertised their objectives in the tobacco colonies, sought the moral support of the planters, gathered statistics about the trade and agreed in advance what price to accept from the French agent.[164] Unfortunately, however, the whole scheme fell through and the association dissolved the following year when some of the members were accused of surreptitiously selling tobacco to the French agent at prices below the one agreed upon.

Ten years later the French purchase, amounting to between 12,000 and 15,000 hogsheads a year, continued to be made by the agent of the Farmers General of the Revenue, but France now began to take tobacco from the outports as well as from London. The agent purchased tobacco from the English merchants "successively, and in small Parcels," thereby rendering its sale "very precarious."[165] In 1737 another unsuccessful attempt was made to form an association for dealing with the French.

In that year a group of merchants headed by Daniel McKircher proposed the formation of a single company which would make purchases in the tobacco colonies, ship the required quantity to England, and sell it on the quay in London to the French agent for an agreed price of two pence per pound cash. They claimed that the handling of large quantities by a single concern would save time formerly wasted in soliciting tobacco from many planters on several rivers, and would reduce freight charges by 25 per cent. In consequence of economy in marketing and transportation, the company would be able to sell the commodity to the French for a farthing a pound less than the current price and still make a substantial profit.

This proposal, involving outright purchase of tobacco in the colonies, appealed to the outport merchants. But it encountered the opposition of London consignment merchants and large planters of the Chesapeake colonies who succeeded in defeating it.[166]

Upon the outbreak of King George's War in 1740, it seemed clear that the trade with the French—by far the most considerable consumers of British colonial tobacco—would again be lost and that the British market would become glutted with the colonial staple. Fortunately, however, such was not the case. By this time tobacco had become an important source of revenue for both Great Britain and France. Both countries were reluctant to forego the revenue, particularly in time of war when money was especially needed, and a *modus vivendi* was reached.[167] The French continued to purchase tobacco in Great Britain as usual, and the Privy Council issued passes to British ships to carry it to France under a flag of truce. Ships regularly put out from London, Bristol, Liverpool, Whitehaven, and Glasgow and landed tobacco at Dieppe, Havre-de-Grace, Morlaix, Bourdeaux, Bayonne, and Marseilles.[168]

As a result, the tobacco trade escaped the catastrophe that befell it in the previous Anglo-French war, and the colonies escaped the extreme depression that they suffered during Queen Anne's War. There was a slight decline in the volume of trade during the years 1744-48, but it was the result of the action of enemy privateers at sea rather than of the loss of the continental market for colonial tobacco.

By about 1750 the production of the Chesapeake colonies amounted to some 80,000 hogsheads, or 72,000,000 pounds of tobacco a year. Of that quantity, three-fourths, or about 54,000-000 pounds, was reëxported to the continent.[169] This volume of trade was maintained, with slight reduction, during the French and Indian War, thanks to the continuation of the policy of "business as usual" with the French. In the midst of the struggle between Great Britain and France for maritime and colonial supremacy, the correspondence of planters and merchants regularly included inquiries and information concerning the price offered by the French agent for Virginia and Maryland tobacco.[170]

Until the end of the colonial period, the French were able to manipulate the price of tobacco to their advantage by means of a single purchasing agency. And since they were the principal buyer, what they offered influenced prices not only in London and the outports, but also in the tobacco colonies. When a factor in Virginia heard that the "French Farmers" had ceased buying tobacco, he wrote that so soon as it was "publick" throughout the colony it would affect tobacco prices to a great degree.[171]

Some idea of the skillfulness of the French purchasing agency in forcing down prices may be had from an account written by a Glasgow merchant in 1761. Tobacco, he said, took "a sudden turn to the disadvantage of the Importers" because the French agent stopped buying for a long time during which so much additional tobacco arrived that he was then able to buy it at an unusually low price.[172] In 1763 the French further reduced their usual purchases in London by a half, and were supplied much more cheaply at the outports.[173] By this maneuver, they forced the price in the outports to a new low. A Liverpool merchant, lamenting the "dismal doings" in the tobacco trade, wrote that the Glasgow and Whitehaven merchants had suffered themselves "to be beaten down by the French Agents" to a price of 1⅝d.

per pound with 2 per cent discount and liberty to reject inferior hogsheads.[174]

Although English merchants never succeeded in coping with the wily French agents, they annually sold enormous quantities of colonial tobacco on the continent. The maintenance of this foreign market for the colonial product enabled Virginia and Maryland to flourish long after their staple production exceeded the consumption capacity of Great Britain and it enabled Great Britain to increase her exports to foreign countries and turn the balance of trade in her favor. The volume of exports to the continent continued to increase after the French and Indian War. During the closing years of the colonial period, 1770-75, when the annual produce of the Chesapeake colonies was about 90,-000,000 or 100,000,000 pounds a year, the amount reëxported to the foreign market was between 80,000,000 and 90,000,000 pounds a year.

# British and African Trade

VIRGINIA and Maryland were regarded by English mercantilists as the two most satisfactory colonies on the North American continent, because their inhabitants consumed enormous quantities of British goods and produced almost nothing that competed with the manufactures of the mother country.

On reaching Virginia in 1759, Jonathan Boucher wrote home to England concerning the Virginians that "they toil not neither do they spin, yet Solomon in all his glory was not array'd like one of These." The common planter's daughters dressed in finer clothes every day than English provincials wore on Sundays. And Boucher's own satin waistcoat, which was thought elegant in his native Cumberland, was such that he was nothing amongst the "Lace and Lac'd fellows" of the colony. He therefore concluded that one may see in Virginia "more brilliant Assemblies than I ever could in the North of England, and except Royal Ones perhaps in any Part of it."[1]

Nor was the English cast of life along the Chesapeake confined to clothes. Virginians and Marylanders lavished almost all their energies on tobacco planting and relied upon the proceeds of their crop to purchase almost everything they needed in the way of manufactured goods from Great Britain. In this way the Chesapeake colonies were supplied with all manner of British, continental, and Asiatic goods through Great Britain as an entrepôt:[2] cloth and fabrics, clothes and furniture, linen, china, and silver, pewter, hardware, tools, and building materials.[3]

The value of the annual imports of the Chesapeake colonies from Great Britain rose from about £200,000 at the beginning of the eighteenth century to nearly £350,000 in 1750. In the years 1760-63 the amount averaged more than £500,000 a year, and in 1771 reached the staggering figure of £920,326.[4]

# Tobacco Coast

During the seventy-seven years from 1697 to 1775, the balance of trade between Great Britain and the tobacco colonies, as reflected in the British customs records, was normally in favor of the colonies.[5] Even so, as already stated, the colonists were usually in debt to British merchants. Jefferson in a well-known remark said that these debts became "hereditary from father to son for many generations, so that the planters were a species of property annexed to certain mercantile houses in London," and estimated that Virginians owed at least £2,000,000 sterling to British creditors on the eve of the Revolution.[6]

The explanation of this paradox lies in the fact that import and export statistics ignored services, taxes, carrying and handling charges such as freight rates, customs duties, insurance, and commissions.[7] Hall estimated the freight to amount to £90,000 in 1731, petty charges and commissions on tobacco to be £60,000, and charges and commissions for purchasing goods in Great Britain to be £11,250.[8] At the same time the yield from customs duties on colonial tobacco was about £390,000.[9] In this way the various carrying and service charges swallowed up the difference between imports and exports, and increased the indebtedness of the Chesapeake colonies to Great Britain despite the apparently favorable balance of trade.[10]

Another invisible export of Great Britain was accounted for by the slave trade, carried on largely by British capital, yet not appearing in the statistics of British exports to the Chesapeake because ships involved in it cleared from Great Britain for Africa.

o     o     o

From its establishment in 1663 until the trade was thrown open to all English subjects in 1698, the Royal African Company had a monopoly on the slave trade to England's American colonies. The depression in the tobacco colonies during the two decades following the Restoration, by limiting the demand for Negroes in the Chesapeake colonies, discouraged the Royal

149

African Company from transporting sufficient slaves to meet even the small demand of these colonies.[11] The apparent indifference of the Royal Company to the needs of the Chesapeake caused much complaint and paved the way for "separate traders," as ships not belonging to the Royal Company were called, to trade to the Chesapeake and for colonial vessels to bring Negroes from the West Indies[12] After 1680, when the rise of tobacco prices brought an increased demand for slaves in Virginia and Maryland, the Royal African Company made several half-hearted attempts to supply them, sending the ship *Speedwell* to Gambia River in January, 1685, for 200 slaves to be carried to Potomac River, and the ship *Two Friends* to the Gambia in March, 1685, for Negroes to be taken to James River.[13] As these efforts proved inadequate, the Chesapeake colonies continued to be supplied by separate traders and by colonial vessels, either under license of the Royal African Company or in violation of its monopoly.

The combined trade of the Royal African Company and the separate traders to the Chesapeake amounted to little during the last three decades of the seventeenth century. Between 1671 and 1700, the number of Negroes in Virginia rose from 2,000 to 6,000.[14] It was not until after the opening of the trade in 1698 that slave imports into the Chesapeake became considerable. Between 1698 and 1708 some 6,369 slaves were brought into Virginia, and the Negro population rose from about 12,000 in 1708 to 30,000 in 1730. Between 1698 and 1710 some 6,000 slaves were imported into Maryland, where the black population rose from 4,475 in 1704 to 7,945 in 1710, and 25,000 in 1720.[15] This rapid rise, especially noticeable after 1710, led the Rev. Hugh Jones to observe in his *Present State of Virginia* in 1724 that the country "may be said to be altered and improved in wealth" since 1710 "more than in all the Scores of years before that, from its first Discovery."[16]

The acceleration of these imports during the eighteenth century profoundly affected the human geography of the Chesapeake colonies. As early as 1736 William Byrd II, appalled by the large number of slaves imported into Virginia, wrote that he feared the colony "will some time or other be confirm'd by the Name of New Guinea."[17] And the census of 1790 shows that Virginia and Maryland then had 395,663 Negroes, approximately 57 per cent of all the slaves in the United States.[18]

The flourishing trade in Africans likewise profoundly affected the economic relations of the Chesapeake colonies and Great Britain. During the years 1751-63 the total value of British imports from those colonies exceeded the total value of British exports to them by £804,000. During the same period, however, Virginia and Maryland imported approximately 15,000 slaves which at an average of £35 amounted to £525,000. As 90 per cent of the Negroes were imported by British vessels, the slave trade represented an invisible export for the British to the extent of nearly half a million pounds (£472,500), thereby reducing the adverse balance of trade with the Chesapeake to a third of a million pounds (£330,000), a figure easily swallowed up by other invisible exports such as freight, insurance, customs duties, and commissions.

During the period of the Royal African Company's monopoly and for some time thereafter, when the volume of slave imports into the Chesapeake was small, most of those brought into Virginia and Maryland came from the West Indies. After 1698, however, the activity of the separate traders to Africa increased, and by the second decade of the eighteenth century the Chesapeake received slightly over half its Negroes from Africa.[19] By the middle of the century the volume of imports from Africa reached 90 per cent of the total. Generally speaking, the African trade was largely carried on by British capital and British vessels, while the slaves imported into the Chesapeake colonies from the West Indies were brought in colonial vessels. From 1718 to 1727 Virginia imported slightly over 11,000 Negroes from Africa in 76 vessels, of which only six vessels carrying 649 of them were from Virginia. The remaining 70 ships carrying 10,442 Africans were from Bristol, Liverpool, and London.

Early in the eighteenth century London and Bristol were the most active ports in the African trade. From 1699 to 1708, 39 vessels brought slaves to Virginia, 34 of them of London registry and five of Bristol.[20] When the Board of Trade conducted an investigation of the Negro traffic in 1726, it found that the trade from Africa to the American colonies amounted to 30,000 slaves a year, and that Bristol alone operated 63 ships in the trade, capable of carrying 16,950 Negroes.

The next few decades, however, saw the phenomenal rise of Liverpool in the slave trade, one of the most spectacular commercial developments of the century. By 1752 Liverpool had 53 ships with a combined burden of 5,334 tons in the African trade,[21] and in 1786 Liverpool slavers sold 31,690 slaves for £1,282,690, of which their profit was £298,462 or nearly a quarter of their investment.[22] The interests of Liverpool became so bound up with the slave trade that Thomas Stothard, a local painter of distinction, was moved to depict the voyage of the Liverpool slaver *Sable Venus* from Angola to the West Indies, and the merchants' exchange of the city was decorated with bas-reliefs of blackamoors, elephants' teeth, and "such-like emblematical figures representing the African trade and commerce."[23]

This shift in favor of Liverpool is reflected in Chesapeake imports. Of the 66 British vessels that imported Negroes into Virginia during the years 1710-18, some 23 were from Bristol, 20 from London, 11 from Liverpool, and 12 from other British ports.[24] By 1751-63, however, the distribution of British vessels in the Chesapeake slave trade was 25 from Liverpool, 18 from Bristol, six from London, and three from other ports.

The extent of colonial participation in the traffic was small, especially after the rise of the direct African trade. During the years 1751-63, when the total slave imports into Virginia were 10,548, only 1,293 were brought in by colonial vessels. It is commonly asserted that New England vessels imported large numbers of Negroes from the West Indies to the Chesapeake, but this is not so. New England participation in the Chesapeake slave trade was small and largely confined to importations from Africa. Between 1727 and 1738, some 16 New England vessels brought 540 Negroes into Virginia—an average of only 45 a year. Of these, 447 came from Africa and only 85 from the West Indies.[25] Between 1753 and 1763, some 13 New England vessels brought 869 slaves to Virginia, 755 of them from Africa, and only two from the West Indies.[26]

During the earlier decade 55 Virginia vessels imported 447 slaves, all from the West Indies, and during the latter decade 20 Virginia vessels brought 229 Negroes from the West Indies and none from Africa. Taking all the entries of colonial ships from 1727 through 1744, some 138 of them were Virginia vessels, 92 were Bermuda and West Indian, 34 were New England vessels. Pennsylvania owned 13, Maryland four, and South Carolina two. Of all the entries of colonial ships from 1751 through 1763, some 35 belonged to Virginia, 16 to New England, 14 to Bermuda and the West Indies, and two to Pennsylvania.

Between 1727 and 1769 there were 231 entries of Virginia registry with Negroes. Only one brought slaves from Africa, the 130-ton *Charming Betty* belonging to James LaRoch and Company, which entered in 1750 with 280 Negroes from Africa. All the rest brought them from the West Indies or from other continental colonies. Thirteen vessels in the slave trade not of Virginia registry were built in Virginia, three were of Liverpool, two of Bristol, seven of the West Indies, and one of Boston. All of them were of less than 100 tons except three, the 220-ton *Cunliffe* of Liverpool, the 130-ton *Eugene* of Bristol, and the 100-ton *Barbados Packet*. During the same period nine vessels of Maryland registry imported slaves into Virginia, four of them over 100 tons, one of them over 200 tons. Three Maryland vessels, the 140-ton *Gildart*, the 120-ton *Johnson*, and the 90-ton *Gildart*, belonged to the well-known Liverpool merchants, Richard Gildart and Company. They brought cargoes of 250, 495, and 200 slaves respectively directly from Africa. Another vessel, the 70-ton *Planter* of Liverpool, also belonging to Gildart and Company, was described as Maryland-built. She entered Virginia with 226 Negroes from Africa in 1746.

As the slave trade was regarded as being by far the most profitable trade of the Chesapeake colonies, participation in it was eagerly sought after by colonial merchants and planters.[27] Purchasing Negroes on the African coast at a prime cost of between £4 and £6 per head, the slavers sold them in Virginia and Maryland at average prices ranging from £16 to £20 at the end of the seventeenth century, from £28 to £35 during the first half of the eighteenth, and at about £40 after the middle of the century.[28] Considerable variation existed in the sale price depending upon the age, sex, physical condition and accomplishments of the slave, young adults preferred to old or to children, males preferred to females, and craftsmen preferred to unskilled laborers. The price was also subject to seasonal variation. In the spring and early summer the planters were "abundantly more fond of them," and would give greater prices for them because they were sure of the advantage of their labor in that year's crop, whereas Negroes bought at the latter end of the year would be of little service until the next spring.[29]

Many colonial merchants and planters desiring to enter the slave trade and partake of its rich profits were deterred by want of capital. If they had enough to build and operate a ship, they were in most cases obliged to use it in the British trade to carry their tobacco overseas and import manufactured goods, or in the West India trade to dispose of their surplus grain and procure rum, sugar, molasses, coin, and bills of exchange without which their other commercial activities would have been hampered. In consequence, few Virginians and Marylanders maintained ships in the African trade.[30] However, Chesapeake merchants and planters occasionally acquired part interest in an African voyage, usually in partnership with British merchants.[31] More commonly they imported Negroes in small numbers from the West Indies, an undertaking that was an adjunct to their ordinary commerce with that part of the empire rather than a separate trade like the African slave trade.[32]

Colonial merchants might also participate in the trade by receiving consignments of slaves imported in British ships. As Negroes could not be sold at high prices for ready money because of the shortage of currency in the colonies, the extension of credit—often for six months or a year—was an essential feature of the system of disposing of them.[33] This required the services of a merchant resident in the colony who knew the planters in the area and could estimate the extent to which their credit was good. As a form of participation in the trade, the handling of slaves on consignment involved little capital and little risk, yet proved quite lucrative. The usual commission amounted to 5 per cent on the sales and 5 per cent on the remittances—or about 7½ or 8 per cent on the gross sales.[34] Among the Virginians to import slaves or to receive them on consignment were some of the leading men of the colony: William Byrd, Robert Carter, and Benjamin Harrison, several Nelsons, Randolphs, and Braxtons, as well as merchants like Andrew Sprowle, William Allason, and Neil Jamieson. Among the prominent Marylanders were Daniel Dulany, Samuel Chew, Edward Lloyd, and John Ridout, and merchants like Galloway, Ringgold, Callister, Robert Morris, and Daniel of St. Thomas Jennifer.

Although enormously profitable, the slave trade was extremely hazardous. Masters and crews of slaving vessels bound to the African coast were exposed to excessive heat, unaccustomed diseases, and the violence and plundering of pirates and the King's enemies. An even more serious risk was the mortality of the slaves during the passage. A vessel that reached Virginia in 1702 brought 230 Negroes from Africa, having lost 100 at sea.[35] The

*Customhouse, London, in 1714, with shipping of the period (from Dow, SLAVE SHIPS AND SLAVING, after engraving by John Harris in the MacPherson Collection).*

normal rate was somewhat lower, but occasional instances of high mortality usually received attention in the provincial newspapers. The Boston *News-Letter* in 1760 carried a news item from New York concerning the Bristol slaver *Diamond,* bound from Bonny in Africa to Maryland with 329 Negroes, of which 99 were lost "with the Flux."[36] Other factors in the mortality of slaves were the region from which they came,[37] and the suitability of the vessels for the trade—those not able to "turn well to windward" often lost many slaves before the vessels could clear the African coast.[38]

Another difficulty was the general prejudice against slaving vessels as suitable ships to carry tobacco to Great Britain. They frequently advertised for cargoes in Virginia and Maryland, but usually had to take tobacco at freight rates lower than the prevailing ones in order to obtain full cargoes.[39] It was the general belief that slavers were "never after in a Condition to take in Tobacco." One irate slaver, John Simpson, master of the Guineaman *Black Prince* of London, publicly protested against this idea as "very absurd and ungenerous, and a great Discouragement to bring Negros here." Asserting that his ship was seaworthy, he offered to have a survey made "to clear up all Doubts."[40]

Finally, the necessity of extending credit to purchasers of slaves, often in considerable amounts and for long periods of time, added to the risk.[41] In view of all the trouble, loss, and disappointment in the Guinea trade, one Maryland merchant wrote his partner that he was firmly resolved not to engage in the trade further because "there are more disasters in those Voyages then any others whatever."[42]

During the late seventeenth and early eighteenth centuries the assemblies of the Chesapeake colonies levied duties on imported slaves as a means of raising revenue either for general purposes or for specific ones such as building a statehouse, a capitol, or finishing the governor's palace at Williamsburg.[43] As the volume of slave imports became considerable, however, there arose a desire on the part of the colonists to check the rising black tide. The large number of slaves threatened the Chesapeake colonies with the evils of overproduction of tobacco. Owners of large plantations well stocked with Negroes desired to prevent their poorer neighbors from becoming serious competitors.[44] A few wise ones perceived that the increase of slaves had a detrimental effect upon the whites, inflating their pride, ruining their industry, and disposing them to idleness. Others saw in the increasing numbers of "descendants of Ham" a weakening of the colony from a military point of view and a danger of revolt which might one day "tinge our Rivers as wide as they are with blood."[45] Shortly after arriving in Virginia, Governor Spotswood expressed the current sentiment when he said, "the Country is already ruined by the great number of negros imported of late years."[46]

After about 1710 the assemblies of Virginia and Maryland began to increase the duties on imported slaves with the mixed motive of raising revenue and reducing the traffic. At first they enjoyed reasonable success, but in time the policy of restriction encountered opposition from the Royal African Company and other British merchants engaged in the African trade. In 1723-24 the matter was aired before the Board of Trade, the immediate cause being the Virginia act of 1723 imposing forty shillings per head on imported Negroes. The British slaving interests maintained that such a duty, since it was paid by the importer, constituted a direct tax upon British commerce. They pointed out that the duty of £5 per head on imported slaves that had been imposed by a Virginia act in 1710 and continued in force until 1718 proved to be "such a discouragement to the traders to Africa," that they were forced "entirely to quit that Colony." And they held that the duty prescribed in the act of 1723 was likewise so high that it would discourage further Negro importations, thereby hindering the expansion of tobacco production and affecting the royal revenue. Accordingly, the Privy Council disallowed the act.[47]

In 1728 Virginia again levied a duty of forty shillings per head on imported slaves, ostensibly for revenue purposes. And the Privy Council again disallowed it on the grounds that the duty was too high and was imposed on the importer.[48] Meanwhile, similar Maryland acts laying duties on imported Negroes were ignored by the British authorities, because Maryland was a proprietary rather than a royal colony. This greatly irked the Virginians. Governor Gooch of Virginia told the Board of Trade in 1728 that it was the common topic among the inhabitants of the colony and that they considered it hard that they "who are under his Majesty's immediate Government" should be restrained from using the same means of "securing and improving their Country" that had served the proprietary province of Maryland.[49]

In 1731 the British government sent letters to colonial governors authorizing their assent to acts laying moderate duties on imported slaves, provided that such duties were to be paid by the purchaser.[50] The next year Virginia laid a 5 per cent ad valorem duty on imported Negroes and specified that it was to be paid by the purchaser. In this way the colony obviated the objections of the British merchants and forestalled disallowance by the Privy Council. The law was continued in force until the end of the colonial period.[51] Had Virginia been content with a 5 per cent duty there would have been no further friction between the colonial and home authorities concerning Negro importations. But there were strong high-duty forces in the colony determined to use the duty as a means of restricting the trade.

In 1740 these forces secured an increased duty of 10 per cent for four years.[52] During the French and Indian War, when the urgent need of revenue provided a plausible excuse, the duty was increased to 20 per cent,[53] which caused Negro imports to fall off sharply, deflected the trade to Maryland and North Carolina,[54] and greatly increased the value of slaves already in Virginia. As the exigencies of war prevented interference by

Great Britain,[55] the question of the duty now became a struggle between the old planters who had large numbers of slaves and wished to enjoy a monopoly of them by prohibiting further imports, and the rising generation of planters who wished to purchase slaves but not at abnormally high prices.[56]

In 1761 the low-duty forces carried the day by appending to the bill raising troops for the Cherokee expedition a rider reducing the duty on Negroes to 10 per cent. In spite of vigorous opposition by the large tidewater planters, the bill passed by a majority of one vote.[57] In later years the high-duty party again obtained control of the assembly and on several occasions put through legislation to raise the duty on imported slaves. But the Peace of Paris in 1763, by bringing the war to an end, deprived them of a good excuse for laying heavy duties on the trade. Consequently, the British merchants were once more able to persuade the Privy Council to disallow such acts.[58]

Coming as it did at a time when the colonists were beginning to chafe under imperial restraint, this renewed interference led them to declare that they had "a title to expect to be considered before those trading people in England, whose particular interest it may be" to sell slaves, and that they were anxious, as Lord Dunmore put it, "to restrain the introduction of people, the Number of whom, already in the Colony, gives them Just cause to apprehend the most dangerous Consequences . . . Sufficient to allarm not only this Colony, but all the Colonies of America."[59] In this way, whether justly or not, the Chesapeake colonists came to regard the actions of the British government as designed to enrich the British slave-trading interests at the expense of the welfare and safety of the colonies. This sentiment must be regarded as one of the threads in the pattern of supposed imperial abuses that led to the war for independence.[60]

o    o    o

Another British export to the Chesapeake colonies that may be considered invisible, since it does not appear in the customs records of imports and exports, was the transportation of European immigrants.[61] This passenger trade included "free-willers," who paid their own way, "redemptioners," who paid part of their passage, and "indentured servants" and convicts who were transported and sold in the colonies at the risk and profit of merchants and shipowners. It also included a number of political and military prisoners principally from Scotland and Ireland—supporters of the unsuccessful rebellions of Argyll and Monmouth in 1685 and the Old and Young Pretenders in 1715 and 1746; captives taken at Preston, Dunbar, and Worcester by Cromwell; Scottish Covenanters, unruly Quakers, and Irish taken at Drogheda.

Among the servants, especially the redemptioners, were French, German, and Swiss Protestants, impoverished farmers, refugees from religious persecution, oppressed peasants, artisans, and adventurers seeking to better their fortunes in the New World. Collectively the servants and convicts comprised all kinds of people: many were rogues and vagabonds, the dregs of British society, but many others were ordinary, respectable, lower-middle-class people, and a few were gentlemen by eighteenth-century standards. It has been estimated that perhaps two-thirds of all the immigrants to the colonies south of New York were servants or redemptioners, and the proportion in the Chesapeake colonies was unquestionably high—perhaps the highest of the continental colonies.

The system of temporary bondage as a means of paying the passage of white immigrants to the colonies enabled large numbers of persons to migrate who otherwise would have been obliged to remain at home, and therefore was an important factor not only in their lives but in the rapid peopling of the British colonies. From the point of view of the British merchants engaged in trade to the Chesapeake colonies the immigrant trade was particularly desirable. Tobacco ships, although heavily laden on their homeward passage to Great Britain with the bulky produce of Virginia and Maryland, were but partially laden on their outward passage, and therefore able to carry a large number of passengers at small extra cost. Moreover, tobacco planters suffering from a shortage of labor were always eager to buy servants and convicts in lieu of, or in addition to, Negroes. Servants and convicts, unlike slaves, were bound to servitude for a limited number of years and therefore were less desirable than slaves as unskilled laborers, but they were less expensive, were more apt to understand English, and were usually more adaptable than Negroes fresh from the jungles of Africa. The smaller planters who could not afford to buy slaves often took convicts and indentured servants instead, and the larger planters occasionally took them either to augment their slave labor or to perform specialized functions for which they were equipped by education or experience in the mother country, such as those of overseers, schoolmasters, carpenters, coopers, weavers, and blacksmiths.

The economic wretchedness of the masses in Great Britain and religious and political oppression on the European Continent provided conditions favorable to large-scale migration to the New World. The most powerful stimulus, however, was the interests of the merchants who engaged in the profitable trade of shipping servants. Some merchants made it their principal business—particularly those who contracted to transport convicts; others participated in it along with their activities in the tobacco trade. In either case they eagerly sought candidates for transportation and created a demand which unscrupulous agents arose to satisfy. In the seventeenth century kidnappers, called "spirits," operated in English seaport towns, shanghaiing adults by force and enticing children by offers of candy aboard outward-bound Virginiamen.[62] Various attempts were made by the government to eliminate kidnapping and deceit, but they were ineffectual. Therefore the methods used to procure emigrants continued throughout the colonial period to be somewhat unsavory. If very few emigrants were forcibly transported against their will, many were persuaded to try their fortunes in the colonies as a result of deception and misrepresentation.

Merchants in the trade regularly maintained emigration offices in British cities where indentures were offered to all comers for servitude in the colonies, and energetic agents called "newlanders" or "soul-sellers," wandering through the Rhine provinces of Germany, stimulated migration by picturing America to the gullible peasants as a veritable paradise. This activity contributed much to the great German migration to the American colonies in the middle of the eighteenth century. Many peasants sold their holdings and set out for the New World, but became impoverished en route and were obliged to continue as redemptioners.

Merchants engaged in the passenger and servant trade accepted what money these people had left and transported them on credit to the colonies where they were given a fortnight in which to secure the balance owed for their passage. This was done by borrowing from friends and relatives who had preceded them to the colonies or by indenturing themselves for the sum due. This method was first mentioned in 1728, although in such a way as to suggest that it had been in use for some years, and it appears at first to have been confined to German immigrants.[63] Soon thereafter it was imitated in Great Britain, particularly in connection with the Irish migration to the colonies. Some Englishmen also came as redemptioners, but indentured servitude continued to be important as a means of transporting English immigrants.[64]

The cost of transporting a servant—that is to say, the price of passage—varied between £5 and £6 throughout the colonial period. Merchants in the trade had to clothe, house, and feed servants from the time the indenture was made until they were sold in the colonies. The cost of doing so varied with the length of time the servant waited for transportation, the length of the passage, the delay upon disembarkation before he was sold, and, of course, with the general price level. Various estimates at the end of the seventeenth century place the cost of clothing a servant in preparation for transportation at about £5. These prices, of course, included the shipowner's and haberdasher's profit. If a merchant transported servants on his own ship and supplied them with clothing from his own stock, the cost would be somewhat less. In general, the cost of equipping and transporting a servant (including the cost of maintaining him before the ship sailed) was about £10 or £12 for a servant who was being transported for a planter or other person not a merchant and shipowner, and between £4 and £10 for merchants who carried on the trade in their own ships. Redemptioners who needed no additional equipment and who provided their own food could make the passage for £5 or £6—the cost of their fare.

The prices brought by indentured servants in the colonies varied considerably depending upon the age, skill, health, sex, and even upon the nationality and religion of the servant. Scottish servants were considered the most desirable and Roman Catholic Irish the least desirable.[65] In the early seventeenth century the average price of unskilled servants in the Chesapeake colonies varied from £15 to £20. Skilled artisans brought from £20 to £40, and, in exceptional cases, as much as £60.[66] Redemptioners transported to the colonies were sold for an amount equal to the cost of their passage plus 15 per cent for interest and insurance. In addition, they were charged freight for their baggage. Even so, the trade was not nearly so lucrative as the indentured servant business, and in consequence merchants operating ships in the trade much preferred the latter. Transporting redemptioners was essentially a passenger trade although under special circumstances; transporting indentured servants was a mercantile venture with opportunities for great profit.

An important group of immigrants who came to America in bondage were convicts whose death sentences had been commuted to servitude in the colonies for a stated period of time depending upon the gravity of their crime. The death penalty was mandatory for persons convicted of felonies and in the seventeenth century no fewer than three hundred crimes—including house-breaking and stealing goods of greater value than one shilling—were designated as felonies. Had the laws been rigidly enforced, the extent of judicial slaughtering in England would have been appalling. In practice, however, the apparent cruelty of the law was moderated by the custom of extending "benefit of clergy" (which exempted a convicted criminal from the legal penalty of a crime for the first offence) to all who could read, and, after 1705, to everyone. When the final extension was made in that year, certain heinous crimes such as treason, murder, arson, piracy, burglary, highway robbery, and theft of goods worth more than a shilling were made "non-clergyable," and other offences were later added to the list until by 1769 it comprised 169 crimes.

As the law was tightened, the practice of granting royal pardons to convicted criminals was extended. At the conclusion of each session of the courts, the justices sent a list of convicted felons to the Privy Council with recommendations of mercy, and pardons were issued wholesale under the great seal. Although many earlier instances are known, it became common practice, after the act of 1718 that provided for the transportation of convicts to the colonies, to extend pardons to criminals who stood in jeopardy of the death sentence on condition that they assent to their transportation. They were not legally obliged to do so, and there are isolated instances of convicts who preferred execution to penal servitude in the colonies, but most of them readily sought this avenue of escape from the gallows. Murderers were usually executed unless there was reason to doubt their guilt, in which case they were transported. Petty thieves were usually pardoned without condition of transportation. The bulk of the felons brought to America were convicted of crimes more serious than the latter but not so serious as the former.

Virginia and Maryland, the principal colonies that used white labor, in 1670 and 1676 respectively prohibited further importation of "jaile birds" because of apprehension that "the peace of this collony be too much hazarded and endangered by the great nombers of fellons and other desperate villaines sent hither from the several prisons in England."[67] Another motive as the Virginia General Court freely admitted in stopping the flow of convicts to the colony was to escape the ignominy of being thought "a place onely fitt to receive such base and lewd persons." The cutting off of the Chesapeake colonies as a market for convicts was not a serious problem for the English authorities from 1689 until 1713, because, as a result of King William's and Queen Anne's wars, able-bodied male convicts were absorbed into the army. But after the Peace of Utrecht (1713) which ushered in a comparatively long period of peace in Europe, the army no longer wanted men, and the annual crop of convicts who had their death sentences commuted to transportation could not be sold for want of a market in the colonies.

In 1718 Parliament passed an act that became the cornerstone of the system for the rest of the colonial period. Persons convicted of offences "within the benefit of clergy," such as grand or petit larceny or felonious stealing, might at the discretion of the court be sentenced to seven years servitude in the colonies. Persons convicted of non-clergyable felonies—for which execution was mandatory—and who received a royal pardon for transportation were to be sentenced to fourteen years servitude in the colonies. As the British government did not intend to provide ships to carry convicts overseas, the act authorized the courts to turn them over to merchants who had contracted with the Treasury for their transportation. If the transported convicts returned to England during the statutory period of servitude, they were liable to execution. Merchants contracting to transport felons were obliged to give security that they would fill their part of the agreement. By including persons within the benefit of clergy, who formerly got off scot-free except for being branded in the hand, the act enormously increased the volume of convict transportation to the colonies. Moreover, the act overruled colonial prohibitions and opened Virginia and Maryland as well as all the other colonies to the convict traffic.

Shortly before the passage of the act, the Treasury began to let contracts to merchants for transporting convicts to America and to pay a certain sum of money—£2 at first—for each convict embarked for the colonies. This practice was continued until the Revolution, and the stipulated payment was raised several times until 1727 when it reached £5 per convict from Newgate, and until 1722 when it reached £5 per convict from the counties near London—known as the Home Counties. One of the principal merchants to engage in the trade, Jonathan Forward of London, held a government contract from 1718 until 1739, and traded largely to the Chesapeake colonies. His contract covered Newgate Prison in London and the prisons of the Home Counties—Hertford, Essex, Kent, Sussex, and Surrey. He was obliged to receive from those prisons all the convicts held for transportation regardless of their age, sex, or infirmity, and he was responsible for all the charges for conveying them from the prisons to his ships.

In April, 1739, the Treasury made a new contract on the same terms with Andrew Reid, and he in turn was succeeded by John Stewart in March, 1757. When Stewart died in February, 1772, his partner, Duncan Campbell, sought in vain to renew the contract. By that time the market for convicts was so good that several merchants offered to transport them without charge to the Treasury, and the trade was opened to all takers. Convicts from the provinces were transported by other merchants: Jonathan Forward Sydenham of London in 1768, Samuel Sedgley and Company of Bristol in 1750 (later under the name of Sedgley and Hillhouse), and their successors William Randolph in 1766 and his partner William Stevenson, William Cookson of Hull in 1747, James Baird of Glasgow in 1770, and Patrick Colquhoun of Glasgow in 1772.

Treasury records show that between 1719 and 1772 Forward, Reid, and Stewart conveyed to America some 17,740 felons from London and the Home Counties. Statistics are not available for the provinces, but Duncan Campbell after twenty years experience in the trade stated in 1787 that he always considered the number from the provinces to be equal to the number from London and the Home Counties. It is reasonable to estimate that the total number of felons transported from Great Britain to the American colonies in the eighteenth century was at least 30,000.

A large proportion of these convicts was brought to the Chesapeake colonies. Of the 190 ships that sailed from London with felons, 53 are known to have come to Maryland, 47 to Virginia, and only two elsewhere—one to South Carolina and one to the West Indian island of Nevis. Many others whose destination is unspecified in the records probably came to the Chesapeake colonies as well, since the business relations of the contractors were largely in Virginia and Maryland. Duncan Campbell in later years reported to the House of Commons that during the twenty years in which he engaged in the trade he took convicts only to the Chesapeake colonies. Several contractors for the provinces, including Sydenham and the firm of Sedgley and Hillhouse, had business relations in Virginia and Maryland and shipping most, if not all, of their felons to those colonies. A recent authority estimates that the Chesapeake colonies received slightly more than 20,000 convicts during the eighteenth century, or two-thirds of the total number transported to America.

The increasing numbers of felons transported to the colonies from 1718 until the Revolution gave rise to considerable resentment and fear on the part of Virginians and Marylanders. The first edition of Beverley's *History of Virginia* in 1705 stated, "As for Malefactors condemn'd to Transportation [the Virginians] have always receiv'd very few and for many years last past their laws have been severe against them." But the second edition in 1722 was amended to read, "tho' the greedy Planter will always buy them, yet it is to be fear'd they will be very injurious to the Country, which has already suffer'd many Murthers and Robberies, the Effects of that new Law [the act of 1718] of England."[68] Murders, arson, and robberies became more common in Virginia and Maryland after 1718, especially in those counties where convicts were most numerous. It is well known that Colonel Thomas Lee's mansion was burnt down in 1729 by convicts who resented his activities as justice of the peace in suppressing crime in the Northern Neck.[69] In 1732 the attorney general of Virginia, John Clayton, requested and received a higher salary because "the increase of Criminals of late Years especially since the importation of Convicts from great Brittain" occasioned him additional "Trouble in the prosecution of them."[70]

Imported felons not only composed an unstable and dangerous portion of colonial society, given to crimes of violence, but they also were responsible for spreading disease among the inhabitants. In 1767 Governor Sharpe of Maryland wrote that "Distempers . . . have been frequently brought into this and many other Places in the Province and . . . scores of People have been destroyed here by the Jail Fever first communicated by Servants from on board crowded infectious Ships."[71] Nonetheless, imported felons never lacked ready purchasers and the British merchants who contracted to transport them were able to obtain royal disallowance of colonial legislation designed to prohibit or seriously restrict the volume of the trade.

No one questioned the authority of Parliament to enact legislation opening the colonies to convict importation, but both Virginia and Maryland tried to devise means of nullifying the effect of the act of 1718. The lower house of the Maryland Assembly in 1719 drew up a bill designed to discourage convict importations by making the purchasers responsible for the good conduct of the felons. The upper house postponed the effective date of the bill for a year, and the governor vetoed it.[72] Virginia passed an act in 1722 which, by imposing elaborate regulations, would have rendered the trade so troublesome as to be unprofitable.[73] Jonathan Forward at once petitioned the Board of Trade to urge royal disallowance, and, after hearing his case, the board did as he requested. The act was vetoed by the King on the grounds that it amounted to "a prohibition of any convicts being imported," and therefore rendered the act of Parliament null and void. A similar act passed by the Maryland Assembly was disallowed by Lord Baltimore in 1723 for the same reason.

Both Virginia and Maryland made further attempts to throttle the trade by levying heavy duties on imported felons in the 1750's and 1760's but without success. The only thing accomplished at all was an improvement of conditions on shipboard as a result of a carefully-drawn Maryland quarantine act in 1767, which managed to escape disallowance. Virginia's quarantine acts of 1767 and 1772, however, were both disallowed for technical defects.

Merchants engaged in the convict trade found it extremely profitable, particularly toward the end of the colonial period. Felons sold for between £8 and £20 apiece, according to Governor Sharpe of Maryland. Duncan Campbell testified that the average price was £10, women selling for £8 or £9 and men for from £15 to £25 depending upon their skill and the nature of their trade or craft. The old and infirm brought very little, and sometimes no one would take them without a premium. Campbell transported 348 felons to Virginia at an expense of £1,740 9s. 7d. and sold them for £2,957 9s. Allowing 10 per cent for bad debts and £233 6s. 8d. for commissions to his agent he still made a profit of nearly £700 not counting the Treasury warrant for £5 per convict which amounted to £1,740 and therefore just covered his expenses. His total profit, then, was slightly less than £2,440 for transporting 348 felons. It is not surprising, therefore, that the Treasury ceased paying subsidies for convict transportation after 1772 because of the exorbitant profits enjoyed by the merchants engaged in the trade.

The transportation of felons to the colonies was anything but pleasant for them—unless they were men of means and connections, in which case they rode to the ship in their own carriages, occupied the great cabin on shipboard, and purchased their freedom upon reaching the colonies. The poor felons, however, marched under guard and in chains amidst the hoots and jeers of the crowds from Newgate to the nearest landing, where they were herded aboard a lighter that conveyed them to their ship. Once on board they were chained in groups of six and kept below decks for the entire passage. As sanitary conditions were bad, jail fever and smallpox frequently ravaged the hapless convicts. When the *Honour* crossed to Annapolis in 1720, 20 of her 61 felons died at sea. Two years later the *Gilbert* lost 30 of her 87 felons, and in 1725 the *Rappahannock Merchant* lost 38 of her 95. Conditions greatly improved in the late 1760's and 1770's as a result of Maryland's quarantine act and the installation of portholes and ventilators on convict ships, but Duncan Campbell estimated that he usually lost more than a seventh (15 per cent) of all the felons he transported.

Before reaching port, as Abbot E. Smith has graphically described it, the human cargo aboard a convict ship was refurbished: faces were washed, bodies scrubbed, haircuts given, and clothes cleaned. Sometimes wigs were distributed to improve the appearance of the men. Upon arrival of a servant or convict ship, advertisements in the colonial newspapers gave the date when the sale was to begin and the number of servants or felons and intimated the variety of their skills. But since the market was so good, advertisements were often unnecessary and entire cargoes sold almost immediately upon disembarkation.

The disposal of servants and convicts in the colonies was a sight that would have distressed modern observers. Like slaves— and, indeed, like cattle—these human beings were displayed to the prospective purchasers, who felt their muscles, examined their teeth and mouths, and otherwise formulated opinions of their health, and morals. Late in the colonial period middlemen called "soul drivers" sprang up, who purchased large groups of servants on shipboard and sold them off in the hinterland by driving them like cattle from one place to another.

Once safely in the colonies the felons found themselves provided with a good diet and healthful labor—better conditions, certainly, than in English prisons or metropolitan slums. Many reformed and became useful citizens; many others longed for the familiar purlieus of Wapping and Limehouse. Some of the latter returned to their old haunts after the expiration of their servitude, many more remained in Virginia and Maryland, squatted on poor soil in the pine barrens or backcountry, and formed a wretched, turbulent, lawless part of society—the prototype of the "poor white trash" of a later day.

o o o

As colonial Virginia and Maryland are associated in the popular mind with a one-crop system of agriculture, and as tobacco was by far their largest export, one is inclined to forget that they produced other commodities as well. Having its origin, perhaps, in the economic conditions of the seventeenth century, this tendency toward oversimplification has been encouraged by the generalizations of popular historians. However applicable it may be to seventeenth-century conditions, the concept of Virginia and Maryland producing nothing but tobacco does not hold for the eighteenth century.

Throughout the early colonial period the governments of Virginia and Maryland sought to stimulate industry and encourage diversified agriculture. In 1662 and 1681 Maryland prohibited the exportation of untanned hides in order to foster tanning in the colony.[74] In 1662 Sir William Berkeley of Virginia consulted with the governor and planters of Maryland concerning methods of promoting the growth of hemp, flax, and "other like considerable Comodityes."[75] The same year Berkeley, urged by

172

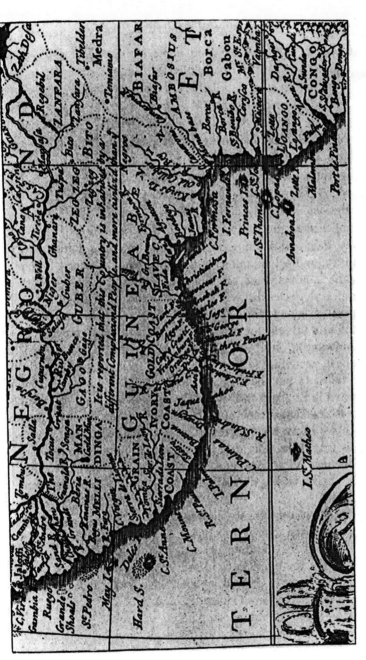

*Map of Guinea Coast, about 1700 (from Dow, SLAVE SHIPS AND SLAV-ING, after map in Churchill's COLLECTION OF VOYAGES, London, 1756).*

the English authorities to send home a shipload of silk, hemp, flax, pitch, and potash,[76] persuaded the Virginia Assembly to pass a law requiring every landholder to plant ten mulberry trees for each hundred acres of land and granting a bounty of fifty pounds of tobacco for each pound of silk produced.[77] In 1682 both Virginia and Maryland enacted laws to encourage the production of linen and woolen cloth.[78]

By 1690, however, it seemed clear that these attempts had failed. Although there was some domestic industry on the larger plantations, it usually supplied the needs of the plantation, producing a small surplus for sale locally and none for export. Some hemp, flax, and cotton were grown and used in a domestic cloth industry, and a few mulberry trees planted and some silk made. But the inhabitants of Virginia and Maryland still devoted their energies almost exclusively to tobacco and were noted for their neglect of commodities for which their soil was known to be suited and famous for their indisposition to apply themselves to manufacturing in order to supply their wants. The Chesapeake colonists, according to Beverley, sheared their sheep to cool them, and failed to put the fleeces to any use. They wore hats manufactured in England and sold in the colonies at a high price rather than make them of their abundant supply of furs. They frequently left hides to rot on the ground, or at best used them to protect goods from rain. The rich forest resources remained practically untouched, Virginians and Marylanders preferring to import their chairs, tables, chests, cart-wheels, and even their birchen brooms.[79]

The eighteenth century, however, saw a marked change in the economy of the tobacco colonies. The rising tide of tobacco production and the resulting price depression made it increasingly difficult for the planters to afford imported English goods. The solution was found, partially at least, in agricultural diversification and in the expansion of domestic industry.[80]

Before 1700 some tobacco planters began to grow wheat and corn on partly exhausted tobacco fields, and in some cases on fresh land, not simply to supply their own needs, but for sale or export. They also began to pen in old-field pastures their cattle, which formerly had been allowed to roam in the woods. And they gave more attention to sheep and hogs. This increased interest in domestic animals made it necessary to raise more corn to feed them. Cereals were further stimulated by the increasing demand for foodstuffs among the rising population of the tobacco colonies, New England, and the West Indies. Moreover, with the great increase of shipping in the eighteenth century, provisioning of ships trading to Chesapeake Bay with flour, ships bread, beef, and pork became a profitable undertaking. Most spectacular of all was the rise of the trade between the Chesapeake and the West Indies in which Virginians and Marylanders exported considerable quantities of wheat, corn, flour, pork, and lumber. This trade stimulated shipbuilding, which in turn fostered ancillary industries: lumber, hemp, cordage, iron, sailcloth, and naval stores.

The increase of cattle, sheep, and hogs brought with it the beginnings of a leather industry. Tanning became more common and a small shoe-making industry arose, producing the cheaper grades of shoes fit for servants, slaves, and the lesser planters. Agricultural diversification increased the supplies of flax, wool, and cotton, thereby encouraging the production of linen, woolen, and cotton both for home consumption and for sale within the colony. The forest industries, already fostered by the increasing demand for houses, tobacco barns, wharves, ships, and hogsheads, were greatly accelerated by the British government's policy of encouraging colonial production of masts, yards, and naval stores. The increasing production of tobacco and the commerce with the sugar and wine islands provided an expanding market for hogshead, barrel, and pipe staves, hoops, and headings, and also for beeswax.

Rising living standards of the eighteenth century brought about a demand for larger and more elegant homes, a tendency to lath and plaster, to shingle and clapboard, to the use of bricks, and to the panelling of rooms. The more elaborate economy of the eighteenth century resulted in an increase in the number and variety of craftsmen and artisans. Finally, agricultural diversification was advanced by the persistent experiments of far-seeing men like Spotswood, Byrd, Ogle, Sharpe, and Washington to find other crops beside tobacco that would sell at a good price in Great Britain: hemp, flax, indigo, and ginseng.

The price of tobacco was generally an index of the industrial activity of the tobacco colonies. When the price fell so low that the poorer planters, particularly on the Eastern Shore and other places where tobacco did not grow so well, were unable to afford to buy necessary supplies from England, there was a spurt of industrial activity in tanning, shoemaking, and in linen, woolen, and cotton manufactures. When the price of tobacco rose, an industrial recession set in, and all but a few abandoned industry for tobacco.

Nicholson pointed out in 1695 that Marylanders were most reluctant to undertake manufacturing, and did so only when tobacco prices were low or imported supplies scarce. Under these circumstances the planters were forced to clothe themselves for, as Nicholson said, "Necessity hath no law, and is the Mother of Invention."[81] Spotswood was of the same opinion about Virginians, asserting that they took to manufacturing more from necessity than inclination.[82] A Virginia councillor in 1713 put it aptly when he said that the people "betake themselves to Manufactures of cotton, flax and hemp, which they would never have thought of, had tobacco but yielded them a living price."[83]

During King William's and Queen Anne's wars the dislocation of trade, the loss of the foreign market for tobacco, and the perennial scarcity of English goods in the colonies drove the Chesapeake colonists, half against their will, to industrial pursuits.[84] By 1695 several cotton gins had been set up in Virginia, one of them at Jamestown, and legislation enacted to encourage fulling mills. On the Eastern Shore of Maryland the counties of Dorchester and Somerset, where numbers of Scotch-Irish had settled, were largely clothing themselves by their linen and woolen manufactures.[85] By 1708 the cloth industry had been brought to such perfection that four Maryland counties not only clothed themselves but sold large quantities of cloth to neighboring counties,[86] and by 1711 one Virginia county annually produced 40,000 yards of "woollen cotton, and linnen cloath."[87]

During the decade after the return of peace in 1713 tobacco prices improved and British shipping to the Chesapeake became more abundant. In consequence, most of the makeshift industry disappeared. In 1728 a British report on wool manufacture in the colonies stated that none of the inhabitants to the southward of Pennsylvania, with the exception of Somerset County, Maryland, "have any temptation or ability to manufacture either wooll or flax to advantage." Somerset County, however, produced a good deal of cloth which "may proceed partly from the soil not being so fit for tobacco, and partly from its being inhabited by people who have been educated and brought up to that sort of business in Ireland."[88]

The depression in the tobacco trade late in the 1720's produced another flurry of industrial activity, much of it of a transitory nature. To quiet the fears of the British authorities, the Virginia Council in 1731 assured them that the shift to manufactures had happened several times before and predicted that so soon as tobacco prices rose again all these "newfangled manufactures" would vanish.[89] Similarily, Governor Gooch of Virginia considered it unlikely that Virginia would develop permanent industries because of the high cost of labor, and because the extreme heat and cold in summer and winter "indispose both whites and blacks to hard working, such as labouring people in Great Britain undergo," for "where the earth produces enough to purchase and supply all the necessitys of life without the drudgery of much toil, men are tempted to be lazy."[90]

Domestic industry, however, continued to play an increasingly important part in the economy of the Chesapeake colonies. Almost every plantation carried on some form of it, and the larger ones carried on a variety. The training of the more intelligent slaves and the utilization of the more skillful servants and convicts in the crafts became increasingly common in the eighteenth century. In 1724 the Rev. Hugh Jones said that "a good Negro" was "worth three (nay four) Score Pounds Sterling, if he be a Tradesman." He also said that Negroes were often sawyers, carpenters, smiths, and coopers.[91] In 1732 Robert Carter bequeathed, among other slaves, "George the Cooper," seven Negro carpenters, and three sawyers.[92]

Toward the end of the colonial period incipient industrialists in the Chesapeake colonies established several small factories for manufacturing cloth. George Washington operated one in 1767-68, producing woolen, cotton, and linen cloth both for his own use and for sale. In 1768 this factory employing one hired white woman and five slave girls, spun and wove 815¾ yards of linen and 1,355½ yards of woolen linsey and cotton for Washington's use. Charles Carroll of Carrollton manufactured coarse woolen and linen cloth on his plantation. Robert Carter had a similar factory at Nomini Hall. And in 1777 the Manufacturing Society of Williamsburg in an advertisement for weavers and spinners, asked for "5 or 6 likely negro lads from 15 to 20, and as many girls from 12 to 15," stating further that "negro girls are received as apprentices."[93]

By the Revolution the Chesapeake colonies were estimated to consume for manufacturing purposes some 4,000 tons of hemp and some 2,000 hogsheads (or tons?) of flax.[94] But the manufactures of Virginia and Maryland, being entirely consumed within those colonies, were not exported. Although they played no direct part in the overseas commerce of the Chesapeake, they were important in the economy of those colonies by providing a ready market for hemp, flax, cotton, wool, and hides and by helping the planters solve the problem of obtaining an adequate supply of goods without going deeper into debt to British merchants.[95] Their rôle in the maritime history of Chesapeake Bay was essentially a negative one: they merely reduced the volume of European manufactured goods imported into the Chesapeake from Great Britain.

o      o      o

Although one of the principal objectives in planting a colony on the shores of Chesapeake Bay was the production of naval stores in order to relieve England of her dependence upon the Baltic for such supplies, Virginia and Maryland did little in this way until the eighteenth century.[96] The English authorities turned their attention principally to New England, which had no convenient staple commodity, and were lukewarm to the development of naval stores in the Chesapeake region for fear of reducing the production of tobacco.

By the end of the seventeenth century, however, war with France and the unsatisfactory state of the Baltic trade placed England in a critical situation. The government anxiously— almost frantically—looked for new sources of supply for the Royal Navy. In answer to inquiries of the Board of Trade in 1697, Governor Sir Edmund Andros said that Virginia produced no naval stores for sale except along the Elizabeth River, where about 1,200 barrels of tar and pitch were made annually. Elsewhere in the colony masters of vessels frequently obtained masts and spars for their own use but not for sale.[97] In Maryland the counties of Talbot, Somerset, and Dorchester on the Eastern Shore alone produced naval stores commercially.[98] The celebrated ship timber, the "streight and lofty pines fit for masts and yards of shipps of all rates," grew on low, level ground adjacent to the swampy headquarters of the Nanticoke, Annemessex, and Pocomoke rivers, convenient to water carriage.[99] Here also tar, standards, knees, and other crooked timbers suitable for the largest English ships were to be had plentifully and cheaply, but "because such things have not bin inquired for, the Inhabitants have not applyed themselves to the prepareing of them."

At the instigation of the English government the Chesapeake colonies at this time enacted a series of laws encouraging the production of hemp, flax, and naval stores.[100] But Virginians and Marylanders, although living in a primeval forest, were preoccupied with tobacco production and for a long time continued to neglect the exploitation of forest products.[101] By 1704 Virginia's tar production amounted to only 3,000 barrels of which some was used in the colony for boats and houses, some sold to masters of ships trading to the Bay, and the rest exported to Barbados, Jamaica, and Leeward Islands.[102] Virginia and Maryland together sent on the average no more than twelve lasts of pitch and tar to England during the years 1701-05.[103] Even the English Naval Stores Act of 1704,[104] which provided encouragement for colonial naval stores in the form of bounties and the removal of customs duties, had little effect on the Chesapeake colonies. During the years 1707-11 the average annual export of pitch and tar from Virginia and Maryland was only slightly more than twenty-four lasts, and during the years 1712-14 only thirty-seven lasts, nine barrels.[105]

Colonial authorities did everything in their power to encourage naval stores production. The Maryland Assembly made hemp and flax current in part payment of debts.[106] Governor Spotswood of Virginia proposed that naval stores be accepted as payment for duties on tobacco,[107] and undertook to produce them in quantity on his large holdings in the frontier counties.[108] William Byrd, who grew hemp on his plantations, recommended the prompt payment of bounties and the acceptance of naval stores instead of money in the payment of quitrents.[109]

Notwithstanding the encouragement of the colonial governments and the interest of prominent individuals like Byrd, few tobacco planters turned their energies to naval stores. In those parts of the country where tobacco grew poorly a few persons began to produce pitch and tar. But for the most part they were ignorant and shiftless—"the meanest of the people"—with little skill and no integrity, people who had no concern for the reputation of their commodity, but whose sole objective was to pass off their produce on the merchant.[110] In consequence, the quality of their tar and pitch was extremely poor: the tar was full of water and the pitch mixed with sand, dirt, and other matter to make it weighty.[111] Colonial attempts to improve the quality failed, but improvement was eventually brought about by an act of Parliament that laid down rigid specifications for the production and preparation of tar and pitch.[112]

Hemp, on the other hand, was produced by more responsible planters and came to acquire a good reputation. William Byrd's hemp, the English rope-makers declared, was as good as the best from the east country: it had a "fine grain" and took tar "as well as any."[113] And in 1725 the officers of the Woolwich Royal Naval Yard certified that some of the Virginia hemp submitted by Colonel Spotswood proved to be "considerably superior" to the best Russian, and equal in strength to the best Riga hemp.[114]

The *Maryland Gazette* in 1729 carried an advertisement addressed to "any Persons, that are willing to try their Fortune in propagating the Hemp Manufactory," offering hemp seed at eight shillings, currency, per bushel, and also free advice "in all its Secrets" by "a very ingenious Artist in that Occupation."[115] Hall in his *Importance of British Plantations* asserted in 1731 that hemp will grow in the Chesapeake colonies as well as anywhere, but that it was not yet produced in quantity there, except by William Byrd.[116] Twenty years later Douglass, in his *Summary of British Settlements,* stated that "they raise in the uplands, quantities of hemp and flax."[117]

The great boom in hemp, however, did not occur until 1765 when the indigo bonanza collapsed. When it became apparent that indigo would not enrich everyone who planted it, many converted their fields to hemp until one observer thought that hemp

*Negroes being carried out to a slave ship, and castles on the Gold Coast (from Dow,* SLAVE SHIPS AND SLAVING, *after engraving in Churchill's* COLLECTION OF VOYAGES, *London, 1756).*

would soon become the staple of the Rappahannock River,[118] and another reported that it was now the article which in everyone's mind "is to effect all purposes."[119] By the end of the colonial period the Chesapeake colonies produced about 5,000 tons of hemp a year, some 80 per cent of which was consumed locally and 1,000 tons exported. Considering each ton to be worth £20, the value of hemp produced in Virginia and Maryland on the eve of the Revolution was £100,000 a year, or nearly a seventh of the value of the annual tobacco crop.[120] The value of the hemp exported, however, was only £20,000 plus £8,000 in bounties from the British government.

Next to hemp, the most successful of the naval stores in the Chesapeake colonies was lumber. In 1694 an experienced shipwright, Gerard Slye, urged that whereas Virginia and Maryland could supply Great Britain with pitch, tar, and deal plank, New England was better fitted to do so because of its infinite number of pine trees, but that the Chesapeake colonies could supply better masts and bowsprits than New England, "the Land being richer, the trees are much bigger and taller and the rivers more convenient to take them in."[121] Notwithstanding these advantages, the Chesapeake colonies produced relatively few masts for sale, although they produced many for local consumption. In 1700 only two large and three medium-sized masts were exported to England from Virginia and Maryland. In 1706 only two small masts, and in 1711 only a dozen small ones were exported. After 1715, however, the number began to increase: eight large, fifteen medium, and four small ones; in 1716, three, ten, and one; in 1717, eighty-six, twelve, and seventeen.[122] Even so, the volume produced was modest, and all but a small proportion of them consumed locally, repairing ships in the tobacco fleet, refitting the coastwise and West India vessels, and building new ships.

It was only the smaller kinds of wooden products—pipe, barrel, and hogshead staves and headings—that were exported in quantity.[123] In 1730 Governor Gooch estimated that Virginia exported to the West Indies, clapboards, shingles, and staves worth £1,000 a year.[124] The next year Hall asserted that Great Britain annually imported lumber from the tobacco colonies worth £15,000.[125] Thereafter the production of lumber increased steadily.[126] In later years almost every vessel that cleared for the West Indies, the Azores and Madeira, and many that cleared for Great Britain carried a partial cargo of lumber. Many a British ship returned home with three or four hundred hogsheads of tobacco and five, ten, or even fifteen thousand staves, and smaller quantities of heading.

When tobacco was scarce, as it was in 1758 and 1761, ships that could not obtain a full cargo of tobacco completed their lading with naval stores and lumber. In the fall of 1758 a Virginia merchant wrote that of the ships that had gone out with the fleet that year, there were "many partly and wholly Loaded with Lumber."[127] One shop, the *Christian* of Glasgow, carried only sixty-eight hogsheads of tobacco, having completed her cargo with 5,086 hogshead and 13,348 barrel staves, twenty-one dozen hogshead hoops, and staves and headings for ten hogsheads.

The same year another Virginia merchant, Francis Jerdone, wrote that a certain shipmaster had unsuccessfully tried to obtain a cargo of tar and pitch, adding that his "last shift" must be lumber, because other cargoes were not to be had on any terms.[128] Later that year he wrote that scarcely a one of the Bristol ships in York River obtained a full lading: one of 500-hogshead capacity having sailed with only 100 hogsheads aboard, another of 470 with only 300, and a third of 300 with only 170. Two other ships in James River with 800-hogshead capacity could not get a single hogshead of tobacco.[129]

The short crop of 1760-61 coincided with the appearance of an unusually large number of ships in Chesapeake Bay. In consequence, the factors and masters again turned to naval stores and lumber in order to complete cargoes. Being unable to get a full lading of tobacco for the brigantine *Beaufort* of Liverpool, William

Allason on the Rappahannock sent his assistant to Nansemond to purchase enough pitch, tar, and turpentine to fill her hold after taking in all the tobacco he could procure.[130] But he was too late. Several vessels had gotten there before him and were loading all the available commodities preparatory to sailing for Great Britain.

Between 1743 and 1754 Virginia's annual exportation of pitch, tar, and turpentine rose from 8,000 barrels worth £2,670 to 10,000 barrels worth £4,000. In 1736 the quantity declined, probably as a result of the French and Indian War, to 4,697 barrels of tar worth £2,113 13s. and 827 barrels of pitch and turpentine worth £454 17s.[131] But production increased after the war, and on the eve of the Revolution Virginia and Maryland annually exported masts, plank, staves, pitch, tar, and turpentine to the value of £55,000, a figure second only to the value of tobacco exported from those colonies. The Chesapeake's exports of naval stores, including hemp as well as lumber, amounted to £76,000 a year, or about a tenth of the value of the annual tobacco crop.[132]

o     o     o

For a hundred years after the failure of the Virginia Company's attempts to produce iron at Falling Creek, the possibility of reviving iron production in Virginia was occasionally spoken of, but nothing was done about it.[133] In 1687 William Fitzhugh wrote of "the plenty of Iron mines almost every where in the Country . . . together with the prodigious quantity of wood,"[134] and in 1696 William Byrd I declared his intention to re-establish the iron works at Falling Creek.[135]

Nothing was done, however, until Alexander Spotswood came to Virginia. Shortly after his arrival in 1710 he revealed his interest in iron production and tried in vain to persuade the assembly to establish public iron works in the colony. Upon their refusal to do so, he proposed to the Board of Trade that the Queen establish iron works in Virginia with funds from the Crown revenues,[136] and upon the refusal of the British government to co-operate, Spotswood undertook to establish iron works at his own expense.[137]

In 1714 he transported to Virginia some forty Germans who had come to England from an iron-mining region in Germany, and settled them above the falls of the Rappahannock at a place he called Germanna. Some years later—the exact date has not been established—the mine and a blast furnace were in operation. In 1723 Spotswood was shipping iron to Bristol and selling firebacks, frames for chimneys, pots, dogs, as well as frying, stewing, and baking pans in Williamsburg.[138]

In Maryland an iron forge was established near the head of Chesapeake Bay in 1715 by the celebrated Principio Company, an organization composed largely of English capitalists, ironmasters, and merchants. The first bar-iron exported to England from the American colonies was made there in 1718. In 1724 the Company established the Principio Furnace, and the next year Augustine Washington joined the Company, developed mines on his lands in the Northern Neck of Virginia, and built the Accokeek Furnace which operated from 1725 until 1752.[139] This became one of the largest furnaces in the colonies, and consumed such quantities of ore that in 1729 the Company's sloops were insufficient to keep the furnace going, and an additional sloop had to be hired at Annapolis to carry 200 tons of ore to the furnace from Maryland.[140] By 1750 the Accokeek Furnace was producing over 400 tons of iron a year, about one-sixth of the total production of Virginia and Maryland combined.[141]

The example of the Principio Company and Spotswood was soon followed by others in both colonies. In 1728 Spotswood, encouraged by the new development, visualized the colonies as the future source of supply of pig iron for Great Britain, thereby relieving the mother country of her dependence upon foreign countries for iron.[142] In 1730 Governor Gooch reported that five furnaces were in operation in Virginia,[143] and by 1762 there were eight furnaces and ten forges in Maryland.[144] The Principio Company produced half the iron exported by Maryland. The second largest concern, the Baltimore Iron Works, operated a furnace and three forges and owned numerous buildings, teams, carts, and 30,000 acres of land. Charles Carroll owned a fifth interest in it and derived £400 sterling a year from his investment. Benjamin Tasker's fifth interest at his death was sold for £5,200 sterling.[145]

One of the peculiarities of the iron industry of the Chesapeake colonies was that the Northern Neck of Virginia, the site of several thriving furnaces and forges, was a part of the princely domain of Lord Fairfax, who insisted upon one-third of all iron ore mined as his feudal right. As Lord Baltimore did not choose to exercise his mineral rights, much of the ore used at Accokeek, Occoquan, and Neabsco in Virginia was brought from Maryland.[146] From an early date the ore from Patapsco River had the reputation of being the best. In 1729, therefore, the Principio Company sent sloops to get ore, and in 1736 considered moving its works to the Patapsco, "it being the source of good ore, and convenient to uninterrupted navigation."[147] The necessity of carrying ore from one river to another and also lightering the pigs and bars to ships for exportation, led the iron companies to purchase and rent sloops and schooners for the purpose and gave a maritime flavor to iron production in Virginia and Maryland.[148]

River freight was a nuisance, but it was a small item in the cost of production. In 1760 William Allason charged four shillings per ton for freighting twelve tons of pig iron down the Rappahannock from Newpost to Micou's Landing.[149] In 1763 Thomas Ringgold of Chestertown offered to send a craft across the Bay to bring thirty tons of iron to Chestertown for five shillings a ton "as Customary."[150]

A certain amount of bar-iron was consumed locally in the Chesapeake colonies, where it was used in shipbuilding, blacksmithing, and foundries. Although usually sold for cash or bills of exchange,[151] bar-iron was occasionally bartered for other commodities and sometimes used to pay debts. The *Maryland Gazette* in 1746 carried an advertisement of "Merchant Bar-Iron" to be sold "for Wheat . . . or for ready Money,"[152] and in 1766 a man in Frederick County, Maryland, who was about to sell a hundred bullocks, wrote to a merchant in Norfolk that "through the Scarsity of Cash" he might be obliged to take bar or pig iron for them and asked the merchant if he would accept iron in part payment of a debt.[153]

Some iron was occasionally shipped to other colonies, though the practice was not common. In 1739 iron was exported from Virginia to North Carolina.[154] In 1750 an observer in Portsmouth, Rhode Island, wrote that iron "for Shipwork" and "all other uses" came chiefly from Maryland, Virginia, and Pennsylvania.[155] In 1769 Maryland bar-iron sold in Philadelphia for £22 10s. currency per ton.[156] More commonly, however, iron was shipped to Great Britain, where there was a good market for it and where it could easily compete with Swedish and Russian iron as a result of the exemption of the colonial product from customs duties by the Iron Act of 1750.[157]

Iron was lightered to convenient wharves or to the anchorage of vessels, loaded aboard by the ship's company, and stowed in convenient spaces between tiers of tobacco hogsheads in the hold. At first pig iron suffered considerable breakage as a result of careless handling. Later, the shipmasters learned to lower the pigs gently into the hold to avoid damage.[158] The amount of iron carried by a single ship was seldom less than ten tons and usually not more than sixty tons. Typical ship clearances of the period list a cargo of six or seven hundred hogsheads of tobacco, several thousand staves, a quantity of iron from ten to sixty tons, and perhaps a cask of skins.[159] Sometimes iron was used for ballast, as in 1763 when Thomas Ringgold tried to obtain twenty-eight tons of iron for Captain Kenney of the ship *Three Brothers* of Bideford. "If I can procure him Iron," Ringgold wrote his partner, "I shall get his Ballast which I want to compleat my Wharf."[160]

The Principio Company in 1769 considered London the best and Bristol the second best market for bar-iron. Bristol was the best market for pig iron, then London, and then Liverpool.[161] The shipment of iron was complicated by the fact that shipmasters occasionally refused to take it unless consigned to their owners.[162] On several occasions the agent of the Principio Company was obliged to ship iron to Bristol by way of Glasgow in order to consign it to the Company's representative there.[163] Thirty-four pigs or seventy bars generally constituted one ton. The customary commission for shipping iron amounted to one shilling sterling, or a shilling and threepence Virginia currency, per ton.[164] The freight to Great Britain, being based on cargo space rather than weight, was low for iron. In 1732 Spotswood computed the total cost of freight, customs, and commissions to be thirty shillings per ton of iron. As pig iron sold in England for £6 per ton Spotswood estimated a gross profit of £4 10s. per ton. Allowing for the cost of operating mines and furnaces, he estimated a net profit of £3 per ton.[165]

By 1730 Virginia and Maryland annually exported to Great Britain over 1,500 tons of pig iron, besides smaller quantities of bar-iron. Between 1730 and 1750 the average annual export of pig iron from the Chesapeake colonies exceeded 2,000 tons.[166] During the same period the average annual exports of pig iron from all the American colonies was about 2,200 tons. Consequently, the Chesapeake accounted for no less than 90 per cent of the colonial exports of pig iron to Great Britain during those years. After 1750 the rise of the iron industry in Pennsylvania reduced the Chesapeake's preponderance in the trade. At the end of the colonial period the value of the annual iron exports from Chesapeake Bay to Great Britain was £35,000.[167]

o    o    o

The fur trade, which was so important in the early days of Virginia and Maryland, steadily declined after the middle of

189

the seventeenth century. In the 1630's Claiborne, operating from his base on Kent Island, shipped £5,000 worth of furs to England in six years.[168] By the end of the century, however, the total annual value of furs exported from Maryland was only £648.[169] Indian disorders on the western frontier discouraged fur traders there and, in consequence, fully 80 per cent of the colony's furs came from the Eastern Shore, where the Indians were peaceful and harmless. In 1695 half of Maryland's furs were exported from the district of Pocomoke, comprising the lower Eastern Shore. In the course of the next half century, the supply became exhausted. An observer writing from Oxford, Maryland, in 1743 declared that "there's no such thing as getting any Skins here within the bounds of Reason." He found only half a dozen for sale, and had to pay as much for raw skins there as he had paid for well dressed and well made breeches in England.[170]

In Virginia, as in Maryland, the fur trade played an important part in the economic life of the colony in the early days. Before tobacco became accepted as currency, beaver skins were at first used thus.[171] After the middle of the seventeenth century the large merchant-planters controlled the trade, while the small planters, who were interested in land rather than furs, favored an aggressive Indian policy—pushing the Indians to the west and building forts—to protect the frontier. The efforts of the small planters culminated in failure with the suppression of Bacon's Rebellion in 1676, and thereafter the fur trade continued without the limitation which such a policy would have entailed.

North Carolina, a large producer of furs and skins, lacking navigable rivers, found it convenient to carry these commodities overland to the Elizabeth River for shipment to England, thereby swelling the volume of Virginia's exports. In 1700 some 58,152 furs and skins were sent to England from Virginia.[172] Thereafter, Indian wars in the Carolinas, the imposition of duties on exported furs and skins by Virginia, and possibly the scarcity of English goods in the colonies suitable for the Indian trade caused a de-

*Boston lighthouse of 1716 and typical American square-topsail sloop of period (from mezzotint by William Burgis, 1729, at The Mariners' Museum).*

cline. By 1714 Virginia exported only 22,722 furs and skins, slightly more than a third as many as she exported fourteen years before.

In 1714 a small group of merchants, including Robert Cary of London, succeeded in obtaining a monopoly of the fur trade through the establishment of a regulated company by a Virginia act in that year. This Indian Company apparently did not have sufficient capital to increase the colony's trade with the Indians, and, by its monopoly, cut out many individuals who would otherwise have engaged in the trade.[173] William Byrd II, who vigorously opposed the company, told the Board of Trade in 1716 that "when the trade was open to everyone, there might be six or eight [of] the most considerable merchants that sent cargoes . . . and very great quantities of skins were imported from Virginia . . . he having himself sent hither 50 or 60 hogsheads of skins in a year." Another deponent said that formerly the trade was carried on by about thirty merchants, chiefly however by four or five of the largest ones, and estimated that "if there was no Company, the value of £8,000 in manufactures of this kingdom would be sent" to Virginia each year.[174] The next year two prominent London merchants, Perry and Hyde, joined Byrd in his opposition and succeeded in ending the monopoly of the Virginia Indian Company.[175]

The opening of the trade, however, did not bring about recovery. In 1730 Governor Gooch reported the value of beaver, buck and doe skins, otter, raccoon, and other furs to be but £1,500 a year.[176] This may be accounted for, partially at least, by the imposition of duties on exported furs and skins for the support of the College of William and Mary.[177] These duties, sixpence upon every tanned hide and threepence upon every raw hide, imposed in 1693 and 1705, were raised in 1744 to the exorbitant figure of five shillings and two shillings sixpence respectively,[178] and instead of producing more revenue, they served only to throttle the trade and divert North Carolina furs and hides to

Charleston rather than Virginia ports.[179] Eventually realizing its mistake, the colony in 1752 reduced the export duty to sixpence per hide,[180] but it was too late to recover the lost trade. During the years 1764-69 the total number of furs and skins exported from the district of Rappahannock was less than 10,000, and yielded a net duty to the College of only £30 7s. 8½d.[181] On the eve of the Revolution, the value of furs and skins exported from Virginia and Maryland, according to a contemporary estimate, amounted to £25,000.[182]

o     o     o

Among the lesser products of the movement for diversified agriculture were flax, indigo, and ginseng. These commodities, though cultivated before the middle of the eighteenth century, enjoyed little attention on the part of Virginians and Marylanders until late in the colonial period. When it became increasingly difficult to make a good living from tobacco alone, planters and merchants turned their attention to these commodities, among others, in search of a second staple for the tobacco colonies.

By the middle of the eighteenth century it was reported that in Maryland great quantities of hemp and flax were produced in the uplands, and that in October, 1751 sixty wagonloads of flaxseed came into Baltimore from the back settlements.[183] In 1753 Maryland exported 100 hogsheads and 100 bags of flaxseed.[184] And by the end of the colonial period the Chesapeake colonies produced 9,000 hogsheads, of which 7,000 worth £14,000, were exported to Great Britain, and the rest used in the colonies.[185]

After the Parliamentary act of 1748 encouraging the production of indigo in the American colonies, some Virginians began to grow it. As early as February, 1749, Governor Gooch told the Board of Trade that he had published the act in the *Virginia Gazette* and that "as soon as they can get the Seed, many intend to try what they can do."[186] In 1756 a Virginia merchant wrote that the shortage of tobacco and corn was so serious that "Sundry of our Gentlemen in this Country are going this year upon Indigo."[187] The next year a merchant on James River spoke of the "great quantity of Indigo" made on that river and asserted that the planters who had "gone upon the Indigo" that year will "profitt" three, four, and some five times as much as had they continued in tobacco. In consequence, he said, "nothing else is talked of here but of Indigo."[188] One planter shipped over 20,000 pounds of indigo to Bristol in 1759.[189] But indigo proved to be no better staple than tobacco. By 1761 the English market was glutted and a London merchant, after apologizing for the low price it fetched, admitted that he saw no prospect of improvement.[190] By 1765 indigo was abandoned altogether, and the Virginia planters became enthusiastic about hemp which was then expected to become the second staple of the colony.[191]

William Byrd II, one of the first to experiment with ginseng in the Chesapeake colonies, sent some to England at least as early as 1738.[192] And before long, others did likewise. In 1753 and 1754 Robert Carter of Nomini sent two casks of ginseng to London, consigned to James Buchanan. Of that consignment Buchanan sent 127 pounds to China where it sold well, but the remainder sold poorly in England. The handling costs and commissions amounted to £14 9s., leaving a net profit of £18 3s. 10s.[193] But ginseng was too scarce and difficult to cultivate, and its market in England insufficiently elastic, to admit of its becoming an important staple. Byrd realized this, saying that "it is an absolute Rarity," that it was hard to grow in a garden, and that the seed "is 20 months in the Ground before it comes up and the Root ten years before it grows fit for use."[194] He philosophically resigned himself to the scarcity, declaring that "its vertues are so great that mankind is not worthy to have it in plenty." Nothwithstanding these difficulties, a certain amount was sent to Great Britain along with other medicinal roots. By the end of the colonial period the Chesapeake colonies exported sassafras, snake-root, and ginseng worth £7,000 a year.[195]

o     o     o

Taking an over-all view of British commercial history during the eighteenth century, the period 1700-63 witnessed a great expansion in the overseas trade of Great Britain, particularly with her own colonies.[196] In 1701, when the total value of English overseas commerce amounted to £13,490,000, the five most important trading areas were Holland (£2,635,000), the American colonies (£1,760,000), Germany (£1,730,000), Spain (£960,000), and East India (£884,000). Of the various branches of American trade, which was second only to Dutch trade, Barbados was first with £460,000, the Chesapeake[197] a close second with £435,000, Jamaica third with £340,000, and New England fourth with £119,000. The value of English trade with the Chesapeake amounted to 25 per cent of England's entire trade with the American colonies. Considering imports and exports separately, the Chesapeake was the origin of £236,000 of English imports, or 71 per cent of the value of imports from the continental colonies. English exports to the Chesapeake amounted to £200,000, or 56 per cent of the total English exports to the continental colonies.

By 1763 British overseas trade amounted to £27,825,000, or about double what it was in 1701. The American colonies in 1763 comprised the most important area to which Great Britain traded, the value of Anglo-American commerce being £7,500,000. Germany was second with £3,360,000, Ireland third with £2,410,-000, Holland fourth with £2,385,000, and East India fifth with slightly less than £2,000,000. Within the American colonial trading area, Jamaica was first, the Chesapeake second, the Carolinas third, and Barbados fourth. The other continental colonies were of small consequence as far as British trade was concerned, New England being eighth, Pennsylvania ninth, and New York tenth.

1763  BRITISH TRADE WITH AMERICAN COLONIES

1 Jamaica ............................................................................ £1,744,000
2 Chesapeake Colonies ...................................... 1,197,000
3 The Carolinas ............................................. 532,000
4 Barbados ............................................................ 467,000
5 Guadaloupe ...................................................... 423,000
6 Martinique ........................................................ 356,000
7 St. Christopher .............................................. 340,000
8 New England ................................................ 334,000
9 Pennsylvania .................................................... 322,000
10 New York ........................................................ 293,000

The value of British trade with the Chesapeake was 16 per cent of the total value of British trade with the American colonies, and 39 per cent of the value of British trade with the continental colonies. Of British imports from the continental colonies, 54 per cent came from Chesapeake Bay; of British exports to those colonies, 30 per cent were sent to Chesapeake Bay.

It will be seen, therefore, that while British overseas commerce increased approximately 100 per cent between 1701 and 1763, British trade to her American colonies increased 425 per cent. During the same period the value of British traffic with Chesapeake Bay increased 175 per cent. As a result of the increasing consumption of British goods by the rapidly growing northern colonies,[198] and as a result of the phenomenal rise of South Carolina as a producer of rice and indigo,[199] British Chesapeake trade, although increasing handsomely in value, declined in relative importance from 64 per cent to 39 per cent of the total value of British commerce with the continental colonies. Even so, the Chesapeake remained the most important British trading area on the North American Continent, and throughout the colonial period British imports from Chesapeake Bay, with the exception of a few years, amounted to more than half the value of the total British imports from the continental colonies.

## CHAPTER SIX

# American and South-European Trade

THE American and South European trade of Chesapeake Bay was founded on grain rather than tobacco, and, unlike its British and African trade, was carried on primarily by American capital in colonial vessels. It consisted of three parts: (1) trade with the West Indies; (2) trade with the "Wine Islands" (Madeira, Cape Verde, and the Azores), Portugal, Spain, and Italy; and (3) trade with the northern American colonies. Grain was by far the largest export to all three areas, with lumber (staves, headings, shingles, and trunnels), naval stores, foodstuffs (pork, biscuit, beans, butter, peas, hams, and beef), tobacco, geese, candles, cattle, and beeswax augmenting the cargoes. The principal imports were rum, sugar, molasses, salt, ginger, cocoa, cotton, lime juice, citrus fruit, Spanish coin, and an occasional Negro slave from the West Indies; wine, citrus fruit, salt, and bills of exchange from south Europe; and codfish, mackerel, rum, furniture, woodenware, and foodstuffs (cheese, malt, biscuit, and peas) from the northern colonies.

These cognate trades were by no means entirely distinct. Barbadian or Bermudian vessels often entered Chesapeake Bay en route to or from New England. Madeira wine was occasionally brought to Virginia and Maryland from the northern or West Indian colonies, and Yankee vessels frequently imported Antigua, Barbados, and Jamaica commodities into the Chesapeake and exported Virginia and Maryland grain to the West Indies.

Despite tobacco's dominance of Chesapeake agriculture, some attention was always paid to cereal crops. At first the colonial authorities sought to insure an adequate food supply by requiring every tobacco planter to grow at least two acres of corn. This law, being difficult to enforce, was widely evaded. But with the founding of other English colonies in America, the planters of Virginia and Maryland discovered it to be to their interest to produce enough corn not only for their own consumption but for export to New England and the West Indies. Thus private enterprise came to the aid of public policy. From the middle of the seventeenth century onwards, with the exception of a few crop failures and a few embargoes for military purposes,[1] Virginia and Maryland annually exported large quantities of grain—mainly corn at first, then wheat and flour as well.

According to Governor Gooch, Virginia in 1730 exported between 10,000 and 20,000 bushels of corn worth one shilling and sixpence per bushel and double that quantity of wheat, worth two shillings sixpence a bushel.[2] In 1743 Gooch reported that Virginia shipped to Portugal and Madeira 12,000 bushels of corn worth £600, 8,000 pounds of beeswax worth £400, and 50,000 pipe staves worth £150. To Portugal, Madeira, and the West Indies, Virginia exported 20,000 barrels of pork and beef worth £44,000 and 20,000 bushels of wheat worth £2,000. To the West Indies alone she exported 100,000 bushels of corn worth £5,000, besides bread, flour, peas, tallow, myrtle wax candles, and large quantities of hogshead and barrel staves and shingles.[3] Eleven years later Virginia grain shipments had doubled and her beef and pork exports increased by half.[4] About this time (1753) Maryland annually exported 110,567 bushels of wheat, 154,741 bushels of corn, 6,327 barrels of bread and flour, 430 barrels of pork, 420 bushels of peas and beans, 170 barrels of herrings, a million staves and headings and two million shingles.[5]

By the end of the colonial period the two Chesapeake colonies annually exported wheat worth £40,000; corn, beans, and peas worth £30,000; and pork, beef, hams, and bacon worth £15,000; besides lumber and naval stores (a considerable portion of which went to the West Indies and Wine Islands) worth £55,000. The total exports of the Chesapeake in the inter-colonial and south European trade, then, exceeded £120,000 sterling a year,[6] or about a sixth of the value of the tobacco trade on the eve of the American Revolution. The production of foodstuffs in the Chesapeake colonies was then in such a flourishing state that in 1775 an Englishman wrote home from Yorktown that "Virginia is the most Plentiful Country for Provisions in the Known World . . . [and] could furnish Scotland and Ireland with every Morsel of Beef those inhabitants could consume."[7]

o o o

During the seventeenth century the grain trade of the Chesapeake was carried on largely by New England and West Indian vessels. These small ketches and sloops came laden with New England and West Indian products and occasionally with Madeira wine, and annually dispersed into the many rivers and creeks of the tidewater, where the shrewd, sea-going Yankee peddlers chaffered their wares from plantation to plantation in return for Virginia and Maryland grain.[8] The New Englanders were unpopular in the Chesapeake colonies because of their close bargaining and because they did not scruple to conduct an illicit trade with slaves for stolen goods.[9]

In the course of the first half of the eighteenth century, as the Virginia and Maryland merchant marine grew, an increasing proportion of the West India trade was carried by Chesapeake-owned vessels.[10] An English visitor to Maryland in 1736 noted that "a new Face seems to be overspreading the Country; and, like their more Northern Neighbours," the planters "in great Numbers have turned themselves to the raising of Grain and live Stock, of which they now begin to send great Quantities to the West Indies."[11] The conversion to grain was particularly marked on the Eastern Shore of Maryland where tobacco production had been in a declining state since the end of the seventeenth century.[12]

In consequence, Maryland's export trade to the West Indies became centered on the Eastern Shore, particularly at Chestertown. A compilation of the average grain exports from the

Eastern Shore of Maryland for the years 1770 to 1775 shows that Chestertown exported 130,000 bushels of wheat, 5,000 barrels of flour, and 50,000 bushels of corn a year and Georgetown, Kent County, 50,000 bushels of wheat, 3,000 barrels of flour, and 10,000 bushels of corn. The leading grain counties were Kent, Cecil, and Queen Anne's. The total annual exportation of the Eastern Shore of Maryland was 613,000 bushels of wheat, 29,000 barrels of flour, and 243,000 bushels of corn.[13]

As the production of pork and corn are interrelated, it is to be expected that where the latter is grown in quantity the former is found in abundance. As early as 1730 Governor Gooch asserted that pork was one of the principal exports of Virginia, amounting to 3,000 barrels worth £3,750 a year. Moreover, he noted that "of late" Virginians had begun to raise stock and export beef.[14] Douglass later wrote of the "vast numbers of swine or hogs" that ran wild in the Virginia and Maryland woods, that when salted and barreled formed a "considerable branch of the export of these colonies," and told of a merchant-planter in Virginia who in 1733 salted up 3,000 barrels of pork.[15] In Maryland the pork of Kent, Cecil, and Queen Anne's was superior to that of the counties that produced little corn, for hogs could not be fattened without it.[16] After the middle of the eighteenth century, pork was plentiful and cheaper on the Eastern Shore than on the Western.[17]

Although the upper Eastern Shore was the source of great quantities of the grain Maryland exported to the West Indies, much of it, particularly after 1760, was not shipped directly but by way of the rising port of Baltimore. All of Chestertown's flour exports and 30,000 of her 130,000 bushels of wheat went by way of Baltimore during the years 1770-75. All the grain exports of important centers such as Worton, Fairlee, and Gray's Inn Creeks, Langford's Bay, and Eastern Neck Island (amounting to 23,000 bushels of wheat, 1,000 barrels of flour, and 15,000 bushels of corn) went by way of Baltimore, as well as substantial portions of the grain exports of the rest of the Eastern Shore. This, in conjunction with Baltimore's extensive Western Shore trade in tobacco, grain, and flax, explains the meteoric rise of that port in the quarter century preceding the Revolution. In 1770 Baltimore was described by a customs official as "the Greatest Market for all kinds of Goods of any place" in Maryland,[18] and William Eddis, about the same time, referred to it as "the grand emporium of Maryland commerce."[19]

In Virginia the West Indian trade became increasingly concentrated after 1700 in the lower district of James River, especially at Norfolk. As that port grew and developed an increasingly large merchant marine of her own, she very soon combined a West Indian trade with her Carolina trade. Between 1700 and 1730 Norfolk gradually ousted most of the New Englanders from Virginia waters and became the principal entrepôt for West Indian goods in Virginia. In 1739 William Byrd II warned the Norfolk merchants not to purchase Maryland instead of Virginia wheat because it would "bring the New England Men again amongst us, who will send a great many West India Commoditys and consequently lessen the Consumption of yours and will also furnish us with Wine for our Wheat, which we must let them have, if we cant otherwise dispose of it." "These," he added, "must be the Effects of our wheat being left upon our Hands we must truck it for what we want and have those Commoditys from Forreigners, which we used to have from you."[20] Norfolk maintained her supremacy in the trade and by 1764 was said by Governor Fauquier to have "almost wholly engrossed the West Indian and grain trade" of Virginia.[21] Although the New England vessels were reduced to a small share of the trade, they were not altogether excluded from Virginia,[22] and they retained a proportionally larger share of Maryland's West India trade.

The West India trade proved a blessing to Virginians and Marylanders. It encouraged them to diversify their agriculture, thereby giving them something to fall back on when tobacco was scarce or prices low, and it offered profitable employment for their merchant marine, many vessels of which were too small to engage successfully in the tobacco or slave trades. Merchants and large planters entered it as a sideline to dispose of their surplus grain and to obtain rum, sugar, molasses, and salt for sale to the neighboring small planters and cash to give for their tobacco. Factors who kept retail stores in the tidewater were obliged to supply their customers with what they wanted in order to keep their custom, and they sometimes were obliged to accept grain in return for European goods. A Virginia factor informed his Glasgow employers that it was essential that he be kept constantly supplied with salt, rum, molasses, and sugar, otherwise the local planters would not sell him tobacco and would deal at other stores.[23]

When competition for the purchase of tobacco was keen, it was advantageous to offer at least a part (often as much as half) of the purchase price in cash,[24] and the use of coin was of further advantage in that there was a 15 per cent discount on duties on imported liquors and slaves when paid in cash.[25] The West India trade, then, was a necessary corollary of the tobacco trade, especially of the outright-purchase system that came in the course of the eighteenth century to engross three-quarters of the tobacco trade of Virginia and Maryland. Plantations with good land for raising wheat and corn, which were located near navigable water, were advertised as "suitable for the West India Trade," and sloops and schooners that were "well ceil'd" and fit for the grain trade sold briskly in the Chesapeake colonies.[26]

The short voyage to the West Indies had a decided advantage over the much longer one to Great Britain.[27] Moreover, the trade, being seasonal, could conveniently be combined with the south-European trade. A vessel could make a voyage to Madeira for wine and return in time to take a cargo of wheat or corn to the West Indies. As wheat was ready for export earlier than corn or pork, a vessel returning from Madeira or Lisbon too late for the former could sail for Barbados and the Leeward Islands with the latter. Wheat was normally exported in the fall, and pork and corn in the spring.[28]

Timing a voyage to the West Indies was important. Unless vessels reached those islands soon after the middle of June, they were apt to have difficulty in selling their grain and obtaining a cargo of sugar. Barbados planters were in the habit of shipping their crop as soon as it was ready in order to take advantage of the first market abroad and to escape damage by hurricanes, which were much more frequent during the late summer and fall. And as the continental colonies produced more grain than the British West Indies could consume, Chesapeake vessels sought to take advantage of an early market in the sugar islands. By October the Leeward Islands were usually drained of sugar and rum and glutted with American grain.[29] Moreover, wheat and corn were sometimes damaged by heat if sent to the West Indies during hot weather. John Collins, master of the brig *Hazard* of Norfolk, wrote to Neil Jamieson from St. John's, Antigua, after a thirty-four day passage, that "all the Corn is Heated," and there remained not "one Grain of good Corn on board."[30] And a Maryland vessel reached Barbados in May, 1758, with 464½ bushels of merchantable corn and 70 bushels of damaged corn.[31]

In shipping grain to the West Indies an ideal cargo, as suggested to a Norfolk merchant in 1764, was 1,000 bushels of wheat, 1,000 bushels of corn, 100 barrels of flour, six to eight barrels of beeswax, 40 to 45 barrels of pork, plus rice, white-oak staves, pine boards, and tar.[32] In order to keep the cost of shipping low, it was desirable to load grain at a single landing rather than at several different ones. In consequence, merchants and planters accumulated quantities of grain at one place in order to make it attractive to prospective buyers.[33] Goods imported from the West Indies often had to be transported inland for sale, therefore it was imperative that the rum and sugar be carefully put up in strong, tight, and well-hooped casks.[34]

It sometimes happened that the vessels employed in the West India trade by Chesapeake shippers, being too small to accommodate the desired amount of grain, were dangerously overloaded. When the small snow *Fortune* sailed from Portsmouth, Virginia, in 1765 with 1,314½ bushels of corn, 76 barrels of light flour, 20 barrels of pork, and a large quantity of red and white-oak staves and headings, she would have taken more corn but was filled to capacity: even the master's stateroom was piled high with corn.[35] In time of peace this practice endangered the vessels by rendering them unseaworthy in bad weather, and in time of war it reduced their speed and rendered them particularly vulnerable to enemy privateers that swarmed the Caribbean Sea.

Lured by opportunities for enormous profits, Chesapeake vessels set out in war time for the West Indies with the slimmest chances of crossing the privateer-infested waters of the Caribbean. The dire effects of the French and Indian War upon the merchant marine of the Chesapeake colonies are described elsewhere; it is enough to note here that the war vastly stimulated the Chesapeake grain trade to the West Indies, rendered it extremely hazardous, threatened with ruin many of the merchants and shipowners who participated in it, and offered the prospect of wealth to those few who were fortunate enough to get their grain through to the starving islanders and their return cargoes back to the Chesapeake where West India commodities were greatly in demand.

It is difficult to say with certainty what quantity of West Indian goods was annually imported into the Chesapeake colonies, accurate statistics being altogether wanting. One may reasonably deduce both from the frequency with which one meets references to them in the accounts and letterbooks of the period and from the estimates of the value of Virginia and Maryland products shipped to the West Indies that the quantity was considerable. The value of Chesapeake exports in the three branches of the grain trade, as we have seen, amounted to about £120,000 a year, just prior to the Revolution. It is certain that more than half of this went to the West Indies, so that the value of West

India commodities imported must have exceeded £60,000, and probably approached £80,000 annually.

o   o   o

By the middle of the eighteenth century, when the production of grain for export by the British continental colonies far exceeded the consumption of the British West Indies, the French, Dutch, and Spanish islands in the West Indies were normally short of grain, and a trade with these foreign colonies inevitably sprang up which continued with or without the assent of the British authorities. The navigation laws did not prevent American grain from being shipped to the foreign West Indies in time of peace, but after 1733 they did proscribe by means of prohibitive duties the importation of foreign sugars into the British colonies.

In time of war the exportation of provisions to foreign plantations was forbidden. The French and Spanish authorities, on the other hand, nominally prohibited British colonial vessels from trading to their West Indian possessions. Chesapeake vessels that engaged in trade to Martinique, Guadaloupe, Surinam, and Hispaniola ran afoul of French, Dutch, and Spanish laws— which, however, were but intermittently enforced and then principally by Spain—when they entered the ports of those islands, and they ran afoul of British laws when they endeavored to freight a salable commodity for Virginia and Maryland consumption. As the trade was lucrative and colonial customs officials usually complaisant, it was frequently engaged in. During the Anglo-French wars of the eighteenth century when the French West Indies were cut off from Canada and France, the price of provisions rose sharply in those islands. Despite enemy privateers, colonial embargoes on grain, and parliamentary legislation, Chesapeake shippers like their northern brethren could not resist the temptation to make a fortune in this trade.

Illicit trade to the West Indies began early. At first it consisted largely of smuggling Barbadian rum into Chesapeake Bay to avoid payment of colonial import duties on liquors. Occasionally it involved export of tobacco, in violation of the navigation acts, to foreign colonies—especially the Dutch West Indies—and the illegal importation of European goods.[36] Frequently the trade was conducted in foreign—usually Dutch—vessels. Toward the end of the seventeenth century, by which time Dutch vessels had been almost completely excluded from the Chesapeake, the trade was carried on by Chesapeake-owned vessels and by pirates who disposed of ill-gotten Dutch, French, and Spanish as well as English wares to the inhabitants of Virginia and Maryland.[37]

In 1682-83 the pirate William Dampier and twenty of his men spent a year in Virginia, where they disposed of their loot of cacao, hides, European goods, earthenware, and brandy gathered by buccaneering in the West Indies. Dampier later said that Virginia was a good market for loot and a good place to provision vessels, for there was a chronic shortage of European goods in the tobacco colonies and a perennial abundance of food.[38]

Accomack on the Eastern Shore of Virginia seems to have been a favorite resort for pirates. In 1683 two pirates, Edward Davis and John Cook, came to Accomack from the West Indies with several prizes, and subsequently joined Dampier and fitted out a vessel for an extended piratical voyage around the Horn to the coasts of Chile and Peru, and to the South Seas. They traded their captured wines for provisions and naval stores and set out on their wild adventure. Some years later, in 1688, Davis returned to Virginia with two henchmen, John Hinson and Lionel Delawafer, in the ship *Batchellour's Delight* after a successful career in the south Pacific and the three were prevailed upon by Governor Nicholson under threat of legal action to endow the proposed college (later the College of William and Mary) with a part of their plunder.[39]

The spectacular pirate John James, who wore a gold chain around his neck, flourished a gold toothpick, and occasionally employed the alias "Captain Kidd" in order to frighten people, entered the Chesapeake in 1699 in the well-armed ship *Alexander*. He captured a Bristolman, the *Maryland Merchant*, in Lynnhaven Bay and told its master that he needed provisions and "would rather pay for necessaries than be obliged to take it perforce." James informed the captive mariner that the *Alexander* had £3,000,000 in gold and silver aboard, and that he "designed no prejudice to the English Nation," so long as he obtained the supplies he required, but James was not hospitably received. The militia of the maritime counties was alerted, and the pirate sailed away with nothing except the plunder of several vessels he took in the Bay.[40]

The same year a pirate named Andrias Gravenreadt entered the Chesapeake, sailed up the Bay, and anchored his sloop in Severn River, Maryland, with a quantity of gold and a cargo of muslin, calico, coral, and 91 pounds of "Dragon's blood" (a bright red gum or resin derived from the *Calamus Draco* palm tree and used in painter's colors and varnish). But his plans for trading in Maryland were disrupted by the governor, who had received advance notice of his intentions and who was waiting for him. Gravenreadt's sloop was seized, tried, and condemned.[41]

After about 1702 piracy gradually declined and became a negligible factor in the illicit trade of the Chesapeake.[42] More common was smuggling carried on by regular trading vessels. Until about 1730, when the grain trade of Virginia and Maryland became considerable, one of the principal commodities exported to the West Indies was tobacco. It was smuggled to the English islands there in order to avoid the plantation duty of one penny per pound established by the Navigation Act of 1673 or to foreign colonies to avoid confiscation for violating the Navigation Act of 1660 which designated it an enumerated article and limited its exportation to England and the other English colonies. Sometimes the smuggling was accomplished by passing off a hogshead of 800 or 1,000 pounds as one of 400 pounds, thereby paying no more than half the plantation duty; at other times the naval

*Frigate careened (from G. Groenewegen, VERSCHEIDE SOORTEN VAN HOLLANDISCHEN SCHOEPEN DOOR).*

officers were persuaded to omit from the certificates the number of pounds of tobacco upon which the plantation duty had been paid, so that the customs officials in the English West Indies were unable to detect frauds.[43] A third way was to take on quantities of tobacco clandestinely after having cleared the vessel with the customs officials;[44] and a fourth was to pack tobacco in bread casks and cover the ends with a layer of flour.[45]

Trading with pirates and running tobacco to the West Indies in order to avoid the plantation duty never reached serious proportions. It gradually declined after 1700 and disappeared altogether after the establishment of the warehouse inspection system in 1730. A more important form of illicit trade—and one that continued to increase in volume during the eighteenth century—was the grain and sugar trade with the foreign West Indies. In the Chesapeake colonies the Norfolk merchants were among the first to engage in it. By 1700 sugar and molasses were cheaper in Guadaloupe, Martinique, and Santo Domingo than in Barbados, Antigua, and Jamaica. During the next thirty years the merchants of Norfolk, like those of other English colonial ports, carried on a considerable trade with the French West Indies, exporting corn, pork, and beef and importing sugar and molasses.[46] Prior to 1733 the British government permitted this trade during peacetime but prohibited it during the several Anglo-French wars.

But a well-established trade, desired by both sides, cannot easily be cut off even in time of war by a distant power whose immediate interests are not involved. As the continental colonies could find no other outlet for their surplus grain and as the profits were unusually large in wartime, the trade increased rather than diminished just when it became technically illegal.[47]

In 1710 Governor Spotswood of Virginia seriously endeavored to detect the persons who engaged in illicit trade to Curaçao and St. Thomas. Being convinced that the trade was carried on chiefly from the lower district of James River, he examined the books of the customs officials there and compared the clearings of vessels with certificates of discharge of their cargoes in West Indian ports. But he found that they revealed nothing; the smugglers had carefully covered their tracks. Then he interrogated various masters and mariners who engaged in the West India trade, but obtained no evidence that could be used as grounds for prosecution.[48] In Maryland, charges were brought against the governor, John Hart, for having illegally imported foreign wines and sugars in partnership with some of the principal inhabitants, and for having "so farr awed or influenced" the customs officials that they made no entry of the goods. But Hart denied the accusation and forwarded the Council's unanimous opinion that there was no trade from Maryland to the French settlements in America, and in this opinion the customs officials of Maryland unanimously concurred.[49]

The problem of detecting illicit trade in the Chesapeake colonies was an insoluble one. Because of the extent of the Bay and the large number of navigable rivers and creeks, it was impossible for the collector and naval officers of each district to attend to collecting duties, examining registries, making entries and clearances, and issuing cockets, and still have time to inspect each vessel while it loaded. Moreover, the attitude of the populace was hostile toward overzealous customs officials, and the provincial courts not infrequently exonerated smugglers against whom the customs officials had proceeded.

Various solutions were proposed and attempted, but most of the former were impracticable because they were too expensive and most of the latter ineffectual because of the configuration of Chesapeake Bay and the temperament of the inhabitants. Small armed vessels stationed in the Chesapeake by the Admiralty and the occasional use of mounted surveyors employed to maintain a constant vigil in certain areas where smuggling was suspected proved hopelessly inadequate.[50] Governor Gooch, who favored the use of riding surveyors and searchers in the counties near the Capes where smuggling was concentrated, fully realized that great diligence on the part of collectors and naval officers could alone reduce illegal trade. Even then they could not possibly prevent the smuggling of small quantities of prohibited goods "where there are so many landing places remote from the inspection of any officer, and the country people ready on all occasions to assist the offenders in the concealment thereof."[51]

The Molasses Act of 1733, brought about by the political pressure of the British West India sugar interests, sought to suppress all trade with the foreign sugar islands, even in peacetime, by placing a prohibitive duty on the products of those islands. Strict conformance with this act would have ruined many merchants of the northern colonies—particularly New England—and would have been a blow to the prosperity of Virginia and Maryland by restricting the market for their grain and by reducing their supplies of rum, sugar, and molasses. But in practice the act was universally evaded. Jamaica became the principal center of illicit trade with the French West Indies. Continental American vessels cleared for home from Jamaica ostensibly with full cargoes, but actually with empty sugar casks, and stopped at Santo Domingo en route to take on an entire cargo of foreign sugar.[52]

After 1737 when the Jamaica trade was suppressed by the British authorities, the interchange of American colonial and French West India produce usually took place at neutral ports such as the Dutch islands of St. Lucia, St. Eustatia, St. Thomas, and Curaçao and at the British Virgin Islands.[53] This trade involved a considerable amount of deception on the part of the shippers—forged clearance papers, partial entries, and mis-labelled packages—and also a certain amount of connivance on the part of customs officials. The smaller vessels, however, avoided these intricacies and simplified the procedure by lading and discharging their cargoes secretly at out-of-the-way creeks and coves, eluding the customs officials altogether.[54]

In considering the question, it must be remembered that smuggling was not then regarded as a heinous crime. In England illicit trade was widely carried on, sometimes by "gentlemen of rank and character," and in America the Molasses Act of 1733, as it was not enforced, was universally considered a dead letter.[55] Moreover, the British West Indies did not produce sufficient rum and sugar for British and colonial needs, and the increasing scarcity of these commodities in the colonies operated as a strong incentive to illicit trade.[56] King George's War and, to an even greater extent, the French and Indian War acted as great stimuli to smuggling between the continental colonies and the foreign West Indies.[57] In 1757 Parliament prohibited the export of colonial grain to any place other than British possessions. As this would certainly have depressed the economy of the Chesapeake colonies and accentuated their scarcity of rum and sugar, Virginians and Marylanders engaged in illicit trade on a larger scale than ever before.[58]

One form of smuggling much in vogue in the northern colonies during the French and Indian War was trading by means of cartels or "flag-of-truce" vessels sent from the continental colonies to French islands in the West Indies ostensibly to exchange prisoners of war captured by colonial privateers. Governor Fauquier of Virginia, however, scrupulously avoided commissioning flags of truce and, instead, sent French prisoners-of-war to England aboard tobacco ships.[59] Governor Sharpe of Maryland also refused to authorize cartels, but some Maryland merchants living near the head of the Bay sent Maryland grain to the French West Indies aboard Pennsylvania flags of truce.[60]

The favorite form of illicit trade with the enemy during the French and Indian War was known variously as the "Mount" or the "Cape" trade. The former was named for Monte Cristi, a port on the northwest corner of Spanish Santo Domingo, and the latter for Cap François in French Santo Domingo, directly opposite Monte Cristi. Chesapeake vessels in common with northern vessels went to Monte Cristi, took on a Spanish master and crew, obtained a Spanish passport, and sailed under Spanish colors to

Cap François where their grain was exchanged for French sugar. Then they returned to Monte Cristi to pick up their original crews, and sailed for home under their own colors.[61]

When the governors of Virginia and Maryland heard of this trade and ordered the customs officials to be particularly vigilant, Chesapeake shippers revived an old procedure that was legally foolproof: they sent out letter-of-marque vessels or privateers by prearrangement to pretend to "capture" their friends' vessels just as they came out of the "Mount" laden with foreign sugar. These vessels together with their contraband cargoes were in due course condemned in the court of vice-admiralty and the proceeds turned over to the owners of the privateers who then divided them with the original owners of the offending vessels. In this way foreign sugar could lawfully be sold in the colony, although the same commodity could not legally be imported.[62]

The British authorities and colonial governors made strenuous efforts to throttle the Mount trade after 1759 and enjoyed success to the extent of seizing and condemning a number of vessels. But the trade continued until suppressed by the French authorities in 1764.[63]

It is impossible to ascertain the extent to which Virginians and Marylanders participated in contraband trade to the West Indies. The nature of the business led merchants who engaged in it to destroy their papers for fear of detection. In consequence, few surviving collections of Chesapeake mercantile papers include very much information pertaining to the trade, although these few are sufficient to give a clear picture of the methods used. Recent historians of the West Indies—McClellan, Pares, and Pitman— agree that the part played by Virginia and Maryland shippers in illicit trade was very small compared to that of the merchants of New England and the middle colonies. And this conclusion is buttressed by official correspondence of the period. Governor Fauquier assured the Board of Trade in 1763 that the regulations in force in Virginia were "pretty effectual to suppress illegal

Trade," and told Lord Halifax the next year that "this Colony stands as clear of illicit Practices in Trade, as any Country that trades at all; in so much that The Men of War stationed on our Coast think it hardly worth watching."[64] Governor Sharpe of Maryland also reported to Lord Halifax in 1764 that "very few, if any, of the Inhabitants of this Province have been concerned in Vessels employed in carrying on any illicit Commerce."[65]

o   o   o

Throughout the seventeenth century Virginia and Maryland received most of their Portuguese and Spanish wines from Great Britain, New England, or the West Indies. The gradual decline of tobacco prices, however, gave impetus to diversification of agriculture and trade in the Chesapeake colonies, and at the end of the century a direct grain trade with the Wine Islands, Madeira and the Azores, sprang up.[66]

As early as 1677 Virginia petitioned in vain for an exception to the Navigation Acts whereby she might export tobacco to Madeira and the Canaries.[67] Failing this, both Virginia and Maryland occasionally shipped grain to Portugal and the Wine Islands in return for a cargo of their stimulating product to gladden the hearts of the tobacco planters.[68] The trade continued during the early eighteenth century,[69] and by 1715 was recognized to the extent that the Maryland Council saw fit to publish the King's proclamation concerning Algerine passes for vessels trading to Portugal, the Canaries, and the Mediterranean.[70]

In 1715 a Philadelphia merchant to whom a quantity of corn was owed by an Eastern Shore planter wrote his Maryland correspondent to collect and ship it to the West Indies or Lisbon, but not to Madeira, as he had recent news of the low prices it was bringing there that year.[71] But the trade was of little account until the middle of the eighteenth century. In 1729 the naval officer's account for the district of York River, Virginia, showed but one entry from Madeira, a cargo of 70 pipes of wine, for the preceding six months and there were no imports into the other districts of the colony during the same period.[72] In 1731 the Maryland Assembly informed the governor, Benedict Leonard Calvert, that only "a few vessels have gone to Madeira, and others of the Portuguese islands, one, two, or three in a year, and for several years none."[73]

After about 1740 the Portuguese and wine-island trade began to grow in volume, probably as a result of the expanding Chesapeake merchant marine, rising grain production, and increasing demand for wine and for Portuguese salt to be used in the fisheries and in preserving meat.[74] The normal cargoes for export to southern Europe and the wine islands consisted of wheat, flour, corn, beeswax, pipe staves, hoops, and some beef and pork. The return cargoes usually consisted of port, sherry, fayal, Canary, and Madeira wine, Lisbon salt, Seville oranges, citrons, lemons, figs, vinegar, and bills of exchange; of these Madeira wine formed by far the greatest part.[75]

As colonial wheat was esteemed inferior to British wheat, with which it had to compete in southern Europe, Chesapeake merchants were careful to load the best quality and to assure their Portuguese and Spanish correspondents that it was "clean of all dust" and "Equal to most from England."[76] But English wheat continued to outsell American wheat and commanded a better price until the shortage curtailed its exportation and enabled American wheat to capture the market.[77] In 1764 a London merchant firm told a Norfolk (Virginia) merchant who contemplated shipping wheat to southern Europe that the price of wheat in Virginia was about half the price in London, a price differential that should fully compensate for the longer voyage from the Chesapeake as opposed to the shorter one from Great Britain. They warned him of the greater risk of damage "by Heating" on a long voyage in low latitudes, and urged him to ship the grain in bags notwithstanding the additional cost entailed.[78]

It was important to time the arrival of cargoes so that they would reach southern Europe between October and June in order to take advantage of the peak of the market and to avoid damage to the grain by the summer heat.[79] Another difficulty connected with the trade was that Chesapeake importers occasionally suffered a loss of wine from leaky casks as a result of the use of insufficiently seasoned staves and heads. But the wine-island merchants could fall back upon the explanation of improper stowage or, indeed, that the staves were of Virginia or Maryland origin.[80] Sometimes southern European merchants entered the Chesapeake trade either with their own ships or by obtaining a part interest in a cargo of grain,[81] but the bulk of the trade was carried on by colonial vessels.

For a time (in the 1730's) Chesapeake vessels were almost driven from the Wine Islands by the competition of New England and New York vessels,[82] but they managed to retain a share of the trade and subsequently (after 1740) to improve their position. Some vessels specialized in the wine trade; others combined it with the British and West India trades. John Fisher, master of the schooner *Hollister* of Chestertown, bound to Madeira in 1747, advertised that "any Gentlemen inclinable to Write for any Wines on Freight back, may depend on its being taken in at the common rate given in Madeira," but declined to handle orders of less than 20 pipes at any other port than Annapolis or Chestertown, a requirement that favored the merchant and large planter at the expense of the small importer.[83]

The competition of the northern colonies was less harmful to the Chesapeake merchant marine trading to southern Europe than the effects of King George's War. As the trade of the Chesapeake colonies to that part of Europe did not enjoy convoy protection, it was extremely vulnerable to enemy action in time of war. Governor Gooch asserted in 1749 that little trading had existed between Virginia and Madeira during the late war.[84] The same year Governor Ogle reported that Maryland had little trade with any foreign plantation except a few ships a year to Lisbon, Madeira, and some of the other Portuguese wine islands.[85]

After 1750, however, the trade expanded and increasingly became, not simply a means of obtaining wine and salt for colonial consumption, but a means of disposing of the ever-growing surplus of Virginia and Maryland grain.

This development, which was not confined to the Chesapeake colonies but was general in the British continental colonies, soon resulted in a satiated market in the Wine Islands. As early as 1754 a Madeira mercantile house informed a Maryland merchant-planter that, as a result of recent shipments, the island was glutted with flour and Indian corn from America as well as with wheat from England.[86] As Maryland and, to a lesser extent, Virginia turned more and more to wheat, that commodity was shipped in greater quantities to the Wine Islands and, when the supply exceeded the demand there, to Lisbon, Barcelona, Cadiz, and Leghorn where, as a result of a series of crop failures in France, Sicily, and Italy, grain brought good prices. By 1765 Maryland alone exported about 150,000 bushels of wheat to Lisbon and the Mediterranean.[87]

The Mediterranean grain market, however, suddenly collapsed in 1766. As a result of bumper crops in Europe and large exports from Great Britain and the American colonies, wheat would not sell at any price and shippers were obliged to reload their grain and look elsewhere for a market. Chesapeake merchants with quantities of wheat on their hands were at a loss to know where to send it. One bewildered speculator, who had counted on turning his wheat to good account in southern Europe, remarked, "Who could have thought the Eastern Marketts woud have so Soon failed?"[88]

The collapse of the eastern market, however, was only temporary. After 1768 the Portuguese and Spanish market for American wheat revived, partly as a result of poor crops in Italy, Spain, and southern France,[89] and partly as a result of declining British exports—Great Britain at this time ceased to export and began its long career of importing grain. In 1769 three ships and four brigs sailed from Chestertown, Maryland, to Lisbon, one ship to Cadiz, and one snow to Oporto laden with wheat.[90] A Maryland ship's charter party the same year provided for freight rates for wheat and flour to be shipped to Lisbon, Cadiz, Malaga, Alicante, Barcelona, Marseilles, Genoa, Leghorn, and Naples.[91] Until the outbreak of the war for independence, the annual export of grain from the Chesapeake to the eastern market remained high.[92]

o    o    o

As soon as other English colonies were established in America, an intercolonial trade sprang up between them and the Chesapeake. At first the newcomers to New England wanted cattle and grain, and they were supplied with these commodities from Virginia and, later, Maryland.[93] In time the trade embraced all the other continental colonies. The principal exports of the Chesapeake colonies to their continental neighbors in the eighteenth century consisted of corn, wheat, and flour, together with such minor items as tobacco, pig iron, pork, lard, tallow, beans, peas, rye, potatoes, flaxseed, walnut and hickory plank, naval stores, hemp, sails and cordage, deer and otter skins, and myrtle wax.

In return the Chesapeake colonies received quantities of European goods, West India commodities, and a variety of other items such as foodstuffs (codfish, mackerel, cheese, raisins, cranberries, apples, hops, and, on rare occasions, lobsters), beverages (New England "kill Devil" rum, beer, cider, chocolate, coffee, and Madeira wine), naval stores (tar, pitch, and turpentine— principally from North Carolina), whaling products (train oil and blubber), woodenware, furniture, bricks and ships' figureheads (from Boston), an occasional horse and carriage, and simple manufactured goods from New England such as axes, buckets, and ironware. Most of the exports were the produce of Virginia and Maryland, but the bulk of the imports (except from North Carolina) consisted of European or West Indian products.

Another feature of the trade is that, with the exception of tobacco, lumber, and naval stores from North Carolina that were merely passing through Virginia enroute to Great Britain, the imports of the Chesapeake from the other colonies were largely consumed in Virginia and Maryland, whereas a considerable proportion of the exports from Chesapeake Bay to the other continental colonies were employed by those colonies in trade with the West Indies and Wine Islands. Hence, whereas the Chesapeake merchant marine was employed exclusively in transporting the produce of Virginia and Maryland to the places where it was consumed and the produce of other colonies to the Chesapeake for home consumption, the vessels of the northern colonies engaged in a carrying trade between Chesapeake Bay and the West Indies and southern Europe, and between Chesapeake Bay and northern Europe by way of Great Britain.

Although vessels from most of the colonies engaged in this carrying trade, the bulk of it was conducted by vessels from New England at first, and then, after about 1730, by Chesapeake, Bermuda, and West India as well as New England vessels.[94] Similarly, the bulk of the continental intercolonial trade of the Chesapeake was also carried in New England vessels. And so strange was the northern coast to Chesapeake mariners, that when a Virginia merchant sought to charter a Chesapeake sloop in 1760 to send a cargo of corn to Boston, he could not find a Virginia master who was sufficiently acquainted with the New England coast to make a voyage there during the winter season.[95]

As might be expected, there was a considerable amount of trade at the head of Chesapeake Bay between Maryland and Pennsylvania, and at the southern end of the Bay between Virginia and North Carolina. The trade with Pennsylvania which sprang up late in the seventeenth century consisted of imports of foodstuffs (flour and bread), West India commodities, and horses in return for cash, bills of exchange, and European goods. Overland transportation, which accounted for most of this trade, took place across eight different portages ranging from five to thirteen miles in length between the headwaters of the Eastern Shore tributaries of Chesapeake and Delaware Bays. Of these the one from Bohemia Landing, near the present Elkton, to the head of Appoquinimink Creek was the principal thoroughfare of Maryland-Pennsylvania overland trade.[96]

Many Marylanders resented this trade, in particular during Queen Anne's War, because in return for Pennsylvania commodities Maryland was obliged to export European goods which were generally scarce in the Chesapeake colonies and especially so during that war.[97] In 1704 the Maryland Assembly forbade the importation of grain, beer, malt, and horses from Pennsylvania as a means of checking the flow of European goods from Maryland to the north, for the Pennsylvanians had nothing else with which to purchase them.[98] In later years, however, when Maryland was a great grain-producing colony, Pennsylvania merchants regularly purchased corn, wheat, and flour in Maryland—especially on the Eastern Shore—in order to complete cargoes of vessels bound to the West Indies, and Philadelphia prices of grain, rice, salt, biscuit, pork, beef, naval stores, West India commodities, lumber, and Madeira wine were advertised in the *Virginia Gazette*.[99]

Two Philadelphia Quaker merchants, William Fishbourne and Ennion Williams, carried on a considerable trade on the Eastern Shore of Maryland during the years 1711-21, buying corn and shipping it in their sloops to Philadelphia, Bermuda, Barbados, Lisbon, or Boston, depending on current prices. If corn was dear in Maryland, they exchanged it for cash or bills of exchange. If at the same time tobacco was cheap, they exchanged their corn for it and exported the tobacco.[100] Similarly, the Maryland merchants Samuel Galloway of West River and Thomas Ringgold of Chestertown, in addition to their activities in shipbuilding and the tobacco, West India, and wine trades, also supplied Eastern Shore grain to Samuel Mifflin and Joseph Saunders of Philadelphia, and gave bills of exchange drawn on English merchants to

Thomas Willing and Robert Morris of Philadelphia for cash.[101] As early as 1737 Philadelphia was the usual place for Maryland merchants to cash bills of exchange in order to get Spanish and Portuguese gold and silver for use in the West India trade.[102]

Trade between Virginia and North Carolina, largely centered at Norfolk, was the principal reason for the growth of that seaport. The commerce of Virginia, being largely dispersed along the many rivers and creeks of the tidewater, did not require a port below the fall line. Norfolk, however, developed as a port for North Carolina, whose inlets and rivers were too shallow or treacherous to admit large ships. Beef, pork, tallow, hides, tobacco, and naval stores from the shores of Albemarle and Pamlico sounds, were transported in small sloops and schooners around by sea to Norfolk or carried from the back country overland to Great Bridge or Suffolk at the head of navigation respectively of the Elizabeth and Nansemond rivers, and from there by flatboat to Norfolk for trans-shipment overseas. Similarly, a large part of the European goods consumed in North Carolina came by way of Norfolk which, despite its location in Virginia, was really the principal entrepôt for North Carolina—or rather for the northern portion, for Charleston performed a similar function for the southern. The interposition of the vast Dismal Swamp between Norfolk and much of North Carolina formed a natural barrier to this trade, which was not fully overcome until the canal-building era which followed the colonial period.

Just as Marylanders resented the Pennsylvania trade, Virginians (other than the merchants of Norfolk, Great Bridge, and Suffolk) resented the North Carolina trade because it drew off to that colony European and West India goods from Virginia, where there was normally a scarcity. In addition, as we have seen, Virginians considered it a grievance that inferior North Carolina tobacco, by being shipped from the lower district of James River, passed for Virginia tobacco in England, thereby lowering the general reputation of the quality of the Old Dominion's crop.

Virginia's attempts to exclude North Carolina tobacco from the Chesapeake enjoyed success for a period of years but were eventually defeated by royal intervention. After 1731, when the Privy Council set aside all Virginia acts intended to restrict North Carolina trade,[103] the trade between the two colonies grew apace. By 1733 Virginia annually received £50,000 worth of North Carolina products.[104] On the eve of the Revolution North Carolina annually exported £75,000 worth of produce by land to Virginia.[105]

o     o     o

The inhabitants of the Chesapeake region, as might be expected, made use of their well-stocked waters, and fish played an important part in the colonial diet. Many fish were taken by hook and line. Michel said that fish were in such abundance in the rivers that those who have a line can catch as many as they please,[106] and Oldmixon reported that they often "tire the Sportsmen with taking them; whereas in England they are generally tired for want of it."[107] Burnaby told of some gentlemen who fished for sturgeon in canoes and caught above six hundred of them with hooks "which they let down to the bottom, and drew up at a venture when they perceived them to rub against a fish."[108]

The sponsors of the proposed academy at Providence, New Kent County, Virginia, considered "the fine fishery" there a great inducement, as it "will admit of an agreeable and salutary exercise and amusement all the year."[109] And at the end of the colonial period Fithian recorded in his journal that while he and Councillor Carter were being rowed in a "battoe" from Machodoc Creek out into the Potomac and around into Nomini Bay, they saw fishermen in canoes in great numbers, "almost constantly taking in Fish, Bass and Perch."[110] He also recorded that at Nomini Hall they dined on fish every Wednesday and Saturday all summer, including rock, perch, and crabs, as well as sheepshead and trout.[111]

But fishing was by no means confined to gentlemen or engaged in only for sport. Those who lived along the rivers caught fish for themselves and their families, taking advantage of the fact that herring and shad came annually to the heads of the rivers to spawn.[112] Many of the great planters tapped this source of food for their "people," as the slaves were often called. William Beverly of Blandfield in 1740 ordered a twenty-fathom seine, eelpots, twelve dozen perch hooks, and a dozen perch lines.[113] George Washington, who never neglected a good fishery, ordered a forty-fathom seine in 1760, specifying that it was to be "well Rigd — not to be above 8 Feet deep — to have spare twine and 150 fathom of Rope to haul her by."[114] And in 1766 he paid seven pounds to John Snowden for repairing and rigging his seine.[115] Francis Lightfoot Lee also ordered a seine for his own use from a London merchant in 1773.[116]

Some enterprising colonial merchants imported seines to dispose of to planters and others interested in fisheries.[117] Landon Carter advertised in the *Virginia Gazette,* "Just Imported from Liverpool, and to be disposed of, a Fine FISHING SEINE, 75 Fathom long; 36 Feet deep in the Middle, five eighths of an Inch Mesh; Ends 21 Feet, seven eighths of an Inch Mesh."[118]

There is also evidence that weirs and fishpots were used in colonial days, especially in Susquehanna River. In 1760 the inhabitants living near that river protested against a bill passed by the Maryland Assembly "to Prevent the making or Repairing of any Fish Dams and Pots on the River Susquehannah." They considered this an infringement of their rights and pointed out that owing to that river's peculiar configuration, rocks, and current, there was "no Hawling of Sains." Fishing could be performed there only by means of dams and pots; nature, they said, "seems to have form'd it for no other way of Fishing." In lieu of the prohibition intended by the bill, they advocated legislative regulation of fishpots, prescribing the distance between laths in order to preserve the young fish.[119]

In spite of the tapping of this source of food by the inhabitants of Virginia and Maryland, the fisheries of the Chesapeake were slow to develop as an industry of commercial importance. Not a single instance of the exportation of fish from Maryland to England between 1696 and 1715 is known, and it is probable that none was previously exported from the Chesapeake either to Great Britain or to the other American colonies.[120] About 1750 Dr. Charles Carroll wrote his son, the barrister, then in London, that the great variety and abundance of fish in the Bay and rivers, especially the herring and shad, "might be turned to Considerable Advantage in Trade were it improved or looked into."[121]

About the middle of the eighteenth century, however, a change occurred. In 1753, according to the proprietary records, Maryland exported one hundred and seventy barrels of herring,[122] and in 1762 Benjamin Mifflin, passing through Chestertown, recorded that a man who had sold 400 barrels of herring in the West Indies at twenty shillings a barrel the year before intended to put up 500 barrels the next year.[123]

In Virginia, as in Maryland, this decade saw the beginning of a fish trade. In 1766 George Leslie of Hampton wrote a Norfolk merchant that he had a recipe for curing sturgeon, that he had already sent a consignment to the West Indies, and suggested exporting some either to the West Indies or London.[124]

Toward the end of the colonial period a few enterprising men became aware of the possibilities of Chesapeake fisheries and undertook to work them on a commercial scale. Among the first of these was George Washington, who operated a well-established herring and shad fishery in the Potomac as early as 1760.[125] By 1770 he contracted with merchants in Alexandria for the sale of all he caught there up to 500 barrels a year. Robert Adam agreed to pay Washington three shillings a thousand for herring and eight shillings fourpence a hundred for shad.[126] Several large fisheries in James River near Richmond, belonging to William

Byrd III, were advertised in 1767 as being worth £2000 and £600 and renting for £100 and £30 respectively.[127]

In the 1770's large quantities of Virginia salt herring were sold in the West Indies, especially Jamaica. Washington shipped herring to the West Indies in return for a cargo of rum, coffee, sugar, and oranges.[128] The herring at first were occasionally badly cured or packed, but after a little experience his men learned how to salt them and lay them in a barrel properly. Thereafter Washington was proud of the product of his Potomac fishery and in 1773 wrote a Norfolk merchant, to whom he consigned 80 barrels of herring, that he had never sold a barrel of his fish for less than fifteen shillings at his landing, knowing that they were "equal, if not superior to any that is transported from this Country" and in "no danger of spoiling by keeping, being well cured, and well pack'd in tight Cask." He went on to say that some of the same catch sold in Jamaica for twenty-five shillings a barrel when other herrings from Virginia brought only ten or at most twelve shillings six pence a barrel.[129]

Although the sea off the Virginia Capes abounded with fish of various sorts, there is little evidence that Virginians and Marylanders engaged in deep-sea fishing before the Revolution.[130] What little activity there was in colonial days was on the part of the people living near the Capes. About 1770, when a certain person sought a land grant for a large part of Cape Henry, a number of inhabitants of Princess Anne County, Virginia, informed President Nelson of the Council of Virginia "that for many Years past a Common Fishery hath been carried on by many of the Inhabitants of the said County and others on the Shore of the Ocean and Bay" and that "during the Fishing Season the Fishermen usually encamp amongst the said Sand Hills of Cape Henry and get Wood for Fuel and Stages from the Desart." They also asserted that "very considerable quantities of Fish are annually taken by such Fishery."[131] When the Commonwealth of Virginia ceded two acres at Cape Henry to the federal government in 1790 for a lighthouse, a proviso inserted in the deed of cession reserved the right of Virginia citizens to "the privileges they now enjoy of hauling their seines and fishing on the shores of the said land."[132]

Whales were occasionally seen off the coasts of Virginia and Maryland. So early as 1692 Governor Copley of Maryland commissioned Edward Greene of Somerset County to be a whaling officer and instructed him to secure drift whales that might be stranded on the Atlantic coast of the province and to prevent people of the neighboring colonies from interloping.[133] In 1698 Virginia forbade the killing of whales in the Bay, a practice which had "poysoned" great quantities of fish and made the rivers "noisome and Offensive."[134] A large whale washed ashore on Smith's Island, off Cape Charles, in 1747, and under orders of Colonel John Custis some thirty barrels of spermaceti oil were obtained from it.[135] On rare occasions whales entered the tributaries of the Chesapeake, as when some mariners from a Scottish vessel anchored off Jamestown in 1746 spied a fifty-four foot whale in the James and after a thrilling pursuit in the ship's longboat drove the creature ashore and killed it.[136]

But the inhabitants of Virginia and Maryland were content to wait until nature, in the form of an unruly sea, washed the carcass of a whale upon their shores. They showed no enterprise as far as the whale fishery was concerned, with the single exception of the cruises of the sloop *Experiment,* which was fitted out at Norfolk early in 1751 for the express purpose of engaging "in the Whale Fishery on our Coast."

In May, 1751, the *Virginia Gazette* announced with pride that the *Experiment* had returned with a valuable whale, and expressed the hope that her success would "give Encouragement to the further Prosecution of the Design" which "will tend very much to the Advantage of the Colony."[137] A month later the *Gazette* reported that the *Experiment* brought three whales and a part of a fourth into Norfolk, and had sailed on another cruise.[138] The *Experiment* continued her prosperous ventures the following year, entering Norfolk in April, 1752, with three more whales.[139] But the undertaking, although successful, was not emulated by other Virginia or by any Maryland vessels during the rest of the colonial period.[140]

The growth of commercial fisheries in the Chesapeake colonies was retarded by a provision of the navigation laws that permitted New England and the middle colonies to import salt directly from southern Europe but forbade the southern colonies to do so. This seeming inequity was in reality a part of the overall plan of the imperial authorities to encourage fisheries in the northern colonies, Newfoundland, Nova Scotia, Quebec, New England, New York, and Pennsylvania, and to discourage them in colonies possessing a marketable staple like tobacco, rice, and sugar. To the inhabitants of the southern colonies who seldom achieved an imperial outlook, however, the action of the British government smacked of the rankest discrimination. In spite of vigorous and repeated protests and petitions, in which Lord Baltimore and many prominent British merchants joined, the Chesapeake colonies throughout the colonial period were denied the right to import salt directly from southern Europe.

Many attempts were made to produce salt locally, but the relatively low salinity of Chesapeake water defeated all efforts. Virginia and Maryland were obliged to obtain their salt either from Great Britain, the West Indies—especially Turks Island and Tortuga, known as the "Sallitudes"—or indirectly from southern Europe—Spain, Portugal, and the Isle of May in the Cape Verdes—by way of Great Britain or the northern colonies at double the cost of transportation.[141]

This provision of the navigation laws was resented in Virginia and Maryland not only because of its discrimination but also because English salt was considered too weak for curing fish and American salt was of "too corroding a Nature." George Washington expressed the opinion of the fishing interests when he asserted that "Liverpool Salt is inadequate to the saving of Fish, and therefore useless in this business . . . Lisbon is the proper kind of Salt for Fish."[142]

The detested provision of the law was occasionally violated, but not on a large enough scale to relieve the salt shortage. Consequently, an excessive price of salt remained characteristic of the Chesapeake colonies until the Revolution. In 1705 a cargo of salt from Bermuda sold in Maryland at "8 times what it Cost." During King George's War salt that cost fivepence per bushel in England brought from three to five shillings in Virginia. During the French and Indian War salt costing fivepence halfpenny in Liverpool brought one shilling sixpence or two shillings in Virginia.[143] In consequence, Governor Gooch complained to the Board of Trade that Virginia "labours under difficulties" for want of salt, and Dr. Charles Carroll thought that freedom to import salt from Spain and Portugal, by rendering it plentiful and cheap, would stimulate the "taking and Curing fish for Exportation as some do now, but trifling to what may be done."[144]

As nothing was done, Edward Montague, the agent for Virginia, informed the imperial authorities in 1763 that although the waters of the colony abound with fish, "the great Difficulty and Expence in procuring Salt proper for that Purpose not only prevents that Branch of Commerce from being extended, but also their curing a sufficient Quantity for their own Consumption."[145]

o   o   o

In addition to the overseas trade of Virginia and Maryland, which involved hundreds of topsail vessels, there was a considerable amount of maritime activity within Chesapeake Bay—between one colony and the other, between Eastern and Western Shores, between one river and another, and up and down each river—which involved a larger number of small vessels that dotted the Bay and rivers with small sails. Hogsheads of tobacco to the number of a hundred thousand annually were conveyed in small sloops and flats from the landings nearest the plantation prize-houses to the local warehouses, and, after inspection, lightered aboard large tobacco ships anchored in the channels or mouths of the rivers. European and West India goods were carried from incoming vessels up rivers and creeks to the fall line, to river towns, or to the network of retail "stores" operated by factors of British merchants in the tidewater.

Grain, pork, lumber, and naval stores were gathered by sloops and schooners at various landings and conveyed to Baltimore, Norfolk, or roadsteads where outgoing ships awaited the completion of their cargoes. Iron ore was carried from deposits conveniently located near navigable water to furnaces elsewhere in the Bay country, and pig and bar iron sent to ships about to sail for Great Britain or the northern colonies. Travellers were sped on their way across rivers, creeks, and the Bay itself by a multitude of ferryboats, and sheriffs, members of the colonial assemblies, and clergymen of the established Church were carried to and from the seats of government of their respective colonies to return writs, attend the general or provincial court, and to confer with the commissaries of the Bishop of London and their fellow clergy in provincial convocations.

Merchants and factors travelled back and forth across the Bay and rivers to buy tobacco and grain, to sell their imported wares, to arrange freight, secure cargoes, superintend lading, and collect debts. Fishing vessels, then as now, cast their nets for shad, herring, and other fish, or netted crabs and tonged for oysters. Everywhere maritime activity was much in evidence, and visitors to Chesapeake Bay seldom failed to comment on the large number of vessels they saw in the Bay.

It was important to planters and merchants in Virginia and Maryland to have their goods from Great Britain and the West Indies consigned to the right river, otherwise they lost them, or at best were put to the additional trouble and expense of having them shipped in a sloop or schooner around to the river on which they lived. George Washington instructed a London merchant never to send him any goods "but in a Potomack Ship," so that they will arrive in good time and in good order, "which never yet has happened when they come into another River."[146] Goods sent to a wrong river, being often unclaimed or misplaced, were frequently advertised in the colonial newspapers, sometimes by the person in whose custody they were placed, sometimes by the owner.[147]

Inter-river transportation, besides being troublesome, added considerably to the cost of goods. A Williamsburg merchant who hired a sloop in 1725 in order to convey goods from ships anchored elsewhere was obliged to pay £8 a month for it.[148] A Virginia factor told his Glasgow employers who sent goods to the Rappahannock instead of the York that "tis a very great loss to you in Sending goods to that or any other River but where they are to be disposed of," and that the charges of inter-river transportation "amount to near the value" of the goods.[149]

Another inconvenience was the loss of time spent in trying to secure Bay craft to transport goods. An Eastern Shore factor in Maryland told an English merchant that goods must be sent in ships bound to Choptank, Wye, or Chester rivers, not to Virginia or any western-shore Maryland river except the Severn, as "we have so little Commerce with them that, except Annapolis, we are as long receiving answers to our Letters from thence almost as from England."[150]

In cases where the payment of debts was made in commodities rather than money, the custom of the Chesapeake country decreed that the cost of river transportation devolved upon the creditor. This helps to explain the price differential in favor of cash sales. William Allason of Hobbs' Hole (now Tappahannock), endeavoring to collect a debt in tobacco from a Norfolk merchant in 1757, asked him to ship it on board a small vessel to the Rappahannock and charge the craft hire to him.[151]

Ten hogsheads of rum were shipped from Antigua to Norfolk in 1759 for £11 5s. (or 22s. 6d. per hogshead) and from Norfolk to Rappahannock River for £2 10s. (or 5s. per hogshead), nearly a quarter of the freight rate from Antigua to Virginia. The ten hogsheads were then rolled from a landing at Tappahannock to the merchant's warehouse for 1s. 3d., and two of them were subsequently shipped around to Potomac River at the cost of 12s. (or 6s. per hogshead).[152] It will be seen that the cost of transportation of a hogshead from Rappahannock River to Potomac River was greater than from Norfolk to Tappahannock, and that the total transportation costs of the two hogsheads that eventually reached the Potomac were £1 13s. 7½d. per hogshead, or about 84 per cent as much as the freight on a hogshead in normal years from the Chesapeake to Great Britain (at £8 per ton consisting of four hogsheads).

Freight rates within the Bay varied from time to time, but were always rather high considering the distances involved. In 1761 the freight for six hogsheads of rum from Norfolk to Alexandria was £3 (or 10s. per hogshead).[153] And in 1764 thirteen hogsheads of tobacco were shipped from Potomac River to Norfolk for only £3 18s. (or 6s. per hogshead).[154] In June, 1760, freight from Mattaponi River (one of the main headwaters of the York) to Falmouth at the head of navigation on the Rappahannock was 6s. per hogshead.[155] By October the same year it was 5s. 6d. per hogshead.[156]

Transportation of goods from one point to another on the same river was relatively even more costly. Nine hogsheads of tobacco were carried from the falls of Potomac to Alexandria, a distance of less than twenty miles, for £1 16s. (or 4s. per hogshead).[157] This may have been more expensive on Potomac River than in southern Virginia because of the scarcity of flats for hire on that river.

Despite these charges, there was a great deal of transportation within the Bay, particularly after the rise of tobacco and grain production in the piedmont, and by the eve of the Revolution Norfolk and Baltimore had become centers of a network of local shipping routes reaching out to all parts of the Bay. The intensity of small-scale maritime activity was so great, particularly in the spring, summer, and fall, that visitors to the Chesapeake marvelled, as did an Englishman who crossed the Bay in 1736, at the "Infinity of Sloops and Barks that appeared everywhere around," and the "whole Fleet of Vessels in the Offing, tumbling in the Calm, and reeling their lofty, unsteady Heads."[158]

# Part III

## SHIPPING

## CHAPTER SEVEN

# Ships and Shipbuilding

Iᶠ a mariner with a spyglass stood on a bluff overlooking Lynnhaven Bay or Hampton Roads early in the nineteenth century, he would have had little difficulty identifying the rig of incoming vessels. Ships, barks, snows, brigs, brigantines, schooners, and sloops by that time were well-defined rigs. But this had not always been so. A century earlier a mariner would have been hard put to it to classify the rig of vessels seen at a distance. The conventional rigs of more recent times, the product of upwards of a hundred and fifty years of gradual evolution, were still in a state of flux at the beginning of the eighteenth century.

In the year 1700 the square sail was dominant on large vessels. During the next hundred years two divergent tendencies occurred simultaneously. Fore-and-aft mainsails and spankers tended to replace square sails in the interest of maneuverability, particularly on smaller vessels, such as brigs and snows, and gaff sails supplanted the lateen mizzens. Larger vessels, increasing in size, tended to multiply the number of square sails by adding more "top hamper." Thus, while all kinds of vessels discarded square spritsails and sprit-top-sails in favor of fore-and-aft-headsails—staysails, jibs, and flying jibs—larger vessels superimposed square topgallants on topsails, royals on topgallants, and in light breezes added studding-sails.

Moreover, experimentation was in vogue. A square sail was occasionally added here, a fore-and-aft sail there, and the results observed on a voyage. Not infrequently a vessel was converted from one rig to another.[1] Sometimes one rig was improved upon by the addition of one or more features later identified with another rig. The square-topsail schooner *Baltick* of Salem, *ca.* 1765, with all the features of a brigantine including a fore course and a main staysail, differed only in that it also had a gaff-headed foresail.[2]

While this evolution was in progress, it was almost impossible to tell for certain the rig of a vessel.[3] From a distance snows and brigs with square main-topsails closely resembled each other. Similarly, the subspecies of brig characterized by emphasis on fore-and-aft sails closely resembled a square-topsail schooner.[4] The *Fair Lady*, 45 tons, of Charlestown, entered the port of Oxford as a schooner in 1759, cleared once as a schooner and once as a brig in 1760.

The only easily distinguished rigs were the ship because of its three masts and the sloop because of its single mast. But even this cannot be considered invariable. Experimentation occasionally reached those vessels and in specific cases obscured the features that have since become characteristic of the rig.[5]

Before the Revolution there was no clear-cut distinction between the brig and the brigantine. A vessel entering as a brig and clearing as a brigantine, might be described both as a brig and a brigantine in the same letter, charter party, port book, or bill of bottomry. At that time the term brig was no more than an abbreviation for brigantine and cannot be taken to imply a difference of rig. Only when the two divergent tendencies of fore-and-aft and square rig had produced a well-defined differentiation—late in the eighteenth century—can the two terms be considered to refer to distinct rigs.

If a generalization can be made, it is that except for spankers, staysails, and headsails, square sails remained dominant and increased in number on the larger vessels—ships, snows, and the larger brigs—whereas fore-and-aft sails made great inroads and became dominant on the smaller brigs, schooners, and sloops.

The sloop and schooner rigs, both supposed to have originated in the Netherlands and to have been known in England in the seventeenth century, proved peculiarly well-adapted to American coastal conditions.[6] The sloop, appearing in North America before 1630, subsequently became the most common colonial rig.[7] The schooner, appearing by 1700 or shortly afterwards, also became popular.[8] After undergoing considerable development here both eventually emerged as distinctively American types.[9]

Originally confined to small boats, the sloop and schooner rigs were soon improved upon and transferred to vessels.[10] The spritsail of the early sloops was converted to a gaff sail with boom. A bowsprit, a jib, and a flying jib were added. Eventually the larger sloops carried topsails. Under American aegis the schooner underwent an even greater metamorphosis, eventually acquiring booms, bowsprit, topsails, and a variety of headsails. During the second half of the eighteenth century the schooner displaced the sloop as the principal colonial coasting vessel and, during the Revolution, emerged as the most distinctively American rig.

The common size of eighteenth-century Chesapeake vessels is shown in the following table:

| RIG | RANGE IN TONS | RANGE IN TONS OF MAJORITY |
|---|---|---|
| Ships | 50 to 400 | 100 to 250 |
| Snows | 40 to 180 | 90 to 120 |
| Brigs | 40 to 180 | 60 to 100 |
| Schooners | 20 to 90 | 30 to 50 |
| Sloops | 20 to 100 | 20 to 50 |

The smallest schooners and sloops, under twenty tons, were normally confined to the Bay. A few of them, however, engaged in coastwise trade. The schooner *Hannah*, eight tons, built in Virginia in 1740, registered in Annapolis, owned and skippered by John Tolson, entered Annapolis from North Carolina with eighteen barrels of turpentine, five of tar, three of pork, eighty pounds of cheese, ten of beeswax, and five pair of millstones. The sloop *Swallow*, fifteen tons, cleared regularly for Boston; the schooner *Speedwell*, fifteen tons, and the sloop *Ware*, seventeen tons, for Rhode Island.

Size played an important part in the suitability of a vessel for trade. As the brigantine *Beaufort* was unsuccessfully employed in the tobacco trade, Robert Allason urged his brother to sell her, "as she is too Little for the Virginia Trade."[11] For that trade he recommended a vessel of at least three hundred and fifty hogsheads capacity—about ninety tons—whereas the *Beaufort* carried only a hundred and eighty-one hogsheads. Being "a good height between Decks for the Guinie trade," the *Beaufort* was sent to Liverpool for sale. Failing to find a buyer there, she was sent to Glasgow in hopes of being sold for "a West Indiaman."

Ship design in Chesapeake Bay in the early eighteenth century developed slowly. Larger vessels, engaged in trans-Atlantic trade, closely resembled their British counterparts. The requirements of the tobacco trade called for ample cargo capacity; naval convoys rendered ships safe from attack in time of war. There was, therefore, no premium on speed.[12] Smaller vessels, however, were largely engaged in intercolonial and West India trade, frequenting sea-lanes unprotected by the British convoy system. In consequence, their builders were obliged to cater to the demand for speed and maneuverability in order that they might have a chance of escaping capture. This necessity, coupled with the high profits in time of war, fostered the use of fore-and-aft rig and stimulated the evolution of sharper hulls, designed for speed rather than capacity. Bound up as it was with the need for pilot boats, with smuggling and privateering, this development was best exemplified in the clipper-schooners that became famous during the Revolution as "Virginia-built schooners" and at the peak of their development during the War of 1812, as "Baltimore clippers."

The word "clipper," from the archaic verb "to clip," meaning to move the wings rapidly or to fly rapidly, was applied to fast horses and, later, to fast-sailing vessels. In early nineteenth-century usage, "clipper" was understood to apply to the sharp, raking American schooners. About the middle of the century, the term was appropriated to the sharp, heavily-canvassed ships and barks of the "clipper-ship era."

## Ships and Shipbuilding

The most spectacular event in the history of naval architecture in the eighteenth century was the emergence of the Chesapeake Bay clipper-schooner, a trim, rakish craft, with smooth underbody, considerable deadrise, deep drag of keel aft, low freeboard, and a minimum of standing rigging. Prior to the Revolution it was exclusively a local Chesapeake type. The war, however, by creating a demand for this type of vessel, impelled builders all along the coast, north as well as south, to turn out vessels on clipper lines, thereby converting it to a national type.[13] The war also made the clipper-schooner internationally known. Before the end of the century the French, Dutch, and British built schooners and brigs on Chesapeake clipper lines.[14] Reaching Europe in this way, the clipper-schooner foreshadowed the major developments of ship design in the nineteenth century.

In view of the importance of the type, its origin has been the object of considerable interest. The date of its first appearance is not known with certainty, and perhaps will never be known, but it is reasonably certain that it was the result of gradual evolution over a period of years. What it started from and what models influenced it are matters of conjecture.[15]

Of the many hypotheses concerning its origin, attributing it to the influence of Bermuda sloops, French vessels, Swedish fishing vessels of the Delaware, and Mediterranean Xebecs, all but two may be rejected as improbable. For it is reasonably certain that the type of vessel that inspired the clipper-schooner must have been present in Chesapeake waters more or less continuously during the period of its evolution, and there is no historical evidence that Swedish fishing boats or Mediterranean Xebecs ever entered the Virginia Capes before the Revolution.

The same objection is not applicable to the French and Bermuda theories, as there is ample evidence that French-built and Bermuda-built vessels frequented the Bay during the half century before the Revolution. French-built vessels taken during the four Anglo-French wars between 1689 and 1763 regularly traded to the Chesapeake and in a number of instances were owned, operated, and repaired by Virginia and Maryland merchants, skippers, and shipbuilders.[16] French vessels, some of them noted for speed and sharp lines, were therefore constantly present in the Bay, available for close inspection, especially when careened for breaming, graving, or bottom repairs.

Among those registered in the Chesapeake colonies some were considered remarkable for their lines. The schooner *Dolphin*, 25 tons, belonging to Thomas Ringgold and Company in 1759, was "a prime Sailer," characterized by "extraordinary Mould." The sharp construction that made her fast also cut down her cargo capacity, causing her to make two unsuccessful trading voyages. In 1761 Ringgold proposed to his partner, Samuel Galloway, that they use her for smuggling sugar from the French West Indies, a branch of trade in which cargo space was readily sacrificed for speed. Ringgold assured Galloway that the *Dolphin* would "soon fly there."[17] Although this particular vessel may have been too late to influence the development of the clipper-schooner, the fact that French-built vessels were in the Chesapeake throughout the eighteenth century and, occasionally at least, had exceptional speed and unusually sharp lines, provides the necessary conditions for the operation of French influence.

An equally strong case can be made for the theory of Bermuda influence. In the course of the first half of the eighteenth century Bermuda sloops, famous for their speed and weatherliness, enjoyed great vogue among traders, privateersmen, and pirates. Eventually even the British Navy used them. And before the middle of the century they became sufficiently celebrated to have their lines included in Chapman's *Architectura Navalis Mercatoria*.[18] These vessels proved well-adapted to the requirements of Chesapeake trade to the West Indies, an unconvoyed route exposed to attack from enemy warships, privateers, and pirates. And they were used in such service by Virginians and Marylanders from an early date.

## Ships and Shipbuilding

Possibly the "nimble Sloop" impressed by the Virginia Council in 1708 to give chase to the French privateer *Crapeau* was a Bermuda-built sloop, or a Virginia-built one influenced by Bermuda sloop lines.[19] By the 1730's Bermuda sloops were a familiar sight in the Chesapeake. Of the thirty-eight sloops mentioned in the *Virginia Gazette* as having entered or cleared between September 3 and December 31, 1737, no fewer than twenty-five were from Bermuda.[20]

When the Virginia authorities decided to hire a vessel in 1745 to serve as a "Guard la Coast," they chose a sloop described as "Bermuda-built, and a good Sailer."[21] In 1747 Colonel Fairfax loaded a "Bermudas Sloop" for a voyage to Barbados.[22] In 1762 a ship carpenter in Norfolk repaired a "Bermuda Sloop" for Neil Jamieson,[23] and the following year a "Bermudian" was selling salt for corn in Wye River, Maryland, and another in Chester River.[24]

Positive proof that Chesapeake shipbuilders observed and copied the lines of Bermuda-built sloops is afforded by an advertisement in the *Maryland Gazette* in 1761, offering for sale the hull of a vessel on the stocks, "built . . . very much after the Bermudas mould."[25] And the next year Benjamin Mifflin, visiting Annapolis, saw a sloop, brigantine, and ship under construction "by a Bermudian."[26]

Thus the stage was set for the evolution of the clipper-schooner with both French and Bermuda vessel much in evidence. For typological reasons the case for Bermuda influence is stronger. Historically, there is no denying that both influences were present. Possibly the clipper-schooner emerged under the combined influence of sharp-hulled French prizes and raking Bermuda sloops. Whatever the proportions of the two ingredients, fast-sailing vessels were turned out by Chesapeake builders for use as privateers during the French and Indian War.

As early as 1755 Charles Carroll, the barrister, built vessels in Maryland for the British market, one of which, the ship *Mermaid,* was "reputed an extreme well built fine moulded vessel." In describing her to a London merchant, Carroll said that ships of her build and size were much in demand for privateers and store ships, and boasted that it would be both unjust and ungenerous to rank her with the "common rate of American or New England Sale Build Vessels."[27]

Another interesting example of sharp construction was the ship *Hero,* which during the French and Indian War operated as a privateer out of Norfolk.[28] After the war the sharp lines that made her an excellent privateer proved a hindrance in the leisurely pursuits of peace-time commerce. Sent to the River Clyde to be sold, she was appraised by three captains and builders who gave opinion that she was too "sharp in the bottom" to be a profitable ship in the trade of Glasgow and Clydeside and recommended that she be sent to France.[29] Sent to Bordeaux the *Hero* again failed to find a purchaser. Possibly she was too extreme even for the French![30]

Because of the multitude of rivers and creeks as well as the Bay itself, boats were a universal necessity in the Chesapeake tidewater. Shallops, bateaux, canoes, skiffs, wherries, and piraguas were in constant use for transportation, ferrying, visiting friends, and going to church. Flats, Moses-boats, small sloops and schooners served to lighter tobacco and other produce to ships anchored in the channel. Various kinds of smaller vessels and boats were employed as fly-boats or dispatch-boats for communication, as fishing vessels for seining, crabbing, and oystering, and as traders up and down the Bay, from shore to shore, and river to river. In addition, the seagoing ships that traded to the Chesapeake, whether British or colonial, were equipped with longboats, dories, yawls, pinnaces, luggers, and dinghies.

Little is known with certainty about the construction of these boats, except in the case of log canoes.[31] Apart from tenders of British ships, it is probable that most of the Bay craft were locally built.[32] Many of them carried sails as well as oars. After 1700 the use of lateen[33] and square sails[34] on boats declined and yielded to various forms of fore-and-aft rig such as spritsails, gaff sails, lugsails,[35] and leg-of-mutton sails.

Sloop and schooner rigs increased in popularity, eventually becoming the principal rig for small boats. A Swiss visitor saw a single-log canoe in Virginia in 1702 that was sloop-rigged.[36] In 1745 a nineteen-foot boat in Maryland was "rigged with a Boom Sail and Jibb."[37] Before the middle of the century boats as small as twenty feet often were schooner-rigged.[38]

Chesapeake builders used many kinds of wood in small boats, mulberry, sassafras, oak, and cedar being the most popular woods for the timbers and frames. Some yawls and cutters were "deal-built," that is, planked with pine or fir boards. Keelsons were commonly of yellow poplar and upper strakes and gunwales of oak. Stems and sternposts were frequently of mulberry or chestnut and inside fittings sometimes of black walnut. Masts were of cypress or pine, "rowlocks" or thole pins of locust, and oars of ash. Insides, when not painted, were payed with pitch, tar, or turpentine.

When boats were painted, the colors were usually bright—red, blue, green, or yellow—although sometimes black, and rarely pearl-color. The usual color combinations are startling by modern standards. Blue sterns, red rudders and oars, black and yellow strakes, red or pearl-color insides, Spanish brown sternsheets and gunwales, and yellow or blue mouldings occasionally appear in extant records. Bright colors were often combined with turpentine sides. A sixteen-foot yawl with bottom and insides payed with turpentine, had Spanish brown sternsheets and gunwale and yellow mouldings,[39] and a twelve-foot boat with turpentine outside was painted red and blue inside and carried red oars.[40]

Seagoing vessels, similarly, contained many varieties of wood—oak, mulberry, cedar, pine, and chestnut—painted with colors that seem garish today. A Maryland schooner during the Revolution was described as having a lower frame of oak, upper frame of mulberry and cedar, stern and "house pieces" mulberry, stern-post chestnut, and all the plank pine except a strake of oak. The wales were painted yellow, the strake below the wales black, and the rest of the vessel red, yellow, and green.[41]

In general, American-built vessels were not elaborately decorated. In the absence of skilled craftsmanship, emphasis was placed on simplicity and utility.[42] However, it seems clear that some colonial vessels, especially the larger ones, occasionally had a carved billethead or a figurehead and sometimes even carved ornaments on the counter. In 1754 an Eastern Shore factor advertised various European and West India goods for sale, including a "neat carv'd Lyon's Head" fit for a ship of 400 hogsheads burden.[43] In 1746 a thirty-six-ton Maryland schooner had a "Scroll Head."[44] William Allason of Virginia on several occasions imported carved figureheads from Boston for use on Chesapeake-built vessels. One was for a hundred-ton vessel, and according to his specifications, was "a woman's head."[45] One of the few examples of carving on the counter was afforded by a Baltimore schooner during the Revolution that had "two dolphins . . . carved on the stern."[46]

Throughout the colonial period American oak was considered inferior to English oak.[47] William Eddis asserted in 1771 that American oak, though greatly exceeding the British in size and foliage, was far less durable. Colonial oak, he said, attains its "highest state of perfection" in about fifty or sixty years, a much shorter time than English oak. For that reason it is light and porous, and will not endure the "depredations of time" in any degree "equal to that which advances by slow degrees to maturity." Persons of knowledge and experience informed Eddis that an English ship of solid, well-seasoned oak was worth more after a service of twenty years than "the generality of American vessels" after seven years.[48]

What Eddis said was in large measure true. The timber in the generality of colonial vessels was far inferior to English oak in quality and durability. The common variety of American oak could not compare with English oak. Moreover, unseasoned wood was occasionally used, especially in the "sale-built" vessels of New England and elsewhere—ships that were turned out as quickly and cheaply as possible for the British market. In consequence, American-built ships had a bad reputation in England. And with them American oak fell into disrepute.

After about 1750, however, the colonists built some vessels of live-oak, a magnificent American wood that is heavier and more durable than English oak. This practice eventually helped to raise the reputation of American timber and ships.[49] And there is evidence that certain woods in the Chesapeake colonies also acquired a good reputation for shipbuilding purposes.

Vessels for sale in Virginia and Maryland were often specified as having "a good Frame,"[50] being "well built, of the best Materials,"[51] and with "season'd plank."[52] Contracts for building or repairing vessels called for "good Sound Pitch Pine," or other durable wood.[53] West River, Maryland, had a good reputation for oak; vessels built there by Samuel Galloway and Stephen Stewart usually sold well in Great Britain and were staunch and tight even after years of service.[54] One old brig built of West River wood did not require pumping during a passage from Barbados to Maryland in 1765, although she had a "Single Bottom."

Norfolk-built vessels were also celebrated for their sound timber, especially the heart-pine from the upper reaches of Elizabeth River and the nearby Dismal Swamp. The white oak of Dorchester County on the Eastern Shore, likewise, enjoyed a good reputation—especially the white oak that grew on the Bay side of the county.[55]

o     o     o

It is hard for anyone who knows the Chesapeake and is fond of the water to believe that our colonial ancestors in the tidewater of Virginia and Maryland neglected to go boating purely for pleasure, and yet specific instances of yachting are not as common in the surviving records as one might suppose.[56] The explanation may be that the daily activities of the colonists involved boating to such an extent that they sought diversion in other ways. Moreover, as Englishmen they were inclined to be conservative and therefore apt to seek recreation in the New World after the fashion of their forebears in the Old: cock-fighting, horse-racing, hunting, and tippling. For yachting was scarcely known in England until the seventeenth century, and then only among the court classes.

The earliest use of the term "yacht" in Chesapeake Bay was in 1676 in connection with the *Loyal Charles,* a vessel belonging to Lord Baltimore.[57] She does not appear to have been a yacht in the modern sense, for she carried soldiers as well as mariners, was "compleatly manned Equipped and armed for warr," cruised in the Bay against pirates, boarded vessels, and examined ships' papers.

The next use of the term was in connection with a small vessel that belonged to Major Richard Sewall of Maryland in 1689, called the "yacht Susanna." Little is known about her size, design, or rig, but she was large enough to have a master and three men in the crew. It seems clear that the *Susanna* was a yacht in the modern sense, for she was described as "a small yatch or pleasure boate."[58]

The *Susanna,* however, was an exception. There were so many kinds of boats and small vessels in the Chesapeake, that the need for special types to be used solely for pleasure was not yet felt. When a group of ladies and gentlemen decided to go on a "sailing party," they generally used a sloop or schooner belonging to one of their number.

An interesting example of this kind that occurred shortly after the Revolution is charmingly described in a letter of William Craik of Strawberry Hill to Walter Stone of Port Tobacco, then on a visit to Philadelphia. Craik, while staying with the Ridouts at Annapolis, was included in "a Sailing party in Mr Fell's Boat," consisting of Madam Ridout, her daughter, Miss Blackburn, and Messrs. Weems, Fell, Moore, Washington, Harrison, and Craik. Sailing down the Bay and up the Potomac, they attended the races at Marlborough (a river town, now extinct, that was situated near the mouth of Potomac Creek) and ended up at Strawberry Hill. They must have had a gay time, because Mr. Harrison, according to Craik, "appears to have suffered much by Miss Ridout's Eyes." Not even the illness of Mr. Washington, who broke out with measles, dampened the gaiety of the yachting party.[59]

There is some evidence that certain vessels were more suitable than others for yachting purposes. The *Maryland Gazette* in 1746 carried an advertisement of a new schooner of thirty-six tons, described as being built for the West India or coasting trade, "railed and handsomely finished, with a Scroll Head, fit for a Gentleman's Use."[60] It is clear that by this time gentlemen had use for small vessels as yachts and that such vessels were expected to be handsomely finished and decorated. It does not follow, however, that such vessels were used solely for pleasure. They were used variously and interchangeably for yachting, for transporting commodities from plantation to river town or from one river to another, for visiting and travelling, and for trade within the Bay, to neighboring colonies, or to the West Indies.

A good example is the schooner *Harriot* belonging to Robert Carter of Nomini. In December, 1773, Carter invited Captain Walker, Colonel Richard Lee, and Mr. Lancelot Lee to accompany him aboard the *Harriot* to the Eastern Shore of Maryland for oysters. As the gentlemen went for pleasure, sailors were taken "to work the vessel."[61] The following February, Carter ordered the crew to rig and fit his schooner for business.[62] In March the *Harriot* assisted in unloading a coasting vessel that had grounded in the Potomac with a cargo of wheat from Alexandria bound to Philadelphia.[63] In July Fithian described the *Harriot* as "a neat vessel" with a capacity of fourteen hundred bushels.[64] In August the *Harriot* carried a cargo of five tons of iron bars, sixty barrels of bread, and ten barrels of flour to Norfolk.[65] Carter's schooner, used for both pleasure and business, is probably typical of the practice of colonial yachting on the Chesapeake.

Toward the end of the colonial period there appeared a full-fledged yacht in Virginia, the *Lady Gower,* belonging to Governor Lord Dunmore. Unfortunately, however, we know nothing about her except that she arrived at Burwell's Ferry on James River in September, 1771, "in four Days from New-York . . . with Part of his Excellency's Retinue, Baggage, &c."[66]

By this time yachting had become sufficiently common in Virginia to obtain legislative recognition. The Virginia act of 1772 for cutting a navigable canal from Archer's Hope Creek to Queen's Creek, through or near Williamsburg, specifically exempted pleasure boats from the ordinary toll or duties for passing through the canal.[67]

Of pleasure boating on a smaller scale there are more frequent instances. Fithian's journal contains a number of them. Mr. Atwell of Machodoc Creek had a "light neat Battoe" which had been built especially for the purpose of carrying the young ladies and others of his family to Nomini Church.[68] Robert Carter also had a boat for that purpose. One Sunday, while on his way to church in Carter's boat, Fithian observed that Nomini Bay was alive with boats and canoes, some going to church, some fishing, and some "Sporting."[69] In 1774 a group of girls at Nomini Hall went boating "for exercise and amusement."[70] And Fithian, while visiting Mr. Campbell, borrowed his barge before dinner and with several other guests went boating for diversion.[71]

Although there was nothing in colonial days that can properly be described as a yacht race, there were occasional boat races. George Washington attended one on May 7, 1774, in company with Mr. and Mrs. John Parke Custis, Miss Calvert, and Mr. Matthew Tilghman, at Johnson's Ferry on Potomac River.[72]

Another was held in the Rappahannock off Hobbs' Hole, now Tappahannock, late in July and early in August, 1774. On this occasion Captain Dobby of the ship *Beaufort* invited sixty gentlemen and forty-five ladies aboard his ship for the occasion. An awning was stretched from the stern over the quarterdeck to the mizzenmast of the *Beaufort* to protect the spectators from the sun. The jovial and sociable skipper entertained the whole company at dinner. Although they were not "throng'd," the large number of guests made it necessary for them to dine "all at twice," instead of all at once. The races are best described by Fithian:[73]

The Boats were to Start, to use the Language of Jockeys, immediately after Dinner; A Boat was anchored down the River at a Mile Distance—Captain *Dobby* and Captain *Benson* steer'd the Boats in the Race—Captain *Benson* had 5 Oarsmen; Captain *Dobby* had 6—It was *Ebb-Tide*—The Betts were small—& chiefly given to the Negroes who rowed—Captain Benson won the first Race—Captain Purchace offered to bett ten Dollars that with the same Boat & same Hands, only having Liberty to put a small Weight in the Stern, he would beat Captain *Benson*—He was taken, & came out best only half the Boats Length.

On gala occasions such as regattas and on occasions of official rejoicing, vessels were in the habit of dressing ship, that is, displaying all their flags. In 1688 the Maryland Council in proclaiming a holiday in honor of the birth of the Prince of Wales ordered all ships in the rivers and harbors of the province to "spread their flaggs and discharge their guns in token of joy."[74] And on St. Andrew's Day, 1761, the election of the mayor, aldermen, and council of the city of Alexandria was attended by great pomp and ceremony involving a grand procession with drums, trumpets, and flying colors. Ships in the harbor participated by displaying their flags and streamers and firing their guns the whole afternoon.[75]

Nothwithstanding the paucity of evidence of specially constructed yachts, the Chesapeake during the eighteenth century developed a type of vessel that later exerted a profound effect upon yacht design. Sometime before 1745—the exact date is unknown—the pilot-boat evolved in the Bay. Probably influenced by the Bermuda sloop, the pilot-boat soon acquired schooner rig and came to be characterized by sharp lines, low freeboard, deep drag of keel aft, hollow quarters, simplicity of hull and rig; in fact, by all those things that are characteristics of the clipper-schooner. Though not well adapted to the needs of trade because of its small cargo space, this trim craft, distinguished for speed and seaworthiness, proved ideal for yachting. Its lines were adopted for that purpose at a later date when that sport became fashionable among men of sufficient means to be able to afford the luxury of owning vessels solely for pleasure.[76]

Almost all schooner yachts until about 1870 were built on the lines of pilot-boats.[77] The most conspicuous triumph of the type was the victory of the yacht *America* in 1851. Her unexpected success in racing against the best contemporary English yachts, by profoundly shocking the English, brought about considerable changes in yacht design there as well as here.[78]

o     o     o

Shipbuilding in the Chesapeake colonies, like all other industries, was slow to make headway against the prevailing belief that tobacco production was the easiest road to wealth. Before the end of the seventeenth century, however, a well-developed shipbuilding industry existed in the Chesapeake colonies.[79] In 1697 Governor Sir Edmund Andros reported that Virginia had recently built eight ships, eleven brigantines, and fifteen sloops for which carpenters, iron work, rigging, and sails had been brought from England.[80] And the evidence from Maryland is even more impressive. A report of the sheriffs of the several counties in 1698 reveals that there were thirteen ships, nine "vessels," six pinks, twelve brigantines, seventy sloops, and fifty-one shallops owned or built in the province besides a great variety of small boats.

Most of the shallops and some of the sloops were engaged in Bay trade. Even so there were between a hundred and a hundred and ten seagoing vessels. The tonnage is not specified in all cases, but of the sixteen vessels of which the tonnage is given, the average burden approached 150 tons.

From the sheriffs' reports it is observable that shipbuilding in Maryland was concentrated upon the Eastern Shore, especially Talbot and Kent counties. In the former alone there were eleven ships and pinks, two brigantines, nineteen sloops, and seven shallops. One ship built there but owned in England was of 450 tons. One pink was of 400 tons, two ships of 300, a pink of 120, a ship of 90, a pink of 70, and another of 50 tons. The average tonnage of Talbot County ships and pinks amounted to 180 tons.[81]

Early in the eighteenth century the Chesapeake merchant marine declined almost to nothing as a result of losses in Queen Anne's War. By 1708 the number of Virginia-owned vessels was inconsiderable, many of her recently-built vessels having been taken by the enemy on their first voyage.[82] In the same year the governor of Maryland reported that his province had practically ceased building ships because of the loss of their small vessels trading to the West Indies.[83]

The end of the war in 1713 brought renewed activity in ship-building. From that time onwards, references to vessels built in Virginia and Maryland steadily increase. After the establishment of the colonial gazettes, scarcely an issue was without an account of a launching, usually "to the great Joy and Satisfaction of all the Spectators," or an advertisement of the sale of a Virginia-built or Maryland-built vessel.

By 1730 the farseeing colonial merchant-planters realized the importance of shipbuilding as an economic diversification and of owning ships as a means of providing cargo space for their tobacco in years when ships were scarce and freight rates high. In that year the reputed poet-laureate of Maryland, Ebenezer Cook, in *Sot-Weed Redivivus, or the Planters Looking-Glass,* urged the

inhabitants of the Chesapeake country to build and operate their
own merchant marine.[84]

> Nor shou'd Crop Merchants correspond,
> On t'other Side the *Herring-Pond,*
> Their pick'd and cull'd *Tobacco* send,
> In weighty Cask, to some sly Friend,
> Unless in Vessels of their own,
> And Ships here built, as shall be shewn.

Realizing that such a thing was more easily said than done, the
author sought to counter the arguments of those who considered
shipbuilding on a large scale a practical impossibility.

> How shall these floating Castles be
> Equipp'd and fitted for the Sea?
> A Doubt not difficult to solve,
> Wou'd such (in Pence abound) resolve,
> As the *Phoenicians* did of old,
> To plow the Seas in Vessels bold;
> Which *Draft-men* best know how to mould.

For, he went on to say,

> Materials here of every kind,
> May soon be found, were Youth inclin'd,
> To practice the ingenious Art
> Of Sailing, by *Mercator's* Chart.

> The Woods with *Timber Trees* abound;
> Near *North-East,* Iron may be found,
> The best that ever yet was made,
> As *Vulcans* say, on Anvil laid.

> From *Hemp* and *Flax,* may *Canvas Sails*
> And *Ropes* be drawn, that seldom fails,
> In stormy Winds, to act their Part,
> If twisted well by human Art.

Thus, he sums up:

> Nothing is wanting to compleat,
> Fit for the Sea, a trading Fleet,
> But Industry and Resolution,
> Wou'd quickly heal our Constitution,
> Were we unanimously bent,
> Impending Evils to prevent.

The colonists, he concludes,

> Can ne'er think to grow Rich and Great,
> But by an Independent State;
> Or hope to thrive, unless we try,
> With Canvas Wings abroad to fly.

As though responding to the clarion call of *Sot-Weed Redivivus,* Virginians and Marylanders turned increasingly after 1730 to shipbuilding, an industry fostered by the changing economic conditions during the half century preceding the Revolution. The great rise of the industry in Virginia and Maryland occurred in these years.

The Chesapeake country, as Cook pointed out, was well adapted by nature to shipbuilding. Its large number of navigable rivers and creeks rendered an unusually large area accessible to the sea. The abundance of oak, mulberry, pitch-pine, and other woods close to navigable water and the numerous swamps provided a ready supply of timber, tar, pitch, and turpentine.

On the other hand, the industry was retarded in the early days by a scarcity of skilled workers, by a shortage of capital, and by want of a local supply of iron, cordage, and sailcloth. These shortages in due course were overcome by the migration of shipwrights to the colonies, by apprenticing new ones, by forming partnerships between merchants and planters to secure sufficient capital, and by importing the necessary shipchandlery from England.

The migration of shipwrights to America began in the seventeenth century and by 1724 had reached such proportions that the master shipwrights of Thames River represented to the King that since 1710 the number in Great Britain had diminished by one half.[85]  Among those who came to the Chesapeake was Andrew Tonnard, formerly of Deptford, who came in the early 1690's and settled on the Eastern Shore of Maryland.  In 1697 he owned a 40-hogshead sloop in Kent County, and had built a 50-ton pink, three 40-ton sloops, and a 40-hogshead sloop.[86] Seeing great promise in the Chesapeake country, he proposed in 1704 that shipyards be erected in Maryland and fourth-rate men-of-war built for the Royal Navy, a suggestion that was not acted upon.[87]

The periodic depressions in the tobacco trade, particularly in those areas where the quality of tobacco was low, drove men away from the cultivation of that crop and increased the potential labor supply.  As shipbuilding tended to be concentrated in those very regions, many displaced planters became apprenticed to skilled shipwrights from overseas and learned their trade.

After about 1730 shipwrights and ship carpenters appear with increasing frequency in the records and, by the middle of the century, represented a substantial craft.  Some became well-to-do like Mr. James Rookings, a ship carpenter of Prince George County, Virginia, who died in 1751 leaving a comfortable estate including an unfinished snow on the stocks, household goods and kitchen furniture, two "very good Silver Watches," cattle, horses, sheep, hogs, several boats, and two Negro ship carpenters.[88]

At first shipwrights settled in the country on convenient navigable rivers.  But as towns grew up and shipbuilding became increasingly concentrated, they soon gravitated to such seaport towns as Norfolk, Annapolis, Chestertown, and to rivers like West River, Maryland, which was the site of a large shipyard.[89]

Ship chandlers soon began to appear to meet the increasing demand for equipment for vessels.  In 1745 Thomas Fleming did a thriving business "at the Sign of the Top-sail Sheet Block" near the Annapolis market house, selling "all Sorts of Blocks for Shipping" and making pumps for vessels.[90] A few years later Nicholas Maccubbin and Lancelote Jacques actively competed with one another in the ship-chandlery line. Maccubbin advertised cables, log and lead lines, deep-sea lines, sewing and boltrope twine, oakum, compasses, glasses, sailcloth, anchors, grapnels, and ballast shovels. Jacques advertised sail-duck, cordage, ship's colors, bunting, "Lanthorn Horns," scrubbing brushes, mops, compasses, and "other Sorts of Ship Chandlery."[91]

Gradually, as the eighteenth century progressed, various industries ancillary to shipbuilding sprang up. After 1718 there was an iron industry in the Bay county. In 1736 an Irish sailmaker, John Conner, operated a business in Annapolis.[92] In 1747 Stephen West of Londontown on South River advertised for a skilled hand at spinning hemp for sailcloth, cordage, and at laying rope.[93] The next year he had a ropewalk in operation making all sorts of cables, cordage, and rigging for ships, and also sail-twine, log lines, deep-sea lines, and marline.[94]

Bedingfield Hands and Company operated a ropewalk at Chestertown in 1748, making and selling cables of all sizes and cordage of every sort, for ships and small vessels.[95] A ropewalk in Annapolis, belonging to Ashbury Sutton, the shipbuilder, was described the same year as "a compleat Rope-Walk, cover'd 360 Feet, with a good Rope House."[96] In 1753 William Bicknell, a sailmaker in Annapolis, advertised that he made sails for ships, snows, brigs, schooners, and sloops "as good, . . . as cheap, and as well-fitted as any brought from Europe."[97] Lord Adam Gordon, visiting Norfolk in 1765, listed a very fine ropewalk among the "conveniences of every kind for heaving down, and fitting out large Vessels."[98] And among the house-owners in Norfolk in 1776 were two sailmakers and three blockmakers.[99]

When the Dutch skipper De Vries was in Chesapeake Bay in 1635 and found his ship leaky, he had to return to New Amsterdam to heave down and caulk his vessel, "which I could not do in the English Virginias."[100] The same situation existed in Virginia in 1700 when H.M.S. *Shoreham,* the guardship on the Virginia station, had a "fowle" bottom and loose rudder.[101] Two years later, however, Captain Moodie of H.M.S. *Southampton* fitted up a convenient place at Point Comfort for careening royal warships and urged the Virginia Council to appoint a caretaker.[102] This the Council did, establishing the annual wage of five pounds for the purpose.

These facilities at Point Comfort must have been for large ships, because careening vessels for purposes of breaming, graving, and caulking had long been common, for smaller vessels at least. In 1708 a group of English tobacco merchants persuaded the Privy Council to disallow a Virginia act of 1706 requiring all ships to be measured in such a way that they had to be careened, on the grounds that there was no place in Virginia where it could be done.[103] On the other hand Beverley in his *History of Virginia,* published in 1705, speaks of protecting vessels from the teredo by coating their bottoms with pitch, lime, and tallow and by burning and cleaning the bottoms as soon as the worm season was over.[104] Moreover, careening was necessary for repairs— replacing keels, planks, or rudders—caulking seams, and for sheathing.

Sheathing was practiced in the Chesapeake at least as early as 1696, when the twenty-seven-foot sloop *Spywell* had her sheath "layd on" some years after she had been built.[105] In later years it became more common. William Johnston, a Virginia factor, provided "Sheathing Stuff" for the ship *Buchanan* in 1739, and in 1763 a Petersburg merchant ordered from Norfolk a number of pine logs between 30 and 36 feet long for the purpose of sheathing a ship.[106]

The large number of ships trading to Chesapeake Bay from Great Britain and the West Indies made repairing and refitting an important activity in Virginia and Maryland. Ships of the

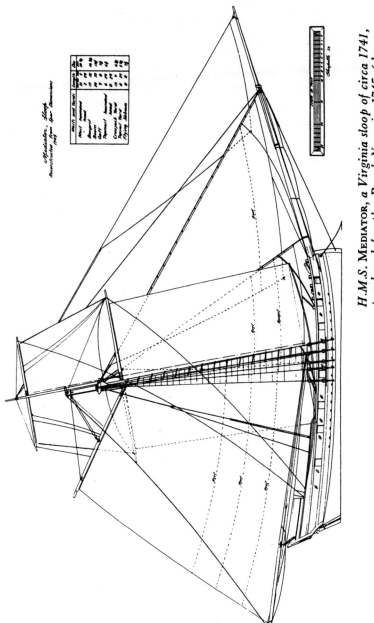

*H.M.S. MEDIATOR, a Virginia sloop of circa 1741, purchased for the Royal Navy in 1745 (drawn by Howard I. Chapelle from Admiralty Records).*

era of sail were frail things, subject to wear and tear, and liable
to damage. Even under favorable conditions shrouds, lines, and
other cordage had to be renewed often, sails sewed and patched,
decks pitched, and seams recaulked. Under adverse conditions,
such as storms at sea, collisions in convoy, or brushes with pirates
and privateers, masts were sprung, yards and bowsprits broken,
top-hamper carried away, sails torn, rigging entangled, and planks
stove in. Repair of this kind of damage gave employment to
a large number of carpenters, sail, and block makers, glaziers, and
ironworkers, and provided a ready market for ship chandlery,
masts, timber, iron, hemp, pitch, tar, and turpentine.

Although done in various rivers and creeks along the shores
of Chesapeake Bay, repairing and refitting tended to become
centered in certain places, notably Norfolk, Annapolis, Chestertown, and Baltimore. The principal center, Norfolk, had the
advantage of being near Dismal Swamp, a rich source of lumber
and naval stores. Being near the Capes, Norfolk also had the
advantage of being easily reached by incoming ships that had
sustained damage in their passage. Moreover, that town enjoyed
unusually fine facilities for work of this kind and possessed a
large class of skilled artisans specializing in shipbuilding.

Alone among the other Chesapeake ports, Annapolis closely
rivalled Norfolk. The gay little capital of Maryland also had good
dock facilities, several shipyards, several ropewalks, and a number
of ship chandlers. In other respects her situation was less ideal:
the town was not near a good supply of timber and naval stores
as were Norfolk and Chestertown, and, like the latter, its harbor
was not deep enough for the largest vessels of the late colonial
period. Even so, its reputation as a supply and refitting center
was equal if not superior to that of Norfolk until well past the
middle of the eighteenth century.

When the snow *Endeavour,* bound from Cape Fear to England,
was forced to put into the Chesapeake in 1749 to repair a leak,
the pilot at Cape Henry recommended Annapolis as the most

advantageous in either Virginia or Maryland.[107] Similarly the ship *Greyhound* after losing all her anchors in a gale while anchored off Point Comfort just prior to sailing for England in 1754 instead of putting into Norfolk almost in sight, ran up to Annapolis because the master thought it the most likely place to find ship chandlery.[108]

Norfolk, however, enjoyed great popularity with West India vessels trading to the Chesapeake. Vessels from Bermuda, Barbados, and Antigua commonly resorted to that port for supplies, repairs, and refitting rather than to Annapolis.[109] Moreover, Norfolk repaired those vessels that were too large to sail up the Severn to the docks and shipyards of Annapolis.[110] A visitor in 1765 declared that Norfolk had a depth of water sufficient for a forty-gun ship and conveniences of every kind for heaving-down and fitting out large vessels.[111]

In the third quarter of the century Norfolk grew fast, greatly extended its commercial and shipbuilding activities, and became the principal seaport of Chesapeake Bay. The phenomenal rise of Baltimore was in progress, but that port did not finally become the "Queen of the Chesapeake" until the Revolution laid Norfolk in ashes and broke her commercial supremacy.

This flurry of colonial industry—iron, hemp, cordage, and sails—may have helped foster colonial shipbuilding, but failed to replace imported British ship chandlery. The colonial supply of craftsmen fell short of the demand, and the quality of their workmanship seldom measured up to the best British standards. Consequently, many colonial shipbuilders continued to import from England all the necessary ironwork and cordage for their vessels rather than patronize local industries, and when English merchants had vessels built for them in the Chesapeake, they usually sent over the necessary ship chandlery.[112]

The locally-manufactured equipment was generally considered inferior to British materials. Ringgold wrote Galloway in 1764 that he needed boltrope for the sails of their brig, but urged him to procure the "best English" rigging because the colonial product was only half worked and therefore "good for Nothing."[113]

Carelessness of workmanship was a common complaint. A sloop caulked by Stephen Stewart at Galloway's yard at West River in 1770 was so poorly done that by the time she reached Chestertown enough water had leaked in to cover the sand ballast. When heaved down, she proved so bad that the carpenters could drive their irons through the seams by hand, without using mallets. It required more than 100 pounds of oakum to re-caulk her.[114]

o     o     o

In the half century after the appearance of the *Sot-Weed Redivivus,* some quite large vessels were occasionally built in the Chesapeake Bay country, like William Roberts' 400-ton ship in 1746[115] and a 425-ton ship built on Nanticoke River in 1747.[116] But these were exceptional. Most vessels built for the tobacco trade were between 100 and 200 tons, and vessels built for the West India trade were considerably smaller.

The most spectacular development in Chesapeake shipbuilding in the half century before the Revolution was the expansion of the Virginia and Maryland merchant marine composed largely of small vessels engaged in the West India trade. Being much smaller than tobacco ships, these vessels required less capital, could be built more easily, and proved less of a risk. Many of them were lost to the enemy during King George's and the French and Indian wars, but the high profits in the grain trade in time of war served as a stimulus for the replacement of the vessels lost and therefore greatly encouraged shipbuilding.[117]

The end of King George's War did not put an end to the shipbuilding boom. In 1749 Governor Gooch of Virginia asserted that many ships were being built in that colony both for British merchants and for colonial shipowners.[118] The demand for ships continued throughout the French and Indian War to such an extent that a British merchant in 1757 who desired to have a tobacco ship built in Virginia could not find a yard or shipwright that was not already overworked, and eventually had the work done in New England.[119] Furthermore, colonial merchants desiring vessels built sometimes searched several rivers in both colonies without finding a ship carpenter who could take additional work.[120]

As might be expected, the excess of demand over supply soon brought rising costs. Charles Carroll the barrister in 1755 told a London merchant that shipbuilding in Maryland could no longer be carried on except at a great expense and risk,[121] and William Allason reached the conclusion in 1758 that it was cheaper to buy ships in the West Indies or in Great Britain than to build them in Virginia.[122]

Finally, in 1766 the bubble burst as a result of the collapse of the grain market in the Mediterranean, Spain, Portugal, and the Wine Islands. The demands for ships fell off sharply both in the Chesapeake and abroad. Builders like Galloway and Ringgold could no longer find a market for their ships, and were at a loss to know what to do with them.[123] They bided their time and kept in correspondence with merchants in Great Britain, Spain, and Portugal, hoping for better times.[124]

The foreign market for American ships recovered in 1768 to the great relief of colonial shipbuilders.[125] But the continued high costs of production made shipbuilding a more risky and less lucrative undertaking than it had formerly been. In 1771 Galloway complained of low returns and high costs, declaring that if his new ship, the *Caroline,* did not bring more than £1,200 he would give up the business.[126] And William Reynolds of Yorktown tried to sell his brigantine *Courtney* in Portugal, the West Indies, and London, ultimately succeeding in doing so but not at a good price.[127]

Accurate statistics are not available for a quantitative estimate of Chesapeake shipbuilding in colonial times. But enough information has come down to us to give some idea how extensive it was. Using the Annapolis Port Books for 1756-75, a Baltimore antiquary some years ago compiled a list of Maryland-built vessels which, though necessarily incomplete, is valuable as an indication of the amount and type of shipbuilding that was carried on during the quarter century prior to the Revolution.[128] The list contains 386 vessels aggregating 32,000 tons and averaging 85 tons. It may be broken down in this way:

### MARYLAND-BUILT VESSELS, APPEARING IN ANNAPOLIS PORT BOOKS, 1756-1775

| | |
|---|---|
| Ships | 98 |
| Snows | 37 |
| Brigs | 66 |
| Schooners | 111 |
| Sloops | 74 |

There is no comparable list of Virginia-built vessels, but the *Virginia Gazette* for the years 1736 to 1766 contains 1,675 reported entries and clearances of vessels, of which 413 have their home port specified.[129] One hundred of these were Virginia-owned and, although there is no way of telling for certain, probably Virginia-built.

They may be subdivided as follows:

### VIRGINIA-OWNED VESSELS, APPEARING IN THE *VIRGINIA GAZETTE*, 1736-1766

| | |
|---|---|
| Ships | 6 |
| Snows | 12 |
| Brigs | 24 |
| Schooners | 20 |
| Sloops | 38 |

A comparison of the above two tables reveals little that is significant except Maryland's preference for schooners and ships as opposed to Virginia's fondness for sloops. But this distinction is not borne out by other statistics.

An analysis of the 281 vessels that were registered at Annapolis between 1733 and 1750[130] indicates a preponderance of sloops over schooners:

### VESSELS REGISTERED AT ANNAPOLIS, 1733-1750

| | |
|---|---|
| Ships | 35 |
| Snows | 15 |
| Brigs | 34 |
| Schooners | 69 |
| Sloops | 123 |

According to the most reliable statistics for colonial shipbuilding, those given by Lord Sheffield, the British colonies in America from Florida to Newfoundland built 453 vessels, of 21,370 tons, in 1769.[131] Virginia and Maryland built 47 vessels, of 2,613 tons, or about 12½ per cent of the total tonnage. New England, the great shipbuilding area, accounted for 13,435 tons or nearly 63 per cent of the whole. Next to New England, the Chesapeake colonies were the largest shipbuilding area, exceeding the combined production of New York, New Jersey, and Pennsylvania on the north, and equalling the combined production of the two Carolinas, Georgia, West Florida, the Bahamas, and Bermuda to the south.

By 1771 when the total colonial production reached 490 vessels aggregating 26,150 tons, the number of ships built in the Chesapeake colonies declined to 37, but the tonnage increased to 3,323 tons, thereby retaining the same proportion to the total, 12½ per cent. As a result of the decline in numbers and the increase of total tonnage, the average burden of vessels built in the Chesapeake rose from 56 tons in 1769 to 90 in 1771.[132]

### COLONIAL SHIPBUILDING FOR 1771—BASED ON LORD SHEFFIELD'S STATISTICS

| Colony | No. of Ships | Total Tonnage | Average Tonnage |
|---|---|---|---|
| Maryland | 18 | 1,645 | 91 |
| New Hampshire | 55 | 4,991 | 90.8 |
| Georgia | 6 | 543 | 90.5 |
| Virginia | 19 | 1,678 | 88 |
| South Carolina | 7 | 560 | 80 |
| Pennsylvania | 21 | 1,307 | 62 |
| Massachusetts | 125 | 7,704 | 61.6 |
| New York | 37 | 1,698 | 46 |
| New Jersey | 2 | 70 | 35 |
| Connecticut | 46 | 1,483 | 32 |
| North Carolina | 8 | 241 | 30 |
| Rhode Island | 75 | 2,148 | 28.5 |

o    o    o

It may be concluded that the Chesapeake in the half century before the Revolution became a shipbuilding center second only to New England in the American colonies. Although always remaining far behind New England in both number and tonnage of vessels, the Chesapeake colonies eventually built vessels of an average tonnage much greater than those of the north—probably because of the large number of small fishing craft built in New England. Moreover, out of the obscurity resulting from missing records, the Chesapeake clipper-schooner emerged and during the Revolution became a national type. That this fine vessel originated in the Chesapeake region speaks well for the ingenuity and vision of the Virginia and Maryland shipbuilders.

Equipped by nature with everything requisite to the industry, these colonies wanted only capital and skilled labor—and a willingness to leave off tobacco planting—to blossom out as a shipbuilding center. When those requirements were met in the half century before the Revolution, the Chesapeake region took its place after New England as the foremost shipbuilding center in America.

## CHAPTER EIGHT

# The Merchant Marine

During the century and a half after Rolfe successfully grew tobacco at Jamestown the production of the leaf rose
to staggering proportions, reaching ultimately a hundred million
pounds a year.[1] The enormous quantity and great bulk of the
Chesapeake staple required a considerable merchant marine to
carry it abroad.

As early as 1633 some thirty or forty vessels traded to Virginia.[2]
Two years later the number was thirty-six.[3] By 1667 between
eighty and one hundred vessels traded to the Chesapeake colonies, probably two-thirds of them to Virginia and one-third to
Maryland.[4]

By the end of the seventeenth century the annual tobacco fleet
consisted of "near 150 vessels, whereof about fifty are of between
four and five hundred tons, loaded with from seventy to eighty
thousand hogsheads of tobacco."[5] Judging from the Virginia
convoy of 1704 the average burden of vessels in that trade was
170 tons.[6] At this rate the total tonnage of the tobacco fleet must
have exceeded 25,000 tons.

But the vessels in the Virginia convoy of 1704 were probably
largely London-owned, and London ships generally exceeded
outport vessels in burden. Morriss found the average London
ship in the Maryland trade, 1689-1715, to be 170 tons and the
average outport vessel 80 tons.[7] Supposing that eighty of the
hundred and fifty vessels were London-owned and seventy out-
port-owned, a proportion which from other sources seems a
reasonable assumption, the total tonnage of the fleet would
equal 19,200.

However, the report specifically states that fifty of the tobacco
ships were between 400 and 500 tons. These fifty alone amounted

to at least 20,000 and possibly as much as 25,000 tons, leaving one hundred vessels unaccounted for. Few tobacco ships were less than 50 tons. And at an average of 50 tons, which is certainly smaller than probable, the remaining hundred vessels amounted to 5,000 tons. By a conservative estimate, then, the tobacco fleet at the beginning of the eighteenth century amounted to at least 25,000 and possibly as much as 30,000 tons.

In 1702 as in 1697 the Virginia fleet numbered about one hundred and fifty ships, carrying 75,000 hogsheads of tobacco.[8] In 1706 the number reached the unprecedented figure of three hundred ships, the "greatest Fleet that ever went from the tobacco Plantations." As it resulted in a disastrous glut of the tobacco market in England, English merchants became more cautious in dispatching vessels to the Chesapeake.[9] For the remainder of the colonial period a mild scarcity of ships was characteristic of the tobacco trade.[10]

During Queen Anne's War Chesapeake trade with Great Britain fluctuated from £200,000 to £450,000, averaging about £330,000 a year.[11] After the Treaty of Utrecht there was a marked improvement in the trade. During the years 1715 to 1717 the Chesapeake branch of British commerce was carried by 448 vessels of 64,660 tons. The average per year was about 150 vessels of 21,553 tons.[12] As the total trade of Great Britain with her colonies at this time employed about 60,000 tons of shipping, slightly more than a third of the British merchant marine trading to the colonies came annually to Chesapeake Bay.

In the years 1715-17 the total clearances of the British merchant marine amounted to 5,663 vessels of nearly 420,000 tons. About one-sixth of these vessels engaged in colonial trade. But as the ships trading to the European continent made several voyages while those bound to America made one, the Board of Trade concluded that the trade between Great Britain and the American colonies "imploys at least one fourth part of the shipping annually clear'd from this Kingdom."[13]

266

Even that did not adequately represent the importance of Britain's colonial trade, for, as the Board of Trade pointed out, the re-exportation of colonial products from Great Britain to the European continent employed nearly half as many ships as engaged in the trade directly to the colonies. Therefore, about three-eighths or 37½ per cent of the merchant marine of Great Britain carried cargoes of colonial production.[14]

During the long interval of peace between Queen Anne's and King George's wars, the volume of trade between the Chesapeake and Great Britain steadily increased from £442,000 in 1720, to £623,000 in 1740. And along with it the merchant marine in the tobacco trade continued to grow.[15]

Governor Hart of Maryland in 1720 estimated the annual fleet to that province at one hundred vessels averaging 130 tons, operated by 1,600 seamen.[16] As Virginia at that time exported about the same or a slightly larger number of hogsheads than Maryland, the total tonnage of the tobacco fleet in 1720 must have been 26,000 and the number of mariners about 3,200.

Hall estimated that the British tonnage employed in trade to the Chesapeake in 1731 amounted to 24,000 and asserted that 200 tons of shipping require twenty men.[17] At this rate the British vessels in the Chesapeake trade employed only 2,400 mariners. But Hall's estimates were theoretical and the tonnage he assigned to the trade was merely a minimum, making no pretension to the actual.

An interesting feature of the tobacco trade is that it required an amount of shipping out of all proportion to the value of the commodity. The total value of the goods exported from Jamaica to Great Britain in 1730 amounted to £533,517, from Barbados £368,326, and from the Chesapeake £346,823, yet the tonnage of British vessels trading to the Chesapeake was twice as great as that to Jamaica and nearly two and a half times as great as that to Barbados. Chesapeake Bay therefore employed more British shipping than Jamaica and Barbados combined, although the value of the exports of those two islands amounted to considerably more than twice that of the Chesapeake colonies. The explanation is simply that the staple of Chesapeake Bay was of great bulk and small value per pound, while sugar, molasses, and rum were of relatively small bulk and great value.

In 1740 the number of British ships trading to Virginia and Maryland was two hundred.[18] Robert Dinwiddie, as Surveyor General of the Customs for the Southern Part of America, made a report on the state of the British colonies in 1743 in which he estimated the annual produce of the colonies to amount to £4,980,000.[19]

### PRODUCE OF THE COLONIES, DINWIDDIE'S REPORT, 1743

| | |
|---|---|
| New England | £800,000 |
| Jamaica | 650,000 |
| Virginia and Maryland | 630,000 |
| Barbados | 450,000 |

Of the four most productive colonial areas, the Chesapeake employed the most British shipping—280 vessels—while New England provided employment for only twenty, Jamaica one hundred, and Barbados eighty. On the other hand, New England had one thousand vessels of her own, Jamaica twenty-five, Barbados fifteen, and the Chesapeake colonies seventy.

Dinwiddie estimated twelve mariners to each British-owned vessel and a value of £1,200. For colonial-owned vessels the average crew was six and the value £500. Taking British and colonial vessels together, the merchant marine trading to Chesapeake Bay in 1743 represented an investment of £371,000 sterling and provided employment for 3,780 sailors. The figures for New England were £524,000 and 6,240 mariners, for Jamaica £132,-500 and 1,350 sailors, and for Barbados £103,500 and 1,050 sailors.

Thus the shipping engaged in the New England trade was greater in value and employed more mariners than the other colonial trades. The Chesapeake was second, Jamaica a poor third, and Barbados fourth. But most of the vessels trading to New England were colonial-owned, whereas in the Chesapeake trade most of the shipping was British-owned. As a field for British investment in the form of shipping, the Chesapeake trade was by far the greatest of the several trades within the Empire.

Some idea of the importance which the British government and mercantile interests attached to the tobacco colonies as opposed to other American colonies may be found in this fact.

### COLONIAL TRADE AS A FIELD OF BRITISH MERCANTILE INVESTMENT, 1743

| Colonies | Value of British Shipping | Mariners |
|---|---|---|
| Virginia and Maryland | £330,000 | 3,360 |
| Jamaica | 120,000 | 1,200 |
| Barbados | 96,000 | 960 |
| New England | 24,000 | 240 |

From the point of view of British shipping interests, therefore, the Chesapeake trade was of considerably more value than the combined trade of New England, Jamaica, and Barbados, with that of Pennsylvania, Delaware, New York, and North Carolina thrown in. By the end of the colonial period 330 British ships of between 30,000 and 35,000 tons representing an investment of £400,000 and employing 3,960 mariners regularly traded to the Chesapeake colonies.[20]

The significance of this lies in the fact that commerce was the cornerstone of the British colonial system[21] and that, in consequence, the policies of the imperial government were in large measure shaped by the needs of the mercantile interests of Great Britain. Whenever interests clashed in connection with colonial policy, it was almost always the British merchants and shipowners that were given consideration by the imperial authorities.

This is illustrated by the encouragement the British government gave the colonial shipbuilding industry. It is certain that this policy was injurious to the British shipbuilding industry. Colonial-built vessels could be built less expensively than British-built ships and readily undersold the latter in the home market. The master shipwrights in England, as we have seen, informed the King in 1724 that their trade had "very much decayed" as a result of the great number of ships built in the American colonies,[22] and the Board of Trade estimated that their number had diminished by one-half chiefly owing to the accelerated colonial shipbuilding industry.[23] But their protest was in vain. An abundant supply of cheap vessels served the interests of British merchants and shipowners, and in imperial policy their interests were paramount.

o   o   o

After the revocation of the Virginia charter in 1624 the trade of the colony was thrown open to independent traders. The responsibility for keeping the colony supplied, formerly the Virginia Company's concern, now shifted to the English government. When Sir George Yeardley went to London in 1625 to secure a supply of necessities for the colony, he found that the Privy Council had anticipated the needs of Virginians by issuing orders to the municipal authorities of London, Plymouth, and Southampton to send a ship with supplies to Virginia.[24]

The opening of the Virginia trade attracted a number of English ships so that during 1626-27 the colony was more plentifully supplied with goods than it had been under the aegis of the Virginia Company. A London merchant, John Preen, testified in 1628 that he had sent four supplies to the colony, presumably in three years.[25] During the rest of the seventeenth century the Chesapeake country was well supplied with shipping from England and, before 1660, from the Netherlands as well.[26]

London did not at first obtain the preëminence in the trade that she had by the end of the century. From the beginning outport vessels were quite as active. The Virginia fleet in 1665 consisted of ships from Bristol, Weymouth, Dartmouth, Hull, Plymouth, Bideford, and Barnstaple as well as from London. One fleet of twenty-one vessels included nine from Bristol. Eighteen of thirty-one ships that sailed from Virginia in May, 1666, were Bristolmen.[27] And in November that year thirty ships at Bristol were loading for a voyage to Virginia.[28] In 1667 several Dutch vessels, nine Bristol merchantmen, two London ships, and seven from other English ports traded in Virginia waters.

Bristol appears to have been the chief English port in the Chesapeake trade from 1650 until 1685. Certainly it was by far the leading outport in the trade. So great was Bristol's activity that in 1690 the customs authorities complained that the shipping of that port absorbed a larger number of mariners than the Admiralty had allotted to it.[29]

By the end of the seventeenth century, however, London had become the most important city in the tobacco trade. According to the calculations of one scholar, thirty-seven of the seventy-two vessels that traded to Maryland, on the average, each year from 1692 to 1699, were from London.[30] The tonnage of these London ships ranged from 50 to 360, averaging 170. The outport vessels were much smaller, the largest being 250 and the average about 80.

London's tonnage in the Maryland trade during the last decade of the seventeenth century, then, amounted to 6,290 as opposed to 2,800 for all the outports combined. London, therefore, owned more than two-thirds of the merchant marine trading to that colony. As Maryland's annual exportation of tobacco was about half that of Virginia,[31] the total shipping in the Chesapeake trade about 1700 must have been close to 30,000 tons. And if London's share in the Virginia trade was as great as it was in the Maryland trade, the tonnage of London vessels engaged in the tobacco trade was about 20,000.

Judging from a fleet of forty-eight vessels that sailed for England from the Chesapeake in 1703, London's share had risen to nearly three-quarters of the whole:[32]

## TOBACCO FLEET OF 1703

|  | London | Outports | Total |
|---|---|---|---|
| No. of ships | 36 | 12 | 48 |
| No. of Hogsheads of tobacco | 11,440 | 3,878 | 15,318 |

In the course of the eighteenth century London gradually lost its preponderance in the tobacco trade as a result of increased activity on the part of the outports, especially the rising northern ports of Liverpool and Glasgow. By 1728 London merchants bitterly complained of their declining share in the trade, admitting that year that nearly half the tobacco imported into Great Britain came by way of the outports.[33] Glasgow, in particular, made a spectacular rise. By 1727 that city imported about 10,000 hogsheads a year, as opposed to London's 18,000.

Between 1736 and 1766 the *Virginia Gazette* carried notices of 937 entries and 738 clearances of vessels. In most cases the home port of the vessel is omitted, but in 409 instances this information is included. The following tables show the ownership of vessels trading to Virginia classified according to rig.[34]

## ORIGIN OF VESSELS TRADING TO VIRGINIA, 1736-66

| Home Port | Ships | Snows | Brigs | Schooners | Sloops |
|---|---|---|---|---|---|
| Great Britain | 165 | 21 | 18 | ...... | 2 |
| Virginia | 6 | 12 | 24 | 20 | 38 |
| Maryland | ...... | ...... | ...... | ...... | 2 |
| New England | 1 | ...... | ...... | 9 | 15 |
| Middle Colonies | ...... | ...... | ...... | ...... | 4 |
| Carolinas | ...... | ...... | 5 | 2 | 5 |
| West Indies | ...... | 1 | ...... | ...... | ...... |
| Bermuda | ...... | ...... | ...... | ...... | 57 |
| Totals | 172 | 36 | 47 | 31 | 123 |

The records of the ports of Annapolis, Oxford, and Patuxent in Maryland for the years from June 25, 1745, to June 25, 1747, reveal a similar distribution of ownerships of vessels trading to that province.

### ORIGIN OF VESSELS TRADING TO MARYLAND, 1745-47

| Home Port | Ships | Snows | Brigs | Schooners | Sloops |
|---|---|---|---|---|---|
| Great Britain | 60 | 10 | 7 | ...... | 1 |
| Maryland | 7 | 1 | 2 | 16 | 23 |
| Virginia | ...... | ...... | 1 | 7 | 6 |
| New England | 7 | 4 | 10 | 32 | 38 |
| Middle Colonies | 1 | ...... | 2 | 1 | 2 |
| Carolinas | ...... | ...... | ...... | 5 | ...... |
| West Indies | ...... | ...... | ...... | 1 | 2 |
| Bermuda | ...... | ...... | .... . | ...... | 5 |
| Totals | 75 | 15 | 22 | 62 | 77 |

The significance of these statistics is unmistakable. The larger vessels trading to the Chesapeake—both ships and snows—were principally British-owned. The brigs were divided, a slight majority being colonial-owned. The schooners and sloops, on the other hand, were overwhelmingly of colonial ownership.

As we have seen, ships, snows, and the larger brigs engaged in the tobacco trade, while the smaller brigs, schooners, and sloops engaged in the sugar and wine trades. In other words, ships, snows, and the larger brigs traded between the Chesapeake and Great Britain and were largely British-owned, while schooners, sloops, and the smaller brigs traded to the West Indies and southern Europe and were largely colonial-owned.

A majority of the smaller vessels trading to Chesapeake Bay were of Virginia or Maryland registry, but a great many New England vessels of small size traded to Maryland. A large number of Bermuda sloops trading to Virginia was a peculiarity of that colony.

## COLONIAL SHIPYARD SCENE

Over-mantel panel from Spencer Hall, Kent County, Maryland, originally the home of Mr. Richard Spencer. Ships were built at Spencer Hall in colonial times and the place was generally called "The Shipyard." It lies at the head of a branch of Gray's Inn Creek, a tributary of Chester River, and large ships once came to a landing here. The panel is about seven feet long by twenty inches wide, painted in oil, and is in a fair state of preservation. It shows vessels of many colonial types in harbor, all flying the British flag, which indicates that it is of pre-Revolutionary date, in all probability circa 1760. The panel is in the Maryland Historical Society Museum in Baltimore.

# The Merchant Marine

Breaking down the figures from the *Virginia Gazette* in order to show the distribution of vessels of various rigs among the ports of Great Britain, we find the following:

### BRITISH-OWNED VESSELS TRADING TO VIRGINIA
#### *VIRGINIA GAZETTE*, 1736-66

| Home Port | Ships | Snows | Brigs | Schooners | Sloops |
|-----------|-------|-------|-------|-----------|--------|
| London | 88 | 2 | ...... | ...... | 2 |
| Bristol | 41 | 10 | 2 | ...... | ...... |
| Glasgow | 12 | 4 | 2 | ...... | ...... |
| Whitehaven | 5 | 3 | 5 | ...... | ...... |
| Liverpool | 4 | 2 | ...... | ...... | ...... |
| Lesser Outports | 15 | 2 | 9 | ...... | ...... |

London, then, was the home port of more than half the British-owned ships trading to Virginia, Bristol of about a quarter of them, and Glasgow of a tenth. Whitehaven and Plymouth, which had a substantial share in the tobacco trade about the middle of the seventeenth century, lost ground by the middle of the eighteenth. Bideford, formerly well represented in Chesapeake waters, almost disappeared from the trade. Liverpool's number of ships, although not impressive in comparison with that of London, Bristol, and Glasgow, consisted of unusually large tonnage and valuable cargoes, for Liverpool specialized in the slave trade.

The most striking feature of the British-owned snows is that London owned very few. The London merchants preferred ships, leaving the lesser vessels to the outports. Bristol, Glasgow, Liverpool, and Whitehaven were the home ports of most snows trading to Virginia and Maryland.

In the case of British-owned brigs, London is conspicuously unrepresented; a few were London-owned, but they were rare. The brig, like the snow, was characteristically an outport vessel. Bristol, second only to London as the home port for ships trading to Chesapeake Bay, likewise owned few brigs. Glasgow, Whitehaven, and the lesser outports owned most of the brigs in the trade. The smallness of the average brig as opposed to the average ship or snow made it preferable for merchants of limited capital. This explains its popularity with the merchants of the smaller outports.

Slightly over a thousand of the entries and clearances reported in the *Virginia Gazette* between 1736 and 1766 designate the rig of the vessel. The following table shows the distribution of rigs among vessels trading to Virginia in those years:

RIGS OF VESSELS TRADING TO VIRGINIA,
1736-66 (ROUND FIGURES)

| | |
|---|---|
| Ships | 450 |
| Snows | 100 |
| Brigs | 100 |
| Schooners | 85 |
| Sloops | 300 |

About half of the vessels trading to Virginia that specified their home ports were British-owned, a quarter Chesapeake-owned, and a quarter owned in the other British colonies in America. As the British-owned vessels were largely ships and snows of considerable tonnage, and the colonial-owned vessels mostly schooners and sloops of light burden, Britain's share in the Virginia trade was preponderant. An observer near the end of the colonial period estimated that six-eighths of the merchant marine trading to the Chesapeake belonged to merchants in Great Britain, one-eighth to British merchants occasionally resident in the colonies, and one-eighth to natives and other permanent inhabitants of Virginia and Maryland.[35]

Judging by the figures for the Virginia convoy of 1704, the average size of vessels in the tobacco trade at that time approximated 170 tons.[36] By 1716 it had declined to 140, by 1720 to 130, and by 1775 probably to 90 or 100.[37] Against this may be set the average tonnage of colonial vessels. Vessels registered in

Maryland averaged 36 tons in 1735, 42 tons in 1740, 44 in 1745, and 60 in 1750.[38]

How these stood in relation to the entire British merchant marine can be seen in the fact that in 1754 Great Britain owned 4,000 vessels of 320,000 tons, of which half were coasters averaging 75 tons and half in foreign trade, averaging 85.[39] For the entire British merchant marine, the average tonnage was only 80 tons.

The tobacco trade, therefore, employed vessels that were considerably larger than the average, while the intercolonial trade, especially from Chesapeake Bay to the West Indies, employed vessels of considerably less than average British tonnage.

The explanation of the gradual diminution of the average tonnage of vessels in the tobacco trade and the gradual increase of that of Chesapeake-owned vessels is that the eighteenth century witnessed increased activity in the tobacco trade of the British outports, the vessels of which were of smaller burden than London-owned ones. As the outports obtained an increasingly large portion of the trade, the average tonnage of tobacco vessels declined. In the colonies the century saw an accumulation of wealth that made it possible for colonial merchant-planters to own vessels of size. In a word, the London tobacco trade decayed, and Chesapeake shipping passed increasingly into the hands of the smaller merchants and shipowners of the outports and of Virginia and Maryland.

o     o     o

As the ownership of vessels required capital beyond the means of most colonists, few Virginians or Marylanders owned ships before the end of the seventeenth century. Those who invested in shipping commonly owned a share in several vessels, rather than owning one outright. The profitable growth and sale of tobacco as well as the importation and retailing of European and West India goods depended upon securing sufficient cargo space at reasonable freight rates, and as scarcity of shipping was the normal condition, the larger planters and merchants soon realized the importance of investing in ships as an adjunct of their principal occupation.

Among the handful of Virginia shipowners of the late seventeenth century were Edmund Scarborough, who owned several, and John Page, who had an interest in two or three.[40] William Fitzhugh, though slow to invest money in ships, had been won over by 1696.[41] William Byrd I owned one—or at least an interest in one—as early as 1684.[42] In later years he complained that his ships proved unprofitable investments, but admitted that ownership of vessels proved advantageous in securing cargo space for his tobacco, particularly when shipping was scarce.[43]

During the last decade of the century colonial investment in ships accelerated, Virginia and Maryland merchants and planters often obtaining part interest in English vessels.[44] The desire to invest capital in this way may explain the boom in shipbuilding that took place in Maryland, and to a lesser extent, in Virginia in the 1690's. Though most of the larger vessels were built with English capital, a few colonists acquired a part interest in them, and the smaller vessels were almost entirely colonial-owned.

The naval officer records of the Port of Williamstad (later known as Oxford), Maryland, for the year 1699 contain the clearance of the ship *Elizabeth* of Liverpool, a vessel of 358 tons, built in Maryland in 1698, and registered at Annapolis, although one of her four owners was master and the other three were Liverpool merchants.[45] Another ship, the *Blew Birds Delight* of Choptank, a vessel of 130 tons, was built, owned, and registered in the colony. And the records for the Port of Annapolis in 1698 and in 1699 show a number of vessels—mostly brigs and sloops, ranging in size from 20 to 70 tons, that were owned and operated by inhabitants of Maryland.[46]

Furthermore, it is reasonable to suppose that some of the twenty-one ships, many of the six pinks and twelve brigs, and a large majority of the seventy-one sloops listed in the Maryland survey of 1698 were colonial-owned. This constituted a fairly respectable merchant marine for the province at that time—one that was not again possessed by Maryland for many decades.[47]

Most of the vessels owned and operated by Virginians and Marylanders in the early eighteenth century engaged in the West India trade. And as that route was not provided with convoys, the loss of colonial vessels in time of war was extremely serious. In consequence, each of the Anglo-French wars of the century greatly diminished the merchant marine of Virginia and Maryland. By 1708 the flourishing merchant fleet of Maryland had been reduced to a few brigs and sloops, not a dozen in all,[48] and Virginia owned only eight brigs and two sloops.[49]

After the Treaty of Utrecht the colonial merchant marine revived. As early as 1721 Maryland owned four brigs and twenty sloops, and by 1730 Virginia's merchant fleet consisted of one ship, six brigs, and sixteen sloops.[50] The rapid rise of Norfolk as a port during the long interval of peace between Queen Anne's and King George's Wars helped build up the Virginia merchant marine, which by 1742 consisted of four ships, six or seven brigs, two or three snows, seven or eight schooners, and five or six sloops.[51]

Again following a sharp reduction during King George's War, the Chesapeake merchant marine began to increase after 1748. Less than two years after the war Governor Gooch reported that Virginia owned and operated sixty sea-going vessels navigated by 500 mariners, besides numerous small craft employed in Bay trade and lightering large ships.[52] Maryland likewise greatly expanded her merchant marine, which by 1756 amounted to sixty vessels of 2,000 tons, employing 480 sailors.[53]

After the disastrous French and Indian War, which reduced the Maryland merchant fleet to thirty vessels of 1,300 tons and 200 mariners in four years, although the number of ships built in the colony doubled, the customary post-war revival took place.[54]

By 1762 Virginia owned 102 vessels of 6,168 tons employing 827 sailors.[55] Maryland similarly recouped her losses.

From the earliest times the advantages of a provincial merchant marine were appreciated and the growth of one encouraged. The assemblies of Virginia and Maryland passed acts that reduced the payment of duties by vessels owned in their respective colonies. In 1661 Virginia exempted vessels owned in the colony from the ten-shilling duty on each hogshead exported, and granted a bounty of 50 lbs. of tobacco per ton (later raised to 200 lbs. for larger ships) on seagoing vessels built in the colony.[56] In 1669 Virginia shipowners received exemption from the castle duty— later called port duty—of 1s. 3d. per ton.[57] In subsequent years the Virginia Assembly passed acts laying a duty of threepence per gallon on liquors imported in British ships and half that amount on those brought in by Virginia-owned vessels.[58] Likewise, ships owned in the colony were exempted from half the naval officers' and collectors' fees.[59]

The Maryland Assembly enacted similar laws designed to encourage the growth of a native merchant marine. In 1661 a port duty of a pound of gunpowder and three pounds of shot for every ton was levied on all vessels "not properly belonging" to the colony.[60] Another act of 1694 levied a duty of threepence per ton on all vessels entering the province except those built and owned by its inhabitants, and rigged the fees of naval officers and collectors for entering and clearing vessels so that Maryland-owned ones paid from one-quarter to one-half the rate charged ships of British or other colonial ownership.[61] In addition, the assembly laid a double duty in 1704 on furs exported by non-residents of the province, and in 1723 a duty of a shilling per barrel on pork imported by nonresidents.[62] And by an act in 1715 the duty of threepence per gallon on imported liquors and that of twenty shillings per head on Negroes and Irish servants imported need not be paid if brought in by vessels belonging to inhabitants of the province.

Quite naturally resenting this kind of discrimination, British merchants and shipowners in many instances succeeded in obtaining royal disallowance of such colonial acts. After 1710 the exemptions from port duties and the two-shilling hogshead duty disappeared from the statutes of Virginia, and after 1748 the half exemption from naval officers' and collectors' fees is not to be found.[63] When Virginia tried in 1730 to exempt colonial vessels from half the duties on imported liquors, a group of London merchants petitioned the Board of Trade and secured an order-in-council in 1731 disallowing the act.[64]

This imperial interference caused a great deal of resentment in Virginia against the British government for acceding so completely to the desires of British merchants. Their dissatisfaction was aggravated by the fact that while Virginia was thus prevented from encouraging a native merchant marine in this way, Maryland, perhaps because it was a proprietary colony, continued to levy differential duties for many years without interference from Great Britain.[65]

Yet despite the opposition of British merchants and the compliance of the London authorities, discrimination in one form or another in favor of colonial-owned vessels continued to exist. Even in royal colonies like Virginia by the passage of acts of short duration and by other legislative legerdemain, colonial-owned vessels continued to enjoy a favored position. As late as 1771 a Virginian wrote his London partners in connection with a ship of Virginia construction they owned, that "it will be a saving of about fifty Pound a Voyage for her to remain under our Register, in Impost Tunnage &c."[66]

Apart from exemptions from colonial duties, the ownership of vessels proved a great advantage to the large planters and merchants of the Chesapeake colonies. The wealthier planters often had widely scattered plantations and diverse interests. They not only had tobacco hogsheads to ship to Great Britain, but also wheat, corn, iron, and lumber. Men like Robert Carter of Nomini

Hall, who owned interests in iron mines, forges, mills, and farms, constantly employed schooners and sloops for transporting goods from one river to another, for collecting cargoes, lightering large ships anchored in the channels of rivers, and for the exchange of grain and lumber for West India products and south European wines.

In the tobacco trade likewise, the ownership of vessels proved of great advantage to the colonists. The larger planters generally shipped their own tobacco on consignment to London to be sold on their account. Consequently, they were quite as concerned as the merchants who bought the crops of small planters to secure adequate cargo space at reasonable rates. In times of scarcity of ships the owners and part owners of vessels, quite naturally, received preference in the freighting of such ships. This served as a powerful inducement to both merchants and planters to invest in vessels.[67]

In the course of the eighteenth century, therefore, it became increasingly common for a Virginia or Maryland merchant-planter to own one or more vessels, or to have an interest in many. Many of the leading families of both colonies had shipping interests: Washingtons, Carters, Custises, Byrds, and Braxtons, as well as the leading merchants of Norfolk and the river towns. And in Maryland, Dulanys, Taskers, Chews, and Ridgelys appear in lists of owners of vessels along with merchants of Annapolis, Chestertown, and Baltimore.

Some of these shipowners had more than one vessel. Samuel Galloway operated two ships, a snow, a schooner, and a sloop at the same time.[68] His little fleet totalled 450 tons and employed 67 mariners. Colonel John Lewis owned the brigantine *Priscilla* in 1737, and the brigantine *Pretty Betty* in 1738.[69] Between 1757 and 1760 Thomas Ringgold of Chestertown owned the schooner *Chester*, 50 tons, and the sloop *Henrietta*, 40 tons. But by 1766 Ringgold had decided "never to puzzle . . . with more than one at a time."[70] Benjamin Harrison owned several ships as well as a shipyard.[71]

## The Merchant Marine

Some merchants owned more than one vessel of their own and, in addition, had an interest in several others. Richard Bennett had an interest in eight vessels. In 1734 he and Ashbury Sutton owned the 90-ton snow *Samuel.* The next year Bennett was part-owner with Samuel Chew, Jr., and James Heath, of the 50-ton sloop *Adventure.* In 1736 he and Caleb Clarke owned the 60-ton brigantine *Rebecca.* In the same year Bennett and John Bartlett owned the 40-ton schooner *Hopewell.* By 1742 Bennett owned her outright. Shortly thereafter, he joined the partnership of John Wallace and Company of Chestertown which included Wallace, George Steuart, James Calder, and Bedingfield Hands. In 1744 this firm owned the 75-ton schooner *Bennett,* in 1745 the 140-ton *Charming Nancy,* and in 1748 the 200-ton ship *Ogle.* Meanwhile, in 1747, Bennett and William Addams owned the 20-ton sloop *William and Mary.*[72]

While in partnership with Bennett, Calder, Steuart, and Hands, John Wallace also owned vessels outright or else in partnership with others. In 1757 Wallace owned the 60-ton brigantine *Nancy* and the 50-ton brigantine *Achsah.* At the same time he and Henry Baker owned the 70-ton snow *Alexander.*[73]

Between 1734 and 1749 Patrick Creagh of Annapolis owned fourteen vessels:

### VESSELS OWNED BY PATRICK CREAGH, 1734-49

| Rigs | Tonnage |
|---|---|
| Ships | 200, 100 |
| Snows | 100, 85 |
| Brigs | 50 |
| Schooners | 50, 30, 20, 20 |
| Sloops | 35, 30, 30, 20, 20 |

In all, Creagh owned 790 tons of shipping.[74] Thirteen he owned outright, the other one he shared with Dr. Charles Carroll.

Another Maryland shipping magnate was Levin Gale, who between 1734 and 1742 owned nine vessels:

## VESSELS OWNED BY LEVIN GALE, 1734-42

| *Rigs* | *Tonnage* |
|---|---|
| Ships (1) | 95 |
| Snows (0) | ...... |
| Brigs (4) | 35-50 (range) |
| Schooners (2) | 45, 30 |
| Sloops (2) | 30, 12 |

Gale's vessels totaled 432 tons.[75] Five of the nine belonged to him alone. Of the others, he owned the ship *Levin and Leah,* 95 tons, together with Matthias Gale; the brigantine *Martha,* 35 tons, together with Captain Arthur Dashiel; the brigantine *Brereton,* 55 tons, with Robert Henry and John Williams; and the schooner *Sarah,* 30 tons, with Edward Chambers, Robert Graham, and Aaron Lynn.

Occasionally a Chesapeake merchant shared the ownership of a vessel with a merchant in Great Britain or in other colonies. The 65-ton brigantine *Maryland Merchant* registered at Annapolis in 1744, belonged jointly to Daniel Cheston of Maryland and William Gibbs of Barbados.[76] In 1747 the 70-ton brigantine *Cookson* belonged jointly to Anthony Bacon of London, Henry Lowes and John Williams of Maryland.[77] In 1749 Foster Cunliffe and Company of Liverpool took Robert Morris of Maryland into partnership with them in the snow *Oxford.*[78]

It sometimes happened that a vessel was registered in the name of a number of owners, as members of a firm or company. The 60-ton schooner *Baltimore* in 1735 belonged jointly to Charles Carroll, Charles Carroll, Jr., Dr. Charles Carroll, Daniel Dulany, and Benjamin Tasker, as members of the Patapsco Company.[79]

Although the average size of vessels in the colonial merchant marine was small, there are a few instances of large ships owned and operated by colonists. William Roberts of Annapolis owned two ships in 1746, one of 400 tons and the other of 150, besides several smaller vessels.[80] James Russell had a 300-ton ship.[81]

Vessels of 200 tons were even more common. And in Virginia Neil Jamieson of Norfolk had several vessels of 200 tons built, as well as one of 190, and one of 176½ tons.[82]

Between 1734 and 1750 thirty vessels of 100 tons or over were registered in Maryland, ten of them of British or New England ownership, and twenty of them Maryland-owned. The following table reveals the size of the latter:

### MARYLAND-OWNED SHIPS, 1734-50

| Tonnage | Number |
|---------|--------|
| 300 | 2 |
| 200 | 4 |
| 150 | 5 |
| 140 | 3 |
| 120 | 1 |
| 100 | 5 |

Between 1753 and 1776 Maryland built one hundred and twenty-six vessels of 100 tons or more.[83] Thirty-six of these were over 200 tons; the largest was 320 tons. Only six of the ships over 200 tons were of British registry, the remaining hundred and twenty of them being registered in Maryland.

Although incomplete, these statistics enable us to see that by the end of the colonial period Maryland had a respectable merchant marine.

Nothwithstanding the fact that ownership of vessels required considerable accumulation of capital, the desire to own ships was so strong that merchants were occasionally led into the error of investing too large a proportion of their wealth in ships. William Reynolds, the Yorktown merchant, wrote John Norton in 1773 that he had involved himself too much in shipowning, finding that "it requires more money than I cou'd have thought." In consequence, Reynolds was obliged to sell his brigantine and content himself with only his schooner.[84]

The same desire for vessels occasionally led a merchant to build a vessel that proved too large and costly for him. The gazettes of the two tobacco colonies often carried advertisements of the sale of new vessels that had made but one voyage.[85] If the merchant ran out of money before the vessel was completed, he either sold her on the stocks[86] or negotiated a bill of bottomry whereby he borrowed enough money to complete her in return for an interest in her first voyage.

When William Roberts of Annapolis ran out of money while his 400-ton ship, *Rumney and Long,* was under construction, he entered into a contract with James Russell by which the latter paid the former £1,000 sterling to enable him to finish the ship. The loan was made at a thirty per cent advance, to be repaid within twenty days of the safe arrival of the ship at London.[87]

It was customary in bills of bottomry to make the vessel itself as well as all the other goods and chattels of the owner security for the loan. Should the loan and the specified interest not be paid at the conclusion of the first voyage, the vessel was at all times afterward "lyable and Chargeable" for the payment of the debt. But if the vessel should be lost at sea on her first passage, the loan was cancelled and the owner relieved of all liability to pay either the money advanced or the interest.[88]

## CHAPTER NINE

# Masters and Mariners

F ROM their earliest days, the natives of the Chesapeake tidewater were part landsmen and part watermen, a combination that is not surprising in a region composed of alternate strips of land and water. In view of the natural setting in which they grew up they were quite naturally as much at home on one element as on the other. The navigable creeks and rivers that interlace the land were the haunts of their childhood. There is scarcely a native of this region who never swam in the waters of a tidal creek, or who never ventured forth upon the waters of a broad estuary in a leaky boat with a makeshift sail. There is scarcely a native who never rounded a point in the teeth of a gale, who never missed his stays and grounded upon a sandbar, or who never netted crabs and tonged for oysters.

Almost every planter, great and small, had a boat of one kind or another. Canoes, bateaux, punts, piraguas, shallops, flats, pinnaces, and sloops—"Bay Craft," as they were called collectively —appear with monotonous regularity in the seventeenth and eighteenth century records of Virginia and Maryland. Rivers and creeks had to be crossed, social calls to be made, large tobacco ships anchored in the river channels to be lightered, and fishing, oystering, and crabbing to be done. For all these purposes, as well as for ferrying and piloting, Bay craft were needed.

Each planter as a rule was quite capable of sailing his own boat. Where assistance was necessary, it was provided by slaves or indentured servants. Except for the larger sloops and schooners, Bay craft seldom required regular crews. In consequence, not-withstanding their active maritime life, Virginia and Maryland, unlike the New England colonies, produced a very small class of professional mariners.

As late as 1697 Governor Andros of Virginia informed the Board of Trade that there were in the province few or no seamen.[1] A survey in Maryland the same year revealed but seventy-one seamen in the colony, thirty-five of them belonging to Kent County alone.[2] The next year Andros explained to the home authorities that the reason why there were no mariners in Virginia was that the few that settle there turn planters and "leave the sea wholly."[3]

A decade later the situation had improved somewhat. Colonel Jennings asserted in 1708 that the Virginia-owned vessels employed about 200 seafaring men, but complained that of those, few were able mariners. Skilled seamen generally gravitated toward the middle colonies where they received greater encouragement than in the tobacco colonies.[4]

During the seventeenth and early eighteenth centuries no important class of mariners arose in the Chesapeake country because of lack of trade, competition with the northern colonies for sailors, and the conviction that tobacco planting was a surer way to prosperity.

As the eighteenth century progressed, however, developments occurred that modified pre-existing conditions. After about 1730 when Chesapeake activity in the West India trade rapidly increased, a native merchant marine was built up. This created the demand, and the increasing population of Virginia and Maryland, together with the rise of ports like Norfolk, Annapolis, Chestertown, and Baltimore, provided the source of supply of mariners.

By 1730, when the tobacco trade of the Chesapeake employed at least 2,400 British seamen, Virginia could boast no more than 184 mariners and Maryland, a few years later, little more than half that number.[5] These seafaring men—290 for the whole Chesapeake—were engaged in overseas trade, principally to the sugar and wine islands. In addition to them were the crews of the small sloops that were constantly employed in the Bay, transporting country commodities from one river to another. These, said Governor Gooch, "can't properly be termed seamen, being for the most part planters with negroes."[6]

The number of mariners in Virginia had increased by 1745 to 220, of which about 50 were English sailors discharged or deserted in the colony, and the remaining ones natives.[7] Gooch estimated the number in 1747 to have risen to 300 native mariners and 100 British seamen.[8] Two years later he reported that Virginia's merchant marine employed 500 sailors.[9]

Meanwhile, Maryland's number was growing at about the same rate, increasing from 106 in 1733[10] to 120 a decade later.[11] By 1756 it had risen to 480.[12] This advance was retarded, however, by the disastrous effects of the French and Indian War upon the Chesapeake merchant marine. By 1760 the number of mariners in Maryland had fallen from 480 to 200.[13]

After the conclusion of peace, revival was rapid. By 1764 Virginia had 827 seamen[14] and Maryland, if she preserved her usual ratio with Virginia, about 400. At this time, when the Chesapeake merchant marine employed about 1,200 mariners, the British-owned vessels trading to the Chesapeake were manned by nearly 4,000.

Throughout the colonial period many inducements lured captains from the sea. For one thing, in the seventeenth century before the rise of factors and stores, the master of a ship trading to the Chesapeake was obliged not only to navigate his ship but also to dispose of the cargo, purchase tobacco, and engage freight. From activity of this sort it was but a short step to settling down and becoming a merchant in his own right. Then, too, tobacco was king, and seafaring men were no less willing than other orders of humanity to pay court to the "sovereign weed." An account of Virginia written in 1649 reported that most of the masters of ships trading there eventually acquire houses, plantations, and servants.[15] In consequence, it was a natural transition for captains in the Chesapeake trade to forsake their calling and become planters.

The same factors that drove British masters from their vocation operated to prevent the rise of a large class of native seafarers. Between the Scylla of tobacco planting and the Charybdis of tobacco trading, few Virginians and Marylanders left their native waters to sail upon the high seas with a quarterdeck under their feet. In the course of the eighteenth century the tide turned and, with the economic diversification of the tobacco colonies, set in the opposition direction.

With the rise of Norfolk as a seaport and with the building up of a native merchant marine, the number of native masters gradually increased. It was a fairly lucrative profession, not because of the salary but because of the perquisites and contacts.[16] As a class the Norfolk masters ranked next to the merchants in wealth and influence.[17]

In all parts of the Chesapeake country they were friends of the great planters, frequently visiting the mansion houses and dining at the tables of the tobacco "nabobs." Moreover, many shipmasters found it an easy transition from quarterdeck to counting-house or to shipyard. And it is not uncommon to find sea captains blossoming forth as merchants, ship chandlers, shipbuilders, or operators of taverns and ferryboats.

In view of the opportunities and of the position of the profession, it is not surprising that members of the better families were occasionally drawn into it. We find masters of Chesapeake vessels bearing distinguished Virginia names like Randolph, Washington, Tyler, and Mason, and prominent Maryland names such as Calvert, Ogle, Chew, and Eager.

Merchants and planters entertained widely varying opinions of English captains that traded to the Chesapeake. So much responsibility attached to the master of a vessel that he was apt to be blamed for everything that did not conform rigidly to the expectations of shipowner and freighter. If for any reason a chartered ship reached its port late, the captain was suspected of incompetence.[18] If the cargo was not stowed away before the

*Calm Day (from oil painting by Peter Monamy, 1670-1749, in Chatterton, OLD SEA PAINTINGS, London, 1928).*

expiration of the lay days, the master was thought negligent.[19] If goods were damaged in transit, the skipper was considered careless.[20]

In many instances the causes of the trouble were heavy weather, desertion of the crew, or storms at sea.[21] Then too, if cargo was not made available for lading, the captain could scarcely be considered responsible for running through his lay days and demurrage, but he seldom received the benefit of the doubt.

On the other hand, captains sometimes were at fault. A Baltimore County factor to whom the ship *Baltimore* was consigned in 1748 charged that the master, John Anter, disobeyed his instructions and failed to load his ship. Instead of collecting tobacco at Elkridge Landing, Gunpowder and Bush rivers, Anter "used his Freighters very Ill" and "almost constantly was Employed at his own Business in his Store or either on board or in a Tavern rendring himself incapable of Business."[22]

Drink, it seems, was the downfall of more than one sea captain! Stephen Hooper, master of the ship *Ranger,* belonging to John Hanbury of London, while in his cups at a tavern in Annapolis was publicly overheard to say that his ship was "a damned old Ship and he wished that he had ne'er Come in her."[23] Whispered abroad, this soon led planters who formerly shipped their hogsheads in Hanbury's ships to switch to other vessels as a result of Hooper's slander.

The Maryland shipbuilder, Dr. Charles Carroll, had more than his share of trouble with bibulous skippers. In 1743 he dispatched Joel Hutchinson, master of his schooner *Annapolis,* to Barbados and Tortugas with the injunction, "Remember that Idleness is the Root of all Evil, and Drunkeness is the soil Wherein that Root must Flourish."[24] But the skipper does not appear to have profited from the worthy doctor's homily. Four months later Carroll wrote Codrington Carrington, a Barbados merchant, that "Hutchinson has made a Drunkener Voyage than my former Skippers."[25] Hutchinson returned from Barbados in ballast instead of going to the "Sallitudes,"[26] and explained his action by saying that he was chased by an enemy privateer. His story didn't ring true to the suspicious Carroll, who told Carrington, "I believe the Tier of Rum you let him have was the ocation." In despair, Carroll observed that he must desist from trade until he met with better skippers.

Perhaps the most acid opinion of sea captains was entertained by William Byrd II, who wrote:

> They are commonly men of no aspiring genius, and their understanding rises little higher than Instinct. When they go out of their ships they are out of their Element. They are most of them arrant Sea Calves, and the Tritons that Swim under the water are just as wise as those that sail upon it. The most they can be brought to do, is, sometimes to deliver a Letter, and if they happen to have superior parts, they may be Instructed perhaps to call for an answer. One may as soon tutor a monkey to speak or a French woman to hold her tongue as to bring a Skipper to higher Flights of Reason.[27]

But all planters were not so outspoken as Byrd. Indeed, on occasion a tobacco planter entertained a favorable opinion of a master and even went the length of recommending him to a shipowner. George Washington wrote Robert Cary, the London merchant, recommending Captain McGachin in complimentary terms.[28]

In retrospect it must be said of the eighteenth-century skippers that they were seldom properly appreciated. It is true that some of them were rascals, given to double-dealing, negligence, and strong drink. Nevertheless, as a class, masters usually navigated their vessels with admirable skill in the face of every kind of hardship. In addition to putting up with unruly and deserting sailors and contending with the ever-present danger of storms and shoals, sea captains—particularly those of the colonial merchant marine—were frequently exposed to the cruelty and robbery of pirates and privateers.

Moreover, some trades were extremely hard on one's health. The Swiss visitor, Michel, on a visit to Virginia in 1702 observed that sailors in the slave trade were sickly and yellow in their faces when they survived at all.[29] Some years later the Eastern Shore factor, Callister, tried to dissuade his brother from entering the Guinea trade, which he called "a murdering Trade, in every respect." He likewise declared the West India trade to be quite dangerous "for Life or health."[30] And Washington wrote that a master he knew who had been in the convict trade to Virginia considered it a service "neither consistent with his Inclinations or Health to persevere in."[31]

There is no doubt that life was hard on the high seas and that it was fraught with danger and unpleasantness. Many a master was cut off in his prime like the Virginia-born John Booth, aged thirty-four in 1748, whose gravestone records that

> Whilst on this variant stage he rov'd,
> From Port to port on Ship board drove.
> Sometimes the wished-for haven reached,
> But twice his bark was stranded on the beach.
> No other coffin but the ship, the Sea his grave
> But god the merciful and just,
> Has brought him to the haven safe in dust
> . . . . . . . . . . . . . . .
> His sails unfurled his voyage tis o'er,
> His anchors gone he's safe on shore.[32]

o    o    o

Because of the hardships of life at sea, it was a common occurrence for British sailors to desert their ships while in Chesapeake Bay. As early as 1690 the desertion of seamen became so widespread that Governor Nicholson issued a special proclamation with a view to suppressing it.[33]

Shipmasters were required to give bond for £1,000 that they would return the same number of sailors to England that they had brought out. To make mariners less dissatisfied with their lot, the governor warned masters to observe all contracts with seamen with scrupulous care. And in the event of any violations on the part of captains, the sailors were encouraged to complain to the nearest justice of the peace.[34]

On the other hand, deserting mariners could expect no sympathy from the colonial government. The law forbade anyone from entertaining a fugitive sailor. No ferryman could carry a seafaring man across a river without a note from his master authorizing him to travel, and all persons in the colony were vested with the right to arrest runaway sailors even without the formality of a warrant.[35]

But the causes of desertion went deeper than dissatisfaction with life aboard merchantmen. Many mariners signed up for long voyages, like those of the tobacco vessels, in order to escape impressment into the King's service in England. For men resolved to avoid the severity of the Royal Navy, no amount of colonial legislation could change their intentions.

Edward Randolph wrote the Lords of Trade concerning these sailors in 1695 that upon reaching the Chesapeake some got ashore and were harbored and concealed by the planters, but a far greater number, in expectation of much higher wages, made their way overland to Philadelphia where they shipped either aboard privateers for shares or upon vessels trading illegally to the West Indies.[36]

As a result of this practice England lost a great many able seamen whom she badly needed in time of war, and the homeward-bound tobacco ships were so weakly manned as to be unable to defend themselves against enemy attacks. Randolph estimated that nearly 100 mariners deserted in 1694 in Maryland alone, most of them succeeding in getting away because of the exceptionally deep snow that winter, which prevented the recovery of the fugitives. As a result, loading was delayed, causing twenty-five tobacco ships to miss the convoy and sail without naval protection.

To remedy the situation in the future, Randolph proposed that one of the outward-bound convoys be stationed in Patuxent River to assist merchantmen in their loading in case many seamen fall sick or run away. He also urged the enactment of legislation imposing the severest penalties upon anyone who enticed or harbored fugitive mariners. The same advice was offered by a group of shipmasters in 1698, when asked by the governor of Maryland how to curtail desertion. As they asserted that Pennsylvania was the principal refuge for runaway mariners, the Council instructed the officials near the head of the Bay to do all in their power to intercept them before they passed into the northern colony.[37]

The assemblies of both Virginia and Maryland in 1702 enacted laws that sought to discourage desertion by such devices as offering rewards for returning runaways, imposing penalties on those who assisted fugitives, restraining sailors from travelling without proper certificates, and limiting the amount of credit to be extended to mariners by ordinary-keepers.[38] The Maryland act limited credit to five shillings per voyage, for ordinary-keepers were in the habit of harboring sailors who had become too heavily indebted to them.

But these acts proved ineffective. Two years later desertion was still so common that a group of English merchants trading to Virginia and Maryland petitioned the Queen to order the governors of those colonies to aid and assist them in holding together the crews of their ships when in the Chesapeake. The Privy Council issued the desired instructions, but they proved no more effective than the acts of the colonial assemblies.[39] Governor Spotswood in 1711 complained that seamen deserted even from the royal warships in the Chesapeake.[40]

Despite the discouraging results of earlier attempts to stem the tide of desertions by legislation, the colonial assemblies continued to pass acts involving the familiar rewards and penalties. Virginia enacted a law of this kind in 1711, made it perpetual in 1713, and implemented it by supplementary acts in later years.[41]

Nevertheless, all attempts on the part of the colonial and British governments to suppress desertion failed hopelessly. The practice continued throughout the remainder of the colonial period to be a characteristic of the tobacco trade. The gazettes of Virginia and Maryland frequently carried advertisements for runaway mariners, describing their clothes and physical features, and offering generous rewards for their apprehension.

There was a statutory reward for returning fugitive sailors, varying with the distance involved. The Virginia act of 1710 established it at five shillings for ten miles or less and ten shillings for anything over ten miles,[42] but mariners were so scarce that the captains of ships from which they deserted generally offered much higher sums. The rewards advertised in the gazettes of the two Chesapeake colonies varied from as low as twenty shillings to as high as five pounds per sailor.[43]

As British coins of large denomination were rare in the tobacco colonies, rewards for sailors were often in terms of "pistoles," a Spanish gold coin worth about 16s. 9d. sterling, one, two, or three being commonly offered for the culprits.[44]

There was a tendency for the size of the reward to increase during the eighteenth century, particularly in the case of deserters from royal warships. The commander of H.M.S.*Triton* in 1751 offered a reward of four pistoles "over and above the common Allowance" for apprehending deserters.[45]

Desertions became so common that a single issue of a gazette sometimes contained several advertisements for runaway mariners. One issue of the *Maryland Gazette* in 1753 had advertisements for nine sailors and three indentured servants that had escaped from three vessels.[46] Shortly before, five mariners had deserted from a ship in Chestertown.[47] And on another occasion a slaver, the snow *Alexander* of Bristol, lost her entire crew, "every one of [the] Men Except the Officers" deserting.[48] The master was obliged to employ ordinary laborers to remove the snow's ballast while he went to Philadelphia to sign on another crew.

The crews of British merchantmen trading to Chesapeake Bay, being habitually depleted by desertion, had to be augmented in the colony. As a result, the newspapers of the two colonies carried frequent advertisements of openings for mariners, promising high wages and "good encouragement."[49] But masters who had lost seamen through desertion were seldom able to secure replacements in the colonies, there being no source of supply in the Chesapeake country before the rise of Norfolk as a seaport. In consequence, they had no course but to petition the governors of the colonies for relief.

In such cases the governor issued an order to the commander of the royal warship then on the Chesapeake station instructing him to supply the petitioner with one or more seamen from the warship and empowering him to press a like number for his own ship "where they may best be spared."[50]

Impressment was more commonly resorted to in connection with ships of the Royal Navy. When the warship on the Virginia station required more men, her commander applied to the governor of Virginia for authority to impress the necessary number. These requests though freely granted, were often accompanied by some reservation, for instance, that the men were to be impressed only from vessels which had more than a dozen in the crew.[51] Royal ships were also authorized by the governor to impress a pilot when one's services were needed.[52]

Sometimes the commanders of royal vessels took it upon themselves to impress seamen without the troublesome formality of applying to the governor for authority to do so. In 1702 the Crown made it clear that the power of impressment was vested solely in the governor in his capacity as vice-admiral of the colony.[53]

When H.M.S. *Southampton* received orders in 1702 to quit the Chesapeake and sail for Newfoundland, her commander, Captain Moody, reported to the Virginia authorities that he was short of men. The governor therefore ordered all officers, civil and military, and all her majesty's loving subjects to use their utmost endeavors to discover and apprehend all vagrant and runaway seamen and convey them safely aboard the *Southampton*.[54] As the warship was a fourth-rate with a complement of 180 men, it was a serious matter to supply her with an adequate number of men.[55] The Virginia Council had to confess that "all the seamen that can be had in this country will scarce be sufficient to supply H.M.S. *Southampton*."[56]

Great Britain found it so difficult in time of war to obtain sufficient seamen to man her enormous fleet and at the same time to recruit thousands of men for her land forces that the government had to resort to the impressment of mariners. When the War of Jenkins' Ear began in 1739, the British Navy had over one hundred men-of-war in commission and the army sought to recruit between 10,000 and 15,000 troops. Within a few days nearly 1,500 seamen were "pressed" into naval service.[57]

When the news of French preparations for war reached London in 1755, the ships about to sail from the Thames Estuary were detained "on account of the Extraordinary Demand there happens to be at this Juncture for Seamen to Man a Fleet of his Majestys Shipps which are now fitting out with all imaginable expedition."[58]

In the colonies as at home the authorities resorted to impressment for supplying the Royal Navy with seamen. Hampton Roads was a favorite place, because it was the principal roadstead in Chesapeake Bay. Shipowners in time of war often ordered their vessels to stand directly into one of the rivers upon entering the Capes and by no means to call at Hampton Roads, in hopes that the "press" might be avoided.[59] Later, when Norfolk became a thriving port and the principal source of supply of mariners, commanders of royal warships who received authority to impress seamen turned their attention to that town.

On occasion, Royal Navy commanders were not overscrupulous about obtaining authorization in advance. Just such a "bloody riotous plan" was conceived in 1767 by Captain Jeremiah Morgan of H.M. Sloop-of-war *Hornet*. Under cover of darkness, the captain together with several of his officers and about thirty men came ashore in an armed tender. Landing at the public wharf of Norfolk, they made the tender fast across the end, so that her loaded swivel guns might command the wharf. The party then paused at the adjoining tavern to take "a cheerful glass" before pursuing their villainous design.

Thus inspired with "a little *Dutch courage*," Morgan and his men made for the part of town to which mariners habitually resorted, and proceeded to force their way with oaths and threats into the taverns and lodging-houses that seamen frequented. The press gang rushed in, according to one witness, like so many tigers and wolves, seizing every man they could find. Those who made the slightest resistance "they knocked down without ceremony and lugged them away like dogs."

But all did not go quite as Captain Morgan planned. The night watchmen, attracted by the scuffling, gave the alarm throughout the town, calling out "A riot by man of war's men, with Capt. Morgan at their head." The alarm roused a number of townfolk, including the intrepid former mayor, Paul Loyall, who left their homes and gathered to suppress the disorder.

The two parties met face to face near a tree at the head of the wharf. Loyall in a mild, genteel manner approached Morgan and asked the reason for the disturbance. The short-tempered naval officer, infuriated by the interference, presented a drawn sword to his breast and thundered that if Loyall "stirred one foot he would be through his body by G-d." Loyall retained his dignity and calm demeanor, but Morgan, conscious of his predicament, repeated the same words several times and made wild lunges at Loyall.

Finally, the badly-shaken Morgan summoned his armed guards from the *Hornet's* tender and sounded a retreat. After reaching the tender, like a cock that fights best on his own dunghill," he found fresh courage, flourished his sword at Loyall, and "abused him and every magistrate in town in the most scurrilous language."

At this juncture the mayor, George Abyvon, arrived on the scene with one hundred followers. Making himself known, he commanded peace in the King's name. But Morgan "damned him and every man in Norfolk" and ordered his men to fire their swivels. Fortunately the seamen hesitated to apply their lighted matches to the guns, and Loyall calmly dissuaded them from doing so, thereby preventing much needless bloodshed.

Captain Morgan, unable to contain himself, jumped into a small boat, ordered a sailor to accompany him, and rowed out to the *Hornet* in high dudgeon. The Norfolk authorities took about ten of Morgan's men into custody and put them in jail; the rest were allowed peaceably to return to their ship.[60]

The scarcity of mariners in the colonial period and the failure of impressment as a means of counteracting the widespread practice of desertion resulted in high wages for seamen. In consequence, wages were the most serious charge that shipowners had to meet in the operation of their vessels.

In the seventeenth century a master often received as much as £9 a month and an ordinary seaman £1 10s.[61] Bruce has found an instance in which a sailor in 1695 received as much as £2 4s., a mate £4, a ship's physician £3 10s., and a ship's carpenter £3 10s. a month.[62] In Maryland in 1692 mariners on the two Newcastle ships, the *Relief* and the *Ann,* were paid at the rate of £3 5s. a month.[63]

By the middle of the eighteenth century wages of sailors varied considerably, and are often difficult to compare because it is seldom clear whether they are in sterling or colonial currency. Sometimes they ran as high as £5 per month.[64] More commonly they were about £2 10s. to £3 15s. currency.[65] In sterling, wages ran between £1 4s. and £1 10s. a month for ordinary seamen.[66]

In some instances there was a stated sum of money to be paid for the voyage in addition to monthly wages while the ship was in port. The ship *Nympha,* bound from Suffolk, Virginia, to Cadiz, advertised for sailors, promising them £2 5s. currency per month "from the Time of their Entry to the Ship's clearing out in *Virginia,* and Eleven Guineas for the Run, upon their being discharged at Cadiz."[67]

The masters, of course, received the highest wages on shipboard. The master of the ship *Hero* received £4 sterling per month, while ordinary seamen got £1 4s. a month. Sometimes the first mate and sometimes one of the skilled men, like the carpenter, came next. The carpenter of the *Hero* received £3 a month and the "Chief Mate" but £2 10s.[68] Aboard the snow *Hobbestone,* the chief mate got £2 10s. per month, the carpenter £2 5s., the second mate £1 10s., the boatswain £1 12s. 6d., and ordinary seamen from £1 6s. to £1 10s.[69]

On one occasion the sloop *Dreadnaught* paid the first mate £5 10s. currency, the second mate £4 10s., the boatswain and the gunner £6 each, the carpenter and the armorer £5 10s. each, and ordinary seamen between £3 and £5 a month.[70] On another occasion the same vessel paid wages at the rate of £4 10s. for the first mate; £4 for the second mate, boatswain, carpenter, armorer, and gunner; £3 for the cooper; and between £2 and £3 15s. for ordinary seamen.[71]

From these examples it will be seen that after the master, the first mate and carpenter vied for the highest wages. Only in rare cases were the boatswain and gunner paid more than the first mate, but it was common for them and the carpenter to receive as much as the second mate or more. Indeed, in some cases an experienced ordinary seaman received as much as the second mate. It is clear that the second mate, particularly on colonial vessels, was little more than an apprentice—probably a mere youth—learning the art and science of navigation.

The lot of the mariner in colonial days was a curious mixture of good and bad. On the one hand the scarcity of seamen led the British and colonial governments to encourage the profession and to maintain scrupulously their rights in courts of law. It was a common occurrence for mariners to sue a vessel for back wages. In many instances their cause was pleaded by the most distinguished members of the legal profession.[72] In almost every case of this sort, even in some in which the master alleged neglect of duty on the part of the seamen, the courts found for the plaintiffs. No right was more rigorously maintained in colonial courts than the right of mariners to their stated wages. Consequently, it was not uncommon for ships to be condemned in the county courts before 1696 and in the vice-admiralty courts after that date to be sold to meet the sailors' claim to wages.[73]

The mariner was also assured by law of "good and sufficient diet and accommodation" and of protection against "immoderate correction."[74] Every opportunity was afforded him to seek redress in the courts in the event of mistreatment. In addition, he was exempt from the petty duties of landsmen such as serving in the militia.[75] Masters were forbidden to discharge a sailor because of illness "without taking due care for his . . . maintenance and cure."[76]

On the other hand life at sea was extremely hard. As Captain John Smith pointed out in 1626, "Men of all other professions, in lightning, thunder, stormes and tempests, with raine and snow, may shelter themselves in dry houses, by good fires, and good cheere; but those are the chief times, that Sea-men must stand to their tackelings, and attend with all diligence their greatest labour upon the Deckes."[77] Then, too, even the "good and sufficient diet and accommodation" promised by law was atrocious and inadequate by the standards of landsmen. Indeed, Smith was of the opinion that the want of proper food at sea had caused the loss of more men than had been slain in any naval battle since the Spanish Armada.

As for discomforts at sea, Smith reminded the would-be sailor that "there is neither Alehouse, Taverne, or Inne to burne a faggot in; neither Grocer, Poulterie, Apothecary, nor Butchers shop."[78] And on top of these privations, the mariner had to put up with the overbearing arrogance characteristic of shipmasters of the colonial period.

Although the sailor was legally protected against "immoderate punishment," he was subject to whipping which in practice was severe enough. The mariners aboard the Liverpool snow *Hannah* in suing the master, Captain Edward Prescott, in the Maryland Vice-Admiralty Court, testified that "the repeated Barbarity Inhumanity and Ill usage" they had received at his hands kept them in "Continual Apprehension of the Danger of their Lives." They deposed that through "Violent Beatings with Illegal Weapons . . . many of the Mariners on board the Said Snow . . . fell a sacrifice to the Savage and Brutal Passions of the said Edward Prescott."[79]

On their part the masters often complained that their mariners had "turbulent and refractory Tempers," and that "sailors are of all men least Capable of Submitting to the authority of their Commanders, when they find themselves under no fear of correction."[80]

When a ship was in Chesapeake waters, the seaman found himself hedged about by irritating regulations calculated to discourage desertion. He was forbidden to go ashore without leave. He was not allowed credit at ordinaries beyond a certain limited amount. And he could not cross a ferry or travel overland any distance without written permission from his master. On top of that the mariner was at all times subject to impressment into service aboard vessels of the Royal Navy where conditions were even worse, discipline more severe, and punishments more cruel, and from which he might not desert with impunity.

Fear of impressment into naval service was so great in the eighteenth century that it was not uncommon for sailors to desert from a merchantman as soon as she made port, in order to escape possible impressment.[81] Then, too, the mariner, particularly on colonial vessels, was exposed to capture by enemy privateers or by pirates, who not infrequently ill-treated prisoners.

The crew of the Virginia sloop *Friendship,* which was taken three leagues off St. Martin, was unceremoniously put into a longboat and obliged to row ashore. The crew of another captured vessel was left to languish in a filthy prison at Cap François for several months before being sent to France and thrown into the dungeon of Denan Castle. They wrote that they were "quite stripped of our clothing," and "were short of provisions," and despaired of ever returning home alive.[82] The mate of the *Flying Fame,* Nehemiah Mills of Elizabeth City, Virginia, became "ransomer" or hostage for his ship in 1709, and as such continued a prisoner at Brest for eleven and a half years "under the greatest hardship, with no more than the bare prison allowance of bread and water."[83]

By the custom of the country, seamen on board ships in the tobacco trade were obliged to go ashore and fetch the hogsheads that were intended for their ship. If the plantation lay inland, the sailors had to roll the hogsheads from the barns to the landings. This sort of work was a little out of a mariner's line. The exertion required to roll a half-ton cask a mile or two over rough roads under a burning summer sun was accounted a great hardship, as it left their hands full of slivers and their throats choked with dust. To make matters worse, the insularity of Englishmen and the conservatism of those who follow the sea led them to "go sweltering about in their thick Cloaths all the Summer, because they used to do so in their *Northern* Climate; and then unfairly complain of the heat of the Country."[84] To relieve their discomfort they drank cool spring-water and new cider to excess, or devoured unripe fruit that grew along the rolling roads. Instead of being assuaged, they developed "Fluxes, Fevers, and the Belly-Ach; and then, to spare their own Indiscretion, they in their Tarpawlin Language, cry, God D--- the Country."[85]

The disgruntled mariners naturally enough conceived a great dislike for Virginia and Maryland and were responsible for the currency which unfavorable opinions of the Chesapeake colonies received in England, particularly in respect to the unhealthfulness of their climate.[86] In 1727 a pamphlet appeared in Annapolis which set forth a sympathetic description of the seaman's lot.[87] It charged that rolling hogsheads was "unfit for Men" and could easily be done by horses. It urged that the cessation of the custom would remove the reproach which the tobacco colonies "but too justly" lay under, "of being one of the worst countries in the Universe for Sailors."[88]

By that time many complaints had been made by merchants and masters as well as by mariners.[89] In response, the Maryland Assembly in 1727 passed a regulation requiring planters to roll their own hogsheads to within a mile of a convenient landing. For doing so there was a statutory allowance of sixpence per mile and for neglecting or refusing to do so, a fine of one hundred pounds of tobacco.[90]

Complaints against this act were so numerous that it was repealed the following year. No other legislation was enacted concerning the rolling of hogsheads until 1730 in Virginia and 1747 in Maryland, when the acts establishing the warehouse-inspection system permanently relieved shipmasters of the liability to fetch tobacco from inland plantations.[91]

The seamen of colonial days, like those of all other periods, were a rough-and-ready lot—blasphemous, quarrelsome, and not infrequently licentious. Often maimed and scarred by their dangerous vocation, they acquired a grizzled appearance from exposure to the weather and from diseases to which their unbalanced diet afloat and their immoderate sprees ashore made them susceptible.

In contemporary accounts they are often described as being "emaciated," having a "thin face," a "Maimed eye," "swell'd Legs," sores on their shins, or being "pitted by smallpox."[92] Sometimes they were described as having "Sun-burnt Freckles" and "short Sunburnt Hair." They usually wore distinctive garments—referred to as a "sailor's habit"—which consisted of dark grey or blue "fearnought" jackets, sometimes a "green sailor's jacket," "striped" or "striped and check trowsers," and a "small round hat" or "tarpaulin."[93]

Mariners occasionally fell afoul of the laws of the colonies against blasphemy. A Florentine sailor, Carlo Arabella, who was in Chester River in 1709, had a particularly unfortunate encounter with the law. He accidentally spilt some scalding pitch upon one of his feet and in "a great passion" flagrantly violated Maryland's severe laws against blasphemy. Haled into court, the poor fellow was fined £20, ordered to have his tongue bored three times, and sentenced to six months imprisonment. Having no money the voluble Italian languished in a Maryland jail until he was pardoned by Queen Anne.[94]

Had Carlo Arabella been familiar with provincial laws, he would have been well advised to hold his tongue in Maryland and save his profanity until he got to Virginia. For in the latter colony, by the acts of 1691 and 1696, the fine for swearing, cursing, or profaning God's name was only one shilling, although in 1699 it was raised to five shillings.[95]

Brawling among seamen was as common in the eighteenth century as in any other. In 1753 two sailors on a ship in Chester River fell to quarreling. Apparently their vocabulary gave out before their anger died down, for they soon grappled with one another. In the course of their struggle they tumbled overboard and, being unwilling to stop fighting, were drowned. Their bodies upon being recovered were buried in one grave, where, the *Gazette* assured its readers, "they lie peaceably together."[96]

On another occasion some sailors at Chestertown got into a brawl with some of the Earl of Loudoun's soldiers whom Governor Sharpe had quartered there. The confusion was increased by the town boys joining battle on the side of the soldiers. When the fray was over and the dust settled, it was discovered that a sailor had been killed. Two men were charged with murder, but the mariners were sufficiently sporting to appeal to the governor in their behalf, and the two men were pardoned.[97]

*Portrait of an eighteenth-century shipmaster (from Branch and Brock-Williams, A SHORT HISTORY OF NAVIGATION).*

## Masters and Mariners

In the graveyard at West Point on York River is a fragment of a tombstone that undoubtedly once covered the mortal remains of a colonial mariner. The inscription—very much restored—reads: [98]

> Though Borea's blasts and Neptune's waves,
> Have tossed me to and fro,
> In spite of both by God's decree,
> We anchor here below.
> Here now do I at anchor lie,
> With many of our fleet.
> Yet once again we must set sail,
> Our Saviour Christ to meet.

# Part IV

## WARFARE

## CHAPTER TEN

# The Convoy System

It must have been an inspiring sight in the seventeenth and eighteenth centuries to watch from Cape Henry a tobacco convoy file out of Chesapeake Bay between the sandy foreland and Middle Ground Shoal and spread its canvas to the prevailing westerlies. Nowhere else in the British Empire could an observer see a more impressive demonstration of the maritime nature of the old colonial system. Here, stretching out before him, was a vast, richly laden fleet of one hundred and fifty or two hundred ships bound for England with the annual produce of two of her most prosperous colonies. Here, indeed, was the embodiment of the maritime intercourse between colonies and the mother country upon which the economic structure of the Empire rested.

It was the more remarkable in that the tobacco trade, which by the end of the seventeenth century was one of the most important and lucrative branches of England's overseas commerce, was a comparatively recent development. A hundred years earlier not a single Englishman lived on the shores of Chesapeake Bay and not a single pound of colonial tobacco was imported by the home country. By 1700 Virginia was the largest and Maryland the third largest of the English colonies in America: together they had one hundred thousand inhabitants and annually exported seventy thousand hogsheads of tobacco to England, enriching the royal treasury by £300,000 a year. Considering the tobacco, the shipping employed, and the English manufactures consumed by the colonists, Virginia and Maryland were computed to be worth £1,000,000 a year to England.[1]

Because the lucrative Chesapeake trade required protection at sea, the convoy system was instituted as a safeguard against the depredations of enemy ships and privateers. Occasional references to convoys appear earlier, but convoying as a regular system was first developed by Spain in the sixteenth century to protect her rich plate-fleets from the Dutch and English "sea dogs." In the following century, when the Netherlands and England became rival naval powers, they too were obliged to institute convoy systems for the protection of their merchant marine. The Dutch, for example, had to convoy merchantmen through the English Channel as early as 1652, and both the English and the Dutch convoyed their vessels trading to the Baltic for naval stores.[2]

The Anglo-Dutch wars exposed Chesapeake Bay to naval attack and also endangered the sea-lanes of English commerce. In 1664 and again in 1673 the Dutch entered the Bay and captured or destroyed many ships in the tobacco fleet. Even more serious was the threat to the tobacco trade represented by the Dutch privateers—known as "capers." These vessels swarmed in English coastal waters and harried the commerce of the "scepter'd isle."

As early as 1662 the merchants and shipowners concerned in the Chesapeake trade petitioned King Charles to order all vessels trading to the Bay to sail for England in May, June, July, and August of that year.[3] The request was denied on that occasion and again when it was renewed in 1664. During the second Dutch war, however, the Dutch privateers dealt the trade such a serious blow that the government was forced to take measures to provide protection.[4]

In June, 1665, at the request of several London tobacco merchants, the Privy Council instructed the Lord High Admiral to detail a competent convoy of warships to sail out to meet the incoming tobacco fleet and escort it from beyond soundings, past Land's End, to safety.[5] At the same time the English authorities instructed the governors of Virginia and Maryland in 1666 to order homecoming vessels to sail together in fleets for their mutual protection, and to depart only on certain dates.[6]

By acceding to the King's order to associate and return in company, ships in the Chesapeake trade were considered to be in a better position to defend themselves against Dutch attack on the high seas.[7] The instructions promised that armed escorts would be sent out to meet the fleet at the other end, and expressed the hope that "prevention may be had against a repetition of the great losses sustained last summer in their voyage homewards."[8]

This action on the part of the Privy Council was timely, for early in 1666 eight capers were at sea lying in wait for the Virginiamen, and six more were in port ready to join their fellows.[9] In May, 1666, one of these capers attacked the tobacco fleet about sixty leagues west of Ireland, falling upon the *Alexander,* a large Bristolman laden with 600 hogsheads of tobacco. Instead of coming to her rescue as they had promised, the captains of the other ships remained on their course. The *Alexander* put up such a long and valiant resistance before surrendering that the other ships of the Virginia fleet escaped.[10] The owners of the *Alexander* later set forth to the Privy Council that had the rest of the fleet "endeavoured her Recovery acording to the expresse Agreement of all the Masters," she would have been saved and the caper captured. They also represented that the loss of its cargo increased the price of tobacco in the other ships, and therefore petitioned the King that "an Averidge may be set upon the said Fleete for their equall concernment in the Losse."[11]

Other losses occurred in September, 1667. A Dutch man-of-war chased a Virginiaman from Land's End to Lundy Island, forcing her to run into King's Road for shelter.[12] During three years, 1665-67, Bristol alone lost fifteen ships together with cargoes amounting to 9,300 hogsheads of tobacco.[13] In 1673 two Dutch capers took the ship *Joseph* within soundings while on her homeward passage from Virginia to England. On this occasion Charles II carried the whole question of Dutch privateering before the States General of the Netherlands. The English Ambassador, Sir William Temple, did what he could to obtain a favorable decision, but without success. Finally in 1674 King Charles wrote to the Prince of Orange, but even the personal intervention of the King failed to bring the issue to a satisfactory conclusion.[14]

In addition to the Dutch capers, Spanish and French vessels preyed on English shipping. In 1674 a Spanish man-of-war took the *Thomas and Mary* of Virginia, while bound from Jamaica to the Chesapeake, plundered its cargo valued at £6,000, and "most barbarously used" the captain and crew. Acting upon a petition from its owners, the Privy Council brought the case through regular diplomatic channels to the attention of the Spanish court, but without success. The Privy Council then sent a special emissary, and decided that if he failed the King would grant "Letters of Reprizall" according to the law of nations.[15] As was expected, the Spanish Court received Cooke, the special emissary, coldly and gave no satisfaction. The owners of the *Thomas and Mary*, presumably, got their letter of reprisal.[16]

The extent of the indignity to which English vessels were subjected in the absence of naval protection may be seen in the experience of the Virginiaman *The Little Dogger* which, on her return voyage to England with tobacco, was taken by French privateers, plundered of 1,000 hogsheads, and dismissed with the insolent expression, "Goe and tell your King of it."[17]

From the outset the fleet-and-convoy system seems to have been welcome, for after 1665 English merchants and shipowners frequently petitioned the Privy Council to assign escort vessels for the tobacco fleet.[18] In one instance, however, the system broke down completely. On September 30, 1676, because of Bacon's Rebellion in Virginia, the Privy Council placed an embargo on English shipping bound to Chesapeake Bay. On this occasion the action of the government was unpopular, and the embargo was generally evaded. Many vessels cleared for Barbados or other West India islands, and once at sea proceeded directly to Virginia or Maryland.[19] Finally, on December 6, 1676, at the request of several prominent London merchants, the authorities terminated the fiasco by lifting the embargo.[20]

After Bacon's Rebellion, enemy depredations on English commerce continued. In 1689 several merchants trading to the

*H.M.S.* Success *and H.M.S.* Norwich *off Yorktown, 1755 (from Ms. journal of* Voyage of H.M.S. Success and H.M.S. Norwich in Nova Scotia and Virginia 1754-56, *at The Mariners' Museum).*

Chesapeake, in requesting a convoy, earnestly represented to the King that they had suffered much by the capture of eleven "capital" ships by the French, and that Virginia and Maryland depended wholly upon them for clothing and other necessities, tactfully adding that every ship taken represented a loss in customs duties of between £5,000 and £10,000.[21] Impressed by this loss of royal revenue, the King ordered a convoy for the Virginia fleet.[22]

With a view to supplying the royal navy with men on the outbreak of King William's War, the English authorities imposed quotas of seamen upon each of the trades in which English merchants engaged. In 1690 London was allowed 400 mariners for the Chesapeake trade, a number far short of its needs. The merchants vigorously protested that the ships fitted out for the tobacco trade required 1,000 or 1,200 men, pointing out that the restriction had led to cutthroat competition between shipowners for seamen. In view of the fact that Virginia and Maryland were thought to be well supplied with goods, the merchants petitioned the King to impose an embargo on all shipping to Chesapeake Bay.[23]

Accordingly the English government forbade the sailing of ships to Virginia or Maryland and ordered the governors of the tobacco colonies not to allow ships to sail from the Bay except in fleets or with convoy.[24] This action, it was thought, would render secure a branch of commerce that was enormously valuable to the Crown and kingdom, for at this time the annual tobacco fleet consisted of nearly 150 ships carrying from 70,000 to 80,000 hogsheads. The revenue that flowed each year into the treasury from tobacco duties approached £300,000 sterling.[25] Little wonder, then, that the Board of Trade in 1702 assured the Lord High Admiral that the trade of Virginia and Maryland deserved "a most particular regard!"[26]

The English government, in fact, did everything in its power to provide enough shipping to bring home the annual tobacco crop. It raised the quota of seamen for London vessels engaged in the Chesapeake trade from 400 to 800 in 1690, and to 1,000, plus a quarter of that number of foreign mariners, in 1691.[27] It freely granted permits to sail without convoy to all vessels of superior armament or exceptional speed.[28] And in order to provide additional cargo space, the Privy Council in 1690 instructed warships acting as escorts in the Chesapeake trade to receive and freight tobacco to the extent of ten tons of freight for every hundred tons burden.[29]

These expedients, however, all proved inadequate. The quota of seamen assigned to the London ships was insufficient. The granting of permits for sailing without convoy resulted in the loss of many of the finest vessels in the trade to enemy privateers. And the practice of allowing warships to compete with merchantmen in freighting tobacco discouraged shipowners and diminished rather than increased the shipping employed in the trade.[30]

Tobacco planters were hard put to find cargo space for their crop, and in the course of the 1690's shipping became so scarce that freight rates soared to the unprecedented height of £17 per ton, a figure never again reached in colonial times.[31] This made the transportation of tobacco unprofitable, so that even the small quantity that eventually reached England brought the planters no profit.

By 1703 the situation was desperate. More than half the tobacco crop of Virginia and Maryland remained in those colonies for want of ships. As the Oronoco variety would not keep for as long as a year, most of it was expected to be worthless by the time the next annual convoy was ready to sail. The sweet-scented variety would keep, but not without losing weight. The treasury was therefore expected to lose much of its normal revenue from the tobacco trade, a loss it could ill afford in time of war.

Moreover, the scarcity of ships and the resulting dearth of English goods in the colonies forced the colonists to curtail their tobacco growing and engage in makeshift woolen and cotton manufactures.³² In a word, England's relations with her tobacco colonies depended upon the maintenance of adequate maritime intercourse, and now that this was impaired the economic ties of the imperial system began to weaken.

The trouble with the convoy system was that it was haphazard, the embargo was incomplete, and the interests of the merchants of the various cities were divergent. There was no fixed date of sailing for convoys, and the number of them sent each year varied without sufficient notice. The granting of permits for single sailing was carried to unwise extremes. The merchants of London desired an early departure of the Chesapeake convoy, while those of the outports insisted upon a late departure. To complicate matters further, the London merchants favored one annual convoy, while the outport merchants opposed it, believing that between the sailings of convoys vessels should be allowed to leave as soon as they were ready.³³

Notwithstanding these disagreements and the shortcomings of the system in the early days, it was the generally-accepted opinion by the end of the seventeenth century that convoys were the only possible expedient in time of war for securing the Atlantic shipping lanes of English commerce. The outbreak of Queen Anne's War, therefore, precipitated a warm discussion of the proper means of improving the system and increasing its effectiveness.

The failure of the merchants of London and the outports to agree upon the sailing date of the convoy to the Chesapeake forced the English authorities to make the decision independently of the merchants. In 1702 the Lord High Admiral laid before the Privy Council a proposal for dispatching two fourth-rate warships by the end of January, 1703, to Chesapeake Bay, there to be joined by two others from Vice-Admiral Benbow's West Indian Squadron. These four would then convoy the homeward-bound tobacco fleet, leaving Virginia the following July. Meanwhile, two fourth-rate warships were to convoy a fleet to the Chesapeake by the end of August, 1703, and return to England in April, 1704.³⁴ The

Privy Council agreed to the proposal and issued orders putting it into effect and enjoining the governors of the tobacco colonies to take care that no ships should sail out of the Capes without convoy.[35]

This novel arrangement, involving two convoys to the Chesapeake in a single year, caused considerable complaint from all sides.[36] Colonel Quary, a conscientious royal official in the colonies, wrote from Virginia in May, 1704, that "Noe Trade belonging to England is worse manedged than the tobacco trade." The want of regularity, both as to the sailing date and to the number of convoys each year, he said, led to confusion and uncertainty in the colonies.

The planters, ignorant of whether there would be a second convoy in any year, did not know whether to sell their crops at a low price in the colony or hold out for more and run the risk of having them left to spoil. They did not know whether to engage freight for their hogsheads at exorbitant rates, or hold back their crops in expectation of a second convoy and lower freight rates. The merchants, on the other hand, taking advantage of the uncertainty, placed extravagant prices on their goods and cargo space, and low prices on tobacco.

To remedy the situation Quary proposed a single annual convoy, to reach Chesapeake Bay before the beginning of November, when the northwest winds set in, making it difficult for square-riggers to enter the Bay, and to leave for England the following April or May.[37]

Quary's proposal was sound. What was needed was greater regularity rather than greater frequency. And since the tobacco colonies produced one crop a year, one annual fleet was sufficient to carry it home. According to Quary, this would fix the price of tobacco in the colonies, in England, and all foreign markets, then all persons concerned would buy "briskly," being well assured that no other supply would come until next year's fleet.

But the English tobacco merchants were still sharply divided on the issue. Those who dealt largely in tobacco on consignment, most of whom were in London, favored the single-fleet proposal. Those who bought and sold tobacco on their own account, most of whom were in the outports, feared that one annual fleet would glut the English market, and encourage the colonists to hold out for high prices. Instead, this group of merchants desired to keep the market open and therefore insisted upon two convoys annually.[38]

The controversy raged for several years, during which the government continued its haphazard method of sending convoys. In 1706 some forty ships were delayed in their passage, and could not be ready in time to leave Chesapeake Bay with the convoy. In February, 1707, the Board of Trade recommended that a second convoy be sent that year, or, alternatively, that the embargo be lifted and the forty ships allowed to sail when ready after the departure of the convoy.[39]

Meanwhile the Board of Trade, having been won over to Colonel Quary's proposal of several years before, succeeded in obtaining its approval by the Lord High Treasurer, the Commissioners of the Customs, and the Admiralty. Finally, on February 20, 1707, the Privy Council formally acceded to it and issued orders putting it into effect. The annual convoy was to reach Chesapeake Bay in October each year and leave for England in May, by which means the convoy and fleet would avoid the "Badd Seasons" in the Bay and the "Worm, which in the Hott Months is so prejudicial to them."[40] This gave the merchants time to sell their goods, and the planters time to cure their crops and prize their hogsheads. The Lord High Treasurer pointed out the further advantage that during the winter the mariners manning the tobacco ships were not needed in England for her majesty's service.[41]

The plan won the wholehearted support of the colonists in Virginia and Maryland, and after 1707 became an accepted feature of the convoy system.[42] In later years, however, during King George's and the French and Indian wars, the sailing date of convoys frequently changed. In 1745, for example, H.M.S.

*Mermaid* convoyed a fleet to England, sailing from Hampton Roads as late as December 15;[43] in 1748 H.M.S. *Hector* sailed on September 2;[44] and in 1757 the convoy left the Chesapeake on September 15.[45]

After its reorganization the convoy system greatly relieved the scarcity of ships and goods in the colonies, but did not entirely eliminate it. After 1707 the scarcity resulted from the fear on the part of English merchants and shipowners that they might send too many ships and too plentiful a supply of goods. This happened in 1721 when Robert Carter reported over forty ships in Rappahannock River and the same number in York River. "We have a swarm of ships in all our rivers," he wrote, and "it's impossible . . . they should all find tobacco." As a result, the freight rate, which during Queen Anne's War had been £13 or £14 per ton, now fell to £8.[46]

In order to avoid a repetition of this glut of ships, the British merchants thereafter sent fewer. In fact, they became over-cautious. When the planters made appeals for more shipping, the British government offered adequate naval protection for the trade, but the British merchants could not be induced to venture a sufficient number of vessels to satisfy the colonists. For the rest of the colonial period a mild scarcity of ships and goods was the normal condition in the tobacco colonies.[47]

During King George's War the convoy system seems to have broken down—particularly in the years 1744-48. From the beginning, French and Spanish privateers were active both in British waters and off the Virginia Capes. The shipping route between Great Britain and Chesapeake Bay was imperilled at both ends. In May, 1742, seven vessels were taken off the Capes by a Havana privateer.[48] In February, 1744, twenty-one ships, including several Virginiamen, were captured in the English Channel by a St. Malo privateer.[49] In the latter case, Walter King wrote Colonel Thomas Jones that he thought it was entirely owing to the government's neglect in not having a squadron of men-of-war cruising in the Channel.

The next year three Bideford vessels on their homeward passage from Maryland were taken by French privateers, two carried into San Sebastian and the other one into Morlaix.[50] In July, 1745, five privateers, one of them of 36 guns, took several tobacco ships homeward bound off the Virginia Capes.[51] In August news reached Annapolis that two more Bideford ships, bound to Maryland, had been captured off the English coast by privateers from San Sebastian and St. Malo.

The worst blow of all, however, was the "melancholy News" that twenty merchantmen under convoy of two men-of-war, many of them bound for Chesapeake Bay, were taken on June 12, 1745, in the English Channel by the Brest Squadron, consisting of nineteen men-of-war.[52] In October the brig *Onslow,* bound for London, was captured by a French privateer and carried into Quebec.[53] The supplement to the *Gentleman's Magazine* for December, 1745, listed sixteen vessels taken while bound to or from the Chesapeake. Several were victims of the St. Malo privateers *Sultana* and *Hermione.*[54]

The years 1744 and 1745 were, perhaps, the worst in the maritime history of the Chesapeake since the last Anglo-Dutch war. There was a slight improvement in 1746 and 1747, but the year 1748 was scarcely less disastrous than 1744. In May, 1748, two vessels laden with tobacco were taken on their homeward passage, one in or near the Downs.[55] That spring, when the Chesapeake was insufficiently guarded, privateers boldly entered the Bay and took a number of ships in the mouths of the rivers and even within sight of Fort George on Point Comfort.[56]

The seriousness of the situation can be seen in the violent fluctuation of marine insurance rates. By May, 1744, the rate had risen from its normal peace-time level of 3 or 4 per cent to 12 and 15 per cent for the outward passage and 20 to 25 per cent for the homeward passage.[57] By September, 1744, the losses to the enemy were so serious that the London brokers refused altogether to insure a vessel bound for the Chesapeake, and the Bristol brokers talked of 40 and 50 per cent.[58] The following January, 1745, the rate was 20 per cent for the homeward passage.[59] By 1748 insurance home again rose to 25 per cent.[60]

Freight rates, like insurance rates, are a good indication of the state of trade at any given time. They indicate the amount of shipping employed in relation to the amount of goods to be transported, and they indicate indirectly the risk involved, because the shipowner must meet his insurance premium out of the proceeds of the freight. In the early years of King George's War, freight rates were low, between £6 and £8 per ton. By 1744, however, they had risen to £16 per ton, the highest since 1691.[61] During 1745 they varied from £13 to £14,[62] and continued at about that level throughout 1746, 1747, and the early months of 1748.[63] In April, 1748, they rose again to £16.[64] After the news of the peace was received, freight rates declined sharply, settling by October, 1748, at £7 or £8 per ton.[65]

In retrospect we may say that except for the years 1744-48 the convoy system after its reorganization in 1707 was a success. It maintained maritime intercourse between Great Britain and her colonial possessions, and it enabled merchants to carry on their trade in time of war without undue risk or excessive losses. The best proof of this is the difference in the insurance rates for vessels sailing with convoy and for those sailing without convoy.

During the French and Indian War the premium for sailing to Virginia with convoy was 5 per cent, and for sailing without convoy between 10 and 12 per cent.[66] There was, in addition, a sliding scale of rates for vessels sailing part way with convoys bound for places other than Virginia and Maryland, with the last leg of the passage without convoy.

In 1757, when the rate for sailing to the Chesapeake without convoy was 12 per cent and for sailing with the Virginia convoy was 5 per cent, the premium for vessels bound to the tobacco colonies, coming with the West India convoy, was 7 per cent. If they came with the English Channel convoy, which protected them

*English Man-of-War Saluting (from painting by Peter Monamy, 1670-1749 in Chatterton, OLD SEA PAINTINGS, London, 1928).*

from enemy privateers off the English coast, and sailed without convoy after that, the premium was 9 per cent.[67]

In 1759, when the rate was 10 per cent for vessels sailing without convoy to the Chesapeake, it was 5 per cent for ships coming with the Virginia convoy, 6 per cent for those with the West India, Pennsylvania, New York, or New England convoys, and 8 per cent for those with nothing but the English Channel convoy. The next year, when the base rate had risen to 12 per cent, the premium for the Virginia convoy stood at 5 per cent; that for the other North American convoys, at 6 per cent; that for the East or West India, the Straits, the African, or the Portuguese convoys, at 8 per cent; and that for the Channel convoy, at 10 per cent.[68]

These figures, of course, apply only to vessels sailing between England and the Chesapeake, and not to vessels from or to other parts of the British Empire. It is also to be remembered that these premiums were not for war risk alone; they covered the usual dangers of the sea as well as dangers from the King's enemies. Moreover, the chances of collision in a fleet of a hundred and fifty or two hundred ships were much greater than in small groups or when a vessel sailed alone. The difference in premiums for ships in convoy and for ships sailing alone, therefore, does not fully reveal the effectiveness of the convoy system in protecting British commerce from the depredations of the enemy. Even so the fact that the rate was almost two and a half times as great for vessels sailing alone as for those in the Virginia convoy is a good indication of the success of the system.

In considering the lack of a convoy system between the West Indies and the continental American colonies, it must be emphasized that the system was established and maintained primarily for the protection of the commerce of the mother country, rather than that of the colonies. The regular convoy routes ran from the island kingdom out to the periphery of the empire like spokes of a wheel. Insofar as colonial vessels used those sea-lanes, they were afforded the same protection enjoyed by British vessels. But the imperial authorities provided no regular convoys for trade routes that did not come to Great Britain.

In consequence, the vital trade route between the American continental colonies and the West Indies was habitually left unguarded. Most of the colonial vessels in the West India trade were small, poorly armed, and poorly manned. They were therefore an easy prey for the enemy. On the return passage in time of war they often joined the convoy that sailed from Antigua or Nevis to Great Britain. Far out at sea, beyond the usual haunts of the French and Spanish privateers, they left convoy and sailed alone to Chesapeake Bay. On the outward passage, however, the Virginia and Maryland vessels bound for the West Indies had no protection at all, and while in Cuban and Hispaniolan waters were frequently taken by the enemy.[69]

The situation had become so acute by 1702 that Lieutenant Governor Bennett of Bermuda wrote the Earl of Nottingham suggesting a convoy for these ships. His reasons, however, were not so much to protect colonial shipowners as to prevent the French West Indies from obtaining provisions by capturing vessels in this trade. Bennett reported that in King William's War the French in the West Indies would have starved had it not been for their success in taking colonial ships engaged in the grain trade. As it was, the French islands became glutted with prize grain, and provisions became cheaper at Martinique than in the English colonies from which the grain had been exported.[70] Bennett's suggestion was ignored, and intercolonial trade, especially between the continental colonies and the West Indies, continued throughout the remainder of the colonial period to be the most vulnerable route of commerce within the Empire.

After 1730 when the trade between the Chesapeake and the West Indies became considerable, the wars with France resulted in great losses to Virginia and Maryland shipowners and merchants. Governor Gooch in 1730 informed the Board of Trade that Virginia exported about 3,000 barrels of pork each year mostly to the West Indies, as well as large quantities of wheat and corn, in return for rum, sugar, and molasses.[71] Shortly after the outbreak of King George's War, shipping in the intercolonial trade had declined to such an extent that freight could scarcely be had from the Chesapeake to the West Indies.[72] At the end of the war Gooch wrote that the West India trade of Virginia had been inconsiderable and uncertain during the war. He added, however, that since the peace it had begun to revive. He also reported that Virginia trade with Surinam, Curaçao, Martinique, and Guadeloupe, which had ceased during the war, was not expected to begin again.[73]

The same thing happened during the French and Indian War, the activity of enemy privateers nearly throttling the West India trade. Captain Hanrick, formerly master of the snow *Nancy,* wrote Samuel Galloway, her owner, in 1757 that she had been taken by a French privateer off Barbados, and reported that eighty-four privateers were operating out of Martinique alone, more than a dozen of them to windward of Barbados. In consequence, that island suffered greatly, some twenty-four ships bound to it having been taken by the enemy in four months' time.[74] Only one Maryland vessel got through to Barbados, and most of the Virginia vessels fell into the hands of the enemy.

As a result, provisions became so scarce in the British West Indies that they commanded unusually high prices, and the restriction of trade led to a shortage of rum, sugar, and molasses in the Chesapeake colonies. William Allason, a merchant in Falmouth on the Rappahannock, wrote to Boston in 1757 that when he was on the Potomac River, four weeks before, West India commodities were scarce and much in demand.[75]

The effect of the depredations of French privateers on Maryland shipping was to cut it in half. In 1756 that colony owned sixty vessels aggregating 2,000 tons, regularly employing 480 mariners.[76] As practically all of this merchant marine was engaged in West India trade, it had been reduced by 1761 to thirty vessels of 1,300 tons and 200 sailors.[77] The decline was categorically stated to be "owing to the Enemies having captured many of our Vessels trading to the Sugar Islands."[78]

The peacetime insurance rate from Chesapeake Bay to the West Indies was about 3 per cent.[79] Toward the end of the French and Indian War the rate rose to 11 or 12 per cent.[80] This was the same as the rate for ships sailing without convoy from Chesapeake Bay to Great Britain, twice the distance. Therefore the risk involved in trade from Chesapeake Bay to the West Indies was approximately twice as great as the risk to Great Britain without convoy. Yet the route from the Chesapeake to Great Britain was provided with regular convoys, while that from Chesapeake Bay to the West Indies was left unguarded.

The explanation is that the trade between the Chesapeake and Great Britain was much more important, provided the Crown with handsome revenues in the form of tobacco duties, and brought rich profits to British merchants and shipowners. The traffic between Chesapeake Bay and the West Indies, on the other hand, provided no revenue for the Crown and was carried on almost entirely by colonial merchants and shipowners. That this branch of commerce, so important to the colonies, was left out of the network of convoys constitutes a serious charge against the impartiality of the otherwise remarkably-enlightened imperial system of the day.

Successful though it was in achieving its principal objective, securing the maritime intercourse between the mother country and the tobacco colonies, the convoy system had many minor defects. Involving as it did the divergent interests of British merchants and colonial planters, of London and outport merchants, of factors, commission merchants, and independent dealers, of importers and exporters, and of shipowners, charterers, and masters, the system necessarily failed to please all concerned. In consequence, it was so hedged about with protests and complaints that one is apt to lose sight of its essential success.

## The Convoy System

The infrequency of convoys to and from the tobacco colonies made it imperative that masters of ships obtain and stow a full cargo before the sailing date of the fleet, or else be forced to choose between sailing with a partial cargo and remaining idle for a year, while the crew deserted, the tobacco deteriorated, and the worms of Chesapeake Bay honeycombed the ship's timbers.

The haste which the convoy system imposed on the shipowners and masters led them to insist upon early deliveries of the tobacco hogsheads for stowage. This, in turn, imposed great hardships on the planters, who had no control over the seasons, and who were often hard-pressed to cure and prize their crops in time. On the other hand, if the sailing date of the convoy were postponed in order to accommodate the planters and masters who were not ready in time, those who were ready considered it a hardship to be forced to wait weeks for their slower competitors.

Besides, the British merchants were usually anxious to receive their tobacco as soon as possible, the early market generally being more favorable. Sometimes certain groups of merchants sought to delay the departure of the convoy from England in order to enhance the value of manufactured goods already in the Chesapeake colonies before the arrival of new supplies.[81]

Considerations of climate also influenced the date of sailing for convoys. If the outward convoy reached the Virginia Capes much after the beginning of November when the northwest winds set in, it might have great difficulty in getting into the Bay.[82] If the homeward-bound convoy failed to leave the Chesapeake by July when the "dog days" began, the mariners were apt to fall sick as a result of the heat and the ships to suffer from the teredo.[83]

The warships acting as convoys caused a great deal of dissatisfaction. They occasionally reached their post late, they competed with merchantmen in offering freight for tobacco, and they sometimes failed to give sufficient notice to mariners as to the sailing date of the convoy. At sea, if the warship went too slow, the faster vessels complained that they were forced to waste time by luffing and rolling uncomfortably in heavy seas, while waiting for the slower vessels to catch up with them.[84] If, on the other hand, the warship went too fast, the slower vessels were obliged to crowd on more canvas than they could safely carry, with the result that some sprung their topmasts and became separated from the fleet.[85] In a fleet of one hundred and fifty or two hundred ships of all sizes, rigs, and speed there could be no speed that would not be too slow for the fast-sailing vessels and too fast for the slower ones. Whatever the commodore of the convoy did, some shipmasters found fault with him.

The captain of the man-of-war that was to convoy the tobacco fleet home to England, in his capacity as commodore of the fleet, set the sailing date and communicated it to the governors of Virginia and Maryland. They in turn forwarded notices to the counties to be posted at courthouses, churches, and other public places. Sometimes the commodore inserted in the provincial newspapers an advertisement containing the information.[86] In addition, personal messages were sent to the masters of vessels lying in the various rivers of Virginia and Maryland.

The news thus noised abroad soon became generally known. Masters hastened to complete their lading and to clear their vessels with the customs officers. The collectors and naval officers of each river hastened to make out clearance papers and take bond from every ship that cleared, to be certain that it would sail with the convoy.[87] Planters and merchants hastened to deliver their last hogshead to the ships in which they had obtained freight and to write home to their friends and business correspondents in time for the letters to be sent with the fleet. There was hustle and bustle on all sides, interrupting once a year the smooth, even course of life in the easy-going Chesapeake tidewater.

Finally, the Maryland vessels, in accordance with orders from the governor, weighed anchor in their respective rivers and sailed separately or in small groups to the mouth of either the Patuxent or the Potomac. When the fleet had gathered, it sailed down the

Bay to Hampton Roads to join the Virginia vessels which meanwhile had collected there.

When the appointed date for departure arrived, the commodore summoned the masters of the vessels and issued long and detailed sailing orders. These listed the various signals to be used at sea to communicate messages from one vessel to another, and especially to communicate the commodore's orders to individual ships. There were signals for anchoring and weighing anchor, for speaking, for announcing a leak, fire, or other disaster, for summoning all masters aboard the flagship, for ordering such maneuvers as tacking, luffing, and passing singly under the man-of-war's stern, and for reporting the sight of land or of enemy ships.

The signals by day were a combination of flags and pennant, of firing guns, and of loosing or furling sails. At night they consisted of lights and the discharge of guns. During a fog they involved firing cannons and muskets, ringing bells, and beating drums.[88]

Then in anticipation of possible enemy attack, the commodore also issued a plan for battle formation. The ships in the fleet were divided into three sections, the commodore to act as admiral-in-chief and to command the main section comprising the larger vessels with the most guns; a vice-admiral and a rear-admiral were designated to command the other two sections. A battle line was drawn up in which each of a selected number of ships in the fleet had a place and a distinctive signal so the admiral could communicate orders to it.[89] And there were detailed fighting instructions consisting of signals for executing maneuvers.[90]

When all was in readiness for the fleet to sail and a "prosperous wind" arose, the commodore gave the signal for departure. (This signal, which varied among convoys, sometimes consisted in loosing the main-topsail and firing one gun, then hauling the main-topsail and firing another; and sometimes in hoisting a blue swallow-tailed pennant at the mizzen-yard and discharging a gun.)[91] Each of the hundred and fifty or two hundred vessels

333

now loosed its sails and weighed anchor. Led by the commodore
the entire fleet threaded its way carefully between Willoughby
Spit and the Horseshoe Shoal and between Cape Henry and the
treacherous Middle Ground. After that the fleet had a thousand
leagues of open sea before it with no landfall until it reached the
Scillies off Land's End.

At sea the convoy fell into regular habits, at least as long as
good weather held. The commodore set the course and directed
the fleet to follow the flagship. Every night at eight o'clock he
fired a cannon to attract the attention of the other ships to the
course. A fire signal was then set so the flagship could be detected
after dark. The entire fleet replied by ringing bells. In "quiet
weather" the sound of hundreds of bells coming across the water
at dusk was delightful and greatly appealed to the passengers.

In thick weather when the fire signal was invisible, the commodore's ships discharged a gun every minute so the fleet could
follow him.[92] After dark each vessel lighted several lanterns—
sometimes as many as four. One was run up to the main truck;
others variously distributed, at the bow, stern, and amidships.[93]
On clear nights the effect of so many lanterns suspended at
various heights above the sea, together with their shimmering
reflection in the water, must have been enchanting.

In spite of all precautions the large number of vessels sailing
together made accidents inevitable. Tacking was difficult in so
large a fleet, and ships frequently came within three or four feet
of one another, to the great anxiety of the ships' companies. Occasionally several vessels collided in tacking, especially at night
or in a fog. Their watches sometimes became careless, and on
the long ocean reaches it was easy to bring one's ship too close
to another without realizing it. Yards and bowsprits became
entangled in the rigging, and the two unfortunate vessels, especially when the sea was running high, bumped dangerously together until separated. The stricken ships set off distress signals
and attracted the attention and assistance of the commodore
and masters of other vessels.[94]

## The Convoy System

It was important to keep the fleet from becoming separated because detached vessels were an easy prey for enemy privateers that hovered around the edges like sharks. The commodore, whose ships usually led the fleet, prevented any merchantman from passing him by firing a solid shot across the bow of the overtaking ship. It was the custom of convoys to fine the offending vessel the cost of the powder and shot fired to restrain her.[95] Toward the end of each day, by which time the fleet had become strung out—the faster vessels pushing forward, the slower ones falling behind—the commodore ordered the forward vessels to luff. This was accomplished by turning the ship across the wind, catching the wind with one sail, and holding the ship back with another. In this position the vessels would remain, hardly moving at all, until the slower ones caught up with them. It was extremely uncomfortable, especially in rough weather, as the luffing ships rolled almost on their beam ends for hours.[96]

Finally, as they neared the end of the long and tedious passage, the mariners and passengers approached the British coast with mixed feelings of dread of hostile ships which frequented those waters, and of relief at the thought that they should soon arrive with their cargoes safely in their home port.

## CHAPTER ELEVEN

# Defense of the Bay

THE seventeenth and eighteenth centuries witnessed a series of titanic struggles between the great maritime nations of Europe for colonial empires. India, Africa, America, and the oceans which lay between them became the theatre of war. In this era of global warfare—the first in history—Chesapeake Bay, in common with other portions of the coast of the New World, found neither solace nor protection in the fact that the broad Atlantic lay between America and Europe. On the contrary, the sea was the highway of imperial ambition rather than a barrier to it, and for that reason the inhabitants of Virginia and Maryland were in almost continual danger—or, at least, in almost continual apprehension—of a naval attack from the enemy, whether Spanish, Dutch, French, or pirates.[1]

In addition to possible enemy naval action in time of war—which actually occurred in 1667 and 1673—there was the constant menace of enemy privateers which hovered off the Capes and harassed the sea-lanes of Chesapeake shipping. On several occasions fears of a "privateer attempt" on the tobacco colonies were aroused.[2] Moreover, even the short intervals of peace in the late seventeenth and early eighteenth centuries brought no respite to the inhabitants of the Chesapeake colonies, for pirates swarmed the coast, and on occasion entered the Bay and plundered ships and plantations. At one time the threat became so serious and prolonged that the Council of Virginia declared the colony to be "as it were, in a continual state of war."[3]

The problem of defense was complicated by the fact that what the Virginians and Marylanders had to defend—their homes, plantations, slaves, and crops—were widely scattered over a large area, and the extraordinary system of natural waterways that

336

made possible the rapid growth of the tobacco colonies now bade fair to be their undoing. The rivers that admitted merchantmen several hundred miles inland also exposed the most remote tidewater plantations to enemy naval attack.[4]

Because of the configuration of the region, forts proved of little use as effective means of defending the country. The entrance to the Chesapeake was so wide that, as Sir William Berkeley wrote, an "enemy's ship may ride out of all possible danger of the greatest cannon in the world."[5] Forts might be built at certain strategic points near the mouths of rivers, but to build and garrison them on a proper scale was quite beyond the means of the colonists. Besides, as one official observed, "Land Fortifications cannot be made sufficient to defend this country from the danger of enemies" for two reasons: first, by means of landing parties they might easily "come upon the backs of those who are to defend the fortifications"; and secondly, the rivers are so broad the guns of the forts cannot command the channels.[6] Hence the colonial authorities reached the conclusion at an early date that the only means of protection was a naval force.[7]

Colonel Francis Moryson, President of the Virginia Council, petitioned the Privy Council in January, 1667, to appoint a frigate to ride in Chesapeake Bay for the protection of ships trading to Virginia.[8] Acceding to his request, the Lord High Admiral ordered a frigate dispatched to what was to be known for the remainder of the colonial period as the Virginia Station. The first ship on this station, the forty-six-gun *Elizabeth,* was in such poor condition that she had to be refitted shortly after her arrival in the Chesapeake. While this was underway, a Dutch squadron of five warships appeared off the mouth of the Bay. Upon learning the condition of the *Elizabeth* from the crew of a small boat they captured, the Dutch boldly entered the Bay flying English colors and, singing out their soundings in English, sailed up James River without exciting the suspicion of the twenty tobacco ships that rode at anchor in Hampton Roads. After taking the unprepared *Elizabeth,* they dropped down the James and captured all twenty of the merchantmen.

The governor, Sir William Berkeley, hastily assembled the militia and endeavored to impress several merchant vessels then in the upper James and York with a view to engaging the Dutch fleet in a naval battle. But the masters of the trading vessels shrank from exposing their poorly-armed ships to the fire of the Dutch men-of-war and procrastinated until the enemy squadron left the Bay. The colony though rich and populous was quite helpless during the five or six days the Dutch fleet rode in Virginia waters. Berkeley's four regiments of militia succeeded in preventing the enemy from sending landing parties ashore, but they could not protect the tobacco ships in the rivers. Neither could they strike back at the enemy in their midst.[9]

This incident impressed upon the English government the importance of stationing an adequate naval force in the Chesapeake, and on the outbreak of the third Dutch War in 1672, two men-of-war were dispatched to the Bay for its protection. While these vessels were at the mouth of James River, a squadron of nine Dutch warships entered the Capes in July, 1673, and anchored in Lynnhaven Roads. The English men-of-war at once prepared for battle by fitting several stout merchantmen with guns and gathering together a full complement of men.[10]

Meanwhile, unaware of the presence of the enemy, eight tobacco ships from Maryland sailed down the Bay and were about to fall into the hands of the Dutch. The situation called for quick action. The two English men-of-war accompanied by six armed merchantmen loosed their sails, weighed anchor, and ventured out of James River to engage the enemy. Four of the armed merchant vessels grounded and one turned back, but the remaining three ships continued and joined battle with six of the Dutch fleet. After three hours the English ships, hopelessly outnumbered and seriously battered, were obliged to retire. But by their extraordinary courage they succeeded in rescuing all but one of the

Maryland vessels. Utter catastrophe was averted, but even so the Dutch managed to capture one Maryland and nine Virginia tobacco ships—a serious blow to the trade and to the revenues of the Crown.[11]

Having learned the importance of naval power from the two Dutch attacks, Governor Sir William Berkeley was quick to use it to advantage in Bacon's Rebellion in 1676. He impressed four merchant ships and eighty mariners into royal service—some for as long as five months.[12] Bacon, also appreciating the value of a navy, assembled a small fleet consisting of an English ship, a bark, and a sloop, and dispatched it to patrol the Chesapeake and prevent Berkeley from attacking the western shore from his Accomack base. Berkeley was helpless as long as Bacon controlled the Bay. But the tide turned against Bacon when twenty-six loyalists under Colonel Philip Ludwell surprised the rebel ship in two small boats and, with assistance from the English mariners aboard, captured Bacon's flagship.[13] Thereafter Berkeley had the great advantage of naval supremacy in the Chesapeake, enabling him suddenly and effectively to attack any part of the western shore.[14]

After the suppression of the rebellion the need for an armed vessel continued to be felt. In 1681 Governor Lord Culpeper recommended the hiring of a small sloop of sixty or seventy tons and ten or twelve guns.[15] Apparently this was not done, for the next year when a pirate entered the Bay and plundered several houses on the banks of York River, the Council had to impress a vessel for the purpose of giving chase to the culprit.[16]

Finding makeshift defense unsatisfactory, the Virginia Council petitioned the home authorities in 1683 for a man-of-war ketch of forty men and twelve guns to supplement the small fort at Point Comfort, which had a garrison of sixty men, for although the fort was a safeguard against disorders ashore, it was ineffective in keeping the peace at sea against pirates. The latter could be done only by means of an armed guardship. To make the proposal more attractive to the Crown, they expressed their opinion that such a ship would also suppress the "frauds of dishonest traders" which cannot otherwise be prevented in this "well watered country."[17]

Meanwhile the need for a guardship became increasingly urgent. With the coast infested by pirates, a Virginian lamented that "our nakedness lays us open to their outrages."[18] To cope with the emergency Governor Lord Culpeper hastily fitted out the sloop *Katherine,* commanded by Roger Jones and manned by eighteen men. But, being too small to engage the pirates, she served only to give "timely notice" of their intended attacks.[19]

Later, Governor Lord Howard of Effingham urged the Lords of Trade in 1683 to send a frigate to Virginia for the defense of the coast and trade. The reasons for dispatching warships to other colonies, he said, prevail with double force here, because the revenue of Virginia "exceeds that of all the other plantations put together." The Commissioners of Customs, believing that a warship on the Virginia station would prove useful in checking irregular trade as well as in protecting shipping from enemy attacks, favored the proposal, and the Privy Council accordingly ordered a ketch fitted out at once and sent to Virginia "to give countenance to his Majesty's Authority . . . for securing his Majesty's Customes, and opposing the Pirates."[20]

After 1684 Chesapeake Bay normally enjoyed the protection of a royal warship. The first of these was the *Quaker* ketch. A few years later she was joined by the *Deptford* ketch. In the 1690's the *Dunbarton, Wolfe, Essex Prize,* and *Shoreham* successively occupied the Virginia station, as well as the advice boat *Swift.*[21] But until the arrival of the *Shoreham* in 1700 the Chesapeake did not have a guardship of adequate size and satisfactory condition. The earlier vessels were small and in some cases unseaworthy. The *Quaker* and the *Deptford* carried only forty men and ten or twelve guns. The latter capsized during a squall in the Potomac, drowning her captain and eight members of the crew.[22]

The *Dunbarton,* although large, proved to be so unseaworthy that she had to be dismantled and broken up in 1691. In the same year the *Wolfe* was aground for five days in Chesapeake Bay on what has ever since been known as Wolf Trap Shoal. In 1698 the advice boat *Swift* grounded near Currituck Inlet and was a total loss. The *Essex Prize* was so small that she was driven off by a pirate after an engagement in Lynnhaven Roads in 1699.[23]

The inadequacy of these vessels was appreciated by the home authorities, but the navy lacked sufficient large ships. As early as 1686 the King resolved to send a fifth-rate frigate of 30 guns and over a hundred men to Virginia instead of a ketch.[24] Although the *Wolfe* was a hired merchantman of about 400 tons, the *Dunbarton* and the *Essex Prize* were only sixth-rates, the former carrying 18 guns and 70 men, the latter 16 guns and 60 men.[25] These small frigates were scarcely more effective than the ketches that guarded the Chesapeake in the 1680's.

Moreover, the Chesapeake guardship was required to perform two entirely different kinds of duty, that of a man-of-war and of a revenue cutter. The smallest vessel of sufficient size to engage large pirate vessels, a fifth-rate frigate, was much too large to board merchantmen in the Bay to inspect their papers or to give chase to petty smugglers. By running up shallow creeks or by holding to shoal waters the illicit trader and small pirate could keep out of striking distance of a frigate and mock its authority.

By 1694 the English authorities had come to realize the nature of the problem, and in that year the Privy Council authorized the governor of Maryland to hire one or more small vessels to serve as revenue cutters. Later it was found more convenient to send a small vessel from England for the purpose.

Meanwhile King William's War centered attention upon the defense of the Chesapeake against a possible naval attack. The secretary of Maryland, Sir Thomas Lawrence, wrote in 1695 that being "open countries" with many rivers, Virginia and Maryland could be defended only by a naval force. He therefore proposed that a frigate of twenty or thirty guns be assigned to each colony together with a sloop or brigantine, a small fire ship, and a quantity of war materials.[26] Along with the many small vessels in the colonies, these would make a sizeable navy for the Chesapeake.

In accordance with Lawrence's suggestion H.M.S. *Essex Prize* was dispatched to Virginia in 1697 and H.M.S. *Swift* to Maryland.[27] It is not clear whether these vessels were selected to serve primarily as revenue cutters as the Treasury wished, or as naval protection as Lawrence wished. In all probability it was the former, for the *Essex Prize* proved hopelessly inadequate for naval defense, and when the *Swift* was wrecked, the vessel sent from England to replace her, H. M. Advice Boat *Messenger,* was described by the governor of Maryland as being serviceable in detecting "foul traders," but too small to be a defense for the coast.[28] The *Messenger* carried only four small guns, but six more were added on her arrival here.

In the short interval between King William's and Queen Anne's wars, 1698-1701, many unemployed privateersmen turned to piracy. In November, 1699, a London merchant told the Board of Trade that in the previous three months more than thirty vessels had been taken and plundered on the American coast.[29] Virginia suffered heavily because of the small size and poor condition of the Chesapeake guardship. In July, 1699, a pirate ship, the *Alexander,* boldly entered the Bay with the express purpose of taking the guardship *Essex Prize* and stripping her of rigging, canvas, and guns.

As the *Essex Prize* with 16 guns and 60 men was no match for the *Alexander* with 26 guns and 130 men, Captain Aldred of the royal frigate dared not risk an open engagement. In consequence, the *Essex Prize* rode safely in shoal water, leaving the pirate free to capture merchantmen at will. While in the Bay the *Alexander* took two trading vessels and plundered them of provisions, ammunition, and equipment.[30]

Governor Nicholson ordered the militia of nearby counties—Norfolk, Princess Anne, Elizabeth City, Accomack, and North-

*H.M. hired ship* WOLF, *1691 (from Ms journal of H.M.S.* WOLF *at British Museum).*

ampton—to be on the alert and to maintain lookouts.[31] But there was little else he could do. The defense of Virginia, like the security of its overseas commerce, depended entirely upon sea power. When that failed, as it did at this juncture, the colony was helpless and without striking power.

This incident brought home to the imperial government the seriousness of the situation. Soon afterwards the Admiralty sent H.M.S. *Shoreham,* a fifth-rate frigate of 28 guns and 120 men, to guard the Chesapeake. Now for the first time the tobacco colonies had reasonably adequate naval protection. When the pirate Louis Guittar entered the Bay in April, 1700, in his ship *La Paix,* it was a different story from that of the incident the year before. So soon as the news reached Captain Passenger of the *Shoreham,* he made sail and bore down on the pirate. A running engagement took place, during which the *Shoreham* badly battered *La Paix* and killed thirty-nine of her crew. Finally, for want of bowlines and braces with which to manipulate her shattered sails, *La Paix* grounded and struck her colors. Three of the hundred pirates that surrendered were hanged, and the rest were sent to England in chains.[32]

The triumph, however, was not an unqualified one. Guittar had taken, plundered, and destroyed five vessels in or near the Chesapeake before the news reached the *Shoreham,* then in one of the rivers. And in 1699 the pirate *Alexander* accomplished a good deal of plundering before the *Essex Prize* knew of its presence in the Bay. To reduce the danger of sudden attack in the future, Nicholson in 1699 instructed the commanders of the militia in Princess Anne, Norfolk, Elizabeth City, Northampton, and Accomack counties to establish lookouts along the coast and Bay until the end of September. One was to patrol Point Comfort, another Smith's Island, and others the seaboard of the Eastern Shore. West of the Capes, a lookout was posted between Cape Henry and Lynnhaven River, and south of them another from the Cape to Currituck Inlet.[33]

Even after the defeat of Guittar in 1700, Nicholson continued the system of lookouts, ordering the militia commanders of the five counties to provide one or more sufficient persons for the purpose. Upon sighting a ship off the coast, these lookouts were to observe her "course, motions and actions," and report to the nearest militia officer if they had any reason to suspect her of being a pirate vessel.[34]

To protect ships coming down the Bay to join convoy at Hampton Roads from pirates "skulking" about the Capes, for in order to clear Horseshoe Shoal a ship had to go near the Capes, Nicholson recommended York River as a more convenient and less dangerous place for vessels from the upper Bay to collect. And as a final expedient for lessening the danger, he authorized the purchase of a small sloop, the *Elizabeth,* to serve as a revenue cutter, a fire ship, and a tender for H.M.S. *Shoreham* and keep the guardship supplied with provisions so that it might cruise constantly about the Capes.[35]

In the spring of 1701 the Admiralty sent a fourth-rate frigate, the *Southampton,* to relieve the *Shoreham* in Virginia, and dispatched the advice boat *Eagle* to cruise in Maryland waters. The *Southampton* was a vessel of considerable force, mounting forty-eight guns and carrying 180 men. The *Eagle,* though mounting no more than ten six-pounders, carried as many as fifty men.[36] Yet even this powerful little squadron proved insufficient for the needs of the Chesapeake. The *Southampton* turned out to be in poor condition, requiring careening as early as February, 1702, and repairing again in March, and the *Eagle* was under the command of the governor of Maryland, who was loath to send her to the Virginia Capes every time the governor of Virginia requested it.[37]

With rumors of a new French war in the air, the Virginia House of Burgesses in September, 1701, resolved that a naval force was the best way to secure the country from an enemy by sea, but that the cost of maintaining it was "altogether inssupportable" by the colony.[38] In this view Colonel Quary concurred, writing in March, 1702, that fortifications in Virginia were useless and urging a naval squadron of force as the only practicable means of defending Chesapeake Bay.[39]

In December, 1702, the Lord High Admiral produced a plan for sending men-of-war to the several American plantations each spring as convoys and having them return in the fall in the same capacity. In this way they might serve as guardships during the time of greatest danger, from early April to late October.[40] The Board of Trade objected to the plan as it affected Virginia and Maryland on the grounds that New England and New York did not need guardships permanently stationed there, but the tobacco colonies because of their many large rivers and the Bay were continually exposed to privateers and pirates. They therefore urged that a ship of force be constantly stationed in Chesapeake Bay, even in the winter season.[41]

Although this change was accepted by the Admiralty, the matter was not permanently settled. Being obliged to remain in the salt water of the lower Bay during the summer months, the man-of-war on the Virginia station suffered damage from the "worm," and had to be sent to Great Britain or to New York to refit every few years.[42] On these occasions a relief vessel was sometimes sent, but the Admiralty sometimes neglected to have this done, being preoccupied with more pressing demands elsewhere. In any event, the colonial authorities found themselves in almost continual anxiety about the guardship on which they depended for the defense of the Chesapeake colonies.

Governor Seymour of Maryland wrote in June, 1707, that the Virginia Capes had been without a guardship for the past year.[43] As a result, the tobacco colonies were exposed to the insult of every "rascally pyrate or privateer" who chose to enter the Bay, burn ships, and plunder plantations. And Colonel Jennings of Virginia, after reporting the capture of six merchantmen off the Capes by a powerful French privateer, warned that its success

would encourage others to frequent Virginia waters. Two privateers, he asserted, could intercept all the trade to and from the
Chesapeake in the absence of a man-of-war on the station.
Whereas "the very name of Guardship," though it be a small one,
would prevent such bold attempts.[44]

To meet the emergency, both Seymour and Jennings wrote to
Governor Lord Cornbury of New York requesting him to send a
warship to protect the Chesapeake from the French privateer.
Acting with promptness, Cornbury dispatched H.M.S. *Triton's
Prize* two days after receiving the news. Seventy miles off the
Virginia Capes she retook one of the merchantmen the French
privateer captured four days before.[45]

Meanwhile the Admiralty received Jenning's letter appealing
for a guardship, but nothing was done until the following February, 1708, when H.M.S. *Garland,* commanded by Captain
Stewart, arrived in the Bay. Having sprung a mast in her passage
the *Garland* was partially disabled and unable to overtake a
Martinique privateer that was capturing vessels one after another
off the Virginia Capes.[46]

A few months after his arrival in the Chesapeake, Captain
Stewart received orders from the Admiralty to convoy the tobacco
fleet to England that summer. These orders were received with
sorrow in Virginia, because they meant that the further pursuit
of the privateer would be interrupted and an opportunity given
it to commit "further spoils" on the coast.[47]

French privateers from the West Indies increased their activity
along the North American coast during the years 1708-09. The
effective disposition of the Royal Navy drove them from British
waters to the less well defended coast of America, just at a time
when Chesapeake Bay was without a guardship for defense.[48]

Shortly after the *Garland* sailed for England, a privateer boldly
entered the Bay and pursued a merchantman from its moorings
at the mouth of York River.[49] Martinique privateers came in
ever-increasing numbers, taking almost every small vessel that

approached or left the Virginia Capes, a state of affairs that had not existed in so extreme a form since the last Anglo-Dutch War nearly forty years before.[50] Finally, in March, 1709, news reached Virginia that a group of French privateers planned a concerted attack on the colony in hopes of obtaining "good booty" in Negroes, plate, and other goods.[51]

In consternation, the Virginia Council, after considering every possible means of defense, petitioned the Admiralty to appoint a fourth-rate frigate to cruise in the Bay and a brigantine or sloop of eight or ten guns to pursue small privateers into shoal waters.[52] Recognizing the necessity of a naval force for the protection of Virginia and Maryland, the Admiralty, in spite of many urgent demands upon the Royal Navy, again appointed the *Garland* to be the Chesapeake guardship and authorized the purchase of a sloop in New England to assist her.[53]

Meanwhile Virginia made all sorts of preparations to repel the expected privateer attempt upon the colony. The militia was made ready, ammunition distributed, lookouts posted, large guns set up to alarm the country upon the appearance of the dreaded privateer fleet, and a brigantine of ten guns and eighty men hired and fitted out.[54] In all, the colonial authorities spent £800 to put the colony in a state of preparedness.[55]

These feverish efforts were apparently not in vain. Jennings wrote the Board of Trade in June, 1709, that the preparation proved useful "in frighting the enemy" from attacking Virginia. At this time enemy privateers made frequent raids on towns on the Delaware and on Currituck Inlet in North Carolina, but carefully avoided Chesapeake Bay.[56]

But though there were no raids on the Virginia coast, small enemy privateers occasionally hovered off the Capes awaiting an opportunity to take small merchant vessels. A few months after the *Garland* had arrived in the Chesapeake and begun her cruising in the lower Bay and near the Capes, Jennings wrote the Board of Trade that the warship was of "too great bulk" to pursue such privateers into shoal waters. He expressed his belief that if the sloop which the Admiralty had ordered to be bought for the Virginia station were in Chesapeake Bay not a single enemy privateer could escape.[57]

Just as the prospect was beginning to look bright for the first time since the outbreak of Queen Anne's War, Virginia received a heavy blow. The *Garland,* while cruising off the coast on November 29, 1709, was wrecked on a sandbar just south of Currituck Inlet. The officers and all except fifteen of the men were saved and a great part of the rigging and stores escaped damage, but as the season of the year was too far advanced, salvage operations had to be postponed until the spring. Meanwhile the tobacco colonies, without adequate protection, lay open to enemy depredations.[58]

In reply to urgent appeals from Jennings, the Admiralty in April, 1710, ordered H.M.S. *Triton's Prize,* a sixth-rate man-of-war, to the Virginia station. Whether she reached the Chesapeake that spring is not known, but by June, 1710, H.M.S. *Enterprize* was on the Virginia station.[59] Being in poor condition, she proved of little use as she had to be sent to New York to refit, and her departure was the signal for the return of a swarm of French privateers.[60]

In May a privateer sloop anchored in Lynnhaven Roads and sent a landing party ashore where they plundered several houses and carried off one inhabitant and several slaves. The next day the privateer engaged the *James* of Plymouth and after a two-hour fight captured her. About the same time another privateer took the *William and Mary* of London and the *Lark* of Falmouth, plundered the latter of several hundred pounds worth of goods and then burned her. Still another captured a Bermuda sloop bound to Chesapeake Bay, and another took two North Carolina sloops. Moreover, the coastal lookouts reported they saw two other vessels burnt at sea.

On top of this, news reached Virginia that a thirty-gun Martinique privateer was headed for the Chesapeake. In August the newly-arrived governor of Virginia, Alexander Spotswood, wrote that since the departure of the *Enterprize* for New York, enemy privateers had taken a great many vessels and kept the inhabitants of the maritime counties "in continual alarms."[61]

Taking an active interest in the problem of defense, Spotswood urged the Board of Trade to establish a victualling station and facilities for refitting at Point Comfort to obviate the necessity of guardships leaving the Chesapeake so frequently. In connection with this, he proposed to build a fort on Point Comfort, the guns of which might protect merchantmen from pirates and privateers, as well as the guardship while it was being careened. Pointing out that the want of sufficient guardships made illicit trade possible and that a thriving trade was being carried on to Curacao and St. Thomas, he requested not only a powerful man-of-war but also a revenue cutter or customs sloop to be stationed in the lower district of James River from which place illicit trade was principally carried on.[62]

Even before Spotswood's proposals reached England, the Admiralty dispatched H.M.S. *Triton's Prize* to the Virginia station, and when Spotswood's letter arived, the Board of Trade readily acceded to his plan for the detection and suppression of smuggling.[63] By the spring of 1711 when H.M.S. *Enterprize* was back on her station at the mouth of the Bay, her commander, Captain Smith, was particularly active in pursuing privateers. In June he captured a French privateer of eighty-eight men. Spotswood sent the prisoners to England rather than to the French West Indies under a flag of truce, in order to avoid all suspicion of an "unlawful correspondence" with the enemy.[64]

Alarmed during the summer of 1711 by the rumor of an impending French naval attack on Virginia, Spotswood set to work to put the colony in a "posture of defense." Finding the militia in poor condition, wholly destitute of ammunition, and not a single piece of mounted ordnance in all Virginia, he wrote to London pleading for arms and powder, adding that without them the colony could not sustain an attack of the enemy. When the munitions finally came as a gift from Queen Anne, Spotswood persuaded the Assembly to authorize the erection of a magazine in Williamsburg to accommodate them,[65] which is the historic building still to be seen on Market Square.

He also "made shift" to build a fort at Point Comfort and erect batteries at the mouths of the principal rivers in the colony. In all, he mounted some seventy guns for the protection of shipping. And for the purpose of keeping watch and spreading alarm, he commissioned a small spyboat, the *Jenny and Mary,* to sail every morning to the Capes, return every night to Point Comfort, and anchor under the guns of the fort. Her commander, Joseph Bannister, received orders to spread the alarm upon sighting the dreaded French squadron either by returning to the fort to report, or, if time did not permit, by hoisting an ensign or jack at the topmast head as soon as it could be seen from the shore and by continuous firing of guns until the country appeared to have taken alarm.[66]

Although the expected attack did not occur, the preparations continued for several months. Finally, in February, 1712, the Virginia Assembly felt secure enough to refuse to pay the cost of maintaining the spyboat even though everyone conceded that it was frugally managed.[67]

Oddly enough, Spotswood gave permission to the two guardships on the Virginia station to leave the Chesapeake in the winter of 1711-12 to convoy a fleet of merchant vessels to Barbados, and to join the West India Squadron of the Royal Navy. Why he did so while the French attack was still expected is a matter of conjecture. Perhaps he had confidence in his forts as adequate means of defending the colony. In any event, the West India Squadron fell in with a fleet of seventeen sail of French merchantmen bound for Martinique, taking twelve of them including the man-of-war that convoyed them. The *Enterprize* of the Virginia station had the distinction of capturing the French warship.[68]

*Model of a sixth-rate frigate of the 1745 establishment (from* THE MARINERS' MIRROR, *Vol. 18, 1932, plate XI).*

In the spring of 1712 H.M.S. *Severn,* while convoying the Virginia fleet, took a powerful French privateer of 180 men that had infested the mouth of the Chesapeake for some time. Soon afterwards Queen Anne's War ended, but not the threat to the Virginia coast, for many unemployed privateersmen now turned to piracy, so that even the twenty-gun frigate sent to Virginia in June, 1713, proved inadequate.[69] During the summer months a single pirate off the Capes took six of the best ships in the trade. Fortunately, the pirate and its prizes were captured by H.M.S. *Shoreham,* but several others continued to "skulk" about the mouth of the Bay, awaiting their chance.

The losses as a result of piracy became so considerable that a group of British merchants trading to Virginia and Maryland petitioned the Privy Council for more protection, setting forth that there was only a small guardship of 18 guns in the Chesapeake. As a result, H.M.S. *Valeur* arrived in the Bay by June, 1715.[70]

The Peace of Utrecht in 1713 brought an end to hostilities in Europe, but not in America. Relations between Great Britain and Spain continued to be strained, and for seven years after the peace the Spanish in the West Indies carried on a desultory, undeclared war against British commerce.[71] Spanish colonial governors continued to issue letters of marque to privateers, and Spanish courts to condemn British vessels as prizes. British ships that ventured into Spanish ports were generally seized on some trifling pretext.[72] Colonial vessels taken by *guarda-costas* many leagues beyond Spanish territorial waters were condemned without regard to international law.[73] Spanish privateers infested the American coast and as late as 1720 one sailed into Chesapeake Bay and took several prizes. By this time a treaty of peace had been concluded between the two countries, and Spotswood succeeded in forcing the Spanish authorities to restore these vessels to their owners,[74] but in 1721 Spotswood estimated that Spanish depredations on the Virginia coast had cost the colonial government nearly £1,000.

During the same years piracy reached unprecedented heights. So many former privateersmen took up that profession that lawful trade to the West Indies was nearly paralyzed.[75] To provide for the security of Virginia vessels trading to the West Indies, Spotswood in 1716 commissioned the privateer *Virgin,* Captain Harry Beverley, to sail to the Bahamas, one of the principal nests of pirates, to make inquiries as to their strength and designs.[76] But the *Virgin* fell a victim to a Spanish man-of-war which, in violation of international law, carried her into Puerto Rico where she was condemned as a prize.[77]

To cope with the threat of piracy, the Royal Navy reinforced its West India Squadron, and the King offered amnesty to all pirates who would surrender before a certain date and promise to mend their ways. Although many were tempted to do so at first, their ardor cooled when it became apparent that they would be expected to relinquish all the wealth they had accumulated through their piratical exploits. Of the few who took advantage of royal amnesty, most subsequently reverted to piracy after giving honest pursuits a brief trial.[78] The efforts of the home government to suppress the plague of pirates during these years failed hopelessly. The colonies, therefore, were obliged to defend themselves.

Looking with suspicion upon the nest of pirates in the Bahamas as a possible base for future attacks on Chesapeake shipping, Spotswood asked the Admiralty for an additional guardship in 1716.[79] His request, however, was denied, for in May, 1717, he reminded the Board of Trade of his predictions the previous year and reported that the number of pirates had greatly increased. To reduce them now, he said, would require "no inconsiderable force." When the *Shoreham* which had just arrived to serve as the Virginia guardship was ordered to return to England, he begged that she be left in the Chesapeake even though her condition was so poor that she could not undertake a long cruise in pursuit of pirates.[80]

In the spring of 1717 several merchantmen were taken by pirates off the Virginia Capes, perhaps before the arrival of the

354

*Shoreham.*[81] In the summer of 1718, however, two warships, the *Pearle* and the *Lyme*, were in Virginia waters. It was men from these ships that Lieutenant Maynard of the *Pearle* led on the famous expedition from the Bay to Ocracoke Inlet, North Carolina, in November, 1718, in which he defeated and killed the notorious pirate "Blackbeard," and brought back in irons to Williamsburg those of his men who survived the engagement.[82] The presence of these two warships afforded the Chesapeake temporary protection, for although there were still some pirates on the coast, the guardships prevented their taking any vessels entering or leaving Chesapeake Bay.[83]

But this satisfactory state of affairs did not last long. During the winter of 1719-20 when the Bay was again inadequately protected, several vessels bound to Virginia were taken and plundered by pirates.[84] In the same year, as we have seen, a Spanish privateer illegally entered the Chesapeake and took several prizes.[85] Upon his return from England in 1720, William Byrd II wrote the Earl of Orrery that pirates "swarm in this part of the World," at least seventy sail haunting the American coast,[86] and Robert Carter, complaining of the plague of pirates and privateers, considered it a "most egregious shame" that so fine a colony should be exposed to depredation by every "picayune rogue."[87] He urged a London merchant to stir up his colleagues into a concerted clamor to procure more naval protection for Chesapeake Bay.

The next year Carter repeated his lamentation and Spotswood made another plea for guardships. Telling of the pirate Roberts whose ship mounted 50 guns and carried 240 men and who was reported to be planning an attack on Virginia, Spotswood asserted that not one of the guardships on the American coast was powerful enough to encounter it. A forty- or fifty-gun ship, in his opinion, was absolutely necessary to convoy merchant ships to sea, and a smaller vessel such as a sloop or brigantine, to pursue "little pickeroons" in shoal waters.[88]

As on previous occasions, Spotswood sought to meet the emergency by hastily erecting batteries at strategic points for the protection of anchorages. He mounted some fifty-four guns at the mouths of the James, York, and Rappahannock in 1721, and the next spring assured the Board of Trade that the colony was secured against attacks by pirates and other enemies on its "sea frontiers."[39]

Roberts' expected attack on the colony did not occur, and after 1720 pirates became increasingly rare. Though they occasionally hovered off the Capes, their prizes were few. Piracy was on the wane. Moreover, merchant vessels sometimes carried sufficient guns to be able to ward off attacks. The ship in which William Byrd II crossed to Virginia, he wrote in 1723, "has so much the ayr of a man of War, that no modest Pyrate will venture to attaque her."[90] And it became increasingly common for merchantmen to capture pirate vessels—though doubtless only "modest" ones.[91]

In consequence of Spotswood's activity in suppressing piracy by putting the colony in a state of defense, by securing more naval protection, and by dispatching the expedition that exterminated Blackbeard and his gang, Virginia acquired a bad reputation with pirates. Indeed, when Roberts planned his attack on the colony in 1721, he was reported to have said that it was to avenge the pirates executed there.[92] When Spotswood wished to return to England in 1724 he was afraid to cross the ocean for fear of reprisals, for many pirates had sworn to wreak vengeance upon him for cutting off the arch-pirate, Blackbeard, and for making so many "of their fraternity to swing in the open air of Virginia."[93]

The pirate John Vidal plundered several vessels off the coast in 1727, but with his apprehension and trial the chapter of Chesapeake piracy ended. Thereafter, the only cases of piracy were petty ones, the seizure of small boats within the Bay by escaped slaves or outlaws, that technically are piracy, yet that bear little resemblance to the kind of activity associated with that word at the end of the seventeenth and early in the eighteenth centuries.[94]

Although pirates disappeared from Chesapeake maritime annals, privateers remained and continued to play an important part in its history. The cessation of armed conflict with Spain in 1720 proved premature, for no permanent solution of the disagreements between that country and Great Britain was found. From that time until the Treaty of Seville in 1730, Spanish vessels commissioned as privateers continued to prey on British shipping. Although West Indian waters were the principal theatre of their depredations, they occasionally came as far north as Chesapeake Bay. In 1724 a Spanish vessel took a New England brigantine, the *Prudent Hannah*, within two leagues of Cape Charles,[95] and in 1727 Governor Gooch of Virginia wrote the Duke of Newcastle that two privateers from Havana recently took seven vessels within forty leagues of the Virginia coast.[96]

By 1730 these attacks had increased to such an extent that Gooch thought it wise to rehabilitate the batteries that Spotswood erected in 1721 in anticipation of an "attempt" on the colony by the pirate Roberts. After ten years of neglect, these batteries were in a sad state of dilapidation. The wooden platforms that supported the cannons had rotted away in the damp Virginia climate. The battery on James River was entirely gone, its guns lying in the sand on the beach. Gooch therefore concluded that it was essential to rebuild these forts of more durable material, but admitted that the cost of doing so and of maintaining sufficient garrisons would be quite beyond the financial abilities of the colony.[97]

The next year Gooch urged the British government to authorize the erection of a fort at the mouth of James River, and requested the Board of Ordnance to send out a dozen thirty-six-pounders, four eighteen-pounders, carriages, and a quantity of shot.[98] But his efforts proved unnecessary. The Treaty of Seville in 1730 put an end to the undeclared war with Spain and ushered in a decade of unprecedented peace for the Chesapeake country. For the first time in three-quarters of a century the Chesapeake required no guardship, the tobacco fleet needed no convoy, and Virginia and Maryland had no fear of attack.

After the peaceful decade of the 1730's, King George's War must have seemed even more destructive than it really was. As early as the spring of 1741, Spanish privateers once more swarmed on the Virginia coast and greatly harassed Chesapeake merchantmen.[99] The following spring a privateer from Havana appeared off the Capes and took seven vessels in less than three weeks.[100]

With the outbreak of war, naval protection was again required by the tobacco colonies. In 1742 H.M.S. *Hector,* commanded by Sir Yelverton Peyton, Bart., appeared on the Virginia station.[101] The next year H.M.S. *Hastings,* under the command of Lord Banff, served as the guardship for the Chesapeake. The latter in its passage to Virginia took the French vessel *Pallarcha,* richly laden with a cargo valued at £36,000, and, later, off the Virginia coast, a Spanish privateer of 80 tons, 70 men, ten carriage guns and twenty-four swivels.[102]

Realizing like Spotswood how unreliable a naval force was, Gooch set to work to rehabilitate the batteries at the mouths of the principal rivers, and having unbounded faith in forts as a means of defending the Chesapeake, he built a brick fort in 1742 at Point Comfort. Called Fort George, this substantial building mounted twenty-two guns.[103]

In the spring of 1745 while the Chesapeake was without a guardship, a report circulated that a squadron of seven French men-of-war had arrived at Martinique, two of 80 guns, two of 70, two of 60, and one of 36, along with twenty-eight transports and a land force of upwards of three hundred men.[104] As no one knew where the "Fury of the French" would fall but all knew that no single colony was strong enough to repel such a powerful force, the rumor struck terror into the hearts of the English colonists in the Chesapeake region and elsewhere along the Atlantic coast.

Doing what he could to prepare a defense, Gooch ordered the militia kept in readiness and posted constant lookouts along the seacoast. The inhabitants of exposed stretches of coast he urged to drive their cattle away so that in the event of an invasion, the enemy would not be too easily supplied with provisions. And in view of the absence of a guardship on the Virginia station, Gooch hired, armed, and fitted out a Bermuda sloop to serve as a "Guard la Coast." The French invasion did not materialize, but enemy privateers came in increasing numbers to harass Chesapeake shipping.

Early in 1745 the *Cunliffe*, Captain John Pritchard, sailed out of the Bay homeward bound for Liverpool. Nine leagues north of Cape Clear, she made out two sail dead ahead, a large snow and a deeply laden ship, presumably a privateer and her prize. At a quarter past eight the snow "loos'd her fore and main Top-sails, haul'd up her main Sail, hoisted a French Jack upon her Ensign Staff," and bore down on the English merchantman. Pritchard cleared the decks for action and displayed British colors. Then after a running engagement until noon, the *Cunliffe* "turned one Reef" of her topsails to make the privateer bear harder. This caused the enemy snow to ship so much water that she was obliged to close her gun ports.

About 2:00 P.M. Captain Pritchard was struck in the head by a musket ball as he was leaning over the side of the quarter deck "Hero like," to see if the guns were pointed "so as to do Execution." Then, according to the account, shot flew as thick as hail. But the ship's company, notwithstanding their small number and the miserable condition of their vessel, were resolved "to get clear or die." They ran up a bloody flag at the mainmast truck to show that they would neither give nor receive quarter, and, at the same time, gave three loud huzzahs. Continuing the chase until 5:00 P.M., the French privateer eventually tired of the pursuit and left. As the *Cunliffe* was heavily laden and in poor condition, manned by only thirty-eight men and boys, whereas the privateer mounted twenty carriage-guns besides swivels, and carried two hundred men, the *Maryland Gazette,* swelling with national pride, gave opinion that "French Superiority in Number is in no wise adequate to true English Courage."[105]

359

The years 1745-48 proved to be particularly trying ones for the tobacco colonies. Dozens of Virginia and Maryland vessels as well as British ships trading to the Chesapeake fell a prey to enemy privateers operating from continental or West Indian ports. Havoc was wrought in the tobacco trade, freight became extremely scarce and freight rates ruinous. Chesapeake Bay was so inadequately protected that enemy privateers often entered the Bay and plundered ships in the very heart of the country.

In 1745 five French privateers cruised off the coast, taking prizes at will, and capturing at least one ship within the Virginia Capes.[106] In 1748, by far the darkest year in Chesapeake maritime annals since the last Dutch War, a sloop at anchor off the mouth of York River was carried off by a privateer,[107] and the *Maryland Gazette* reported nine vessels captured in the Bay or off the Capes. One of the latter, a Norfolk schooner, was taken and plundered within sight of the fort at Point Comfort. A snow and a sloop were captured "back of the Horse-Shoe." The two men-of-war then on the Virginia station, H.M.S. *Looe* and *Hector,* cruised constantly—almost frantically—in an attempt to cope with the swarm of privateers. Finally, the colonial authorities fitted out and armed a small vessel to assist the warships in the hope of clearing the Bay and coast of the "Pests of Trade" that swarmed in a greater degree than had ever before been known in the tobacco colonies.[108]

The activity of these war vessels helped to stem the tide. The *Looe* took a Spanish privateer of a hundred and fifty men, as well as a smaller vessel. Before long there were so many captured French and Spanish privateersmen in Virginia that Gooch had to hire a vessel, the *Mermaid,* to serve as a cartel. She took them to Havana under a flag of truce and exchanged them for British prisoners of war.[109] By June the *Looe* had captured another Spanish privateer, after which enemy depredations declined to such an extent that the *Maryland Gazette* considered the coast clear.[110] Shortly afterwards the *Hector* in company with the sloop *Otter* arrived in Hampton Roads with six prizes they had taken.[111] At this juncture King George's War came to an end, and the Chesapeake colonies returned to peaceful pursuits for another six years.

Not long after the end of the war a violent storm in the Bay wrecked Fort George at Point Comfort. Colonel Thomas Lee, then acting governor, on visiting the site found the fort surprisingly shattered and laid in ruins, all the guns dismounted and "Honey-coomb'd." As for the other batteries in the colony, they were quite out of repair, their guns almost all unfit for use.[112] Lee proposed turning Fort George into a battery to save the cost of rebuilding the fort. He also proposed a combined fort and lighthouse to be built at Cape Henry, which, he said, would serve as protection for both Virginia and Maryland, whereas a fort at Point Comfort could protect only James River. As the main channel between the Capes passed within pistol shot of Cape Henry, a battery of twenty-four-pounders there would make it unsafe for the larger enemy privateers to enter the Bay, or, if they should do so, merchantmen could anchor safely within range of its guns.

Nothing came of Lee's proposal. When Governor Dinwiddie gave an account of the state of the colony in 1755, he said that there were no forts in the dominion. Fort George, he added, having been built on a sandy foundation was destroyed by the "Sea and Weather." Five years after its destruction nothing had been done to rebuild it. The two small batteries at Yorktown and Gloucester Point, although useful to protect merchant vessels in the York River, were of little value as defense against an enemy with force enough to attack them from the land. Indeed, a powerful enemy ship might run up the river and demolish them both with ease. Consequently, Dinwiddie concluded that without British naval vessels in time of war, Virginia would be subject to "the Insults" of small privateers.[113]

Upon the outbreak of the French and Indian War, the Chesapeake colonies were once more faced with the prospect of enemy invasion. Dinwiddie reminded the London authorities in 1755 that although he had been very solicitous in putting Virginia in a defensive position in case of an invasion by sea, the absence of fortifications made it necessary for the colony to depend on warships sent them from England for their protection.[114]

In this war even more than in previous ones, the British government failed to provide adequate naval protection for the Chesapeake. By January, 1757, the Admiralty had sent nothing more than a twenty-gun frigate to the Virginia station.[115] A group of the most prominent London tobacco merchants, petitioning the King to take more care of their trade, asserted that they apprehended the most fatal consequences to themselves as well as to the "most Essential Trade" of the kingdom unless a larger naval squadron were sent to the Chesapeake. The populous northern colonies, they complained, received the support of royal troops, while the southern colonies, though "no less interesting" to Great Britain, remained defenseless both by sea and land against the French. They therefore implored more protection for the tobacco colonies in order to defeat the objective of the French to bring about the destruction of the British nation through the conquest of the American colonies.[116]

The colonists made similar pleas. Dinwiddie wrote a letter to the Board of Trade and another to the Admiralty in January, 1757, the formal language of which failed to disguise his outraged feelings. Reminding them that the great Bay of Chesapeake bordered on both Virginia and Maryland and that they were open countries without any fortifications to repel enemy attack, he estimated their annual exports to amount to at least 100,000 hogsheads of tobacco beside large quantities of grain, pork, and other produce. He then politely intimated that they could scarcely disagree that such valuable colonies require and deserve a much better protection than a twenty-gun ship.[117]

A month later, a group of Bristol merchants trading to the Chesapeake also petitioned the King to provide more naval protection for Virginia and Maryland against the incursions and attempts which may be made upon them by "such Implacable Enemies" as the French and Spaniards.[118] But in spite of these pleas, the Admiralty did not provide the protection requested. Toward the end of the war a French naval squadron cruising off the Virginia coast, although it did not attack the colony, played havoc with the tobacco trade, taking so many ships that by August, 1761, the Glasgow underwriters refused altogether to insure vessels bound to the Chesapeake.[119] Also humiliating to the Old Dominion was the capture and plundering of the schooner *Peggy* of Hampton, while crossing the Bay bound to Oxford on the Eastern Shore of Maryland in August, 1761, by a French privateer of eight carriage and twelve swivel guns.[120]

It is apparent that at no time did the Chesapeake receive what might be called sufficient naval protection. This rich seat of commerce was left exposed to devastating attacks from enemy warships, privateers, and pirates. Indeed, it was one of the weakest spots in the armor of the British Empire, but the entire blame for the deficiency cannot be laid at the door of the imperial authorities. The British Empire was far-flung and its enemies powerful upon the sea. The paramount function of the Royal Navy was to defend the British Isles from invasion and to protect the vital sea-lanes of British commerce from enemy depredations. These objectives were achieved, but they strained the resources of the Admiralty to the utmost.

Moreover, it was not unreasonable for the imperial authorities to expect the colonies to prepare their own defense in time of war. In the case of Virginia and Maryland, however, little was done— or could be done. The configuration of the Chesapeake and the scarcity of towns made defense difficult if not impossible except by means of a substantial naval force, and even the wealthy and populous tobacco colonies proved unable to bear the cost of a provincial navy sufficient to cope with an attacking squadron of enemy men-of-war, the constant threat of which cast a dark shadow over the lives of the Chesapeake colonists during most of the years of the colonial period.

## CHAPTER TWELVE

# Prizes and Privateers

ALTHOUGH possessed of no other navy than the royal warships assigned to the purely defensive task of convoying the tobacco fleet and protecting Chesapeake Bay, by means of private armed vessels Virginia and Maryland shared in the offensive against the French and Spanish on the high seas during the four Anglo-French wars from 1689 to 1763. These vessels, owned and operated by private capital, were officially commissioned by the colonial governors in their capacity as vice-admirals of their respective colonies to make war, capture, and destroy vessels belonging to the subjects of princes at war with Great Britain.

Private armed vessels, often called privateers (presumably a combination of "private" and "volunteer") or "letters of marque" (from their commissions) were issued commissions called "letters of marque and reprisal." Originally this commission authorized them to recover by means of depredations on enemy vessels a sum equal to the amount lost by or owed to the recipient by a subject or citizen of the enemy country. Later they were issued upon request to any vessel willing to prey upon enemy shipping.

Privateers played an important part in the wars of the eighteenth century; they augmented the number of warships of a nation without costing the treasury a penny. Later there was a distinction between a privateer and a letter of marque, the former being a private armed vessel whose main business was plunder, the latter primarily a trading vessel armed to resist attack and authorized to capture enemy vessels encountered *en route*. Privateers made "cruises," while letters of marque made "voyages." The similarity between privateering and piracy was recognized by King James I, who called the former *"splendidum furtum."*[1]

The nature of the privateer's activities, revolving as they did around plundering, was hardly distinguishable in practice from piracy, yet legally there was a world of difference. Pirates were universally condemned as cruel and lawless enemies of mankind and, if caught, were liable to be hanged. Privateersmen, on the other hand, were engaged in a legal—though no less destructive— occupation, acting in the name of the King, and, if captured, entitled to the privileges accorded by the law of nations to prisoners of war.

As early as 1660 Virginia enacted legislation authorizing the governor and Council to act as a court of admiralty with jurisdiction over all things pertaining to seafaring including the "causes and actions of reprisalls, of letters of marque." However, there was little privateering in Virginia-owned vessels during the seventeenth century. In answer to some enquiries from the Lords of Trade and Plantations, Governor Sir William Berkeley asserted in 1671 that in the preceding twenty-eight years not one prize had been brought into Virginia, for which reason he thought it unnecessary to have a special court of admiralty.[2] The Lord Proprietor of Maryland, by virtue of the Charter of 1632, enjoyed the dignity of being High Admiral of Maryland with authority to hold admiralty courts in his American palatinate. And although there is evidence that he exercised this right and commissioned a provincial admiral in Maryland, here as in Virginia few prizes were brought in for disposition during the seventeenth century.[3]

Captain John Hurle, master of the ship *Providence* of London, after capturing a French vessel at sea in 1694, brought her into Maryland waters where he petitioned that a court of admiralty be appointed to try the vessel and its cargo of Martinique sugar, gold dust, silver, and "Cocoe Nuts." From the large number of documents relating to the *Providence's* prize, it is clear that the trial and condemnation of a captured enemy ship was something of a novelty in Maryland.

At first there was some doubt about the extent of Governor Nicholson's authority as vice-admiral. The commission of the former governor and that of Nicholson were diligently translated from Latin into English and critically examined by the Council. The Attorney General, George Plater, rendered a legal opinion setting aside the first trial as faulty, whereupon a second court was erected for the trial of the prize.

From the proceeds of the prize a fifth part was deducted for the King, but when the mariners aboard the *Providence* petitioned for their share of the remaining four-fifths, the Council confessed that it had no idea what part of the prize money belonged to them. To be on the safe side, the Council referred the matter to the High Court of Admiralty in England.[4]

While bound to Virginia in 1697 H.M.S. *Harwich* took the French flyboat *St. Ignace* of Bayonne, carried her into James River, and requested a speedy proceeding for condemnation. Apparently the admiralty court established in 1660 had been forgotten, for the Council informed the governor that no admiralty court had ever been erected in the colony. On the advice of the Council, the governor established a new one under the seal of the colony and appointed a judge, register, and marshal. This court was not a permanent one; created specifically to try the *St. Ignace*, its duration was limited by the commission to six days.[5]

Before 1697 no colonial vice-admiralty courts, properly so-called, existed because none of the courts handling admiralty cases in the colonies held commissions from the High Court of Admiralty in England, and without that authority their actions were of doubtful validity. This chaotic state of affairs was rectified by the parliamentary act of 1696 which provided for the creation of regular courts of vice-admiralty in the colonies. After 1697, when the first of these was set up, these courts became a regular feature of colonial life.[6]

With the outbreak of Queen Anne's War in 1702 the question of disposing of prizes again came to the fore. By that time regularly-established courts existed for the purpose, but the law pertaining to prizes was complicated and not well understood in colonial courts. Indeed, prize jurisdiction was the subject of dispute in England, resulting in confusion until it was permanently settled by statutory authority in 1708. Meanwhile, although Virginia and Maryland issued few letters of marque, a royal warship or an English merchantman brought an occasional prize into those colonies.[7]

H.M.S. *Oxford,* commanded by Captain Josiah Moore, took a French prize in the West Indies in 1703 and brought it into Maryland where it was condemned in the Court of Vice-Admiralty. As the *Oxford* was a royal ship, one half of the value of the prize vessel and cargo—worth £6,000—belonged to the Queen. Even this late the condemnation of a prize in Maryland was apparently unforeseen, for the Commissioners of the Prize Office in England had not appointed anyone in the colony to take care of the Queen's share. In the absence of an authorized prize officer, George Plater, then Receiver of Royal Revenues in the District of Patuxent, took the goods into custody and sold them at auction in behalf of her majesty.[8]

At first the procedure of the colonial courts of vice-admiralty, particularly with respect to the disposition of prizes, caused some dissatisfaction in England. In 1696 the officials of the Prize Office commissioned Peter Jennings to investigate concealments or embezzlements of prizes since 1689 in Maryland and other colonies.[9] In 1704 the Board of Trade complained to Governor Seymour of Maryland about irregularities in the manner of granting commissions to privateers, sending him for his guidance copies of commissions and instructions issued in England.[10] The same year the Secretary of State, Sir Charles Hedges, complained to the governor of Virginia about irregularities in the disposition of prizes, urged him to obey the instructions from the Lord High Admiral, and instructed him to appoint officers to take charge of prizes.[11]

A thrilling capture that was much talked about in Maryland took place in 1704 and greatly stimulated colonial interest in privateering. Richard Johnson, master and part owner of the brigantine *Betty* of Maryland, was taken by the French and carried to Martinique. Later, aboard the French barque *L'Ortolan,* 70 tons, bound to France, Johnson was roused by taunts that Englishmen did not know how to fight, and continually threatened by the French captain, Pierre Rolleau, who habitually carried a loaded pistol. Finally, with the assistance of another prisoner-of-war, an English boy, Johnson rose in the night, threw Rolleau overboard, surprised the crew, and brought the vessel into Chesapeake Bay.

A colonial court straightway condemned *L'Ortolan* together with her cargo of 150 hogsheads of brown sugar, 36 of white, and a "parcell" of ginger as a prize. But, as the capture had been made without letters of marque and reprisal, Governor Seymour admitted that he was "a little in the dark" as to who was rightly entitled to the prize. The court declared the prize to be a perquisite of the Lord High Admiral, but referred the matter to the English authorities for final disposition. In view of the fact that the heroic Johnson lost £3,500 by the capture of his brigantine, that *L'Ortolan* and her cargo amounted to no more than £1,500, and that Johnson's exploit "Redounds so much to the Honour of the English Nation," Queen Anne graciously bestowed the prize upon Johnson, reserving only the Lord High Admiral's customary tenth.[12]

The next year Edward Ratchdale, master of the 400-ton Maryland-built *Elizabeth* of Liverpool, captured the *François* of Rochelle, bringing her into Maryland where she was condemned in the Court of Vice-Admiralty.[13] Early in 1706 H.M.S. *Woolwich,* commanded by Captain Robert Thompson, brought to Virginia a French prize that had sprung a leak. As the cargo was in danger of being seriously damaged by water in the hold, Captain Thompson requested prompt legal action. Accordingly, Governor Nott commissioned a Court of Vice-Admiralty without delay and appointed Nathaniel Harrison to be acting prize agent.[14]

In 1708 H.M.S. *Lowestoffe,* a 32-gun fifth-rate frigate commanded by Captain Fane, sent a French prize into Virginia

*Navy Agents Refusing to Pay Prize Money (from drawing by Thomas Rowlandson in The Society of Nautical Research, Annual Report, 1935).*

manned by a prize crew. The French master and one of his men
who were detained in order to give evidence in the condemnation
proceedings had to be subsisted ashore, as provisions aboard the
prize were exhausted. In this connection the question arose as
to who should receive the bill for their accommodations. The
prize agent refused to pay it, so Captain Richard Dennis, acting
in behalf of Captain Fane, carried the matter to the Council
obtaining a decision that the cost of accommodations should be
defrayed out of the proceeds of the prize.[15]

The widespread state of confusion concerning the disposal of
prizes in the colonies led in 1708 to the enactment by Parliament
of a law for the encouragement of trade to America, which laid
down rules governing prize captures. Thereafter the disposition of
prizes rested on a strictly legal basis. But colonial privateering
continued to be discouraged because of the cupidity of the commissioners for prizes, who often delayed the process and augmented their fees, and because of the substantial share of the
proceeds taken by the Crown and the Lord High Admiral.

In order to remove these deterrents and to encourage privateering in the colonies, Queen Anne voluntarily gave up her lawful
share of a fifth of the proceeds of prizes and abolished the office
of prize agent in the colonies.[16]

In 1712 the *Bedford* galley arrived in Virginia with a French
prize, a merchantman laden with sugar, indigo, and cocoa. About
the same time H.M.S. *Severn*, one of the convoys of the Virginia
fleet, took and carried into New York a French privateer of
180 men.[17]

The Peace of Utrecht, as we have seen, did not mark the end
of hostilities between the British and Spanish. One of the most
high-handed actions during this period of desultory warfare was
the Spanish seizure of the Virginia privateer sloop *Virgin* in 1716,
an incident mentioned in the previous chapter.

Captain Harry Beverley, master of the *Virgin*, a merchant
vessel bound to the West Indies on a trading voyage three years

after the Peace of Utrecht, received from the Governor of Virginia letters of marque and a commission to investigate the pirates that were reported hovering around a sunken Spanish treasure fleet on the Bahama Bank and the Island of Providence. His purpose being to investigate rather than plunder, Beverley gave bond to the governor for his "honest and peaceable deportment." Yet because of the danger involved, the *Virgin* was equipped with arms, ammunition, and a privateer's commission—an unusual but apparently not illegal procedure.

At sea the *Virgin* fell into the hands of Don Joseph de la Pena, commander of the Spanish warship *St. Juan Baptista,* who ordered the crew of the Virginia sloop stripped and beaten and the vessel itself rifled. Carried into Puerto Rico, the sloop and its cargo were sold, and the Virginians imprisoned without trial.[18] Spanish captures of this kind continued to be made until the Treaty of Seville in 1730, but no prizes were brought into the Chesapeake during these years.[19]

King William's and Queen Ann's Wars witnessed very little privateering activity on the part of Chesapeake-owned vessels. For one thing privateering required large vessels and considerable capital. For another the normal trade routes of colonial vessels seldom afforded opportunities of encouraging French or Spanish merchantmen until after the development of a considerable West India trade. Moreover, the Crown's share of the prize money and the prize-office system with its interminable delay and its venal officials operated to discourage owners from refitting their ships as privateers. In consequence, most of the prizes brought into Chesapeake Bay for trial and condemnation were either enemy merchantmen taken in the Caribbean or enemy privateers taken in the Atlantic by British merchantmen or royal warships.

By 1740, however, conditions had changed. Colonial capital had accumulated and the Chesapeake merchant marine had grown. Shortly after the outbreak of King George's War there was a flurry of colonial privateering.[20]

## Prizes and Privateers

To combat the serious losses due to Spanish privateers off the coast, the Virginia Council in 1741 appointed a three-man commission to impress and fit out two sloops as privateers to cruise off the coast for three months. These sloops, carrying between 60 and 70 men each, received powder, shot, and small arms from the colony's magazine in Williamsburg. To entice mariners into their crews, the generous salary of forty shillings per month was offered plus a share of all prizes taken. The government assumed responsibility for any damage sustained by the vessels and agreed to pay up to fourteen shillings currency per ton a month hire.

When all was in readiness, the little squadron put to sea under the command of the master of one of the two sloops, Thomas Goodman of the *Ranger*. Shortly after sailing these privateers recaptured a Plymouth ship that had fallen into Spanish hands, but allowed the enemy privateer to escape under conditions that reflected discredit upon Captain Goodman. After sifting all the evidence, the Virginia Council declared that Goodman had acted with negligence and cowardice in the affair, censured him for his action, and ordered an entry in the journal "to stand as a lasting mark of Infamy upon the said Goodman."[21]

In 1742 Governor Gooch of Virginia issued a letter of marque to the ship *Happy,* a 200-ton vessel mounting ten carriage and six swivel guns and carrying a crew of twenty-five men. She was authorized to prey on Spanish shipping only, for Britain and France were not yet at war, but at that time many French vessels sailed under Spanish colors and letters of marque.[22]

A Virginian in England wrote home in 1744 that the trade of Bristol had been almost entirely disrupted by the enthusiasm for converting merchantment into privateers, estimating that sixteen Bristol ships had already been converted. One of them a Virginia-built brig, the *Sea-Horse,* which had been purchased in Bristol for the rather high price of 400 guineas, was refitted as a privateer and sailed under the new name of *Ranger*. After a two-month cruise she returned to port with a rich prize worth between £10,000 and £12,000.

As privateering was a rough game, it required a fairly large vessel. Notwithstanding her initial success, the *Ranger* was considered too small for making war on enemy merchantmen. After her first cruise her owners laid her up and converted her prize, the *Rover,* into a privateer at the cost of £5,000.[23]

About this time, as seen in the previous chapter, H.M.S. *Hastings,* commanded by Lord Banff, while on her way to the Virginia station in 1743, took the *Pallarcha* bound from Vera Cruz to Spain with 180,000 pieces-of-eight, besides a quantity of cochineal, vanilla, indigo, jalap (a Mexican purgative drug), and hides. Though of French registry, the *Pallarcha* had been freighted by the King of Spain. Estimated to be worth £36,000 sterling, the vessel and cargo were condemned by the Virginia Court of Vice-Admiralty. Shortly after arriving in the Chesapeake, Lord Banff took a Spanish privateer of 80 tons, 70 men, ten carriage and 24 swivel guns, cruising off the Virginia capes, which was also condemned as a prize in the colony.[24]

The field of operations of privateers expanded in 1744 when Great Britain declared war on France. Immediately thereafter King George II issued a declaration for the encouragement of privateers. By this instrument, the officers and men aboard warships of the Royal Navy and privateers were granted the proceeds of any lawful prize they might capture, subject only to the payment of the customs duties to which the cargo would have been liable had the goods been imported.

The net proceeds of a prize vessel and cargo taken by a royal warship were to be divided into eight equal parts and distributed according to the procedure laid down in the declaration. Three parts belonged to the commanding officer. One part belonged to the other officers of the rank of lieutenant, including captains of marines and land forces. One part went to the junior officers and the boatswain, gunner, purser, carpenter, master's mate, surgeons, and chaplain. One part was reserved for the midshipmen and the more important petty officers—boatswain's mates, gunner's mates, carpenter's mates, masters-at-arms, yeomen, and coxswains as well as sergeants and corporals of marines. The remaining two parts were assigned to the lesser petty officers, ordinary seamen, and soldiers.[25]

The net proceeds of a prize vessel and cargo taken by a privateer were distributed among owners, officers, and crew in accordance with the agreement entered into by them prior to the voyage or cruise on which the prize was taken. Prizes taken by privateers were free from the control of agents of the Prize Office, but those taken by royal warships had to be handled by prize agents as formerly. These agents, however, had to make final payment to recipients within three years after the date of condemnation. Those shares that remained unclaimed after that period of time were transferred to the Greenwich Hospital.

Captain Walter Codd of the *Virginia* privateer took a Spanish sloop off St. Kitts in 1745, and, shortly after, the French vessel *St. Anne,* bound from Marseilles to Martinique, valued at £5,000. Several months later, in consort with a St. Kitts privateer, he took a French ship bound from Bordeaux to Martinique, worth £15,000.[26]

The same year two London merchantmen arrived in Virginia with a French prize, the ship *Elizabeth.* Condemned as a prize at Williamsburg, she and her cargo of 282 hogsheads of sugar, 4,000 or 5,000 weight of indigo, and a parcel of choice mahogany plank were offered for sale and the handsome proceeds divided between the two London ships. The following fall the cargo of the prize sloop *Experience,* consisting of twenty-five hogsheads of white powdered sugar and a parcel of sail duck and coffee, was auctioned at Norfolk. In Maryland John Bebby, master of the ship *William and Betty* of Liverpool, brought into Potomac River a prize brigantine of 70 tons laden with sugar, rum, ginger, fustick, hogshead staves, pitch, and thirty and a half dozen "Cloaths-Brushes."[27]

Privateers commonly advertised for crews in the provincial newspapers during King George's and the French and Indian

Wars. In 1745 the privateer *Raleigh,* commanded by Mason Miller, advertised in the *Virginia Gazette* that it would sail on a certain day, urging all seamen and others "that have a Mind to go on a Cruise" to apply within a month. Captain Walter Codd, after his successful cruises off St. Kitts, received command of a fine new privateer, the snow *Earl of Stair,* in the fall of 1745. This 150-ton vessel, mounting 18 carriage and 30 swivel guns, and carrying 150 men, was accounted the "compleatest Vessel" ever built in Virginia as a privateer. Codd notified all persons interested to repair to Norfolk "with the greatest Dispatch" and communicate with him.[28]

These rough-and-ready privateersmen were often rather sensitive when their honor was impugned. Mason Miller and his two mates of the *Raleigh* complained that some "ill-designing People" maliciously spread scandal about them, saying that they had "gam'd away" a considerable portion of the proceeds of two prizes they took in the West Indies, and offered a reward of fifty pistoles for information leading to the discovery and conviction of the person who first started the slander.[29]

In 1748 the guardship on the Virginia station, H.M.S. *Hector,* commanded by Captain Masterton, and the sloop *Otter,* Captain Ballet master, arrived at Hampton Roads with six prizes. The *Otter* took two French vessels illegally trading "under Colour of Flags of Truce," and also, with the assistance of the *Hector,* a Spanish privateer schooner with a tender and two prizes. One of the "Flags of Truce" carried 3,000 pieces-of-eight, fifty hogsheads of tobacco, and two casks of silver. The other was laden with rum, sugar, and coin. The same year the Virginia Court of Vice-Admiralty condemned the French prize snow *Fidelity* of Nantes that had been taken by Captains Cornish of the letter-of-marque ship *Winchelsea* and Hutchinson of the letter-of-marque ship *Britannia.* Her cargo consisted of coals, tile, beef, butter, candles, salt, bacon, nails, shoes, slippers, ribbons, earthen pots, arms, linens, shirts, copper and brass ware, and "Chirurgical

Medicines." The vessel and her cargo were exposed to sale at Hampton.[30]

After an interval of peace, 1748-55, France and Great Britain again went to war. And with the official opening of hostilities in 1756, an even greater privateering boom than in King George's War took place. In the summer of 1756 the ship *Industry,* commanded by Matthias Miller, belonging to John Hutchings of Norfolk, fitted out as a privateer. A 200-ton vessel, she mounted twenty carriage and twenty swivel guns and carried 120 men. With a reputation of being well-built, her "Timber all of Mulberry and Cedar," she was known to be a "prime Sailor." Her owner, however, being financially unable to convert her to a ship-of-war, offered to put in £500 and advertised for partners in the venture, the total cost of which was estimated at £4,000 or £5,000. Hutchings proposed that the master and other officers be chosen by the majority of the subscribers.[31] In a similar fashion, the privateer ship *Two Sisters,* James Hanrick master, mounting 18 carriage guns and every way "completely fitted," advertised for "Gentlemen Sailors or Landsmen" who might care to join the crew.[32]

In 1757 the prize ships *Czar of Muscovy* and *St. Vincent,* condemned by the Virginia Court of Vice-Admiralty, were sold at auction at the Swan Tavern in Yorktown together with their guns, apparel, and their cargoes of sugar, rum, indigo, pimiento, coffee, ginger, and cotton. At the same time, in Williamsburg, Andrew Sprowle of Norfolk auctioned thirty hogsheads of claret, twenty boxes of fine salad oil, and twenty boxes of Castile soap, part of a cargo of a prize vessel that had been taken by the *Garland.*[33]

Another Virginia privateer of the French and Indian War was the ship *Hero* of Norfolk, which has already been mentioned in connection with her unusually sharp lines. She was owned by Benjamin Tatem of Norfolk and commanded by Hugh Sprowle. Going to Bermuda on business before the end of the war, Tatem drew up a power of attorney authorizing Henry Tucker of Norfolk to be his agent in his absence to "ask, demand, recover, sue for, and receive all money or moneys, that are now due, or may be due me as prize Money from the Privateer ship Hero."[34]

Maryland got very few prizes during this war, a fact that Governor Sharpe attributed to the considerable distance of the colony's ports from the sea.[35] But Marylanders fitted out privateers just as did their Virginia neighbors. The privateer *Sharpe,* an unusually powerful vessel mounting twenty-six carriage and twenty swivel guns and carrying a crew of 200 men, was fitted out at Chestertown.[36] In the summer of 1758 the privateer ship *Oliver Cromwell,* commanded by John Nicoll, advertised for men. Mounting 16 six-pounders and carrying 120 men, she was esteemed a "prime Sailer." Lying at Annapolis, she proposed to sail in seven or eight days on a cruise "against his Majesty's Enemies."[37] Another Maryland privateer was the snow *Tryal,* commanded by George Freebairn. This vessel had an unfortunate brush with an English privateer, the *Scourge* of London, commanded by Captain Clarke. Freebairn hailed him three times, but Clarke, apparently under the impression that the *Tryal* was an enemy vessel, fired two swivels and three volleys of small arms at her, killing one and wounding several other men.[38]

During the Anglo-French wars a number of colonial vessels trading to the West Indies applied for and received letters of marque which they used as a means of covering up illicit trade in French sugar. As few documents pertaining to this type of smuggling have survived, there is no way of telling how widespread it was. Apparently it appeared early, for Governor Nott of Virginia in 1705 issued a proclamation against collusive, fraudulent, and clandestine captures by privateers, in pursuance of an act of Parliament.[39]

Very little is known about this form of illicit trade in the Chesapeake until the French and Indian War. The papers of Samuel Galloway and Thomas Ringgold throw a great deal of light on it. Ringgold wrote his partner, Galloway, in 1761 that the men-of-war in the West Indies were taking all the vessels that came from Monte Cristi and Cap François, noted centers of smuggling on the Island of Hispaniola, so that "there's no probability of Vessels escaping or of the Trades being carried on but by having the Vessel in the Name of one person or persons and a privateer own'd by a Different person, to attend her and take her coming out of port."

By pretending to capture the vessel laden with foreign sugars, and having her condemned as a prize, the owners of the privateer could then lawfully sell the foreign sugar in Maryland, though the same commodity could not legally be imported. The practice does not seem to have been common in the Chesapeake colonies, for as late as 1761 the colonial officials were unaware of its existence in Maryland and convinced that it was of negligible proportions in Virginia.

The conditions that operated to discourage Chesapeake participation in privateering during the earlier Anglo-French wars had changed by 1740. During King George's and the French and Indian Wars there was ample capital in the Chesapeake colonies to enable privateers to be fitted out, there were many vessels of sufficient size and proper build for the undertaking, and a well-developed West India trade existed enabling letters of marque to combine profitable trading voyages with good chances of encountering rich prizes en route. Moreover, George II continued the generous policy, begun late in Queen Anne's reign, of assigning the Crown's share of prize money to the privateersmen who captured enemy vessels. In consequence, Virginia and Maryland took increasingly to privateering during the last two Anglo-French intercolonial wars with the result that shipbuilding —especially of large vessels—was stimulated, the scarcity of coin and West India commodities relieved by the importation and sale of prize goods, and colonial masters and mariners given the opportunity to acquire experience in a type of marine warfare that was to stand the American colonies in good stead in their struggle with Great Britain after 1775. Even so, privateering was by no means so important in the Chesapeake colonies during these wars as it was in the New England and Middle Colonies, or as it was to become in the Chesapeake during the Revolution and the War of 1812.

# Part V

## CONCLUSION

## CHAPTER THIRTEEN

# Conclusion

ALTHOUGH historians have made much of the importance of tobacco in shaping the society and economy of
colonial Virginia and Maryland, little has hitherto been said of
the importance of Chesapeake Bay. This inland sea—the Mediterranean of America—which rendered the Chesapeake tidewater
"the best water'd Country" by providing it with "the best and
most convenient Navigation unit of any known Country in the
World,"[1] was the principal factor in the development of Virginia
and Maryland.

The presence of the Bay with its network of navigable waterways made the Chesapeake tidewater easily accessible to colonization, opening up a considerable inland region to water-borne
traffic. The navigability of the rivers and creeks made it possible to
adopt as a staple a bulky commodity like tobacco that could not
stand overland transportation.[2] The two together account for the
rapid growth of the tobacco colonies in wealth and population
and help to explain their preëminence among the American
colonies.[3] As one eighteenth-century observer put it, "'tis the
Blessing of this Country . . . and fits it extremely for the Trade
it carries on, that the Planters can deliver their Commodities at
their own Back doors, as the whole Colony is interflow'd by the
most navigable Rivers in the World."[4]

The peculiar property of the Chesapeake tidewater—the land's
extraordinary accessibility to sea-borne traffic—that facilitated
the rapid development of the two colonies and made possible the
adoption of tobacco as a staple, had an adverse effect in discouraging the growth of towns and thereby depriving the tobacco colonies of the social and intellectual advantages of urban communities.

The presence of the extensive network of rivers and creeks
made towns unnecessary in the tidewater.[5] It was only when the

process of settlement reached the piedmont, beyond the head of navigation of the rivers, that large towns developed along the fall line to serve as points of trans-shipment for the hinterland.[6]

The absence of large towns and the accessibility of all parts of the Chesapeake tidewater to navigation were factors in the continuance of the cultural and intellectual dependence of Virginia and Maryland upon Great Britain. Being in close touch with London and the outports through the annual tobacco fleet and having no metropolis to mould colonial thought and stimulate crafts and industries, the inhabitants of Virginia and Maryland continued to grow tobacco and look to the mother country for inspiration and supplies as well for the mind as for the body.

Borrowing the ideas and fashions that were current at home, they reproduced British civilization in miniature on the shores of the Chesapeake insofar as the conditions of the American wilderness permitted. Planters who were of that turn of mind delighted in repeating the gossip and relating the scandals of St. James's. The more serious discussed the theories and practices of the Royal Exchange and followed in the columns of English newspapers the military and diplomatic activities of the kings of France and Prussia, the emperor, the tsar of Muscovy, the "Grand Turk," and innumerable lesser princelings. Those of literary inclination read the *Tatler,* the *Spectator,* Pope, Cowper, and the latest works of Defoe, Richardson, and Smollett. All kinds of agricultural equipment and supplies, clothing, household effects, furniture, and vehicles were imported from the mother country, which gave an English cast to the physical setting of colonial life.[7]

The dependence of Virginia and Maryland upon Great Britain was not limited to social and cultural matters. As the market for the staple commodity of the Chesapeake was in Europe, the welfare of Virginia and Maryland depended upon the transportation of their annual crop to Great Britain. This in turn depended upon the maintenance of an adequate British merchant marine— for tobacco was carried largely in British-owned ships—and, in time of war, on the security of the trade from enemy depredations on the high seas.

Being unable to maintain an adequate merchant marine of their own and incapable of supporting a navy for convoy purposes, the Chesapeake colonies were dependent upon Great Britain for the transportation and safe conduct of their tobacco.

As a result of the configuration of the Bay, with its wide mouth and its many broad estuaries, rivers and creeks, and of the dispersion of the population among widely scattered plantations, the Virginia and Maryland tidewater lay exposed to enemy attacks from the sea. Pirates, privateers, and foreign men-of-war could enter the Chesapeake, sail up the Bay and into the rivers, and take rich prizes with impunity, remaining beyond the range of the greatest cannon known at that time.

The course of events in the seventeenth and eighteenth centuries demonstrated that the Chesapeake could be defended only by a naval force and not by troops, batteries, or forts. The maintenance of an adequate squadron of warships was quite beyond the financial resources of the tobacco colonies.[8] Because of the Bay, then, the Chesapeake colonists were even more dependent upon Great Britain for their defense than were the other continental colonies.[9]

o     o     o

From every point of view except a political one, the Chesapeake tidewater was a single unit. All parts of it produced the same crops, its climate differed but slightly from one part to another, and there grew up in it a plantation society based upon the same staple commodity. There were sub-regional variations—areas that tended to specialize in the production of naval stores or grain—but they should not be allowed to obscure the essential unity of the Chesapeake region.

Colonial observers were fully aware of this unity. Hammond in his *Leah and Rachel* in 1656 stated that the "two Sister Countries" of Virginia and Maryland were "much of one nature, both for produce and manner of living."[10] Lord Culpeper in 1681 informed King Charles that the political turmoil in Maryland required him to maintain troops in his colony, "any disturbance there affecting Virginia as much as if in Virginia itself, there being only a river between them."[11]

In 1705 some inhabitants of the Eastern Shore, complaining of customs irregularities, said of Virginia and Maryland that they were "Contiguous and Neighbour Collonyes and much Under the Same Circumstances and a Joynt Trade has been Carryed on Since Theire Origionall Settlement."[12] The same year the observant Beverley gave opinion that there could not be much difference between Virginia and Maryland, "they being contiguous one to the other, lying in the same Bay, producing the same sort of Commodities, and being fallen into the same unhappy Form of Settlement altogether upon Country Seats, without Towns."[13]

The same view prevailed in Great Britain. A group of London merchants petitioned the Board of Trade in 1724 to disallow a Virginia act laying a duty on slaves imported, in the course of which they asserted that the trade of Virginia was "Exactly of the same Nature as Marylands (which is not the case of other colonys)."[14] Hall writing in 1731 dealt with both colonies as one, saying "I apprehend little can be said of one Province which the other doth not deserve or is not capable of, I will take leave therefore to treat of them as one."[15] And Douglass, writing a quarter of a century later, said "As the colonies or provinces of Virginia and Maryland lie in the same long bay of Chesapeak, we cannot avoid giving a joint account of them . . . principally with regard to their trade and navigation."[16]

As a result of Maryland's having been formed from Virginia, and of the similarity of the two colonies, the term "Virginia" long continued to be applied to both in common parlance. Hammond said "*Maryland* is a province not commonly knowne in England, because the name of *Virginia* includes or clouds it."[17]

# Conclusion

Beverley asserted that "the Name *Virginia* was lost to all except to the Tract of Land lying along the Bay of *Chesapeak,* and a little to the Southward, in which are included *Virginia* and *Maryland*; both which, in common Discourse, are still very often meant by the Name *Virginia*."[18]

This confusion lasted until the end of the colonial period. A letter addressed to Samuel Galloway from Mayne and Company of Lisbon in 1765 carried the address "Annapolis, Maryland" on the outside, and "Annapolis, Virginia" on the inside.[19]

Observers of the seventeenth and eighteenth centuries fully realized the error of dividing Chesapeake Bay into two political units. Sir William Berkeley was particularly vehement in denouncing the dismemberment of Virginia and predicted that it "will in the next Age be found more disadvantagious to the Crown then is perceptible in this."

Speaking of the economic disadvantages, Berkeley pointed out that Virginia could "never make any Lawes for the erecting Staple Commodities, and setting a stop to our unlimitted planting of *Tobacco,* whilst these Governments are distinct and independent, for on frequent tryals when we begin to make provisions for these, our people fly to *Maryland,* and by this means heighten our publick charges, and weaken our defenses against our perpetual enemies the *Indians*."[20]

Berkeley took the same view and complained of the evils that stemmed from the political division of the Bay country. "By this unhappy Accident," he wrote, "a Country which Nature had so well contriv'd for one, became Two separate Governments. This produced a most unhappy Inconvenience to both; for these Two being the only Countries under the Dominion of *England,* that plant Tobacco in any Quantity, the Consequence of that Division is, that when one Colony goes about to prohibit the Trash of that Commodity, to help the Market; then the other, to take Advantage of the Market, pours into *England* all they can make, both good and bad, without Distinction. This is very injurious to the other Colony, which had voluntarily suffer'd so great a Diminution in the Quantity to mend the Quality."[21]

These objections of Berkeley and Beverley are valid. As a result of the division of the Chesapeake country into two political units, Virginia and Maryland were unable to control the volume of tobacco production, they failed to standardize its quality until well along in the eighteenth century, and they never succeeded in agreeing to a uniform size for tobacco hogsheads. On the maritime side, the political dismemberment of the Chesapeake region resulted in failure to build a much-needed lighthouse, disputes over fisheries and navigation in the Potomac, lack of cooperation between Maryland and Virginia in defending the Bay in time of war, customs irregularities and illicit trade along the Potomac and Eastern Shore boundary, and lack of uniformity of laws pertaining to pilots and ferries.

Many of these evils—if not all of them—might have been avoided if King Charles I had not made the blunder of separating the Chesapeake region into two unnatural divisions.

o   o   o

FINIS

o   o   o

# Footnotes

○   ○   ○

# Bibliography

# Abbreviations Used in Footnote Citations

CNHP    Colonial National Historical Park, Yorktown, Va.

CW    Colonial Williamsburg, Inc., Williamsburg, Va.

Depn.    Deposition

f, ff    Folio page or pages

LC    Library of Congress, Washington, D. C.

MHS    Maryland Historical Society, Baltimore, Md.

n    Footnote

NYPL    New York Public Library, New York, N. Y.

p, pp    Page or pages

PRO    Public Record Office, London, England

v    Volume

VHS    Virginia Historical Society, Richmond, Va.

VSL    Virginia State Library, Richmond, Va.

W&M    College of William and Mary Library, Williamsburg, Va.

# Key to Short Titles in Footnote Citations

Following the example set by E. G. Swem, *Virginia Historical Index,* the principal historical publications dealing with Maryland and Virginia history are cited in the footnotes to this work by initials only. In each such citation the number of the volume precedes the initials, the number of the series, if any, follows them and then the page is given. Books, in general, are cited by the author's name only, preceded by the volume number and followed by the page number. Complete particulars concerning the various works cited may be found by consulting the Bibliography at the end of the Footnotes section.

1. *Accomack Wills.* Accomack County Will Book.
2. *Agr. Hist.* Agricultural History (Agricultural History Society, Chicago).
3. *AHR.* American Historical Review.
4. *Allason Letterbook.* William Allason Letterbook, VSL.
5. *Alsop.* NEWTON D. MERENESS, ed. A Character of the Province of Mary-Land, by George Alsop.
6. *Amer. Neptune.* The American Neptune.
7. *Anderson.* ADAM ANDERSON, Origin of Commerce.
8. Andrews, *Col. Per.* CHARLES M. ANDREWS. Colonial Period in American History.
9. Andrews, *Virginia.* MATTHEW P. ANDREWS. Virginia, the Old Dominion.
10. *APCC.* Acts of the Privy Council, Colonial Series.
11. *Arch. Rec.* Architectural Record.
12. Bailey, *Dict. Brit.* N. BAILEY. Dictionarium Britannicum.
13. *Bassett.* JOHN S. BASSETT. Relation between Virginia Planter and London Merchant.

14. *Berkeley.* SIR WILLIAM BERKELEY. A Discourse and View of Virginia.

15. *Beverley.* ROBERT BEVERLEY. History and Present State of Virginia.

16. *Beverley Letterbook.* William Beverley Letterbook, 1737-1744/5, NYPL.

17. *Birket.* JAMES BIRKET. Voyage to North America.

18. *Bishop.* JAMES L. BISHOP. American Manufactures.

19. *BMAM.* British Museum Additional MSS, British Transcripts in LC.

20. Brown's *Genesis.* ALEXANDER BROWN. Genesis of the United States.

21. *Bruce.* PHILIP A. BRUCE. Economic History of Virginia.

22. *Burnaby.* REV. ANDREW BURNABY. Travels through Middle Settlements in North America.

23. *Byrd.* WILLIAM BYRD. History of the Dividing Line.

24. *C.* Calendar of Virginia State Papers.

25. *Cappon.* LESTER J. CAPPON. Iron Works at Tubal.

26. *Carman.* HARRY J. CARMAN. American Husbandry.

27. *Carter Letters.* LOUIS B. WRIGHT. Letters of Robert Carter, 1720-27.

28. *Chalkley.* THOMAS CHALKLEY. Journal of Life, Travels, etc.

29. *Channing.* EDWARD CHANNING. History of the United States.

30. Chapelle, *Baltimore Clipper.* HOWARD I. CHAPELLE. The Baltimore Clipper.

31. Chapelle, *Sailing Craft.* HOWARD I. CHAPELLE. American Sailing Craft.

32. Chapelle, *Sailing Ships.* HOWARD I. CHAPELLE. History of American Sailing Ships.

33. Chapin, *Privateering.* HOWARD M. CHAPIN. Privateering in King George's War.

34. Chapin, *Privateer Ships.* HOWARD M. CHAPIN. Privateer Ships and Sailors.

35. *Charnock.* JOHN CHARNOCK. History of Marine Architecture.

36. Chatterton, *Fore and Aft.* E. KEBLE CHATTERTON. *Fore and Aft.*

37. Chatterton, *Seamen*. E. KEBLE CHATTERTON. English Seamen and the Colonization of America.
38. *C.O.* Colonial Office Papers, PRO, British Transcripts in LC.
39. *Convention Records*. MAX FERRAND, ed. Records of Federal Convention of 1787.
40. Craven, *Va. Co.* WESLEY F. CRAVEN. Dissolution of Virginia Company.
41. Craven, *Soil Exhaustion*. AVERY O. CRAVEN. Soil Exhaustion as a Factor in History.
42. *Cresswell*. NICHOLAS CRESSWELL. The Journal of Nicholas Cresswell.
43. *Crittenden*. CHARLES C. CRITTENDEN. Commerce of North Carolina.
44. *CSPC*. Calendar of State Papers, Colonial Series, America and West Indies.
45. *CTB*. Calendar of Treasury Books. *CTBP*. Calendar of Treasury Books and Papers. *CTP*. Calendar of Treasury Papers.
46. *Custis Letterbook*. John Custis Letterbook, 1717-41, LC.
47. *DAH*. Dictionary of American History.
48. *Dampier*. WILLIAM DAMPIER. A New Voyage Round the World.
49. *Danckaerts*. BARTLETT P. JAMES and J. FRANKLIN JAMESON, eds. Journal of Jasper Danckaerts.
50. *Darnall*. HENRY DARNALL. Transactions of the Merchants in London.
51. *De Vries*. DAVID P. DE VRIES. Voyages from Holland to America, 1632-1644.
52. *Donnan*. ELIZABETH DONNAN, ed. Slave Trade to America.
53. *Douglass*. WILLIAM DOUGLASS. British Settlements in North America.
54. *Durand*. (Durand of Dauphiné) A Frenchman in Virginia. FAIRFAX HARRISON, trans.
55. *Earle*. SWEPSON EARLE. Chesapeake Bay Country.
56. *Eddis*. WILLIAM EDDIS. Letters from America.
57. *EJC*. Executive Journals of Council of Virginia.
58. *Enc. Brit.* Encyclopaedia Britannica.

59. *Falconer.* WILLIAM FALCONER. Dictionary of the Marine.

60. *Field.* THOMAS M. FIELD. Unpublished Letters of Charles Carroll and his Father.

61. *Firth.* C. H. FIRTH, ed. An American Garland.

62. *Fisher.* SIDNEY G. FISHER. Struggle for American Independence.

63. *Fithian.* HUNTER D. FARISH, ed. Journal and Letters of P. Vickers Fithian.

64. *Fitzpatrick.* JOHN C. FITZPATRICK. George Washington, Colonial Traveller.

65. *Flippin.* PERCY S. FLIPPIN. Financial Administration of Colony of Virginia.

66. *Force.* PETER FORCE, ed. Tracts and Other Papers.

67. *Freeman's Jour.* Freeman's Journal or North American Intelligencer.

68. *Gent. Mag.* Gentleman's Magazine.

69. *Geog. Rev.* Geographical Review.

70. *Gipson.* LAWRENCE H. GIPSON. British Empire before the American Revolution.

71. *Goodwin.* RUTHERFOORD GOODWIN. Williamsburg in Virginia.

72. *Gould.* CLARENCE P. GOULD. Money and Transportation in Maryland, 1720-1765.

73. *Guild. Lib.* Guildhall Library, PRO, British Transcripts in LC.

74. *H.* WILLIAM W. HENING. Statutes-at-Large.

75. Hall, *Narratives.* CLAYTON C. HALL, ed. Narratives of Early Maryland.

76. Hall, *Plantations.* F. HALL. Importance of British Plantations in America.

77. *HLL.* House of Lords Library, British Transcripts in LC.

78. *Honyman.* PHILIP PADELFORD, ed. Dr. Robert Honyman's Journal.

79. *Jacobstein.* MEYER JACOBSTEIN. Tobacco Industry in the United States.

80. *JBT.* Journal of Commissioners for Trade and Plantations.

81. *JEBH.* Journal of Economic and Business History.

82. *Jefferson.* PAUL LEICESTER FORD. Writings of Jefferson.

83. *Jerdone Letterbook.* Jerdone Account and Letterbook, 1736-1737, 1738-1744, W&M.
84. *Jernegan.* MARCUS W. JERNEGAN. Laboring and Dependent Classes in Colonial America.
85. *JHB.* Journal of House of Burgesses of Virginia.
86. *Jones.* HUGH JONES. Present State of Virginia.
87. *Jour. Neg. Hist.* Journal of Negro History.
88. *Lee Mss.* Miscl. MSS of Lee Family, LC.
89. *LJC.* Legislative Journals of Council of Virginia.
90. *McClellan.* WILLIAM S. McCLELLAN. Smuggling in American Colonies.
91. *MacInnes.* CHARLES MacINNES. Early English Tobacco Trade.
92. *Mariner.* The Mariner.
93. *Maryland, A Guide.* Maryland, A Guide to the Old Line State.
94. *Maryland Records.* GAIUS M. BRUMBAUGH. Maryland Records.
95. *Maryland Wills.* ANNIE W. B. BELL, comp. Abstracts of Wills in Charles and St. Mary's Counties, Maryland, 1744-1772.
96. Mass. Hist. Soc., *Collections.* Massachusetts Historical Society, Collections, 4th series.
97. *Md. Arch.* Archives of Maryland.
98. *Mereness.* NEWTON D. MERENESS, ed. Travels in the American Colonies.
99. *MG(G).* Maryland Gazette (Jonas Green and Family).
100. *MG(P).* Maryland Gazette (William Parks).
101. *MHM.* Maryland Historical Magazine.
102. *Mifflin.* VICTOR H. PALTSITS, ed. Journal of Benjamin Mifflin.
103. *MNPB.* Maryland Notary Public Record Book, Hall of Records, Annapolis.
104. *Morris, Fore-and-Aft.* EDWARD P. MORRIS. Fore-and Aft Rig in America.
105. *Morriss.* MARGARET S. MORRISS. Colonial Trade of Maryland.
106. *Morton.* LOUIS MORTON. Robert Carter of Nomini Hall.
107. *MPP, Black Books.* Maryland Proprietary Papers, Black Books, Hall of Records, Annapolis.

108. *Mrs. Browne.* MRS. BROWNE. Journal of Voyage from London to Virginia, 1754-1755.
109. *Natl. Geog. Mag.* National Geographic Magazine.
110. *Neill.* EDWARD D. NEILL. Virginia Vetusta.
111. *Nelson Letterbook.* William Nelson Letterbook, CNHP.
112. *Nettels.* CURTIS P. NETTELS. Money Supply of America.
113. *Northampton Wills.* Northampton County Will Book.
114. *OED.* Oxford English Dictionary.
115. *Oldmixon.* JOHN OLDMIXON. British Empire in America.
116. Phillips, *Life and Labor.* ULRICH B. PHILLIPS. Life and Labor in the Old South.
117. Phillips, *Va. Cartography.* PHILIP L. PHILLIPS. Virginia Cartography.
118. *Pitman.* FRANK W. PITMAN. Development of British West Indies.
119. *PMCA.* Proceedings of Maryland Court of Appeals, 1695-1729.
120. *Reynolds Letterbook.* William Reynolds Letterbook, CNHP.
121. *Robertson.* WILLIAM ROBERTSON. History of Virginia and Maryland.
122. *RSMG.* Royal Society MS Guardbook, British Transcripts in LC.
123. *Semmes.* RAPHAEL SEMMES. Captains and Mariners of Early Maryland.
124. *Sheffield.* JOHN, LORD SHEFFIELD. Observations on Commerce of American States.
125. *Smith.* EDWARD ARBER, ed. Travels and Works of Captain John Smith.
126. Smith, *Colonists.* ABBOT E. SMITH. Colonists in Bondage.
127. *Spears.* JOHN R. SPEARS. American Slave Trade.
128. *Spruill.* JULIA R. SPRUILL. Women's Life and Work in the Southern Colonies.
129. Steiner, *Md. Poetry.* BERNARD C. STEINER, ed. Early Maryland Poetry.
130. *Swain.* ROBERT L. SWAIN. Chestertown as a Colonial Port.
131. *T.* Tyler's Quarterly Historical and Genealogical Magazine.

132. *Tatham*. WILLIAM TATHAM. Essay on the Culture and Commerce of Tobacco.

133. *Thomas*. SIR DALBY THOMAS. Rise and Growth of West-India Colonies.

134. *TP*. Treasury Papers, British Transcripts in LC.

135. *Tyack*. N. F. C. TYACK. Trade Relations of Bristol with Virginia.

136. *V*. Virginia Magazine of History and Biography.

137. *VG(D&H)*. Virginia Gazette (John Dixon & William Hunter).

138. *VG(H)*. Virginia Gazette (William Hunter).

139. *VG(P)*. Virginia Gazette (William Parks).

140. *VG(P&D)*. Virginia Gazette (Alexander Purdie and John Dixon).

141. *VG(Pinckney)*. Virginia Gazette (John Pinckney).

142. *VG(R)*. Virginia Gazette (William Rind).

143. VHS *Collections*. Virginia Historical Society, Collections.

144. *Virginia Iron*. KATHLEEN BRUCE. Virginia Iron Manufacture.

145. *W*. William and Mary Quarterly, Series 1, 2, and 3.

146. *Washington Diaries*. JOHN C. FITZPATRICK, ed. Diaries of George Washington.

147. *Washington Invoices*. George Washington Papers, Invoices and Letters, LC.

148. Wertenbaker, *Norfolk*. THOMAS J. WERTENBAKER. Norfolk, Historic Southern Port.

149. Wertenbaker, *Planters*. THOMAS J. WERTENBAKER. Planters of Colonial Virginia.

150. Wertenbaker, *Virginia*. THOMAS J. WERTENBAKER. Virginia Under the Stuarts.

151. *Williams*. LLOYD H. WILLIAMS. Pirates of Colonial Virginia.

152. *Winsor*. JUSTIN WINSOR. History of America.

153. *Wroth*. LAWRENCE C. WROTH. Way of a Ship.

154. *Wyckoff*. VERTREES J. WYCKOFF. Tobacco Regulation in Colonial Maryland.

# Footnotes

## CHAPTER I

1. Will of William Fitzhugh, Apr. 9, 1700, *Lee MSS*, LC.
2. *Chalkley*, 12. 3. Hall, *Narratives*, 31. 4. Hall, *Narratives*, 140.
5. *Chalkley*, 33. 6. A stringer is an inside strake of planking secured to the ribs and supporting the ends of the beams. *OED*.
7. Planeshear, or planksheer, is a continuous planking, covering the timber-heads; the term is also loosely applied to the gunwale. *Ibid.*
8. Quickwork is that part of a ship which is under the surface of the water when she is laden. *Falconer.*
9. Caboose is the space devoted to the cooking facilities of a ship.
10. Halbert Hansen to Samuel Galloway, Dec. 10, 1759, *Galloway Papers*, Box 1742-69, NYPL.
11. Depn. of Stephen Mesnard, June 2, 1749, *MNPB, 1744-96*, B.
12. Depn. of Birstall, Pugh, and Quinby, Dec. 26, 1748, *ibid.*, B.
13. Depn. of John Kuill, Nov. 12, 1749, *ibid.*, B.
14. Steiner, *Md. Poetry*, 1. 15. Chatterton, *Seamen*, 62. 16. *Ibid.*, 64.
17. The Westerlies are stronger in winter than in summer, while the reverse is true of the Northeast Trades. In summer the latter are occasionally felt as far north as 36° N; in winter the Westerlies usually prevail as far south as 30° N. 2 *Enc. Brit.*, 636.
18. *Semmes*, 32. 19. Chatterton, *Seamen*, 125.
20. The Northeast Trade wind is occasionally felt as far north as 36° N, but this generally occurs in spring and summer, rather than in winter. Byrd must have made the passage somewhere between the 30° and 36° parallels. 25 *V*285. 21. 32*V*25.
22. The Downs is a roadstead off Deal, carrying a depth of twelve fathoms and well protected in all but severe southerly gales. 7 *Enc. Brit.*, 565.
23. Chatterton, *Seamen*, 123; *VG(P)*, May 25, 1739. 24. *Chalkley*, 12.
25. 5 *Jones Papers*, LC, 685. 26. *MG(G)*, Oct. 19, 1748.
27. 3 Mass. Hist. Soc., *Collections*, 4th ser., 37.
28. *Neill*, 131. 29. *Ibid.*, 131.
30. *CSPC, 1574-1660*, 231. 31. 1 *Bruce*, 138. 32. 37*V*102. 33. 2*MHM*40.
34. Lndg. Crtfs., Am. Ports, *Guild. Lib.*, 1718-37, LC; *MG(G)*, Mar. 30, 1748.
35. *VG(P)*, July 22, 1737. 36. 24*V*117. 37. 1 *Bruce*, 137.
38. *De Vries*, 54, 112; 1 *Bruce*, 137 n2. 39. Wertenbaker, *Norfolk*, 13.
40. 2*MHM*36. 41. 4*JEBH*528.

42. 2*MHM*40; for examples of quarantine under the act, see 9 *MP, Black Bks.*, pt. 2, nos. 147, 148.

43. *Alsop*, 94. 44. 2*MHM*322. 45. 24*V*10. 46. 17W*(1)*107.

47. 24*V*10; 24*V*277. 48. Mrs. Browne, *Journal, 1754-55.*

49. 24*V*15; 24*V*279. 50. *Mrs. Browne*, Feb. 3, 1755.

51. *Ibid.*, Jan. 27, Feb. 24, 28, 1755. 52. 3 *Force*, no. 10, p. 12.

53. *Ibid.*, 17. 54. 24*V*5; 24*V*11; 24*V*277. 55. *MG(G)*, Aug. 11, 1747.

56. *Mrs. Browne*, Feb. 6, 17, 20, 27, 1755. 57. *Ibid.*, Mar. 2, 10, 1755.

58. *Ibid.*, Dec. 15, 1754; Jan. 12, 20, 1755. 59. 24*V*11; 24*V*277.

60. 24*V*14. 61. *CSPC, 1704-05*, no. 1051, p. 491; *JBT, 1704-08/9*, 93.

62. 90 *CTP*, 1702-07, no. 109, p. 267. 63. 102 *CTP*, 1702-07, no. 120, p. 532.

64. 24*V*13. 65. *Wroth*, 73. 66. 5 *Isis*, 78-80.

67. 4*V*37; 5*V*7.

68. For illustration and description, see Bailey, *Dict. Brit.*, under Back Staff, also 20 *Gent. Mag.*, 112.

69. 11*Old Time New England*, 147-59.

70. William Allason to Robert Bogle, [May 24, 1761], *Allason Letterbook, 1757-70*, VSL; *MG(G)*, Nov. 1, 1753; 3 *Jamieson Papers*, LC, 515.

71. For example, see *MG(G)*, Mar. 25, 1746.

72. Inventory, Muns Bishop, Apr. 14, 1747, *Northampton Wills, 1740-50,* 281; bill, Captain Pine to Barnabas Lorane for sloop *Dreadnaught,* Norfolk, Aug. 29, 1767, 1 *Jamieson Papers*, 87; goods taken by the French from the snow *Two Brothers*, Oct. 27, 1760, *MNPB, 1744-96*, B; inventory, Jacob Rodgers, 1750, *Accomack Wills, 1749-52*, 108; goods ordered from Hanbury & Co., London, by Dr. Charles Carroll, Annapolis, 27*MHM*317. A spyglass listed in the inventory of an estate is sometimes a surveying instrument rather than a navigational one. In the inventory of Daniel Richardson, 1722, a spyglass worth only 4s. is closely followed by a "sett of surveying Instruments": 3 *Bozman Papers, 1730-56*, LC, 569. In other cases, there is no doubt as to the maritime use of the instrument, as for example the "fine Mahogany Spy Glass" that was supplied to the ship *Thistle* in 1763 for £1 5s. by Neil Jamieson: 3 *Jamieson Papers*, LC, 520.

73. 9*V*247. 74. 28*MHM*198.

75. Navigation books commonly appear in colonial inventories of estates, e.g., "a parcell of navigation books" belonging to Robert Tucker, merchant, Norfolk County, Va., 1723: 4*V*361; "Mariners' Jewell" and "Epitome of Navigation": 10*V*399; "Elements of Navigation," 3*T*49; "Moore's Practical Navigator and Seaman's New Daily Assistant" and "Patoun's Treatise of Practical Navigation," offered for sale at Williamsburg, 1775: 15*W(1)*105.

76. *MG(G)*, Apr. 26, 1745, Mar. 25, 1746. See also the proposal for an academy at Providence, New Kent County, Va., in 1770: *VG(R)*, Mar.

1, 1770; 3 *W(2)*55. Among the subjects to be taught were arithmetic, bookkeeping, navigation, surveying, geography, astronomy, the use of the globes, and the calculation of eclipses.

77. 4*V*30; 5*V*13.

78. Captain James Hanrick to Samuel Galloway, Nov. 20, 1764, *Galloway Papers*, Box 1742-69, NYPL.

79. St. George Tucker, Journal, Aug. 14, 1773, *Tucker-Coleman Papers*, CW.

80. 3*Force*, no. 12, p. 5; *Burnaby*, 4; 24*V*15.

81. 2*Beverley*, 2-3; *Berkeley*, 2. 82. 24*V*16.

83. For a detailed account, see the author's "Struggle for the Cape Henry Lighthouse, 1721-91": 8 *Amer. Neptune*, 26.


## CHAPTER II

1. 1 Brown's *Genesis*, 352. 2. 15*W(1)*216; Rev. Hugh Jones to Benj. Woodroof, Jan. 23, 1698/9, *RSMG*, LC, no. 1, p. 183; 4*V*257.

3. 3 *Force*, no. 12, p. 11. 4. *Robertson*, 64. 5. 35 *Geog. Rev.* 219.

6. *Burnaby*, 12-13, 10; *Berkeley*, 4.

7. 5*T*1; William Byrd I wrote in 1690, of his Westover plantation on James River, that "as big ships as any . . . ride within two miles of it:" 27*V*279; 1 *Oldmixon*, 405; Ports of N.A., James River, *BMAM*, LC, 15484.

8. 1 *Oldmixon*, 410; *Burnaby*, 10; Ports of N.A., York River, *BMAM*, LC, 15484.

9. *Burnaby*, 12; Ports of N.A., Rappahannock, *BMAM*, LC, 15484.

10. *Burnaby*, 12, 1 *Oldmixon*, 423; *Mereness*, 407; Ports of N.A., N. Potomack, *BMAM*, LC, 15484.

11. *Burnaby*, 56, says: "near fifty miles for vessels of three hundred tons burthen." Probably an exaggeration; thirty miles would be more exact today.

12. *Burnaby*, 56. 13. *Burnaby*, 57; 2 *Douglass*, 361.

14. Thomas Ringgold to Samuel Galloway, Mar. 9, 1766, Ringgold Letters, 1760-70, *Galloway Papers*, NYPL.

15. Ports of N.A., Pocomoke, *BMAM*, LC, 15484. 16. Ports of N.A., Accomack, *BMAM*, LC, 15484.

17. Henry Callister to Foster Cunliffe & Sons, Aug. 6, 1747, *Callister Papers*, NYPL, f. 81. Speaking of some competitor, Callister said: "The Tobacco they buy is often rolled twenty miles and upward, which is not only a great Charge upon it, but it is always damaged by it and shaken to pieces both inside and outside."

18. 15*W(1)*147. 19. 25*MHM*62. 20. 2 *Beverley*, 5-6. 21. *Berkeley*, 2.

22. Henry Callister to Foster Cunliffe & Sons, July 10, 21, 1745, *Callister Papers*, NYPL.

23. Washington to Robert Cary & Co., May 28, 1762, *Washington Invoices, 1755-66*, LC.

24. Depn. of Edward White, Nov. 6, 1761, *MNPB, 1744-96*, B.

25. The absence of stones in the tidewater region made it unnecessary to shoe horses. Rev. Hugh Jones to Benj. Woodroof, Jan. 23, 1698/9, *RSMG*, LC, no. 1, p. 183; *Burnaby*, 42.

26. 4*V*256. 27. *Earle*, 363.

28. Durand observed that "none of the plantation houses, even the most remote, is more than 100 or 150 feet from a 'crik' [creek] and the people are thus enabled not only to pay their visits in their canoes, but to do all their freight carrying by the same means." *Durand*, 23.

29. Wertenbaker, *Norfolk*, 28-37.

30. As early as 1772, an observer writing from Petersburg said: "For though the Quantity of Tobacco encreases greatly above on the upland [the piedmont], it declines below on the old worn out Lowlands where they can make none without manuring and that too little and at a too great expence:" as a result, wheat became "a kind of second staple:" 15*V*352, 15*V*350. Evidence of the shift to wheat in the upper Bay region may be found in *Honyman*, 4, 8, 9; see also 1 *Chalmers Papers*, Md., NYPL, 52; for soil exhaustion and the silting-up of rivers, see Craven, 13, and Gottschalk on soil erosion in 35 *Geog. Rev.*, 219-38. Alexander Rose wrote in 1768 that "the Impetuous Rains sweep away the whole vegetative Earth from the broken grounds [of the tidewater region] unless they are tended in grain (I mean wheat, etc.), Indian Corn," 33*V*83. For monographs on the river towns, such as Chestertown, Londontown, Dumfries, and Port Tobacco, see 19*MHM*125, 4*W(2)*99, and 40*MHM*-261.

31. 1 *Smith*, 344; *C.O.* 5: 1326, 25-26. 32. 1 *Smith*, 344.

33. 1 *Bruce*, 139 nl; *CSPC*, 1696-97, no. 1252, p. 582. 34. 7*MHM*8.

35. 32*V*26. 36. 1 *Smith*, 344; 3 *Force*, no. 12, p. 5-6; 1 *Bruce*, 131.

37. Hall, *Narratives*, 401; *Burnaby*, 7-8. 38. 2 *Donnan*, 423.

39. *MG(G)*, Dec. 23, 1746; Henry Callister to Foster Cunliffe & Sons, Feb. 23, 1746/7, *Callister Papers*, NYPL.

40. Depn. of Robert Steel, Jan. 13, 1748/9; depn. of Matthew Caverly, Jan. 22, 1748/9, *MNPB*, 1744-96, B.

41. 1 *Smith*, 110-11. 42. Hall, *Narratives*, 151.

43. *CSPC, 1701*, no. 434, p. 227; 13 *Md. Arch.*, 56, 58.

44. 1 *Bruce*, 395; *CSPC, 1661-68*, no. 1625, p. 516.

45. Depn. of Wright *et al.*, Nov. 20, 1745; depn. of Andrew Mills, Jan. 31, 1748/9, *MNPB, 1744-96*, B.

46. *MG(P)*, Feb. 11, 1728/9; *MG(G)*, Jan. 14, 1746; depn. of John French, Dec. 12, 1761, *MNPB, 1744-96*, B.

47. *VG(P&D)*, Sept. 14, 1769; 14*W(2)*165.

48. 3 *Force*, no. 12, p. 7. 49. *MG(G)*, Aug. 9, 1745. 50. 24*V*356.

51. John Custis to (William Byrd II?), Aug. 12, 1724, *Custis Letterbook, 1717-41*, LC, 18; *VG(P)*, Apr. 21, 1738; *VG(H)*, Oct. 12, 1752.
52. *VG(P)*, June 6, July 11, 1771; 22*V*383 n4.
53. 6*V*128; Col. Richard Adams to Thomas Adams, Sept. 30, 1771, VHS.
54. 1*Smith*, 344. 55. 15*W(1)*220. 56. *Firth*, 24.
57. 2 Brown's *Genesis*, 583. 58. 1 *Smith*, 352. 59. *Mereness*, 406-7.
60. 1 Smith, 132; 2 *Force*, no. 7, p. 27; *Alsop*, 40.
61. *Danckaerts*, 123, 126. 62. *MG(G)*, June 7, 1753.
63. *Maryland: A Guide*, 169. 64. 101 *Natl. Geog. Mag.*, 669.
65. Henry Callister to William Whitfield, Aug. 1, 1743, *Callister Papers*, NYPL.
66. 24*V*37. 67. *Alsop*, 32-33. 68. 2 Brown's *Genesis*, 586.
69. Hall, *Narratives*, 80. 70. 2 *Force*, no. 8, p. 17; 22*W(2)*217.
71. 1 *Oldmixon*, 445-46. 72. 1 *Oldmixon*, 445-46. 73. *Honyman*, 9.
74. 1 *Bruce*, 112-13; 2 *Force*, no. 8, p. 17. 75. 1 *Smith*, 114.
76. 3 *Force*, no. 12, p. 4. 77. *Cresswell*, 13.
78. *MG(G)*, July 25, 1750; 17*MHM*374. 79. 24*V*34. 80. 15*W(1)*218.
81. 1 *Smith*, lxii. 82. 24*V*35. 83. 1 *Bruce*, 113; 24*V*35; 1 *Oldmixon*, 446; 1*W(3)*183.
84. 1 *Bruce*, 113; *Semmes*, 28. 85. 24*V*35. 86. 4*V*261.
87. *VG(H)*, Mar. 5, 1752.
88. 1 *Washington Diaries, 1748-99*, 108-9; 2 *Valentine Papers*, 947.
89. 13*W(1)*46; 1*W(3)*180. 90. 78 *Arch. Rec.*, 374-75; *VG(H)*, Mar. 14, 1750/1.
91. 1 *Bozman Papers*, LC, 38, 40. 92. 14*V*374; 1 *Bruce*, 114.
93. 1 *Oldmixon*, 446; *Fithian*, 224; 38*V*356; 22*W(2)*220.

## CHAPTER III

1. *CSPC, 1574-1660*, 38-39; *Eddis*, 19; *MG(G)*, July 29, 1746.
2. *Tatham*, 93; *Gould*, 136-37.
3. *Gould*, 136-37. Rope ferries are still in use in Wicomico County on the Eastern Shore of Maryland.
4. *Chalkley*, 38. 5. *Gould*, 137; *VG(P&D)*, Sept. 7, 1769.
6. *Honyman*, 7-8; *Mereness*, 406; *VG(P&D)*, June 24, 1773.
7. *Fithian*, 130. 8. *MG(G)*, Feb. 17, 1747/8; *VG(P&D)*, Sept. 7, 1769.
9. *Mifflin*, 14; *Honyman*, 7-8; *MG(G)*, July 15, May 13, 1746.
10. *MG(P)*, June 10, 1729; 15 *W(1)*216; *MG(G)*, June 10, Dec. 9, 1746; May 10, 1753.
11. *MG(G)*, April 2, 1761.
12. *Mereness*, 406, 409; *VG(P&D)* Sept. 7, 1769.
13. Depn. of John Bryan et al., Feb. 23, 1760, *MNPB, 1744-96*, B; *Fithian*, 130; *Honyman*, 7-8.
14. 15*W(1)*220; *Eddis*, 4-5. 15. 1 *Bruce*, 421.

16. 1*H*269; 1*H*348; 1*H*411; 2*H*310. 17. 1 *Bruce*, 422-23; 1*C*50.

18. 3*H*218; 3*H*469; 4*H*45. 19. 4*H*92. 20. 4*H*438. 21. *Gould*, 138-140.

22. *MG(G)*, Mar. 29, 1753; *Gould*, 139-40. 23. *Gould*, 140.

24. *Gould*, 141 n78. 25. 6 *Md. Arch.*, 236.

26. *MG(G)*, Apr. 26, May 24, 1745; June 24, 1746.

27. *MG(G)*, June 24, Aug. 5, 1746. 28. *MG(G)*, June 2, Dec. 9, 1746.

29. *MG(G)*, June 10, 1746; Dec. 9, 1746; May 10, 1753; *Mifflin*, 14.

30. *MG(G)*, Oct. 25, Mar. 29, 1753; *VG(H)*, Apr. 22, 1757; see also *Spruill*, 302-4.

31. *MG(G)*, Oct. 12, 1752. 32. *Gould*, 138; *Honyman*, 7-8; *Eddis*, 19.

33. *Mereness*, 405. 34. Sailing Directions, 1739-78, *BMAM*, LC, 27891.

35. A. Smith, *Chart of the Bay of Chesapeake*. This chart by the pilot of St. Mary's was first published in 1776.

36. Swem, *Maps Relating to Virginia*, 41-71 and Introductory Note 37.

37. 4 *EJC*, 253-55, 280, 298; *CTBP*, 1731-34, 241.

38. 4 *APCC*, no. 537, pp. 619-23.

39. Thornton and Fisher, *Virginia, Maryland, Pennsylvania, East and West Jarsey*, in *The English Pilot* (London, 1706), bk. 4, no. 13, btw. pp. 22-23; see also Swem, *Maps Relating to Virginia*, 56-57; 5 *Winsor*, 273; Phillips, *Va. Cartography*, 43. The Thornton and Fisher chart was reissued in the editions of 1737, 1745, 1749, 1755, 1758, 1760, 1767, 1773, and 1775. A Dutch chart of the Chesapeake known as the Johannis van Keulen chart, in Claas Janssoon Voogt, *Le nouveau et grand illuminant flambeau de la Mer* (Amsterdam, 1713), pt. 4, btw. pp. 42-43, and in an earlier undated edition, *ca.* 1700-1710, is almost certainly based on the Thornton and Fisher chart. The 1737 and subsequent editions of *The English Pilot* also contained a large-scale chart—two miles to the inch—of the lower part of the Bay, entitled *A Draught of Virginia from the Capes to York in York River and to Kuiquotan or Hampton* in James River, by Mark Tiddeman. It was 18⅛ by 23⅛ inches, and indicated no latitude or longitude.

40. Walter Hoxton, *Mapp of the Bay of Chesapeack with the Rivers Potomack, Potapsco, North East, and Part of Chester* (London, 1735). The chart bears an elaborate cartouche, the arms of Virginia and Maryland, and a representation of a ship. It is dedicated to "the Merchants of London Trading to Virginia and Maryland," and has eighteen sections, each 15 by 11½ inches. Copy in Md. Hist. Soc.; small-scale reproduction in Matthew Page Andrews, *Virginia, the Old Dominion*, btw. pp. 212-13.

41. Walter Hoxton first appears in Maryland records in 1699, aboard the Richard and Margaret. *PMCA, 1695-1729*, 211, 214.

42. 25 *Md. Arch.*, 329; 50 *Md. Arch.*, 205; 3*MHM*72; 10*MHM*145; 10*MHM*148. When Hyde Hoxton married Susanna Brooke, she was the widow of Walter Smith (*ca.* 1692-1734), one of whose sisters married

Thomas Brooke, another Col. Thomas Addison, and a third Daniel Dulany, and whose son, Walter Smith (1715-43), half-brother of young Walter Hoxton, married Elizabeth Chew.

43. There are two copies of the Hoxton chart in the British Museum, both in poor condition. One is dated 1735, and bears the imprint, "London, Printed for the Author and Sold by B. Betts at the Virginia and Maryland Coffee house near the Royal Exchange and E. Baldwin at Ratcliff Cross." This differs slightly from the one cited in note 40, which says "W. Betts" instead of "B. Betts." The other is undated and has the words "Sold by W. Mount and T. Page on Tower Hill." A third copy is in the Public Record Office, London, and a fourth in the Maryland Historical Society. This information was supplied through the courtesy of Burton W. Adkinson, Acting Chief, Division of Maps, Library of Congress.

44. Swem, *Maps Relating to Virginia*, 71, 72, 82, 83. The edition in the author's possession is the 1794 edition; London, Laurie and Whittle, May 12, 1794.

45. Editions were published in 1776, 1778, 1794, and 1798: see above, *n*44. The 1778 edition was done in Paris, the others in London.

46. An Anthony Smith appeared as a witness in St. Mary's County in 1749, and again in the census of 1776, at which time he was 48 years old and had a five-year-old male dependent. Nothing further is known about him. 24 *Maryland Wills, 1688-1744*, 18; 1 *Maryland Records*, 50. The young boy may have been the Anthony Smith who was active after 1800 and who appears occasionally in the *Maryland Archives*. The federal census of 1790 does not carry the name of Anthony Smith.

47. 4 *Md. Arch.*, 303, 307; *Semmes*, 83; for subsequent references to Rablie in connection with Ingle's Rebellion, see 4 *Md. Arch.*, 513.

48. 2*H*35; *Flippin*, 54-55. 49. 2 *Bruce*, 352-53; 1*C*32.

50. 1*V*363; *CSPC, 1702*, no. 380, p. 268. 51. 1*C*197. 52. 6*H*490.

53. 7*H*581. 54. 17*W(1)*114.

55. Both the act of 1755 and that of 1762 made it illegal for more than two pilots to associate themselves.

56. 7*H*580.

57. Beverley wrote of the Chesapeake in 1705 that "the Experience of one Voyage teaches any Master to go up afterwards without a Pilot." 2 *Beverley*, 4.

58. 10*MHM*12; depn. of Alexander Stewart, Sept. 4, 1754, *MNPB, 1744-96, B.*

59. *Calvert Papers*, MHS, no. 295½, p. 65.

60. For example, even the jolly innkeeper of Annapolis, Samuel Middleton, on occasion served as pilot: *MG(G)*, June 23, 1747. For examples of pilots in Chester and Sassafras Rivers, see depn. of Arthur Savage, Jan. 11, 1757, and depn. of Joseph Bill, March 11, 1762, *MNPB, 1744-96, B.*

61. 4 *MPP, Black Books,* pt. 2, no. 111; *Calvert Papers,* MHS, no. 2, p. 180; 6 *Md. Arch.,* 92, 408; *Gould,* 155.

62. For example, Richard Bryan in 1755 offered to pilot vessels from Annapolis to the Patapsco, about 30 miles by a tortuous channel, for £3; to Susquehanna, about 50 miles, for £5; and to Cape Henry, 145 miles, for £8 6s. 10d., Maryland currency: *MG(G),* Apr. 17, 1755.

63. In going up James River the mean tidal range falls from 2.6 feet at Newport News to 2.0 feet at Jamestown, but thereafter increases to 2.8 feet at City Point, 3.2 feet at Curles, and 3.7 feet at Richmond. In Potomac River the mean tidal range increases from Point Lookout, 1.3 feet, to Blakistone Island, 1.9 feet, then falls to 1.5 feet at Chapel Point, the mouth of Port Tobacco River. Above that point it gradually increases to 2.2 feet at Mount Vernon, 2.8 feet at Alexandria, and 2.9 feet at Washington. See U. S. Coast and Geodetic Survey, *Tide Tables, Atlantic Ocean, 1938.*

64. 1 *Oldmixon,* 414; *MG(G),* Oct. 24, 1754; for the normal tide at Annapolis, see *Burnaby,* 51.

65. 3 *Force,* no. 12, p. 11. 66. 3 *Force,* no. 12, p. 5.

67. *Tatham,* 92; 1 *Bruce,* 445; *Gould,* 156. For an interesting discussion of soil erosion and the silting-up of rivers in this region, see 35 *Geog. Rev.,* 219-38. 68. 2*H*455; 2*H*484.

69. 3*H*46; 10*V*244. The act was renewed in 1705: 3*H*353; see also 6*H*98.

70. 13 *Md. Arch.,* 487-88; *Gould,* 156. 71. *Gould,* 156 n.140; 19*V*89.

72. Samuel Galloway to Capt. Tippell, Sept. 13, 1768, Samuel Galloway Letterbook, 1766-71, *Galloway Papers,* LC.

73. *Prince George's County Records,* X, 109; *Gould,* 156.

74. *Gould,* 157; 6 *MPP, Black Books,* no. 11. 75. *MG(G),* May 31, 1759.

76. Petition, Apr. 21, 1761, 6 *MPP, Black Books,* no. 11.

77. 5*Amer. Neptune,* 205.

78. *Eddis,* 5. The suggestion for the Great Falls canal was made in 1769. The Chesapeake and Delaware canal was suggested in 1679 by Jasper Danckaerts: *Danckaerts,* 127-28. 79. *VG(P&D),* Jan. 16, 1772.

80. *Berkeley,* 7-8. For other attempts to open up the headwaters of rivers, e.g. the James and Chickahominy in 1765, see 8*H*148. Such attempts were much more common after the Revolution.

## CHAPTER IV

1. Andrews, *Virginia,* 10. 2. 1 Brown's *Genesis,* 338-53.

3. 1 Brown's *Genesis,* 384-86.

4. Wertenbaker, *Planters,* 25; 1 *Bruce,* 218, 235.

5. 1 Andrews, *Col. Per.,* 153.

6. Craven, *Va. Co.,* 100-104; 1 Andrews, *Col. Per.,* 139.

7. 1 *APCC,* no. 63; 1 Andrews, *Col. Per.,* 138-39.

# Footnotes · Chapter IV

8. Craven, *Va. Co.*, 195; 1 Andrews, *Col. Per.*, 139-40.  9. *Jacobstein*, 23, 28.
10. *Smith*, 615.  11. 4 Andrews, *Col. Per.*, 19, 35-37.  12. *Tatham*, 109.
13. 3 *Force*, no. 12, p 15: Clayton says that "the same Sort of Seed in different Earths, will produce Tobacco much different, as to Goodness"; John Custis to Philip Perry, 1737, *Custis Letterbook, 1717-41*, LC, f. 73-74, says that he grew oronoco on the Eastern Shore of Virginia, using "the same seed of my York Crops"; 2 *Douglass*, 370n, says of the various sorts of tobacco that "the difference seems to be only from the soil."
14. *U. S. D. A. Yearbook for 1936*, 805-22; 11 *Agr. Hist.*, 44.  15. 2*V*18.
16. Micajah and Philip Perry to John Custis, Aug. 23, 1716, VHS; Sir Thomas Lawrence in a memorial of June 25, 1695, speaks of the "sort of dark tobacco" grown on the Eastern Shore of Maryland: *CSPC, 1692-96*, no. 1916, p. 518.
17. *Darnall*, 7; 1 *Oldmixon*, 448.
18. William Beverley to Micajah and Philip Perry, July 12, 1737, *Beverley Letterbook, 1737-44/5*, NYPL: Beverley hoped that his tobacco would "obtain a good name and become as famous as Mr. Burwell's tobacco."
19. John Mair, writing in 1752, said: "all the tobacco in the country, when brought to the warehouse, comes under one of two denominations, viz.: *Aronoko*, and *Sweet-scented*:"1*W(1)*14.
20. Writing in 1799 after twenty years as a planter in Virginia, Tatham said: "I have not been able to learn from the inspectors themselves (who I have frequently questioned thereupon) that their botanical knowledge is sufficient to distinguish, at this day, one species from another of the blended mass by any leading characteristic . . . and hence (although the law affects to make a distinction) we most generally find all kinds classed in the Oronoko column:" *Tatham*, 4n.
21. Oldmixon considered the thriving of Maryland to be "plain Proof of the Profit of the coarse Tobacco, preferable to the sweet-scented, or rather that which is sold to a foreign Market turns to a better Account every way, than what is made for a home Consumption with more Labour and Cost, and at last with less Gain:" 1 *Oldmixon*, 340.
22. Edward Athawes to John Carter, April 10, 1735, 1 *Carter Papers*, VHS, 15.
23. In Maryland everything was about three weeks later than in the lower part of Virginia: *CSPC, 1696-97*, no. 1253, p. 582.
24. When transplanted they were about four or five inches high: *Carman*, 159.
25. *CSPC, 1696-97*, no. 1285, p. 591.
26. *Alsop*, 69; Phillips, *Life and Labor*, 112-13; 1 *Bruce*, 438-41.
27. In the early days as many as 25 or 30 leaves were grown on a plant. In 1628 this practice was condemned by the Virginia Assembly, and a limit of 12 leaves set on a plant: 1*H*135. James Blair in 1697 told the Council of Trade and Plantations that in Maryland the stalk is allowed

to grow high and carry up to 20 leaves, whereas in Virginia it is cut, and not above 5 or 6 leaves left on it: *CSPC, 1696-97*, no. 1253, p. 582; as a rule only 7 or 8 leaves were allowed to remain. See 2 *Gipson*, 114; *Carman*, 160.

28. *Alsop*, 69-70; Phillips, *Life and Labor*, 113. Alsop, writing in 1666, said: "some twice or thrice they are weeded, and succoured from their illegitimate Leaves that would be peeping out from the body of the Stalk. They top the several Plants as they find occasion in their predominating rankness."

29. *Carman*, 160.

30. The plants were pegged through the stalk to a tobacco stick which was suspended in the barn. The barns averaged about thirty by twenty feet but were occasionally forty, fifty, and even sixty feet long. The proper degree of curing was ascertained by the quickness with which the stem snapped when bent. 1 *Bruce*, 440-41.

31. *Thomas*, 424. 32. Phillips, *Life and Labor*, 114; 14*W(1)*88.

33. Oronoco was bulkier than sweetscented and could not be as tightly prized as the latter. The thinner, finer sweetscented admitted of remarkably close prizing. This accounts for the fact that a hogshead of sweetscented weighed more than a hogshead of oronoco. In 1724 the average hogshead of sweetscented weighed 700 lbs. and the average hogshead of oronoco 600 lbs., although the governor of Virginia estimated that eight plants of both kinds weighed a pound. *CSPC, 1724-25*, no. 487, iii, p. 319.

34. *Tatham*, 79, 117, tells of a crop he bought at South Quay, Prince Edward County, Va., in 1778, the hogsheads of which weighed between 1400 and 1700 lbs. In *MG(G)*, Aug. 20, 1752, it was announced that a hogshead from Corsica Creek, Queen Anne's County, Md., weighed 1969 lbs. gross, and, deducting the weight of the cask, 1829 lbs. net. These were exceptional.

35. *Tatham*, 92-93, describes a tobacco flat as " a kind of flat-bottomed lighter or scow, which draws but a few inches of water, and will take off from ten to twenty hogsheads or more, and convey them to vessels in the channel which frequent the river trade . . . These lighters are very convenient for this purpose, being built with flat bottoms, upright sides of about two feet six inches or three feet, and sloped up at each end so as to ride over the waves with less resistance than a square or blunt end would permit."

36. Henry Callister to Foster Cunliffe & Sons, Aug. 6, 1747, *Callister Papers*, NYPL, 81. "The Tobacco they buy is often rolled 20 miles & upwards . . . it is always damaged by it & shaken to pieces both inside and outside."

37. *Gould*, 144-45. 38. *Thomas*, 424.

39. Major Wilson told the Board of Trade in 1697 that one man could tend 10,000 plants covering about three acres which will produce about three

hogsheads or 15 hundredweight of sweetscented or 10 hundredweight of oronoco tobacco. *CSPC, 1696-97,* no. 1285, p. 591.

40. Phillips, *Life and Labor,* 114-15.

41. *CSPC, 1689-92,* no. 1951, p. 578. 42. *Thomas,* 424.

43. William Fitzhugh to Oliver Luke, July 21, 1692, said: "trading by sea is very difficult & uncertain in these war times, for a Trader, today he may be worth 1000 £ and tomorrow not worth a groat." Fitzhugh lost two crops in three years. 4*V*72.

44. *CSPC, 1689-92,* no. 1951, p. 578. "Little tobacco is on board, and little tobacco stripped owing to the dryness of the season."

45. Washington to Capel & Osgood Hanbury, Aug. 10, 1760, *Washington Invoices,* 1755-65, wrote that "a continued series of Rain for near four weeks has given a sad turn to our expectations . . . a great deal of Tobacco being Drownd, and the rest spotting very fast, which is always a consequence of so much Wet Weather."

46. *Tatham,* 53. 47. *Tatham,* 48; 1 *Bruce,* 443.

48. *Tatham,* 47n, 213-15, recommended the use of skilled professional stowers "of great practice and experience in this art." He tells of the levers and jacks, "made use of in stowing tobacco" by which means "whole casks of tobacco are compressed into a much smaller space than they seem naturally designed to occupy." This practice, he added, resulted in "tobacco which had been *squeezed to death,* as it were, without regard to the proprietor's loss."

49. *Tatham,* 97, observed: "I believe it would not be hard to prove, that negro attendants at the Richmond warehouses have been honoured with applications from England for the choicest chewing tobacco." He also asserted that the losses in this way amounted to "many thousand pounds of tobacco per annum."

50. Edward Hunt & Sons to Robert Carter, Nov. 6, 1770, 1 *Carter Papers,* 81, VHS.

51. William Nelson to James Gildart, July 26, 1766, *Nelson Letterbook, CNHP.*

52. Halbert Hanson to Samuel Galloway, Nov. 25, 1758, *Galloway Papers,* Box 1742-69, NYPL. On another occasion London merchants reported to a planter that a cargo was "much damag'd" because the captain "met with very severe Weather at sea." They hoped the planter would not "impute any fault to us:" Higginson & Bird to William Kenney, Sept. 30, 1718, Higginson & Bird Letterbook, 1718-19, *Galloway Papers,* LC; see also Edward Athawes to John and Charles Carter, Jan. 10, 1738/9, 1 *Carter Papers,* 24, VHS.

53. Francis Jerdone to Neil Buchanan, Nov. 19, 1740, *Jerdone Letterbook, 1736-37, 1738-44,* W&M. See also William Beverley to Micajah Perry & Co., Sept. 19, 1739, *Beverley Letterbook, 1737-44/5,* NYPL.

54. Henry Callister to Cunliffe & Sons, Aug. 6, 1747, *Callister Papers,* NYPL, f. 80; Francis Jerdone to Edward Hunt, May 10, 1757, *Jerdone Letterbook,* 1756-63, W&M; Account of Sale of . . . Tobacco of Robert Carter, 1758, I *Carter Papers,* 35, VHS; James Lawson to Alexander Hamilton, Jan. 31, 1764, *Hamilton Papers, 1760-1800,* MHS; Francis Jerdone to Thomas Flowerdewe, July 15, 1760, *Jerdone Letterbook, 1756-63,* W&M.

55. *MG(G),* July 28, 1757. 56. *Tatham,* 49-50 .

57. For example: Account of Sale of Tobacco of Robert Carter, Jr., 1733, by Edward Athawes, I *Carter Papers,* 3, VHS; see also I *Carter Papers,* 5, 13, 15, 30, 32, 35, 37, 41, 43, 44; *VG(P)* Aug. 5, 1737; Account of Sale of Tobacco of Col. John Custis by Hansbury & Co., July 10, 1740, VHS; *Tatham,* 198-200.

58. William Beverley to Micajah and Philip Perry, July 12, 1737, *Beverley Letterbook, 1737-44/5,* NYPL, said: "we never have our accounts by the Ship that Carries the tobacco but are generally obliged to wait 12 or 18 months longer." Few planters were as cautious as William Fitzhugh who wrote his English consignment merchant in 1695: "I desire you Sir to send my Account Currant by the first ships and send me two or three duplicates for fear of miscarriage, for not knowing how my Account stands, I dare not send for goods though my wants are very great and pressing:" 4*V*416.

59. *Nettels,* 65-66. 60. I *Bassett,* 569-70.

61. Francis Jerdone to Neil Buchanan, Mar. 4, 1741/2, *Jerdone Letterbook, 1736-73, 1738-44,* W&M, told that Mr. Millar "industriously spreads it abroad at all publick places you have cheated him out of £20 besides a great many opprobrious reflections on you."

62. I *Bassett,* 569-70; William Byrd I in 1686 sent "an Indian Habitt" for the little son of his London merchant, consisting of a "Belly Clout, one pair of Stockings and one pair of Mocosins or Indian shoes also Some shells to put about his necke and a cap of Wampum." They were put up in an Indian basket to which was tied "a Bow and arrows," 25*V*129.

63. 2*V*17; 2*V*269; 4*V*415; I *Bassett,* 569-70. 64. 9*V*115; 9*V*124.

65. William Allason, a factor for Baird & Walker of Glasgow, received an annual wage of £60 and the right to sell £120 worth of goods on his own account the first year and £150 thereafter. In the West India trade he shared his commissions with the company. 39*V*112.

66. Francis Jerdone, a factor for Alexander Spiers & Hugh Brown of Glasgow, received a commission of 5% for purchasing tobacco. In 1758 he purchased 227 hhds. for £2996 4d., yielding a commission of £149 16s. See invoice in *Jerdone Letterbook, 1756-63,* W&M, following letter of June 20, 1758.

67. Francis Jerdone to Neil Buchanan, May 20, 1741, *Jerdone Letterbook, 1736-37, 1738-44,* W&M, ordered rum, molasses, and sugar, saying:

"There is a necessity in having these goods without which no Tobacco Purchase can be made;" Mair, speaking of stores, said: "wherever planters find they can be best suited and served, thither they commonly resort, and there dispose of their tobacco," 14*W(1)*89.

68. William Johnston to Neil Buchanan, Oct. 16, 1738, May 7, 1739, Francis Jerdone in *Jerdone Letterbook, 1736-37, 1738-44,* W&M, said "I Endeavour to deal as much in the mony way as I can, tobacco commonly being much cheaper purchased that way" and urged the importation of cash from the West Indies or England "their being an allowance of 15 per cent on payments of Dutys on liquor or Slaves Imported."

69. Henry Callister to William Murray, Apr. 6, 1748, *Callister Papers,* NYPL, 120-21, wrote: "If the planter takes one article of a merchant . . . he must let his whole Crop go to that Merchant, at least a whole hogshead."

70. *Callister Papers,* NYPL, ff. 81, 116-17, 121, 143. In 1747 Callister bought 50 hhds. of "ready" tobacco and about 70 hhds. of tobacco "on the Ground."

71. 39*V*117. These regional agreements were seldom kept; one or more of the factors failed to keep faith.

72. Henry Callister to Cunliffe & Sons, Aug. 6, 1747, *Callister Papers,* NYPL, f. 81; *Gould,* 64-65.

73. Henry Callister to Foster Cunliffe & Sons, July 10, 1745, Dec. 28, 1747, *Callister Papers,* NYPL, ff. 31, 114. Callister wrote: "we give the best Planters extraordinary [prices] for the Advantage of Shippable heavy Tobacco and the Convenience of their Situation."

74. William Nelson to Edward Hunt & Son, Sept. 11, 1766, *Nelson Letterbook, 1766-75,* CNHP, consigned 100 hhds. to a London merchant, saying: "88 of which are of my Crops."

75. These stores were often kept in the planter's house; see 2 *Bruce,* 381. *MG(G),* May 19, 1747, has an advertisement of the sale of "the late Dwelling-House of Mr. William Hardie, at one End of which is a Store."

76. 1 *Oldmixon,* 339-40: "Every considerable Planter's Warehouse being like a Shop, . . . he supplies not only himself with what he wants, but the inferior Planters, Servants and Labourers, and has Commodities to barter for Tobacco," and further on, "These Gentlemen take Care to supply the poorer sort with Goods and Necessaries, and are sure to keep them always in their Debt, and consequently dependent on them." 1 *Oldmixon,* 453-54.

77. The tobacco fleet of 1703 consisted of 36 London ships with 11,440 hhds. and 12 outport ships with 3,878 hhds. *CSPC, 1702-1703,* no. 1366, p. 864; see also *Nettles,* 51 *n*11; *Morriss,* 88.

78. Higginson & Bird to Nathaniel West, Dec. 24, 1718, Higginson & Bird Letterbook, 1718-19, *Galloway Papers*, LC.
79. *Darnall*, 18. 80. *MG(G)*, Apr. 15, 1729. 81. *14W(1)88*.
82. *Morriss*, 43-45; *7W(2)239*.
83. *Berkeley*, 5, says "one Ship from Virginia brings more Money to the Crown, than five Ships of the same burthen do from the Barbados"; in 1669 Berkeley told Lord Arlington that the king derived more revenue from Virginia than from all the West Indian islands together: *CSPC, 1669-74*, no. 73, p. 27. In 1673 Sir John Knight told the Earl of Shaftesbury that "Virginia is of as great importance to his Majesty as the Spanish Indies to Spain:" *CSPC, 1669-74*, no. 1159, p. 530; and in 1683 Lord Howard of Effigham told the Lords of Trade that "the revenue of Virginia exceeds that of all the other plantations put together": *CSPC, 1681-85*, no. 1273, p. 505.
84. *CSPC, 1696-97*, no. 1289, p. 593; 11 *CTB, 1696-97*, 322; *Morriss*, 46; 2*Douglass*, 372; *Tatham*, 288.
85. *7W(2)240*. 86. *Thomas*, 425. 87. *Tatham*, 279-81; *7W(2)240*.
88. *CSPC, 1685-88*, no. 386, p. 99; *CSPC, 1712-14*, Preface, p. viii; Francis Jerdone to Latham Arnold, June 25, 1757, *Jerdone Letterbook*, W&M, 1756-63; *Morriss*, 43-45.
89. *Flippin*, 231; *C.O.* 5: 1329: 167, 237, 327; *C.O.* 5: 1330: 29, 33, 173, 177, 233, 347, 499.
90. The earlier figures are based upon average exports 1700-14, *Morriss*, 31-35; the later figures are based upon statistics in 1*Chalmers Papers*, Maryland, NYPL, 1619-1777, 38.
91. 9 *CTB, 1689-92*, pt. 4, pp. 1408-9.
92. *CSPC, 1696-97*, no. 956, ii, p. 457; Rev. William Dawson to Philip Lee, Dec. 9, 1743, 1 *Dawson Papers*, NYPL, 14-15.
93. *5W(2)252*.
94. 1 *APCC*, no. 565, p. 331; 1 *Bruce*, 390-92; 2*H200*; 3 *Md. Arch.*, 510-12; 5 *Md. Arch.*, 5-6; 1 *Patriotic Marylander*, 36-42.
95. 5 *Md. Arch.*, 6-7, 18; 2*H225*; 2*H229*; 2*H250*; 1 *Col. Recs. of N. C.*, 117; 1 *Bruce*, 393-94; 1 *Patriotic Marylander*, 36-42.
96. 1 *Bruce*, 401. 97. 5 *Md. Arch.*, 361-62; 28*V*117; 1 *Bruce*, 404.
98. In the late 1720's there were plant-cutting riots in Maryland, but they were suppressed before very much tobacco was destroyed.
99. *CSPC*, 1726-27, no. 215, p. 110; no. 844, p. 429.
100. *CSPC, 1728-29*, no. 372, pp. 187-89.
101. *CSPC, 1731*, no. 382, p. 239; *CSPC*, 1731, no. 516, p. 356.
102. William Byrd II to John Custis, Oct 19, 1717, *Emmet Collection*, NYPL, favored the practice and thought that "if every body wou'd agree to Strip all the Sweet Scented Tobacco in the Country, twou'd be a great

advantage to the Trade, because twill Sink the Quantity a fourth part, which proportion they compute the Stalks to amount to."

103. 9 Geo. I, c. 21. 104. *C.O.* 5: 1337: 71: 3.

105. *JBT*, Jan. 1728/9-Dec. 1734, 5, 39. 106. 22*W(1)*57.

107. 1*H*456; 1 *Md. Arch.*, 446; *Wyckoff*, 56-57; Virginia established the size of the hogshead to be 43″ by 26,″ whereas Maryland fixed it at 42″ to 43″ by 26″ to 27.″

108. *JBT*, 1704-1708/9, 433; 8*W(2)*13. 109. 13 *Md. Arch.*, 552-54.

110. *JBT*. 1704-1708/9, 433. 111. *JBT*, 1704-1708/9, 433.

112. *JBT*, 1704-1708/9, 474-75. The specifications in Virginia were those of the act of 1695 as re-enacted in 1706.

113. *JBT*, Feb. 1708/9-Mar. 1714/15, 267-68. The merchants carried the day with their arguments that a difference in the size of the hogshead "would be a very considerable loss to the owners of shipping in the stowage," that ships in the tobacco trade "are built proportionately to the size of tobacco hogsheads, that is, to contain seven hogsheads in depth in the hold; whereas if 2 inches in diameter in the head more were allow'd to the Maryland hogsheads, then their ships could hold no more than six hogsheads and a half in depth, . . . whereby the owners must . . . either crop the hogsheads, or . . . build new ships, or . . . give up the trade."

114. 38 *Md. Arch.*, 128-30; *Wyckoff*, 124 *n*48.

115. 30 *Md. Arch.*, 348-55; 34 *Md. Arch.*, 503; 36 *Md. Arch.*, 596; 37 *Md. Arch.*, 149, 553-55; 38 *Md. Arch.*, 199-207; *Wyckoff*, 124.

116. 13 *Md. Arch.*, 552. Attempts were made to protect the hogsheads while in the hands of shipmasters, who sometimes "cropped" (i.e. cut) them to facilitate stowage. The Maryland act of 1707 required masters to give bond with one surety of £200 sterling that they would not "Cut, Crop, lessen, Diminish, impair, Deface any Tobacco Hogsheads." The penalty was £3 sterling per hogshead. This act was disallowed in 1703 because the penalty was considered too high. *JBT, 1704-08/9*, 474-75; 26*MHM*17.

117. 1 *Bruce*, 452-5; 8*W(2)*12.

118. *CSPC, 1685-88*, no. 1396, p. 418; no. 1397, p. 418.

119. *CSPC, 1685-88*, nos. 1461, 1481, 1482, 1489, 1498; 8 *Md. Arch.*, 45-46; *Wyckoff*, 97-99.

120. The Virginians attributed the king's order to the influence of the London consignment merchants who conceived that the prohibition of bulk "would answer their Particular Interest & profit," and politely told King James II that he was misinformed. *JHB, 1659/60-1693*, 317-19, 322-23. The Marylanders declared that bulk tobacco was a kind that

would be damaged if casked, that it was largely consumed in England thereby paying five pence per pound duty to the crown whereas casked tobacco was largely re-exported, thereby escaping all but one halfpenny per pound duty, and that casking their tobacco would cut off their trade with the outports. 13 *Md. Arch.*, 151, 198-99.

121. *CSPC, 1689-92*, nos. 2075, 2140.

122. 2 *Byrd*, 140-58; 1 *CTP*, 226; 9 *CTB*, 1608; *Wyckoff*, 103.

123. 10 Wm. III, c. 10; 19 *Md. Arch.*, 90-91; *CSPC, 1693-96*, no. 1897.

124. *CSPC, 1702-1703*, no. 993, pp. 599-600; 8*W(2)*13. In 1703, Col. Quary complained to the Board of Trade of the naval officers and collectors in Virginia and Maryland: "I am very confident that no officer ever saw or knew what was shipped . . . but they take the report of the Masters and certify accordingly, which gives all the opportunity imaginable to carry what Bulk Tobacco they please."

125. *CSPC, 1574-1660*, no. 45; 1 *Bruce*, 254; 8*W(2)*14; for examples after 1619, see 1 *Bruce*, 304-6; 1*H*152, 1*H*165, 1*H*190, 1*H*204, 1*H*210, 1*H*225; 1 *Md. Arch.*, 90-91, 97-98, 360; *Wyckoff*, 51-52, 55.

126. *Wyckoff*, 55. 127. *Wyckoff*, 126-27.

128. *CSPC, 172-14*, no. 530, pp. 274-78. Gov. Spotswood said that "This law therefore by obliging all planters to have their tobacco view'd by a sworn officer . . . has made provision against the exportation of all such trash as is said to be allowed by the Customhouse officers in the outports as damaged tobacco, and thereafter frequently re-exported with the benefite of the drawback." See also *CSPC, 1714-15*, no. 188, pp. 82-88; *JBT*, Mar. 1714/15-Oct. 1718, 139.

129. *JBT*, Mar. 1714/5-Oct. 1718, 229-30.

130. *CSPC, 1716-17*, no. 687, pp. 362-63. For the discussion leading to the disallowance, see *CSPC, 1716-17*, nos. 559, 610, 625, pp. 298, 328, 335.

131. *CSPC, 1722-23*, no. 625, pp. 297-98; *CSPC, 1728-29*, no. 796, pp. 414-20; *C.O.* 5: 1337: 72, 1.

132. 4*H*247.

133. Examples: Shockoe's on Col. Byrd's land, Turkey Island on Col. Randolph's land, and others on land belonging to Col. Bolling, Col. Munford, Mr. Bland, Mr. Holloway, Col. Page, Mr. Meriwether, Col. Fitzhugh, and Mr. Conway.

134. *CSPC, 1730*, no. 635, p. 422; *CSPC, 1731*, no. 85, p. 56.

135. *CSPC, 1731*, no. 187, pp. 106-7; no. 363, p. 224.

136. *CSPC, 1732*, no. 149, pp. 97-99.

137. *CSPC, 1733*, no. 248, pp. 145-46; no. 250, pp. 146-47.

138. William Johnston to Neil Buchanan, Dec. 2, 1758, *Jerdone Letterbook, 1736-37, 1738-44*, W&M; *VG(P)*, Jan. 5, 1738/9.

139. 38*Md. Arch.*, 290-94; *Wyckoff*, 128, 129, 140-46, 151-52, 159-60.

140. In 1728, after much bickering between the two houses of assembly, a compromise was reached: production was limited to 7,000 plants per person, and the fees of the clergy and attorneys were reduced one-fourth. Despite the protest of the clergy, the act was passed by the assembly, but disallowed by the lord proprietor in 1730.

141. Daniel Dulany to Lord Baltimore, 1743, *Dulany Papers*, MHS, box 2, no. 17; Gov. Thomas Bladen to Lord Baltimore, Feb. 3, 1743/4, *Calvert Papers*, MHS, no. 1101.

142. Henry Callister to Foster Cunliffe & Sons, Jan. 11, 1744, *Callister Papers*, NYPL, f. 10; same to same, July 10, 1745, *ibid.*, f. 31; *MG(G)*, Apr. 28, 1747, Apr. 5, 1753; *Gould*, 60-61.

143. 44 *Md. Arch.*, 595; *Wyckoff*, 174-77.

144. 14*W(1)*90: The inspectors were "obliged to give oath and bond, with security in £1,000 sterling. Their salaries varied from £25 to £60 currency, "acording to the importance of the place where they serve."

145. Warehouses were situated on "all the rivers and bays of Virginia and Maryland, at the distance of about twelve or fourteen miles from one another," 14*W(1)*90.

146. The term "tare" applied to the weight of the cask itself. The net weight of a prized hogshead represented the weight of the tobacco itself. The gross weight of a hogshead was the sum of the net and tare.

147. A specimen crop note (entries conjectural):

### RAPPAHANNOCK RIVER

FALMOUTH WAREHOUSE, 5TH DAY, JANY. 1738

| MARK | No. | SWEETSCENTED | | | | | | ORONOCO | | | Rec'd of Chas. Carter, Esq. 3 hhds of crop tobo., marks, nos., weights, and species as per margin to be deliver'd us by the said Chas. Carter Esq. or his order, for exportation, when demanded. Witness our hands, Antho. Strothers, Wm. Johnston |
| | | Stemmed | | | Leaf | | | | | | |
| | | Gross | Neat | Tare | Gross | Neat | Tare | Gross | Neat | Tare | |
| c4c xx c.c. ɔc | 71 | 1238 | 1141 | 97 | 1150 | 1052 | 98 | 1047 | 957 | 90 | |

148. *Tatham*, 84-86; 14*W(1)*91.

A specimen transfer note:

---

POTOMAC RIVER　　　No. 34

Yeocomico warehouse, the 10th day of February, 1783. This shall oblige us the subscribers, our and each of our executors and administrators, to pay, upon demand, to Robert More　　　, or his order, at the above mentioned warehouse, five hundred and sixty pounds of good merchantable Aronoko tobacco, according to the directions of the act of assembly for amending the staple of tobacco, and preventing frauds in his Majesty's customs; it being for the like quantity received.

Witness our hands.

DANIEL TEBBS
MATTHEW RUST

---

149. *Tatham*, 84-86; 14*W(1)*92. The inspectors received 2s. 6d. currency in cash for prizing and 30 lbs. of tobacco for the cask.
150. Gov. Gooch told the Board of Trade, Feb. 7, 1731, that the tobacco notes are "accepted as payment at any store or shop" as readily as money. *CSPC, 1731*, no. 67, pp. 47-50.
151. 14*W(1)*92. 152. *CSPC, 1681-85*, no. 319, p. 156; 4 *Donnan*, 56n.
153. 8*W(2)*240.
154. Col. Quary wrote the Board of Trade on 1704, "The present war hath cut us out of the trade of Spain, France, Flanders and part of the Baltic, which took off at least 20,000 hogsheads every year:" 26*MHM*24.
155. Col. Quary said in 1706: "The Dutch and their neighbors in Germany are said to have planted the last year 33,500 hogsheads," *CSPC, 1706-1708*, no. 225, p. 98; 26*MHM*25; 8*W(2)*241.
156. *CSPC, 1706-1708*, no. 225, p. 98. 157. *CSPC, 1706-1708*, no. 483, p. 213.
158. 3*W(2)*250. 159. *CSPC, 1706-1708*, no. 684, p. 342.
160. *JBT, 1704-1708/9*, 397; 2 *APCC*, no. 1044, p. 356. The Board of Trade favored this proposal because the purchase of 360,000 lbs. of tobacco per annum in England would result in the enrichment of the royal treasury by some £9,343:15:0 a year.
161. *CSPC, 1712-14*, no. 319, p. 169; no. 503, p. 251.
162. *CSPC, 1724-25*, no. 291, i, pp. 183-85. 163. *Darnall*, 33-34.

164. *Darnall,* 33-34; *8W(2)*9. To the suggestion that the French agent might buy from the outport merchants rather than yield to the high price of the London association, Darnall replied: "the French cannot supply themselves at the Out-Ports with the Quantity they want; nor in Quality equal to Tobacco at London." Even if they could, the outports would be drained, he said, and "we shall in that Case have the Dutch Market all to ourselves."

165. *VG(P),* Aug. 5, 1737. 166. *8W(2)*9.

167. *3APCC,* no. 602, pp. 796-98. The Privy Council was won over to the idea because it was represented that the French purchased £160,000 worth of colonial tobacco a year for ready money, that sixty ships were employed carrying tobacco to France, and that the kind of tobacco consumed by the French was unfit for any other market.

168. 2 *Douglass,* 372; 3 *APCC,* no. 602, pp. 796-98; 3 *APCC,* no. 602, pp. 796-98.

169. *14W(1)*88; *Tatham,* 279-81.

170. Examples: Walker & Co. to William Allason, Jan. 17, 1758, *Allason Papers,* VSL; William Allason to Baird & Walker, Mar. 1, 1760, *Allason Letterbook, 1757-70,* VSL.

171. William Allason to Baird & Walker, March 1, 1760, *ibid.*

172. Alexander Walker to John Baird and William Allason, Jan. 8, 1761, *Allason Papers,* VSL.

173. Perkins, Buchanan, & Brown to Clement Hill, Jan. 17, 1764, *Clement Hill Papers, 1683/4-1819,* MHS.

174. Charles Goore to Thomas Jones, Feb. 4, 1765, 14 *Jones Papers,* LC, 2683.

## CHAPTER V

1. *7MHM*5. 2. *Morriss,* 58-59.

3. *CSPC, 1689-92,* no. 579, p. 183; *Morriss,* 58. 4. *Tatham,* 284.

5. *Tatham,* 284-85. It was in favor of the colonies during sixty-one years and in favor of Great Britain during sixteen years.

6. 5 *Jefferson,* 28. 7. *Nettels,* 51-52. 8. *Hall, Plantations,* 73-75.

9. Based on statistics in *HLL,* LC, Items no. 126, 131, Film pp. 47, 66.

10. *Tatham,* 198-200, cites the case of a merchant who imported 131 hogsheads of tobacco into Bristol, selling them for £4,912 10s. 9½d. Of this, the various charges consumed £3,604 6s. 7d., including £3,181 11s. 9d. for customs duties, £232 6s. 9d. for freight, £147 7s. 6d. for commission, and £16 13s. for insurance, leaving him a net return of but £1,308 4s. 2½d.; *Morriss,* 37, estimates that a hogshead of tobacco in England about 1730 brought £21 10s. Of this the duties took £16, freight £4, and the merchant's commission 15s., leaving a net profit of 15s. for the planter. *BMAM,* LC, 22265, p. 102.

11. In 1664 Governor Charles Calvert wrote Lord Baltimore that the plan to take 100 or 200 slaves per annum from the Royal African Co. fell through because the Marylanders "are nott men of estates good enough to undertake such a businesse." However, he said, "we are naturally inclin'd to love neigros if our purses would endure it." 4 *Donnan*, 5-7.

12. 4 *Donnan*, 6, *n*1. In 1708 Governor Seymour wrote that previous to 1698 Maryland "has been supplyd by some small Quantitys of Negro's from Barbados and other . . . Islands and Plantations, as Jamaica and New England, Seaven, eight, nine or ten in a Sloope, and sometymes larger Quantitys, and sometymes, tho' very seldom, whole ship Loads of Slaves have been brought here directly from Affrica by Interlopers, or such as have had Lycenses." See also *CSPC, 1708-1709,* no. 197, pp. 150-51; 4 *Donnan*, 21-23.

13. 4 *Donnan*, 10-11, 59-61. 14. *Donnan*, 6.

15. 4 *Donnan*, 19, 14, *n*8; *Morriss,* 80.

16. *Jones,* 53; 2 *Bruce,* 1; in 1719 the Board of Trade was informed that Barbados was overstocked with slaves and that "very great numbers of Negros have been carryed from Thence, both to Martinico, Virginia and all the Leeward Islands:" 4 *Donnan*, 241.

17. 4 *Donnan*, 131-32. 18. *U. S. Census of 1790,* Population, 7.

19. Analysis of the years 1710-18, based on statistics for Virginia in 4 *Donnan*, 175-81: total slave imports 4,415, of which 231 died and 103 were re-exported; of this number, 2,399 were imported from Africa, 1865 from the West Indies and Bermuda, 84 from Carolina, 16 from the Middle Colonies, 13 from New England, and 6 from Great Britain. Statistics for Maryland are wanting: it is probable, however, that the same general conclusions apply equally to Maryland and Virginia.

20. 4 *Donnan*, 172-73. Of the London ships, only six were owned by the Royal African Company. The Royal Company imported 679 slaves; the the separate traders imported 5,692 slaves.

21. *Spears,* 82.

22. *Spears,* 84. The extraordinary activity of Liverpool in the slave trade resulted in the contemporary newspapers becoming filled with advertisements of handcuffs, leg shackles, iron collars, chains, branding irons, and other articles for use in the trade.

23. *Spears,* 18.

24. 4 *Donnan*, 175-87. Of the 70 British vessels importing slaves into Virginia, 1718-27, some 50 were from Bristol, 15 from London, and 5 from Liverpool.

25. 4 *Donnan*, 220-30.

26. 4 *Donnan*, 223-30. The remaining 91 were re-imported from New England, but their point of origin is not recorded.

27. William Allason to Crosbies & Traffords, Aug. 4, 1761, *Allason Letterbook, 1757-70,* VSL.

28. *JBT*, Jan. 1722/3-Dec. 1728, 64-66; 3*V*167; 25*V*262; 2 *Donnan*, 105-6.

29. *CSPC, 1710-11*, no. 21, p. 4; 4 *Donnan*, 90-91.

30. Between 1718 and 1727 some 6 vessels from Virginia imported 649 slaves from Africa. After the rise of British activity in the African trade, this was rare. An exceptional case was that of the *Charming Betty*, 130 tons, of Virginia registry, belonging to James LaRoch & Co. of Bristol, which brought 280 slaves to Virginia from Africa in 1750.

31. Higginson & Bird to Col. Edward Lloyd, Sept. 27, 1718; to Col. Henry Darnall, Nov. 10, 1718, Higginson & Bird Letterbook, 1718-19, *Galloway Papers*, LC; Walter King to Col. Thomas Jones, Feb. 21, 1744, 5 *Jones Papers*, LC, 692; Henry Callister to Ewan Callister, Nov. 12, 1749; to Foster Cunliffe, Oct. 4, 1750, *Callister Papers*, NYPL, ff. 149, 165; 11*W(1)*157; 4 *Donnan*, 140.

32. 4 *Donnan*, 188-234, contains a list of ships importing slaves into Virginia, 1727-69, showing their registry. Of 231 entries in vessels of Virginia registry, only one came from Africa, only 30 entries carry more than 20 slaves, only 7 more than 50. A few merchants made regular imports of Negroes from the West Indies: Benjamin Harrison, Charles, Robert, and John Tucker, Daniel, Edward, and Theophilus Pugh, Cornelius, John, and Maximilian Calvert, Archibald Taylor & Co., John Hutchings, Samuel Barron, Samuel Boush, Andrew Sprowle, and John Perrin.

33. Thomas Ringgold and Samuel Galloway to Fowler Easton & Co., Sept. 17, 1761, Ringgold Letters, *Galloway Papers, 1760-70*, NYPL.

34. William Allason to Robert Allason, July 30, 1759, *Allason Letterbook, 1757-70*, VSL; Samuel Galloway and Thomas Ringgold to James Gildart, Nov. 30, 1762, in 4 *Donnan*, 43. Their terms were 8% on gross sales to remit one half by the ship and the other half in twelve months.

35. 24*V*117. 36. 4 *Donnan*, 35.

37. Slaves bought in "the bite" (the Bight of Biafra, Gulf of Guinea) were "very much subject to mortality in their passage." A cargo brought to Virginia in 1718 from "the bite" was reduced from 313 to 170 in the passage. Higginson & Bird to Col. Edward Lloyd, Sept. 27, 1718, Higginson & Bird Letterbook, 1718-19, *Galloway Papers*, LC.

38. *Ibid.*, same date. Higginson & Bird told Lloyd that "if a vessell will not turne well to windward she generally looses half her slaves before she can get cleare" of the African coast, and "wee understand your Briganteene is no Extraordinary sailor; which she ought to be" for the Calabar trade. On another occasion they wrote Col. Darnall of Maryland that "by the Character wee have had by sundry hands the vessell [Darnall's sloop *Ann*] is very proper for that trade." Same to Col. Henry Darnall, Nov. 10, 1718, Higginson & Bird Letterbook, 1718-19, *Galloway Papers*, LC.

39. Examples: *VG(P)*, June 1, 8, 1739; July 3, 1752; William Allason wrote in 1759 that Guinea ships offered to take tobacco at £7 per ton, when the current rate was £10. He added: "they take it at this Rate by way of Ballast." William Allason to William Corbett, Sept. 18, 1759, *Allason Letterbook, 1757-70*, VSL.

40. *VG(P)*, June 29, 1739. The *Black Prince*, a snow, is described as a "prime Sailer," mounting 16 guns, burden 150 tons.

41. Thomas Ringgold and Samuel Galloway to Fowler, Easton & Co., Sept. 17, Ringgold Letters, 1760-70, *Galloway Papers*, NYPL. Ringgold and Galloway pointed out that credit was indispensable to the slave trade. In selling a lot of 105 slaves, "we refused no offers of a Safe Man even upon 6 & 12 Months Credit."

42. Thomas Ringgold to Samuel Galloway, Nov. 16, 1762, Ringgold Letters, 1760-70, *Galloway Papers*, NYPL: 4 Donnan, 42n.

43. Examples: the Maryland act of 1695, 38 *Md. Arch.*, 51-52; 4 *Donnan*, 14-15; the Virginia act of 1699, 3*H*193; 4 *Donnan*, 66-67.

44. *CSPC, 1722-23*, xxxvii; no. 714, pp. 343-44; no. 777, p. 384; no. 781, p. 385.

45. 4 *Donnan*, 131-32. William Byrd II wrote: "I am sensible of many bad consequences of multiplying these Ethiopians amongst us. They blow up the pride, and ruin the Industry of our White People, who seeing a Rank of poor Creatures below them, detest work for fear it should make them look like Slaves." He also feared a revolt, saying: "In case ther shou'd arise a Man of desperate courage amongst us, exasperated by a desperate fortune, he might with more advantage than Catiline kindle a Servile War."

46. *CSPC, 1710-11*, no. 710, pp. 415-16.

47. *CSPC, 1722-23*, xxxvii; no. 625, pp. 296-97; no. 700, p. 336; no. 797, p. 399; *JBT*, Jan. 1722/3-Dec. 1728, pp. 50, 64-66; 4 *Donnan*, 102-15.

48. *CSPC, 1728-29*, no. 510, pp. 261-62; no. 740, p. 390; 4 *Donnan*, 122-27. The duty was held to be harmful to the Guinea trade, which in turn provided a market for British manufactures, and, therefore, "for Virginia to lay a duty on negroes so purchased is the same thing as laying a duty on the importation of British manufactures."

49. *C.O.* 5: 1321, f. 79; 4 *Donnan*, 122-23.

50. 5 *APCC*, 287; 12 *Jour. Negro Hist.*, 22-23.

51. 4*H*317; *JHB, 1727-40*, xxiii, 131, 165; 4 *Donnan*, 127-31. The act was allowed to lapse from July, 1751, until February, 1752. An act in 1758 made the importers of slaves collectors of the duty and responsible to the colonial government for its payment—a clever legal fiction to avoid threatened disallowment of the act. 5*H*28; 4 *Donnan*, 137-39.

52. 5*H*92. 53. 6*H*466; 7*H*363.

54. William Allason to Robert Allason, July 30, 1759, *Allason Letterbook, 1757-70*, VSL.

55. In 1757 the Rev. Peter Fontaine, rector of Westover Parish, Charles City County, wrote his brother Moses, "All our Taxes are now laid upon slaves and on Shippers of tobacco, which they [the British authorities] wink at while we are in danger of being torn from them, but we durst not do it in time of peace, it being looked upon as the highest presumption to lay any burden upon trade." 4 *Donnan,* 142-43.

56. Gov. Francis Fauquier to Board of Trade, June 2, 1760, in *JHB, 1758-61,* 284-85; 4 *Donnan,* 145; see also William Allason to Halliday & Dunbar, Aug. 19, 1760, *William Allason Letterbook, 1757-70,* VSL.

57. 7*H*383; 4 *Donnan,* 146-47.

58. The act of 1767 was disallowed in 1768. The act of 1769 was disallowed in 1772. By this time it was realized that a duty on the purchaser was the same as a duty on the seller, that "all such Duties must in the end be paid by the Purchaser," and that high duties restricted the slave trade and benefited the colonial slave-holders. 4 *Donnan,* 151-53.

59. *C.O.* 5: 135, ff. 91, 95; 4 *Donnan,* 153-55.

60. In later years George Mason expressed this view in his celebrated dictum that "this infernal traffic originated in the avarice of the British merchants," and that "the British Government constantly checked the attempts of Virginia to put a stop to it." 2 *Convention Records,* 364.

61. This section is based largely upon the recent excellent work, Abbot Emerson Smith, *Colonists in Bondage: White Servitude and Convict Labor in America.*

62. *Jernegan,* 49-50.

63. Smith, *Colonists,* 21, says that Germans rarely came as indentured servants, "as far as we know nearly all who did not pay their own passage went out as redemptioners." The migration of Swiss and German peasants to America, although it began in the 1680's, did not become important until about 1708 or 1709.

64. Two Entry Books of the Port of Annapolis, Patuxent District, Maryland, for the years 1746-75 reveal that during those thirty years 23,347 immigrants entered the port: 9,035 (39%) of them indentured servants, 8,846 (38%) of them convicts, 3,324 (14%) slaves, and 2,142 (9%) German and Irish passengers (i.e. redemptioners). 2*MHM*43.

65. In order to keep down the number of Roman Catholic servants—who were regarded as a disloyal and possibly dangerous element in the population—Maryland in 1699 placed a head tax of 20*s.*—in 1717 raised to 40*s.*—on them at importation. 22 *Md. Arch.,* 497. In order to avoid the imputation of being "Popish recusants" and to escape the 40*s.* duty of 1717, Irish immigrants were encouraged to subscribe to an oath denying "Transubstantiation in the Sacrament of the Lord's Supper." This being considered sufficient proof of Protestantism, the importer was not required to pay the duty. Doubtless the illiteracy of many of the Irish servants and the interest of the importer to avoid the duty

led to collusion and deceit in many cases. For a copy of the oath administered to Irish servants imported into Maryland in the brig *Nancy,* Captain James Park, in 1746, see 1 *Gilmor Papers,* division 2, MHS.

66. Smith, *Colonists,* 38-39. 67. 2*H*509; 2 *Md. Arch.,* 540-41.

68. Beverley, *History of Virginia* (1705), bk. IV, ch. 15, sec. 67. Cf. same chapter and section in 1722 edition.

69. *MG(P),* Feb. 4, 1728/9.

70. 4 *EJC,* 281-82; in order to cope with the situation in Virginia, the colonial government pressed many convicts into military service in King George's War and sent a large number of them in 1740 to the disastrous siege of Cartagena from which few returned. 30*V*256.

71. 14 *Md. Arch.,* 412; see also *MG(G),* July 9, 1767, containing an account of "the deplorable Havock lately made . . . by that horrid contagious distemper, commonly called Jail-Fever"; for a heated discussion of the matter, see the letters of "A.B.," "C.D.," and "Philanthropos" to *MG(G),* July 30, Aug. 20, 1767.

72. 33 *Md. Arch.,* 344-45, 349-50, 425, 431-32, 443-44, 453.

73. 4*H*106; Smith, *Colonists,* 119-20.

74. *Morriss,* 67; 3 *Md. Arch.,* 457; 7 *Md. Arch.,* 206.

75. 1 *APCC,* no. 566, pp. 331-32. 76. *MacInnes,* 143-44.

77. 1 *Bruce,* 397; 2*H*121. 78. *Morriss,* 67; 2*H*503; 7 *Md. Arch.,* 324.

79. 2 *Bruce,* 397-98. 80. 25 *AHR,* 222-24.

81. *C.O.* 5: 719, 18; *Morriss,* 69, 82. *C.O.* 5: 1316: 0, 88; *Morriss,* 69.

83. *C.O.* 5: 1316: 0, 153. 84. *CSPC, 1689-92,* no. 1897, pp. 568-69.

85. *CSPC, 1693-96,* no. 1916, pp. 518-20.

86. 26*MHM*29. 87. *CSPC, 1710-11,* no. 744, pp. 430-32.

88. *CSPC, 1728-29,* no. 490, p. 249. 89. *CSPC, 1731,* no. 473, pp. 326-27.

90. *CSPC, 1732,* no. 406, pp. 228-31. 91. *Jones,* 38-39.

92. 25 *AHR,* 225-29. 93. 11*W(1)*95. 94. *Carman,* 183.

95. 25 *AHR,* 239.

96. 1 Brown's *Genesis,* 37; 2 Brown's *Genesis,* 783-84; 1 *APCC,* no. 368, p. 218; 4 *Force,* no. 12, p. 7; 1 *Bruce,* 41-42, 90; *Morriss,* 52-54. In 1612 the ship *Starr* was sent to Virginia for pine masts. In 1616 Sir Thomas Dale asserted that Virginia was admirable for "the mayntenance of our shipinge (all things nessysarye ther unto, being ther to be had)." In 1637 the ship *Ensurance* fetched four tons of Campeachy wood from Virginia.

97. *CSPC, 1697-98,* no. 550, pp. 264-65; Major Wilson, testifying before the Board of Trade in 1697, stated that they make good pitch and tar in Virginia and send abundance of it to the West Indies. A barrel of 32 gallons was worth 18*s. CSPC, 1696-97,* no. 1285, p. 591.

98. 19 *Md. Arch.,* 541.

99. 19 *Md. Arch.,* 541. The lofty pines "generally grew on low & levell ground near such Creekes & Coves as every high tide can floot them

most comonly within halfe a mile of the water and sometimes not ten rods from it."

100. 3*H*81, 3*H*148, 3*H*254; 19 *Md. Arch.*, 149; 26 *Md. Arch.*, 632.

101. Tobacco production and trade, however, made exacting demands upon the primeval forest. Rev. Hugh Jones to Benj. Woodroof, Jan. 23, 1698/9, 1 *RSMG*, LC, 1, 183, said: "All the low land is verry wooddy like one continuous Forest . . . And tho' we are pritty closely Seated yett we cannot See our next neighbours house for trees." But, he added, in a few years "we may expect it otherwise for the tobacco trade destroyes abundance of timber both for making of hogsheads and building of tobacco houses besides clearing of ground yearly for planting."

102. 3*W(2)*209. Fourteen barrels were considered "a Virginia tun" by shipmasters. Tar sold for 10*s*. or 12*s*. a barrel in 1704; pitch brought double that amount. A barrel contained at least 30 gallons.

103. A "last" was equal to 12 barrels; statistics from *C.O.* 390: 6: pt. 2, pp. 222-34.

104. 3 & 4 Anne, c. 9. The English authorities were anxious not to interfere with tobacco production. "Tho' the Encouragement of the Production of Naval Stores in the Plantations being of the highest Importance to England, yet it is not fitting to be encouraged in those Places which are proper for the Production of Tobacco." Board of Trade to Gov. Seymour of Maryland, Mar. 26, 1707, quoted in *Morriss*, 55.

105. *C.O.* 390: 6, pt. 2, pp. 222-34. England at this time was importing nearly 3,000 lasts of pitch and tar a year, two-thirds of which came from Sweden. From the colonies, in 1709, England received less than 600 lasts. Carolina was first with 359 5/12, New England second with 207 2/3, the Chesapeake third with 15 5/6 lasts. *CSPC, 1710-11,* no. 597, i, p. 340.

106. *CSPC, 1706-1708,* no. 470, p. 194. 107. *CSPC, 1710-11,* preface, xxxiv.

108. 6 *APCC*, Unbound Papers, no. 380, pp. 188-90; *CSPC, 1728-29,* no. 94, pp. 47-53.

109. *CSPC, 1716-17,* no. 506, p. 273; no. 507, p. 273. In 1721 William Byrd II told the Board of Trade that "as to hemp, . . . the taking off the present duty, and continuing the praemium of £6 per ton upon importation . . . would be sufficient encouragement; that the present bounty upon pitch and tar not being well paid, and those commodities bearing . . . but a low price in Great Britain, they would decline making so much of those stores . . . in Virginia." *JBT*, Nov. 1718-Dec. 1722, 328.

110. *CSPC, 1717-18,* no. 699, pp. 355-56.

111. *CSPC, 1717-18,* no. 416, pp. 200-01.

112. *CSPC, 1719-20,* no. 271, p. 141. In 1724 the Board of Trade was acquainted "that there had been several experiments made in Virginia for making of tar, according to the directions of the Act [8 Geo. I], but that the people found it impossible to succeed therein . . . that they

used to make their tar from fallen trees only, and that unless the Government here [Great Britain] would think fit to continue the bounty on tar made after that manner, that branch of trade from the Plantations would entirely cease." *JBT*, Jan. 1722/3-Dec. 1728, 139.

113. *JBT*, Mar. 1714/5-Oct. 1718, 218.

114. *CSPC, 1726-27*, no. 235, pp. 124-26; *1728-29*, no. 106, p. 57.

115. *MG(P)*, Oct. 28, 1729. 116. *Hall, Plantations*, 75-76. 117. 2 *Douglass*, 375.

118. 4 *Jamieson Papers, 1757-89*, LC, 726, 891.

119. William Allason to Alexander Walker, May 21, 1765, *Allason Letterbook, 1757-70*, VSL. In 1768 Allason shipped to Glasgow 3 tons, 14 cwt., 2 qtrs., and 19 lbs. of hemp. Same to Hugh Stewart, Oct. 12, 1768.

120. *Carman*, 183-84. 121. *Morriss*, 54, *n*188.

122. *Morriss*, 134-37. In 1715 Great Britain imported 93 large and 3 middle-sized masts from New England. From Denmark and Norway she received 490 large, 1,318 middle-sized, and 2,249 small masts. *C.O.* 390: 6, pt. 2, no. 240.

123. As early as 1682 Col. William Fitzhugh wrote John Cooper of London that he "intended to have sent you ten thousand Pipe Staves and four hundred feet of two inch black wallnut Plank but could not get freight for them." 1*V*107. He also inquired about the price of ship trunnels, two foot, a foot and a half, and a foot long, and considered sending "40, 50, 60, or 70 thousand," of them to England.

124. *CSPC, 1730*, no. 348, i, p. 216. 125. Hall, *Plantations*, 74.

126. In 1743 Gov. Gooch told the Board of Trade that Virginia annually exported 50,000 pipe staves: *C.O.* 5: 1326, 30; in 1753 Maryland exported 1,095,500 staves and 2,000,000 shingles: *Calvert Papers*, MHS, no. 596; in 1754 Virginia exported pipe heading, barrel staves, and shingles worth £10,000: *C.O.* 5: 1328, 328-29; in 1763 Virginia exported 174,242 feet of scantling and plank worth £844 10s., and 3,231,970 staves, shingles, and lumber worth £9,696: *C.O.* 5: 1330, 542-43.

127. Williamson Allason to Alexander Walker & Co., Oct. 5, 1758, *Allason Letterbook, 1757-70*, VSL.

128. Francis Jerdone to Captain Hugh Crawford, June 10, 1758, *Jerdone Letterbook, 1756-63*, W&M.

129. Francis Jerdone to Speirs & Brown, Aug. 4, 1758, *Ibid.*

130. William Allason to Robert Allason, Mar. 23, Apr. 6, 1761, *William Allason Letterbook, 1757-70*, VSL.

131. *C.O.* 5: 1326: 29-30; *C.O.* 5: 1328: 328-29; *C.O.* 5: 1330: 542-43.

132. *Carman*, 183. 133. *Virginia Iron*, 5-6. 134. 2*V*136.

135. *Virginia Iron*, 5.

136. *CSPC, 1710-11*, no. 437, pp. 234-35; no. 555, p. 317; no. 911, p. 569.

137. *Virginia Iron,* 6. Spotswood was in partnership with Robert Cary, a London merchant.

138. *CSPC, 1722-23,* no. 529, p. 254; 4 *Donnan,* 102. By 1736, according to the parish records, 175 tithables were employed at Spotswood's iron works. *Cappon,* 12.

139. 4 *DAH,* 343. 140. *BMAM,* LC, 29600, f. 13. 141. *Virginia Iron,* 16.

142. *CSPC, 1728-29,* no. 94, pp. 47-53. England annually imported "above 20,000 tons of bar-iron from foreign countries," and was not considered capable of increasing her own iron production by that much because of her diminishing forests. America, on the other hand, was rich in iron ore and plentifully supplied with wood.

143. *CSPC, 1730,* no. 348, i, p. 216. 144. 4 *JEBH,* 522-24.

145. 12*MHM*27; *MG(G),* Mar. 14, 1765. In 1750 Dr. Charles Carroll of Annapolis shipped 100 tons of pig iron to London. In 1752 he shipped 200 tons. 22*MHM*173; 25*MHM*53.

146. *Virginia Iron,* 17. In 1738 Col. John Tayloe, who was owner of the Neabsco and part owner of the Occoquan iron works, petitioned the Virginia Council for permission to import Maryland ore duty free. The reason he gave was that Maryland ore was "for the more easy fluxing" of his Virginia ore. 14*V*236. In 1751 a sloop belonging to Col. Tayloe was in Patapsco River loading ore. *VG(P),* July 11, 1751.

147. *BMAM,* LC, 29600, ff. 13, 15. The Principio Co. recognized the fact that the "Baltimore Iron" had "acquired a pretty good reputation for toughness." In 1753 the Company removed all its hands, stock, and utensils to Maryland. *Virginia Iron,* 16.

148. *BMAM,* LC, 29600, f. 13. William Smith went to Annapolis in 1729 to "hire a Sloop to carry oar." He spoke of the Principio Company's "Sloops not being sufficient to keep the furnace going." He agreed to pay 6*s.* per ton for the transportation of 200 tons of ore from the Patapsco to the furnace. *MG(G),* Feb. 10, 1748, reported the wreck of "a Schooner loaded with Iron, going from Patapsco to West River."

149. William Allason to Robert Allason, Aug. 19, 1760, *Allason Letterbook, 1757-70.*

150. Thomas Ringgold to Samuel Galloway, Ringgold Letters, 1760-70, *Galloway Papers,* NYPL.

151. Bar iron advertised for sale for "Bills of Exchange, Gold, or Paper Money." *MG(G),* Sept. 16, 1746.

152. *MG(G),* June 10, 1746.

153. 7 *Jamieson Papers, 1757-89,* LC, 1583. In 1769 Samuel Galloway shipped 20 tons of pig iron to London, saying: "the Iron was put into my hands to pay a debt:" Samuel Galloway to James Russell, Sept. 3, 1769, Galloway Letterbook, 1766-71, *Galloway Papers,* LC.

154. *VG(P),* Jan. 25, 1739.

155. *Birket,* 12-13; in 1752 bar iron was exported from Virginia to Providence, Rhode Island. *VG(P),* Oct. 12, 1752.

156. William Baxter to Principio Company, Feb. 2, 1769, *Emmet Collection,* NYPL.

157. In 1728 Spotswood wrote the Board of Trade, proposing "the taking off the present duty of 4*s.* per tun . . . and the freeing it from the charge of landing and weighing at the Custom-House keys [quays]:" *CSPC, 1728-29,* no. 94, p. 53. The Admiralty also urged the freeing of colonial iron from customs duties: 6 *APCC,* Unbound Papers, no. 399, pp. 194-96. The Board of Trade was eventually won over: *JBT,* June 19, July 31, 1735. The duty on colonial pig iron was removed by the Iron Act of 1750. Bar iron could be imported into London duty free. In 1757 the privilege was extended to all other English ports: 3 *DAH,* 155.

158. *BMAM,* LC, 29600, f. 15. 159. Examples: *VG(P),* July 15, Aug. 5, 1737.

160. Thomas Ringgold to Samuel Galloway, July 10, Ringgold Letters, 1760-70, *Galloway Papers,* NYPL. Spotswood in 1710 suggested that "iron might be sent home as Ballast:" *CSPC, 1710-11,* no. 555, pp. 313-318.

161. Directions on Shipping of Pig and Bar Iron on Account of Principio Co. given by Thomas Russell to Adams & Underwood, Mar. 20, 1769, *Emmet Collection,* NYPL.

162. 32*MHM*39.

163. Thomas Russell to Michael Harris, July 1, 1768; Francis Phillips to Principio Co., Oct. 26, 1768, *Emmet Collection,* NYPL.

164. Directions on Shipping Pig and Bar Iron; in 1760 Allason charged 5% for handling pig iron. William Allason to Robert Allason, Aug. 19, 1760, *Allason Letterbook, 1757-70* ,VSL.

165. 2 *Byrd,* 51; *Virginia Iron,* 13.

166. *HLL,* LC, Item 185, film pp. 44-45.

167. *Carman,* 183; *Sheffield,* 117-18; Giddens, in 4 *JEBH,* 522-24, states that in 1753 Maryland produced on the average 2,500 tons of pig iron and 600 tons of bar iron a year, about one-seventh as much iron as England produced and six times as much as Pennsylvania.

168. *Semmes,* 58; 5 *Md. Arch.,* 199. 169. *Morriss,* 14.

170. Henry Callister to Robert Whitfield, Jan. 10, 1742/3, *Callister Papers,* NYPL, f. 3.

171. *Semmes,* 67; *Alsop,* 68-69. 172. *C.O.* 5: 1317: 365.

173. Its capital was £4,000, but the act gave "liberty for subscribing 6,000 l. more, when it shall be proper." *JBT,* Mar. 1714/5-Oct. 1718, pp. 163-66.

174. *Ibid.* Byrd vaguely asserted that before the monopoly the fur traders "traded for more than 4,000 l. yearly," and when asked the annual

value of English goods formerly imported to Virginia for the trade, said: "between 4 and 5,000 l."

175. *Ibid.*, p. 230; 4*V*370.  176. *CSPC, 1730,* no. 348, i, p. 216.

177. 3*H*123; 3*H*356; 4*H*431; 5*H*56.  178. 5*H*236.

179. *C.O.* 5: 1327: 160. In 1695 Maryland levied an export duty on furs and hides, and applied the revenue to the free school [King William's School] at Annapolis. The duties were small, ranging from a farthing on muskrats to 9*d.* on bear skins. 19 *Md. Arch.,* 276; *Morriss,* 12.

180. 2 *LJC,* 1084.  181. 1*T*42.

182. *Carman,* 183; *Sheffield,* 114, estimated the average value of furs and skins imported by Great Britain from North America for the years 1768, 1769, and 1770 to be £95,472 10*s.*

183. 2 *Douglass,* 375.  184. 4 *JEBH,* 521.  185. *Carman,* 183.

186. *C.O.* 5: 1377: 89.

187. Francis Jerdone to Hugh Crawford, Feb. 10, 1756, *Jerdone Letterbook, 1756-63,* W&M.

188. William Allason to Alexander Walker & Co., Sept. 1, 1757, *Allason Letterbook, 1757-70,* VSL.

189. *Ibid.,* May 12, 1759.  190. 6 *Campbell Papers,* VSL.

191. William Allason to Alexander Walker & Co., May 21, 1765. "Some years ago great were the expectations from the Cultivation of Indico . . . Now the Article of Hemp is the thing which is to effect all purposes." *Allason Letterbook, 1757-70,* VSL.

192. 9*V*129.  193. 1 *Carter Papers,* VHS, 33.  194. 9*V*129.  195. *Carman,* 183.

196. The following statistics are based upon tables of imports and exports in Adam Anderson, *Origin of Commerce,* V, 42-56. See also *CSPC, 1702,* no. 97, pp. 67-69; *1720-21,* no. 656, pp. 408-49; *HLL,* LC, Item 227, film pp. 70-72; *C.O.* 5: 5: 200-05.

197. In the customhouse books and most other official British accounts of the period, the trade of Virginia and Maryland is treated as one, and no effort is made to break down the statistics into their two component parts. Similarly, the trade of the New England colonies was considered as one.

198. British exports to the continental colonies north of Maryland:

| | | |
|---|---|---|
| 1720—£210,000 | 1750—£ 872,000 |
| 1740— 353,000 | 1760— 1,955,000 |

199. British imports from the Carolinas:

| | |
|---|---|
| 1698—£ 9,265 | 1750—£191,607 |
| 1701— 16,973 | 1760— 162,769 |
| 1720— 62,736 | 1761— 253,000 |
| 1730— 151,739 | 1763— 282,366 |
| 1740— 266,560 | 1764— 341,728 |

## CHAPTER VI

1. In 1709 an embargo was placed on exports of corn from Virginia because of the "long and unusually dry weather for almost the whole past summer" which "burnt up the corn" and occasioned "apprehensions of a great scarcity:" *CSPC, 1708-1709*, no. 765, pp. 479-80. On July 20, 1714, Governor Spotswood asserted that "if there should happen no rain in a week more there will be a great danger of a scarcity of corn:" *CSPC, 1712-14*, no. 726, pp. 371-72. In 1724 Governor Drysdale placed an embargo on export of Virginia corn "in view of the badness of last year's crop of corn and the great export already made thereof:" *CSPC, 1724-25*, no. 257, i, p. 140. Later the same year Drysdale extended the embargo because of a storm that damaged the crops: *CSPC, 1724-25*, no. 487, p. 318; no. 638, i, p. 381. In 1728 Governor Gooch placed an export embargo on "grain, flower and meal" because of their scarcity: *CSPC, 1728-29*, no. 174 (b), p. 85; no. 261, ii, p. 127. Other embargoes were imposed in 1738, 1741, 1756, 1757, and 1758—the last three by order of the British military authorities to prevent the French West Indies from receiving grain. As grain was plentiful in Virginia and Maryland, this hit the grain-growers, caused trade to stagnate, and was accounted a great grievance.

2. *CSPC, 1730*, no. 348, i, p. 216. 3. *C.O.* 5: 1326: 29-30.

4. *C.O.* 5: 1328: 328-29. In 1754 Virginia exported 40,000 bushels of wheat worth £5,000; 250,000 bushels of corn worth £12,500; 10,000 lbs. of beeswax worth £500; 30,000 barrels of beef and pork worth £60,000; and pipe heading, barrel staves, and shingles worth £10,000.

5. 33*MHM*234; *C.O.* 5: 1326: 29-30. 6. *Carman*, 183.

7. Matthew Pope to John Jacob, Aug. 25, 1775, *BMAM*, LC, 34813, f. 88. Pope added: "nine months in the Year 6 men may dine for One Shilling Sterling most ellegantly," and stated that the finest oysters were obtained for one shilling currency per bushel.

8. William Fitzhugh sent 6,240 pipe staves to Barbados in 1683. 1*V*121. William Byrd I in the 1680's maintained mercantile relations with Sadleir and Thomas of Barbados, sending corn, flour, and pipe staves in return for rum, molasses, sugar, and limejuice: 24*V*133, 24*V*353, 24*V*361; but this was rare until the eighteenth century. In 1689 Byrd wrote John Thomas and Co. of Barbados that he rarely heard of a vessel "bound for your parts."

9. Wertenbaker, *Norfolk*, 38.

10. *C.O.* 5: 1359: 40; *CSPC, 1712-14*, no. 11, pp. 6-8; advertisement of West India goods imported into Maryland by the ship *Enterprise* in *MG(P)*, Mar. 11, 1728/9; *Gould*, 13, says that after about 1730 the trade grew brisk.

11. 15*W(1)*5, mispaged as 15*W(1)*147.

12. *Morriss*, 89 *n*20; *CSPC, 1692-96*, no. 1916, pp. 518-20; 6*MHM*224; Henry Callister to Foster Cunliffe and Sons, Aug. 21, 1746, *Callister Papers*, NYPL, f. 68, asserted: "we have been obliged to look abroad [i.e. to the Western Shore] for Tobacco [as] our own place has not been able to supply us, neither do I think it will next Year; the Climate seems to have changed . . . and everything seems to conspire to ruin the Tobacco Trade" on the Eastern Shore. Notwithstanding the decline of tobacco relative to grain, it still remained an important item on the Eastern Shore. See Thomas Ringgold to Samuel Galloway, Aug. 15, 18, 1761, May 12, Aug. 13, 27, 1766, Ringgold Letters, 1760-70, *Galloway Papers*, NYPL; Henry Callister to Foster Cunliffe and Sons, Jan. 11, 1744, *Callister Papers*, NYPL, f. 10.

13. Aggregate of Wheat, Flour, and Indian Corn annually exported from the Eastern Shore of Maryland, on an average, from 1770 to 1775, 1 *Chalmers Papers*, Maryland, NYPL, f. 52.

14. *CSPC, 1730*, no. 348, i, p. 216. 15. 2 *Douglass*, 374-75.

16. Henry Callister to Robert Morris, Aug. 6, 1747, *Callister Papers*, NYPL.

17. Richard Murray to [Samuel Galloway?], Dec. 23, 1758, *Galloway Papers*, Box 1742-69, NYPL. "Pork in our Neighborhood [Anne Arundel County] has rise to a very great price not to be had under 20/ [20s.] upon which I went to the Eastern Shore and got what is wanted at 16/8 [16s. 8d.]"; see also Daniel Wolstenholme to Samuel Galloway, Jan. 12, 1760, *Ibid.*

18. Ports of N. A., Port of Patuxent, *BMAM*, LC, 15484.

19. *Eddis*, 95-98. 20. 36*V*359; Wertenbaker, *Norfolk*, 38-39.

21. Wertenbaker, *Norfolk*, 38 *n*52.

22. Governor Gooch reported in 1741 that Virginia exported to New England "chiefly in their own vessels, which come to trade here, some pork, beef, corn, tallow, and some hides, pitch, wooden ware, and a few European goods," Wertenbaker, *Norfolk*, 38-39.

23. Francis Jerdone to Neil Buchanan, May 20, 1741, *Jerdone Letterbook, 1736-44*, W&M. "There is a necessity in having these goods without which no Tobacco Purchase can be made."

24. William Johnston to Neil Buchanan, Oct. 16, 1738, *ibid.*, "I Endeavor to deal as much in the mony way as I can tobacco commonly being much cheaper purchased that way"; Francis Jerdone to Neil Buchanan, Aug. 5, 1741, *ibid.*, "Tis a very great loss to you, in not Supplying your Stores with [salt, rum, and sugar]. The Best of the trade is carried on with them and little can be done without them."

25. William Johnston to Neil Buchanan, Oct. 4, 1739, *ibid.;* Francis Jerdone to Neil Buchanan, Dec. 10, 1742, *ibid.*, asserted: "Scarce a hogshead [of tobacco is] to be bought for Goods without one half cash"; Henry Callister to William Murray, Apr. 6, 1748, *Callister Papers*, NYPL, f. 121, "Ready Money is the best Trade, and that commands the Market."

26. *VG(P&D)*, Dec. 24, 1767. "To be Sold . . . A Tract of Land, . . . situated on Mattapony river, . . . The land is good for either grain or tobacco, is well timbered, and is a very convenient situation for carrying on a West India trade, lying in the heart of a grain country, where a vessel of 250 tuns burthen may load opposite to the house"; *MG(G)*, Nov. 11, 1746, "To be sold, . . . a new Schooner of about 36 Tons, well built for the West Indies or Coasting Trade, well ceil'd, fit for the smallest grain"; see also vessels advertised with capacity stated in terms of bushels rather than tons or hogsheads, *MG(G)*, June 7, 1753, Jan. 3, 1754, Sept. 16, 1756.

27. William Reynolds to George F. Norton, June 3, 1774, 1 *Reynolds Letterbook*, CNHP, stated: "I can assure you from Experience, there is money to be made by them [schooners] and as an instance can tell you I clear'd £200 by my Schooner in 8 months, our small Vessells make four Voyages in the time a Ship makes one."

28. William Johnston to Neil Buchanan, July 5, 21, 1739, Sept. 8, 1740, *Jerdone Letterbook, 1736-44*, W&M.

29. Thomas Applethwaite to Henry Tucker, Oct. 20, 1765, 6 *Jamieson Papers*, LC, 1201.

30. John Collins to Neil Jamieson, Apr. 21, 1764, 4 *Jamieson Papers*, LC, 718.

31. William Potts to Samuel and Joseph Galloway, May 31, 1758, *Galloway Papers*, Box 1742-69, NYPL.

32. Wertenbaker, *Norfolk*, 39.

33. *MG(G)*, Apr. 14, 1747. "London-Town . . . To be Sold . . . One Thousand or 1200 Bushels of Indian Corn, all at one Landing, fit for Shipping directly."

34. Francis Jerdone to John Tucker of Barbados, Dec. 13, 1759, *Jerdone Letterbook, 1756-63*, W&M, requested his rum and sugar from Barbados to be put in strong casks, "as I have to cart them a great distance on very Rough Roads"; same to same, Oct. 24, 1761, complained of the condition of some of the sugar barrels, and urged Tucker's cooper to "bestow a little more pains on the Casks . . . as I have a very long and rugged way to cart both the Rum and Sugar."

35. John Matthews to Neil Jamieson, Nov. 27, 1765, 6 *Jamieson Papers*, LC.

36. 2 *Bruce*, 328-29; 1 *APCC*, no. 601, pp. 365-67; *CSPC, 1661-68*, no. 597, p. 172.

37. *Morriss*, 129-32. 38. *Dampier*, 53-55.

39. *Williams*, 41-45; *Goodwin*, 13, 361; 7*W(1)*165; 9 *CTB*, pt. 3, pp. 1027-30; pt. 4, p. 1561.

40. *Williams*, 47-51; *CSPC, 1699*, no. 693, p. 382; no. 705, p. 387; no. 711, p. 390; no. 802, pp. 444-45; no. 989, i, p. 539; no. 1034, p. 565.

41. *CSPC, 1699*, no. 530, pp. 286-88.

42. Trading with pirates in the Chesapeake during the period 1680-1700 was largely confined to Virginia; the Lower House of the Maryland Assembly in 1702 informed the governor that "As to pyrates . . . this House say they never knew of any to be harbored or favoured in this Province." *CSPC, 1702,* no. 203, p. 136.

43. 26*MHM*31; Order to Gawin Corbin, Collector for Rappahannock, to observe orders of H.M. Customs Commissioners, Mar. 16, 1693, issued by Governor Francis Nicholson, Nov. 10, 1699, *Emmet Collection,* NYPL, no. 10,553. As a result of this practice, the customs commissioners said, the duty "hath been frequently compounded at little more than half Value"; in 1700 Colonel Quary told the customs commissioners that the quantity of tobacco imported by Barbados increased tenfold in the previous three or four years, whereas the consumption there decreased. The surplus was packed in small parcels and smuggled into England on board the sugar ships without paying duty. Quary was convinced that "the saving of the duty makes it a far better trade than any commodity they can carry from Barbados." *CSPC, 1700,* no. 190, pp. 106-09.

44. *CSPC, 1710-11,* no. 349, p. 170.   45. *CSPC, 1693-96,* no. 1916, p. 520.

46. Wertenbaker, *Norfolk,* 43. The usual procedure was to clear for Jamaica, proceed to some neutral island such as Curaçao, St. Thomas, or Surinam and there exchange their products for French sugars which had been carried there from the French West Indies.

47. Samuel Brise, a mariner who spent four years in Curaçao, told the Board of Trade in 1710 that during his stay there he saw several ships come in from Virginia. *JBT,* Feb. 1708/9-Mar. 1714/5, pp. 114-15.

48. *CSPC, 1710-11,* no. 349, p. 170; no. 437, p. 233; *CSPC, 1711-12,* no. 42, p. 26; in 1716 the Board of Trade told Governor Spotswood: "You are very much to be commended for your care in preventing illegal trade with the French." *CSPC, 1716-17,* no. 186, p. 101.

49. *CSPC, 1717-18,* no. 417, i, ii, p. 201.

50. *CSPC, 1711-12,* no. 42, p. 26. Spotswood proposed in 1711 to establish two searchers for Virginia waters, "furnished with shallops . . . which may be continually running in to the little rivers and creeks," where smugglers were likely to load their vessels, and "cruising in the Bay for examining them after they are clear'd."

51. *CSPC, 1730,* no. 348, i, p. 215.

52. Wertenbaker, *Norfolk,* 44; *Pitman,* 277-78.   53. *Pitman,* 280-83.

54. *McClellan,* 47.   55. *Ibid.,* 48; 1 *Fisher,* 51.

56. An English visitor on the Eastern Shore of Maryland in 1736 found rum extremely scarce and at an exorbitant price, 1*W(1)*3.

57. *C.O.* 5: 1326: 30; *C.O.* 5: 1327: 172; *C.O.* 5: 1328: 329; *VG(P),* Sept. 11, 1746.

58. *McClellan,* 48-50.   59. *Pitman,* 317, 329.

60. Governor Horatio Sharpe to Philip Sharpe, Feb. 8, 1760, portfolio no. 4, folder 54, Hall of Records, Annapolis; Samuel Mifflin to Samuel Galloway, Feb. 11, 1760, *Galloway Papers*, Box 1742-69, NYPL; Daniel Moore to Samuel Galloway, May 21, 1760, *ibid.*

61. In 1757 fourteen British colonial vessels reached Cap François within seven months. In 1759 H.M. Sloop *Viper* entered Monte Cristi and found 29 British colonial vessels engaged in trade, and Admiral Cotes estimated that more than 200 vessels from the continental American colonies traded to Monte Cristi in 1759. *Pitman,* 314, 316-17. Among the Chesapeake merchants who participated in the "Mount" trade were Daniel Wolstenholme, Samuel Galloway, James Dick, and Thomas Ringgold. For an extensive collection of papers dealing with this trade, see *Galloway Papers,* Box 1742-69, and Ringgold Letters, 1760-70, NYPL.

62. Governor Nott of Virginia in 1705 issued a proclamation against "Collusive, fraudulent, and Clandestine Captures by privateers' pursuant to an act of Parliament in the third to fourth year of the reign of Queen Anne. *C.O.* 5: 1315: 35, viii; 3 *EJC,* 558. However, its application to the "Mount" trade was a novelty in 1759. Governor Horatio Sharpe to Philip Sharpe, Feb. 8, 1760, portfolio no. 4, folder 54, Hall of Records, Annapolis.

63. In May, 1759, Capt. Edwards in H.M.S. *Assistance* seized eight colonial vessels near Monte Cristi and carried them to Jamaica where they were condemned in the court of vice-admiralty; *Pitman,* 317. Samuel Mifflin to Samuel Galloway, Feb. 11, 1760, *Galloway Papers,* Box 1742-69, NYPL, said: "The English Men of War are very Industrous in Cruizeing [off Hispaniola] . . . that it is difficult escapeing"; in Jamaica an admiralty judge was reprimanded by the governor and threatened with suspension for acquitting a number of vessels caught trading to the French West Indies: Daniel Moore to Samuel Galloway, May 21, 1760, *Galloway Papers,* Box 1742-69, NYPL; Clement Biddle to Samuel Galloway, Jan. 27, 1764, *ibid.*: "Have now Received Letters from Messr. Mesnier Freres [dated Cap François, Dec. 22, 1763] in which they say 'Our Trade with your Colonys, is by Orders arrived from France to be put an end to.'"

64. *C.O.* 5: 1330: 539-41. Fauquier admitted, however, that "no Regulations can totally suppress it. It chiefly depends on the Diligence, Ability, and Integrity of the naval Officers and Collectors," and he confessed that a few Virginians "have been concerned with some Gentlemen to the northwards in this secret practice"—i.e. the obtaining of false certificates: Governor Francis Fauquier to Lord Halifax, Nov. 20, 1764, *TP,* class 1, bundle 442, f. 341, LC. Fauquier told Halifax that the chief fraud was the shipping of tobacco to the other British colonies without paying "the Duty appropriated to the Support of William and Mary College," mostly by New England vessels.

432

65. Governor Horatio Sharpe to Lord Halifax, Oct. 20, 1764, *TP*, class 1, bundle 442, f. 343, LC.

66. 25$V$133; 25$V$253; 25$V$361; *CSPC, 1696-97*, no. 956, i, p. 455; *CSPC, 1708-1709*, no. 216, i, pp. 159-62; *Morriss*, 81.

67. 1 *Bruce*, 401. 68. 1 *Bruce*, 460; 5 *Md. Arch.*, 449; 23 *Md. Arch.*, pp. 40-41, 316.

69. A vessel from Lisbon was in Maryland in 1706: 26 *Md. Arch.*, 525.

70. 25 *Md. Arch.*, 302-03; see also 23 *Md. Arch.*, 40-41; and for permission to import wines from Madeira and the Azores, 1697, see 23 *Md. Arch.*, 316.

71. William Fishbourne to Daniel Richardson, June 19, 1715, 3 *Bozman Papers*, 502, LC.

72. *CSPC, 1728-29*, no. 796, v, p. 420; *CSPC, 1732*, no. 241, iv, p. 127, shows the importation of only 33 pipes of Madeira wine between Apr. 25 and Oct. 25, 1731.

73. *CSPC, 1731*, no. 375, p. 231. They continued: "This Province has very little trade with any part of Europe beside Great Britain, and that confin'd to a few voyages by three or four small vessels in several years past to Lisbon, which carried grain and lumber thither."

74. Governor Gooch told the Board of Trade in 1743 that Virginia shipped annually to Portugal and Madeira 20,000 bushels of wheat worth £2,000, 12,000 bushels of corn worth £600, 8,000 lbs. of beeswax worth £400, besides 50,000 pipe staves worth £150, and 20,000 barrels of beef and pork, "in return whereof this Colony is supply'd with Wine of the Growth of that Country." *C.O.* 5: 1326: 29-30.

75. *MG(P)*, Apr. 29, 1729; *MG(G)*, Nov. 2, 1752; William Johnston to Neil Buchanan, Mar. 10, 1739/40, Sept. 8, 1740, *Jerdone Letterbook, 1736-44*, W&M; William Beverley to Richard Hill, Dec. 10, 1744, *Beverley Letterbook, 1737-44/5*, NYPL; William Reynolds to Pasleys and Co. of Lisbon, Oct. 11, 1773, 1 *Reynolds Letterbook*, CNHP.

76. Samuel Galloway to Robert Harris and Co. of Barcelona, Mar. 29, 1767, *Galloway Letterbook, 1766-71*, LC.

77. Hill, Lamar, and Hill to Samuel Galloway, July 15, 1754, *Galloway Papers*, Box 1742-69, NYPL.

78. Bogle, Bogle, and Scott to Neil Jamieson, Oct. 24, 1764, 4 *Jamieson Papers*, LC, 861-62.

79. Hill, Lamar, and Hill to Samuel Galloway, July 15, 1754, *Galloway Papers*, Box 1742-69, NYPL. Corn "is not like to rise till next winter when it probably will as the Cheapness makes it Sell faster than usual and as the weavle will destroy a great part of what's here. Flour . . . not being so perishable keeps" a higher price.

80. William Reynolds to Lamar, Hill, Bissett and Co. of Madeira, Aug. 26, 1773, 2 *Reynolds Letterbook*, CNHP; Madeira merchants occasionally assured their Chesapeake correspondents that the wine casks were "all

new and the Sap taken out of most of the Staves." Hill, Lamar, and Hill to Samuel Galloway, Mar. 5, 1754, *Galloway Papers,* Box 1742-69, NYPL.

81. In 1765 a "Merchant of Cadiz" was loading two vessels with wheat at Baltimore and two or three at Norfolk besides four in New York and Pennsylvania. John Taylor, Jr. to Neil Jamieson, Dec. 4, 1765, 6 *Jamieson Papers,* 1274, LC; Scott, Pringle, Cheap and Co. to Samuel Galloway and Stephen Stewart, Sept. 5, 1768, said they would "not scruple to be concerned either a half or one third" in a cargo of Maryland wheat and flour for Madeira.

82. 1 *Oldmixon,* 450. 83. *MG(G),* Feb. 17, 1746/7.

84. *C.O.* 5: 1327: 172. 85. 28 *Md. Arch.,* 469.

86. Hill, Lamar, and Hill to Samuel Galloway, July 5, 1754, *Galloway Papers,* Box 1742-69, NYPL; as grain exports grew in volume, the Chesapeake received increasing quantities of wine, and sometimes sold it elsewhere—usually in the West Indies, rarely in England: William Jarvis to Neil Jamieson, Oct. 11, 1763, 3 *Jamieson Papers,* LC, 579-80. Cecilius Calvert, secretary to Lord Baltimore, thanked Gov. Sharpe for sending a "Stock of Madeira" to the lord proprietor in England, June 20, 1763, 31 *Md. Arch.,* 548; Madeira was considered to be improved by two ocean passages and the meliorating effects of the climate of the Chesapeake colonies.

87. 4 *JEBH,* 524-5; the Cadiz merchant who was in the Chesapeake in 1765 loaded 8 or 9 ships in the American colonies that year, and gave as high a price as 5s. 6d. per bushel for wheat. 6 *Jamieson Papers* ,1274.

88. Thomas Ringgold to Samuel Galloway, July 7, 1766, also Aug. 4, 13, 1766, Ringgold Letters, 1760-70, *Galloway Papers,* NYPL: a cargo of wheat belonging to Ringgold and Galloway after being unloaded at Lisbon was reloaded and sent to Cork in hope of finding a market. The freight and loading charges amounted to £200 sterling. Not only did the wheat sell poorly at Cork, but the brig failed to secure return cargo for America, and therefore made what was accounted a "wretched voyage."

89. March and Tilebein to Samuel Galloway. Aug. 10, 1768, *Galloway Papers,* Box 1742-69, NYPL; The British government placed an embargo on exportation of grain from Great Britain in 1768, Hyndman and Lancaster to Robert Carter, Nov. 2, 1768, 1 *Carter Papers,* 61, VHS; Bond of Robert Carter to Prosper Jackson and Robert Rutherfurd of Leghorn for £1,000 sterling, July 7, 1768, *Carter Accounts,* LC.

90. 27*MHM*234.

91. Charterparty for the *Fitzhugh,* Captain Bishoprich, Nov. 29, 1769, *Galloway Letterbook, 1766-71,* LC.

92. William Reynolds to Pasleys and Co. of Lisbon, July 4, 1772, 1 *Reynolds Letterbook,* CNHP; same to same, Oct. 11, 1773; same to Lamar, Hill,

Bissett and Co. of Madeira, Aug. 26, 1773, 2 *Reynolds Letterbook*, CNHP.

93. In 1634 Sir John Harvey reported that Virginia had sent 10,000 bushels of corn to the relief of New England, and added: "Virginia is now become the granary of all his Majesty's northern colonies." *CSPC, 1574-1660*, viii, 184. Father Andrew White in his Relation of Maryland, reprinted in Hall, *Narratives*, 75, said that Maryland was so "well stored" with corn, that the settlers bought enough for their own needs from the Indians and in addition, enough to send 1,000 bushels to New England; as late as 1723 a Massachusetts man wrote concerning that colony, "tis the reverse of all countrys under heaven, we are all husbandmen yet we want bread . . . no wheat rye barley oats pease or beans but all our cornes come to us from New York Virginia etc." *CSPC, 1722-23*, no. 530, pp. 254-60; in 1750 a traveller at Portsmouth, N. H., observed that New Hampshire imported large amounts of grain from Maryland and Virginia: *Birket*, 10.

94. The activity of these vessels in the trade between the Chesapeake and the West Indies will be discussed at length in Chapter 8.

95. William Allason to William Corbett, Dec. 20, 1760, *Allason Letterbook, 1757-70*, VSL.

96. *Gould*, 128; John Carman advertised in *MG(P)*, June 3, 10, 17, 1729, "Carts and Horses for carrying Goods by Land between the Two Bays of Delaware and Chesapeake, this is, between Apoquinomy and Bohemia Landings." Carman also kept a sloop and hands "to transport Goods and Passengers to any Part of Maryland or Virginia."

97. *C.O.* 5: 1309: 24; 1257: 4; 740: 335; *Morriss*, 82.

98. 26 *Md. Arch.*, 314; 27 *Md. Arch.*, 172, 574; 29 *Md. Arch.*, 238, 310, 328; 30 *Md. Arch.*, 226.

99. *VG(P)*, May 5, 1738, May 25, 1739. Prices for similar commodities in Georgia were also advertised in *VG(P)*, Sept. 10, 1736, to encourage Chesapeake merchants to ship provisions to the newly-founded colony.

100. 3 *Bozman Papers*, LC, *passim*. 101. *Galloway Letterbook, 1766-71*, LC.

102. John Galloway to Charles Willing, July 18, 1737, and *passim*, John Galloway Letterbook, *Galloway Papers*, LC.

103. 3 *APCC*, no. 245, pp. 345-46. 104. Wertenbaker, *Norfolk*, 37.

105. *Crittenden*, 76. 106. 24*V*34. 107. 1 *Oldmixon*, 446.

108. *Burnaby*, 13. 109. *VG(R)*, Mar. 1, 1770; 3*W*(2)54.

110. *Fithian*, 191. 111. *Ibid.*, 224. 112. 12 *AHR*, 327-40; *Morriss*, 10.

113. Invoice of goods ordered from Micajah Perry, enclosed in a letter dated Aug. 13, 1740, *Beverley Letterbook, 1737-44/5*, NYPL.

114. Invoice, Sept. 1760, from Robert Cary & Co., *Washington Invoices, 1755-66*.

115. Ledger A of George Washington, 1750-54, f. 94, NYPL.

116. Letter of Francis Lightfoot Lee, May 15, 1773, *Emmet Collection,* NYPL, 3808.
117. Thomas Ringgold to Samuel Galloway, Mar. 9, 1766, Ringgold Letters, 1760-70, *Galloway Papers,* NYPL.
118. *VG(D&H),* Jan. 7, 1775. 119. *MPP, Black Books,* pt. 1, no. 56.
120. *Morriss,* 11. 121. 25*MHM*63. 122. *Calvert Papers,* MHS, no. 596.
123. *Mifflin,* 7. 124. 7 *Jamieson Papers,* LC, 1498. 125. 23*W(2)*130.
126. 23*W(2)*131. 127. 23*W(2)*130. 128. 23*W(2)*131. 129. 23*W(2)*132.
130. 23*W(2)*1. It was unsuccessfully attempted in the early days of the Virginia colony. De Vries, some years later, attributed the failure of the sturgeon fishery to the fact that "it is so hot in summer, which is the best time for fishing, that the salt or pickle would not keep them as in Muscovy . . . where the climate is colder than in the Virginias."
131. 18*V*57. 132. 5*C*196. 133. 8 *Md. Arch.,* 400. 134. 21*V*76.
135. George Kendall to John Custis, Feb. 2, 1746/7, VHS.
136. *MG(G),* Dec. 23, 1746.
137. *VG(H),* May 9, 1751. An application for a whaling license was made to the Virginia Council in 1710, but there is no evidence that it was followed up. 1*C*140; 3 *EJC,* 244.
138. *VG(H),* June 13, 1751. 139. *VG(H),* Apr. 24, 1752.
140. See letter of Dr. Charles Carroll to Charles Carroll, "Barrister," in 25*MHM*63.
141. 4 Andrews, *Col. Per.,* 109; 2 *Bruce,* 483-86; *RSMG,* LC, no. 1, 36a; 2 *APCC,* no. 241, pp. 102-3; *CSPC, 1702,* no. 89, p. 61; *CSPC, 1722-23,* no. 353, ii, pp. 171-74. Lt. Gov. Hope of Bermuda asserted that most of Bermuda's 50 or 60 sloops "sail for the salt islands, where they take in salt for Virginia, Philadelphia, and New York, etc."
142. *C.O.* 5: 1330: 515-16; 23*W(2)*131.
143. 12 *AHR,* 328; Francis Jerdone to Buchanan & Hamilton, Nov. 21, 1744, *Jerdone Letterbook, 1737-44,* W&M; William Allason to Robert Allason, June 1760, *Allason Letterbook, 1757-70,* VSL.
144. *JBT,* Jan. 1734/5-Dec. 1741, pp. 278-79; 25*MHM*69.
145. *C.O.* 5: 1330: 515-16.
146. George Washington to Robert Cary and Co., Aug. 10, 1760; same to John and James Searl, Apr. 30, 1763, *Washington Invoices, 1755-66,* LC. Washington told Cary that "This year the *Charming Polly* went into Rappahannock and my Goods by her, received at different times and in bad order." See also William Beverley to Micajah Perry, May 24, 1739, *Beverley Letterbook, 1737-44/5,* NYPL, "for the future pray never send any of my goods to James River."
147. *VG(P),* Sept. 24, 1736, Oct. 15, 1736. "A Parcel of English Calf Skins, marked IL, were sent in a Ship to Rappahannock, the last Spring; but cannot be heard of by the Owner. Any Person who will give Information of them to Mr. Robert Munsford, in Prince George County, . . . shall be

thankfully rewarded for his Trouble"; *VG(P)*, Sept. 28, 1739: "A Small Box, with this Direction upon it, T. Adams on York River, Virginia, was brought into York River, this Year, by Capt. Whiting, in the Ship Whitaker; and there being no Bill of Loading given for it, nor Letter of Direction with it, it is therefore left with Mr. Beverley Whiting, Merchant, in Gloucester-Town; of whom the Owner may have it, on paying the Charge of this Advertisement."

148. Account of Thomas Jones, July 13, 1726, 2 *Jones Papers,* LC, 235-36.

149. Francis Jerdone to Neil Buchanan, Apr. 18, 1741; same to same, July 13, 1741, *Jerdone Letterbook, 1736-44,* W&M. On another occasion when a consignment of goods was sent to the Piankitank instead of the York, trans-shipment cost £50 and Jerdone wrote that he "was Obliged to hire a Sloop to send there for them, which has return'd with ¾ of Each Cargo, . . . So Shall be at a double expence before the remainder can be got around." Same to same, Mar. 4, 1741/2.

150. Henry Callister to William Murray of Isle of Man, Apr. 6, 1748, *Callister Papers, 1741-80,* NYPL, f. 120.

151. William Allason to James Parker, Dec. 18, 1757, *Allason Letterbook, 1757-70,* VSL.

152. William Allason's Accounts, *Allason Letterbook, 1757-70,* VSL, 39.

153. 1 *Jamieson Papers,* LC, 64-65. 154. 4 *Jamieson Papers,* LC, 769.

155. Account rendered Robert Douglas, July 1, 1762, *Allason Papers,* VSL.

156. Receipt of Travers Tarpley, Oct. 30, 1760, *Allason Papers,* VSL.

157. Receipt of Michael Taylor to William Allason, Dec. 1, 1760, *Allason Papers,* VSL.

158. 15*W(1)*221.

## CHAPTER VII

1. For example, in 1761 Ringgold converted a sloop to a brig. Thomas Ringgold to Samuel Galloway, Feb. 3, 1761, Ringgold Letters, 1760-70, *Galloway Papers,* NYPL.

2. Edward P. Morris, *The Fore-and-Aft Rig in America,* 190-91, considers the continuance of the mainstaysail even after the addition of the gaff sail on the foremast to be clear evidence that the topsail schooner was nothing but a slightly altered brigantine and that it developed from a brigantine as a result of the addition of the fore-and-aft foresail and not from the small schooner-rigged boats as a result of enlargement and the addition of topsails. This is unquestionably true in the case of the *Baltick.* In other cases, it is likely that topsail schooners developed in both ways.

3. The *John* and *Mary,* Richard Tillidge master, was described in the *VG(P)* as a snow on May 3, Oct. 24, 1737, and Mar. 8, 1738; as a sloop on Nov. 9, 1737; and as a brig on Nov. 15, 1737.

4. Port Book for Oxford, Entry Inwards and Outwards, 1758-73, MHS.

5. Experimentation produced the bark by 1769. Falconer, *Dict. of the Marine,* defined barks as those vessels which "carry three masts without a mizzen top-sail." As for the sloop, Blanckley, *A Naval Expositor,* said that sloops are "sailed and masted as Men's Fancies lead them, sometimes with one Mast, with two, and with three, with Bermudoes, Shoulder of Mutton, Square, Lugg, and Smack Sails." See Morris, *Fore-and-Aft,* 2-3.

6. For the sloop, see Morris, *Fore-and-Aft,* 73, 85-89; for the schooner, *ibid.,* 178, 185-87.

7. In 1652, The sloop *Anne,* belonging to a shipwright in Anne Arundel County, Md., was sold to Edward Lloyd. 10 *Md. Arch.,* 172. Thereafter sloops were increasingly common. See *Semmes,* 77.

8. In 1717 the "Skooner *Marlbrogh*" of Boston, and in 1718 the "Skooner *George*" of Jamaica were trading in Chesapeake Bay. 4 *Donnan,* 181.

9. A French nautical work published in Paris in 1783 refers to the sloop as "bateau d'Amérique." Chatterton, *Fore and Aft,* 180.

10. As early as 1690, the sloop *Amy* was engaged in the tobacco trade between the Chesapeake and London. 26*V*389.

11. Robert Allason to William Allason, Jan. 28, July 22, 1761, *Allason Papers,* VSL; William Allason to Robert Allason, Apr. 6, May 8, 1761, *Allason Letterbook, 1757-70,* VSL.

12. Chapelle, *Sailing Ships,* 30-31.

13. Chapelle, *Baltimore Clipper,* 35-36. 14. *Ibid.,* 30-32.

15. For a fuller discussion of the subject see Arthur Pierce Middleton, "New Light on the Evolution of the Chesapeake Clipper-Schooner," 9 *American Neptune,* 142-47.

16. For a list of French-built ships, brigs, schooners, and sloops that traded to the Port of Annapolis, 1756-75, and for French-built vessels owned or registered in Maryland, see *ibid.,* 144 *n*9.

17. Thomas Ringgold to Samuel Galloway, Feb. 23, 1761, Ringgold Letters, 1760-70, *Galloway Papers,* NYPL. The Dolphin was registered at Chestertown in 1759, owned by Thomas and William Ringgold. She made a voyage to St. Kitts and one to Boston in 1759. The next year she was sold to John Tillotson and registered at Patuxent. In 1760 she made a voyage to Philadelphia and one to Barbados, both commercially unsuccessful. After that, Ringgold suggested to Galloway that they buy her back cheap "under pretense of Rebuilding her for her extraordinary Mould," and employ her in smuggling.

18. Chapelle, *Baltimore Clipper,* 9-10. 19. *C.O.* 5: 1341: 23.

20. For earlier shipping relations between Virginia and Bermuda see J. H. Le Froy, ed., *Memorials of the Discovery and Early Settlement of the Bermudas or Somers Islands 1515-1685* (London, 1877), I, Appendix V, pp. 721-42.

21. *VG(P),* May 23, 1745. 22. *Richard Bland Lee Papers,* LC, no. 367.

23. 6 *Jamieson Papers*, LC, 1209. The bill included the item "To 13 lbs. Spikes for a Keel . . . For a Bermuda Sloop." Since the other items are for repairs, not building, the probability is that Williamson repaired a Bermuda sloop then in Virginia waters, consigned to Jamieson. As she would have to be hove down in order to receive a new keel, her underwater lines could have been carefully studied.

24. Thomas Ringgold to Samuel Galloway, July 10, 1763, Ringgold Letters, 1760-70, *Galloway Papers*, NYPL.

25. *MG(G)*, Sept. 3, 1761.  26. *Mifflin*, 12.  27. 31*MHM*307.

28. 2 *Jamieson Papers*, LC, 430. It is assumed that this ship was built in the Chesapeake, but there is a chance that she was the French prize ship *Hero*, 260 tons, registered in London in 1758, and known to have traded to the Bay in that year.

29. 3 *Jamieson Papers*, LC, 638.

30. 4 *Jamieson Papers*, LC, 888. Since no purchaser was found at Bordeaux, the *Hero* was dispatched to St. Martin to load salt, thence to Lewes, Delaware. In 1765 she was employed in the West Indies trade.

31. See Brewington, *Chesapeake Bay Log Canoes*, pt. 1.

32. Occasionally the colonists imported boats from Great Britain. Thomas Jones of Yeocomico River, in 1763, instructed Captain Woodford of the ship *Magnanimity* to purchase a boat for him in London. The boat, delivered in 1764, was a "clinch Built Cutter 18 Feet Long Built with Wainscot and Panneld in the Stern Sheets" and cost £12 4s. 6d. 12 *Jones Papers*, LC, no. 2345; 13 *Jones Papers*, LC, no. 2464.

33. For use of lateen on small boats in the seventeenth century, see Morris, *Fore-and Aft*, 20-23.

34. Morris, *Fore-and-Aft*, 24-25. The square sail, when used on small boats, was of a shape different from that of the square sail of a vessel; it was higher than it was wide.

35. *MG(G)*, Dec. 7, 1752, advertises a deal cutter that "goes with a Lugg Sail."

36. 24*V*41, "a sloop or canoe . . . made of one piece . . . had two sails [in 1702]."

37. *MG(G)*, Aug. 4, 1745. The account specified that she had a mainsail and a jib; it is clear, therefore that she was sloop-rigged. *MG(G)*, Dec. 9, 1747, mentions a ship's longboat as having "one Mast, a Foresail, and Mainsail." As she had but one mast, the "foresail" was undoubtedly a jib, and the rig that of a sloop.

38. *VG(P)*, Jan. 27, 1737/8; see also *MG(G)*, Feb. 17, 1748. Reference to a "neat sailing Boat, 20 Feet Keel, rigged Schooner Fashion": *ibid.*, April 27, 1758; "A Small new Schooner about 20 Feet Keel . . .": *MG(G)*, Sept. 16, 1756.

39. *VG(P)*, Aug. 14, 1746.

40. *MG(G)*, July 23, 1752. A ship's yawl with turpentine sides was painted black and yellow, with thwarts and inside work red. *MG(G)*, Sept. 16, 1756.

41. *Mariner*, 109; *MG(G)*, Apr. 11, 1754.

42. *Eddis*, 102-3, stated that vessels built in America and sent to Great Britain for sale were "exclusive of particular decorations;" 21*MHM*307.

43. *MG(G)*, Jan. 10, 1754. 44. *MG(G)*, Nov. 11, 1746.

45. William Allason to Capt. James Chalmers, Aug. 12, 1757, *Allason Letterbook, 1757-70;* for another example, see same to William Corbett, Dec. 20, 1760, *ibid.*

46. *Mariner*, 109.

47. In 1717 Sir Thomas Johnson told the Board of Trade that plantation oak did not "come up to our English oak in goodness," *JBT*, Mar. 1714/5-Oct. 1718, 218; see also 2 *Douglass*, 376.

48. Eddis, 102-5. These observations led Eddis to disagree with those who predicted that the colonies would "before many years are passed, become great and formidable as a maritime power." The necessity of rebuilding in order to support a navy "cannot but be attended with expences that that will require immense revenues." See also 3 *Charnock*, 171.

49. 1 *Bishop*, 84-85, 90. 50. *VG(H)*, Nov. 28, 1751. 51. *VG(H)*, June 6, 1751.

52. *VG(H)*, Sept. 12, 1751. 53. 7 *Jamieson Papers*, 1626.

54. Samuel Galloway to (?), Oct. 28, 1766, Galloway Letterbook, 1766-71, *Galloway Papers*, LC. Galloway wrote of a ship belonging to him and Stewart, "I can recommend her for as good a Vessel as was ever built in America": Thomas Ringgold to Samuel Galloway, July 7, 1765, Ringgold Letters, 1760-70, *Galloway Papers*, NYPL.

55. *MG(G)*, Aug. 29, 1765.

56. See Arthur Pierce Middleton, "Yachting in Chesapeake Bay, 1676-1783," 9 *American Neptune*, 180-84.

57. 7 *Md. Arch.*, 137; 17 *Md. Arch.*, 216-17.

58. *CSPC*, 1689-92, no. 785, p. 223; 8 *Md. Arch.*, 163, 164, 174, 176, 251-62. "Major Sewell had not been on any Tradeing designe nor was it a boate for trade nor proffit but pleasure a vessell of the Country made use of upon account of visitts to his friends"; 8 *Md. Arch.*, 258.

59. [William Craik] to Walter Stone, May 12, 1783, *Stone Papers*, LC, 93.

60. *MG(G)*, Sept. 30, 1746.

61. *Fithian*, 38; the Harriot had a 38-foot keel, 14-foot beam, 6-foot depth of hold, and was valued at £140 in 1777. *Morton*, 199. William Lawrence, her master, was a mulatto.

62. *Fithian*, 89-90. 63. *Fithian*, 102. 64. *Fithian*, 196.

65. 2 *Carter Papers*, VHS, 52. 66. *VG(P&D)*, Sept. 12, 1771.

67. 8*H*560. 68. *Fithian*, 190. 69. *Fithian*, 252. 70. *Fithian*, 248.

71. *Fithian*, 101. 72. *Fitzpatrick*, 352. 73. *Fithian*, 201-3.

74. 8 *Md. Arch.*, 44, 58. The next day, Oct. 6, 1688, the Council ordered Capt. Samuel Philipps, "His Lordship's Admirall of Maryland," on board the ship *Baltimore* in South River, to "spread your Colours and discharge your Cannon" and to command all other ships "within your precinct" to do likewise.

75. 4*W(1)*17. 76. Chapelle, *Sailing Craft*, 188. 77. *Ibid.*, 215.

78. Chatterton, *Fore-and-Aft*, 174. 79. Chapelle, *Sailing Ships*, 8-9.

80. *CSPC, 1696-97*, no. 1131, p. 530. 81. 25 *Md. Arch.*, 595-601.

82. *CSPC, 1708-1709*, no. 216, p. 158.

83. *CSPC, 1706-1708*, no. 1570, p. 760; *Morriss*, 11 n142.

84. Steiner, *Md. Poetry*, 48-49.

85. *CSPC, 1724-25*, no. 383, i, p. 242. "By the great number of ships and other vessels lately built . . . in . . . America, the trade of Petitioners is very much decayed, by reason of which great numbers of those able shipwrights . . . for want of work to maintain their families, have been necessitated to withdraw themselves from their native Country into America." See also *CSPC, 1724-25*, Preface, p. xxviii; no. 485, i, pp. 316-17.

86. 25 *Md. Arch.*, 599-600.

87. *Morriss*, 54. A similar suggestion was made in 1694 by Gerard Slye. He thought that New England with its many pine trees ought to supply pitch, tar, and deal plank, and that Virginia and Maryland ought to supply masts, "the Land being richer the trees are much bigger and taller and the rivers more convenient." Warships, he said, could be built in the Chesapeake "for half the charge that they are built for in England." *Morriss*, 54 n188.

88. *VG(H)*, Feb. 28, 1750/1.

89. Examples: Samuel Hastings, ship carpenter at Annapolis in 1728, in *MG(P)*, Dec. 10, 1728; vessels caulked, William Johnston to Neil Buchanan, Dec. 21, 1739, *Jerdone Letterbook, 1736-44,* and depn. of George Kimber *et al.*, May 5, 1769, *MNPB, 1744-96,* B; William Hood of West River, *MG(G)*, Apr. 7, 1747; James Fenn, who "served his Time" as an apprentice on Thames River, came to the Chesapeake in 1738, worked at Annapolis and several other places on the Bay, *MG(G)*, June 15, 1748; Thomas Wilkins of Kent County, *MG(G)*, Mar. 1, 1753; there was a thriving class of ship carpenters in Norfolk. Wages were high —in 1759 they got four shillings and a pint of rum a day. Of the house-owners in Norfolk in 1776, seventeen were carpenters, six ship carpenters. Wertenbaker, *Norfolk*, 18.

90. *MG(G)*, May 24, 1745. 91. *MG(G)*, July 2, 1752.

92. *VG(P)*, Oct. 15, 1736. He was described as "much Pock-fretten and freckl'd in the Face" and as having "Red Hair and Beard." He apparently had learned his trade in Bristol.

93. *MG(G)*, Mar. 17, 1747. 94. *MG(G)*, May 18, 1748.

95. *MG(G)*, May 18, 1748. 96. *MG(G)*, July 27, 1748.

97. *MG(G)*, June 21, 1753. His price was 7s. 6d. sterling per bolt. Bicknell had already made sails for one ship, two brigantines, a schooner, and a sloop for Galloway; for two snows and a brigantine for Dr. Steuart; for a ship, a snow, and a sloop for Roberts; for a brig for Ridgely and Sligh; "and a great deal of Work for Mr. Creagh, and many others, too tedious to mention."

98. *Mereness*, 406. 99. Wertenbaker, *Norfolk*, 18-19.

100. *De Vries*, 108. 101. *CSPC, 1700*, no. 739, xi, pp. 499-500.

102. *CSPC, 1702*, no. 474, p. 317; 2 *EJC*, 237, 240, 262.

103. 3*H*492; *JBT, 1704-1708/9*, p. 412. The merchants also objected that by the method of admeasurement prescribed, they "are obliged to pay double the tonnage they can load . . . that measurement being a fourth part more than the cubical measurement, by which all ships are built." *Ibid.*, 353-54.

104. 2 *Beverley*, 5-6. 105. *C.O.* 5: 1311: no. 10 (xv), p. 511.

106. William Johnston to Neil Buchanan, May 7, 1739, *Jerdone Letterbook, 1736-44*, W&M; 6 *Jamieson Papers*, LC, 1196, 1213; see also William Reynolds to Messrs. Pasleys & Co., July 4, 1772, 1 *Reynolds Letterbook, 1771-83*, CNHP.

107. Depn. of William Palmer, Apr. 15, 1749, *MNPB, 1744-96*, B.

108. Depn. of Alexander Stewart, Sept. 4, 1754, *MNPB, 1744-96*, B.

109. In 1764 Fauquier told the Board of Trade that "the town of Norfolk and James river have almost wholly engrossed the West Indian and grain trade." Wertenbaker, *Norfolk*, 38 *n*52; *BMAM*, LC, 15484.

110. In 1769, *Eddis*, 18-19, said "There is not, however, any probability that Annapolis will ever attain any importance in a commercial point of view: the harbour is not capable of containing many vessels of considerable burthen."

111. *Mereness*, 406.

112. 27*MHM*317; 27*MHM*322; Henry Callister to Foster Cunliffe & Sons, July 10, 1745, *Callister Papers, 1741-80*, NYPL; see also William Allason to Robert Allason, July 14, 1764, *Allason Letterbook, 1757-70*, VSL; 4 *Jamieson Papers*, LC.

113. Thomas Ringgold to Samuel Galloway, June 22, 1764, Ringgold Letters, 1760-70, *Galloway Papers*, NYPL.

114. *Ibid.*, Aug. 10, 1770.

115. Contract [Bill of Bottomry] between William Roberts and James Russell concerning the ship Rumney and Long, Aug. 7, 1746, *MNPB, 1744-96*, B.

116. *MG(G)*, Feb. 3, 1747.

117. Charles Carroll of Doughoregan in 1759 wrote that the profits in the grain trade were such that the "War which at first, as a new thing, was terrible to us, is now our interest and desire." *Field*, 242; 4 *JEBH*, 532.

118. *C.O.* 5: 1327, 171.

119. Francis Jerdone to Speirs & Brown, June 16, 1757, *Jerdone Letterbook, 1756-63*, W&M.

120. William Allason to Robert Allason, Oct. 21, Nov. 27, 1757, *Allason Letterbook, 1757-70*, VSL.

121. 31*MHM*307.

122. William Allason to William Walker, Nov. 8, 1757; to Robert Allason, Oct. 5, 1758, *Allason Letterbook, 1757-70*, VSL; see also 3 *Jamieson Papers*, 579-80.

123. Thomas Ringgold to Samuel Galloway, July 7, 1766, Ringgold Letters, 1760-70, *Galloway Papers*, NYPL.

124. Samuel Galloway to Sedgley Hillhouse & Co. of Bristol, May 28, 1766; to Robert Harris & Co. of Barcelona, March 29, 1767; to James Russell of London, Sept. 29, 1766, Galloway Letterbook, 1766-71, *Galloway Papers*, LC.

125. Samuel Galloway and Stephen Stewart to James Russell, Apr. 19, 1768, Galloway Letterbook, 1766-71, *Galloway Papers*, LC; see also same to Capt. William Tippell, Feb. 22, 1770, *ibid.*; Thomas Adams to John Morton Jordon & Co., Nov. 9, 1770, VHS.

126. Samuel Galloway to Capt. William Tippell, May 7, 1771, Galloway Letterbook, 1766-71, *Galloway Papers*, LC.

127. William Reynolds to John Norton, June 7, 1773; to Mrs. Courtney Norton, Aug. 5, 1773; to John Norton, Jan. 12, 1774, 1 *Reynolds Letterbook*, CNHP.

128. Basil Sollers, *List of Ships and Shipping, 1753-76*, MHS. This list includes vessels of British ownership and vessels owned in other colonies besides Maryland. It includes everything Mr. Sollers found in the Annapolis Port Books that was designated as having been built in Maryland. It is interesting to note that schooners are more numerous than sloops, and that schooners and ships are the most common varieties of vessels.

129. Mrs. Edith Harker, ed., *Seafaring Virginia; or a Table of Ship Entries and Clearances, Compiled from the Virginia Gazette, 1736-1766* (Master's Thesis, Westhampton College, Richmond, 1941).

130. 26*MHM*138.

131. *Sheffield*, 84. The tonnage given is the contemporary registered tonnage. One-third should be added in order to get the gross tonnage according to modern measurement.

132. New England collectively produced 301 vessels aggregating 16,326 tons, or 62½% of the total colonial tonnage, but the average tonnage of New England-built vessels in 1771 was only 54 tons.

## CHAPTER VIII

1. *Jacobstein*, 23, 28.   2. *DeVries*, 53.   3. *DeVries*, 112.
4. *CSPC, 1661-68*, no. 1800, p. 591.   5. *CSPC, 1696-97*, no. 901, p. 438.
6. In 1704, for example, the 127 ships in the Virginia fleet totalled 21,797 tons—an average of 172 tons apiece. *CSPC, 1704-05*, no. 370, i, p. 158.
7. *Morriss*, 87-88.
8. *CSPC, 1702*, no. 793, pp. 491-92; *CSPC, 1702-03*, no. 1372, p. 867.
9. *CSPC, 1706-08*, no. 483, pp. 213-16.   10. 2 Bruce, 336; *Morriss*, 64.
11. *Tatham*, 284-85.   12. *CSPC*, 1720-21, no. 656, p. 430.   13. *Ibid.*
14. As has been said, in the years 1715-17 some 21,000 tons of shipping were in the Chesapeake trade. The proportion of re-exportation of tobacco from Great Britain was, at this time, about two-thirds of the whole. At this rate, the Chesapeake trade must have employed in both direct and indirect transportation about 35,000 tons of shipping.
15. 5 *Anderson*, 42-56.
16. *CSPC, 1720-21*, no. 214, pp. 129-31; no. 656, p. 430.
17. Hall, *Plantations*, 26, 73-74.
18. 3 *Anderson*, 496; 1 *Oldmixon*, 448-49.   19. *C.O.* 5: 5: pp. 200-205.
20. An estimate based on a statement by John Henry, on his Map of Virginia, 14*W(1)*85, that Virginia exported 50,000 or 60,000 hhds. in 17,000 tons of British shipping. See *Tatham*, 195-96, 288. In 1775, 96,000 hhds. were exported by Virginia and Maryland. See 5 *Anderson*, 250.
21. 20 *AHR*, 47.   22. *CSPC, 1724-25*, no. 383, i, p. 242.
23. *CSPC, 1724-25*, no. 485, i, pp. 316-17.
24. 2 *Bruce*, 296-98; *Tyack*, 48 n2.   25. 2 *Bruce*, 298.   26. 2 *Bruce*, 399.
27. 1 *Bruce*, 384-85.   *Tyack*, 51; *CSPC, 1661-68*, no. 1303, p. 422.
29. *Tyack*, 54.   30. *Morriss*, 87-88.   31. *Wyckoff*, 111.
32. *CSPC, 1702-1703*, no. 1366, p. 864.   33. *MG(P)*, Apr. 15, 1729.
34. These statistics are compiled from the list of ship entries and clearances recorded in the *Virginia Gazette*, 1736-66, as they appear in Harker, *Seafaring Virginia*.
35. *Burnaby*, Appendix 2, pp. 133-34.
36. *CSPC*, 1704-1705, no. 370, i, p. 158. But *Morriss*, 87-88, states that the average for London ships was 170 tons, while that for outport ships was 80 tons. In Maryland, 1689-1701, there were about 72 vessels a year, of which 37 were from London. At this rate, the average tonnage for the 72 vessels was 125 tons.
37. *CSPC, 1720-21*, no. 656, p. 430; no. 214, p. 129. Estimate based on a statement by John Henry (see above, p. 1 *n20*) that in 1770 Virginia exported 50,000 or 60,000 hhds. of tobacco, in 17,000 tons of shipping. In 1775, according to 5 *Anderson*, 250, 96,000 hhds. were exported from Virginia and Maryland. Using the proportions of tonnage to hogsheads

that appears in Henry's statistics, the tobacco trade in 1775 must have employed between 30,000 and 34,000 tons of shipping. Anderson states that there were 330 ships in the trade at that time, therefore the average tonnage in 1775 must have been 90 to 100 tons. There is some evidence, however, that the average was higher. In 1760 there were 120 vessels of 18,000 tons in the Maryland tobacco trade: *2MHM*356. At that rate, the average was 150 tons.

38. See Maryland "Commission Book 82," *26MHM*138, *26MHM*244, *26MHM*342; *27MHM*29. In 1756 Maryland's merchant marine consisted of 60 vessels of 2,000 tons—an average of 33 tons. In 1760 the average was 43 tons: 31 *Md. Arch.*, 145; 32 *Md. Arch.*, 23. In 1764 the average tonnage of the Virginia merchant marine was 60 tons. Wertenbaker, *Norfolk*, 45. In 1769, according to *Bishop*, 90-91, Maryland built 20 vessels of 1,344 tons, and Virginia 27 of 1,269 tons. At that rate Maryland averaged 60 tons and Virginia 47 tons.

39. 3 *Anderson*, 591.  40. 1 *Bruce*, 448; 25*V*374; 1 *Bruce*, 448.

41. 1 *Bruce*, 448.  42. 24*V*231; 25*V*134.  43. 1 *Bruce*, 449.

44. *CSPC, 1706-1708*, no. 1570, p. 760.

45. *C.O.* 5: 749: pt. 4; she was undoubtedly one of the ships that were under construction in Talbot County in 1697. 25 *Md. Arch.*, 595-601.

46. *C.O.* 5: 749: pt. 4.  47. 25 *Md. Arch.*, 595-601.

48. *CSPC, 1706-1708*, no. 1570, p. 760.

49. *CSPC, 1708-1709*, no. 216, p. 158.

50. *CSPC, 1720-21*, no. 656, p. 421; but in 1733 Maryland owned 16 sloops, 2 snows, and 1 ship, operated by 106 mariners. *CSPC, 1733*, no. 61, i, p. 49; *CSPC, 1730*, no. 348, i, p. 214.

51. Wertenbaker, *Norfolk*, 44; 14*V*241; *C.O.* 5: 1326: 28-29.

52. 3*V*117; 3*V*123.  53. 31 *Md. Arch.*, 145.

54. 31 *Md. Arch.*, 145; 32 *Md. Arch.*, 23; Gov. Sharpe to Board of Trade, 1761, 1 *Gilmor Papers*, MHS, div. 1, no. 23; Sollers, *Number of Ships Built in Maryland, 1746-75:* 1755—10; 1759—21; 1762—24.

55. *C.O.* 5: 1330: 535-37.  56. 2*H*134, 2*H*122, 2*H*178.  57. 2*H*272.

58. *CSPC, 1726-27*, no. 215, p. 109.

59. *Flippin*, 63.

60. 2 *APCC*, no. 497, pp. 246-50; 13 *Md. Arch.*, 460-62.

61. Portfolio no. 2, folder doc. D, no. 69, Hall of Records, Annapolis.

62. *CSPC, 1731*, no. 434, i, p. 294.

63. *Flippin*, 63.

64. *CSPC, 1731*, no. 251, p. 143; no. 364, p. 224.

65. *CSPC, 1731*, Introduction, p. xxi; no. 567, p. 389.

66. [Thomas Adams?] to John Morton Jordan & Co., Jan. 24, 1771, 1 *Carter Papers*, VHS, 121.

67. William Beverley to Christopher Smith, Nov. 25, 1740, *Beverley Letterbook, 1737-44/5*, NYPL. Beverley complained that "freight being so

hard [to get]" it could "be got only to the Owners of the Ships." Not being an owner himself, Beverley was obliged to leave some of his tobacco in the colony.

68. Entries for June 9, Aug. 4, 1756; June 2, Nov. 21, 1757; Jan. 20, May 12, June 8, 1758, *Annapolis Port Books—Entry Inwards, 1756-75*, MHS.

69. *VG(P)*, Mar. 1, 1737/8; Mar. 23, 1738/9.

70. Entries for Oct. 7, 1757; Apr. 19, 1758; Sept. 23, 1759; June 11, 1760, *Annapolis Port Books—Entry Inwards, 1756-75*. Thomas Ringgold to Samuel Galloway, Jan. 24, 1766, Ringgold Letters, 1760-70, *Galloway Papers*, NYPL.

71. 1*T*142; Benj. Harrison to Wm. Palfrey, Dec. 27, 1772, *Emmet Collection*, NYPL, 422; John Sanderson, Biography of the Signers, *Emmet Collection*, NYPL, 3764-3906, p. 202.

72. 26*MHM*139; *ibid.*, 143, 146, 148, 247, 252, 256, 260, 262.

73. *Annapolis Port Books—Clearance 1756-75, passim*, MHS.

74. 26*MHM*142; *ibid.*, 148, 149, 154, 157, 158, 246, 250, 252, 255, 257, 259, 260, 345, 349.

75. *Ibid.*, 143, 145, 146, 148, 149, 150, 155, 244, 245, 247.

76. *Annapolis Port Books—Clearance 1748, passim*, Hall of Records, Annapolis; 26*MHM*252.

77. 26*MHM*259.

78. Henry Callister to Ewan Callister, Nov. 12, 1749; to Foster Cunliffe & Co., Oct. 4, 1750, *Callister Papers*, NYPL.

79. 26*MHM*145.

80. Bill of Bottomry, Aug. 7, 1746, *MNPB, 1744-96*, B. The ship was registered as 300 tons. See also "Commission Book 82," 26*MHM*253, 26*MHM*259.

81. "Commission Book 82," 26*MHM*254; *Ibid.*, 258, 262, 350.

82. Bill of George Jamieson to Neil Jamieson, Sept. 24, 1761, 1 *Jamieson Papers*, LC, 115-16.

83. Compiled from Sollers, *Number of Ships Built in Maryland 1746-75*.

84. William Reynolds to John Norton, June 7, 1773, 1 *Reynolds Letterbook, 1771-83*, CNHP.

85. Examples: *VG(H)*, Oct. 31, Nov. 28, 1751.

86. *VG(H)*, June 6, 1751; Apr. 17, Aug. 14, 1752: *MG(G)*, June 27, 1748; May 21, 1751; Aug. 29, 1765.

87. Bill of Bottomry for Ship *Rumney and Long*, Aug. 7, 1746, *MNPB, 1744-96*, B.

88. On at least one occasion, George Washington held a bottomry bond. Apparently the owner, Daniel Jenifer Adams, defaulted in his payment, for Washington directed that the brigantine *Anne and Elizabeth* be sold at auction at Alexandria on Mar. 28, 1774, "pursuant to the Condition of a Bottomry Bond." *V(P&D)*, Mar. 10, 1774; 10*V*325.

## CHAPTER IX

1. *CSPC, 1696-97*, no. 1131, p. 530.
2. 25 *Md. Arch.*, 595-601. In this instance it is probable that the figures apply to masters only.
3. *CSPC, 1697-98*, no. 550, p. 264. 4. *CSPC, 1708-1709*, no. 216, p. 158.
5. *CSPC*, 1730, no. 348, i, p. 214; *CSPC*, 1733, no. 61, i, pp. 49-50.
6. *CSPC*, 1730, no. 348, i, p. 214. 7. *C.O.* 5: 1326: 28-29.
8. *C.O.* 5: 1326: 473. 9. 3*V*123. 10. *CSPC, 1733*, no. 61, i, pp. 49-50.
11. Maryland had 20 ships in 1743. Allowing 6 seamen to a ship, the colony must have had 120 seamen. *C.O.* 5: 205: 200-205.
12. 31 *Md. Arch.*, 145. 13. 32 *Md. Arch.*, 23.
14. Wertenbaker, *Norfolk*, 45. 15. 2 *Force*, no. 8, p. 5.
16. By the end of the seventeenth century the master of a small vessel was allowed by custom the perquisite of cargo space to the extent of one ton: 25*V*354; the same privilege was extended to masters in the tobacco trade in the eighteenth century. *Tatham*, 215-17, stated that on Liverpool ships the privilege amounted to four hogsheads—one cargo ton. The chief mate was allowed two hogsheads and the second mate and carpenter one each. He thought the same was true of Bristol ships. Officers on Glasgow ships enjoyed "a privilege with regard to the staves and lock-stocks by which the cargo is secured; and perhaps in some instances the captains have a percentage allowed upon the cargo, and in others share the passage money." Some masters preferring "a little clear gain to their personal comfort" were in the habit of "stowing their cabins with hogsheads of tobacco, as well as the hold and steerage."
17. Wertenbaker, *Norfolk*, 17.
18. Depn. of Darby Lux, June 9, 1748, *MNPB, 1744-96*, B.
19. Depn. of Capt. William Scandrett, June 18, 1746; Depn. of Capt. Edward Ogle, Feb. 26, 1747/8; Depn. of Capt. John Curling, July 11, 1752, *ibid.*
20. 37*V*110. William Byrd complained, on July 10, 1741, that "everything is damaged and broke to pieces . . . partly owing to . . . your Masters tumbling them ashore at Hampton, and tossing them into a Ware house."
21. Depn. of Capt. Isaac Storm, Nov. 7, 1748, *MNPB, 1744-96*, B. He asserted that "the Cause of his Not Arriving Sooner . . . was Not by any Neglect or fault of this Deponent but Intirely Owing to the Damage he received at Sea . . . Occationed by the Violence of the Wind and Seas."
22. Depn. of James Richard, Nov. 26, 1748, *ibid.*
23. Depn. of Constantine Bull, Nov. 25, 1748, *ibid.*
24. 21*MHM*61. 25. 21*MHM*59.
26. "Sallitudes" was a common name for the salt-producing Tortugas in the West Indies.

27. 9$V$249.

28. George Washington to Robert Cary & Co., Oct. 4, 1763, *Washington Invoices, 1755-66*, LC.

29. 24$V$117.

30. Henry Callister to Ewan Callister, Aug. 13, 1744, *Callister Papers, 1741-80*, NYPL.

31. Washington to Robert Cary & Co., Oct. 4, 1763, *Washington Invoices, 1755-66*, LC.

32. 2$W$(1)223. 33. 2 *Bruce*, 348. 34. 2 *Bruce*, 348. 35. 2 *Bruce*, 349.

36. *CSPC, 1693-96*, no. 2198, p. 630. 37. *CSPC, 1697-98*, no. 422, p. 189.

38. *CSPC, 1702*, no. 221, p. 148; no. 501, p. 332; 3$H$400.

39. 2 *APCC*, no. 935, p. 473. 40. *CSPC, 1710-11*, no. 710, p. 417.

41. *CSPC, 1712-14*, no. 603, p. 303; *CSPC, 1728-29*, no. 174(a), p. 85; 4$H$46.

42. 3$H$487. 43. *MG(P)*, June 10, 1729; *MG(G)*, July 19, Oct. 11, 1745; Dec 9, 1747; July 2, 23, 1752.

44. *MG(P)*, July 1, 1729; *MG(G)*, Feb. 24, 1748; May 24, 1753; Sept. 16, 1756.

45. *VG(H)*, Sept. 5, 1751. 46. *MG(G)*, Aug. 9, 1753. 47. *MG(G)*, July 1, 1753.

48. Thomas Ringgold to Samuel Galloway, Aug. 18, 1761, Ringgold Letters, 1760-70, *Galloway Papers*, NYPL.

49. Examples: *VG(H)*, Oct. 20, 1752; *MG(P)*, July 8, 1729; *MG(G)*, Apr. 5, 1753; Aug. 12, 1756; Jan. 19, 1758.

50. *CSPC, 1702*, no. 222, p. 151.

51. For example: *CSPC, 1701*, no. 1168, p. 739. 52. *Ibid.*

53. Instructions to Gov. Nicholson, Dec. 12, 1702, *C.O.* 5 (no reference number—volume is temporary).

54. *CSPC, 1702-1703*, no. 103, p. 80. 55. *VG(P)*, Sept. 28, 1739.

56. *CSPC, 1702-1703*, no. 103, p. 80. 57. *VG(P)*, Sept. 14, 1739.

58. 7 *Jones Papers*, 1131, LC.

59. William Allason to Capt. William Scott, Aug. 12, Oct. 25, 1757, *Allason Letterbook, 1757-70*, VSL.

60. *VG(P&D)*, Oct. 1, 1767; Wertenbaker, *Norfolk*, 17-18.

61. 2 *Bruce*, 347. 62. 2 *Bruce*, 347-48. 63. 8 *Md. Arch.*, 334, 445.

64. Bill for wages &c. of sloop *Dreadnaught*, Norfolk, Sept. 14, 1761, 1 *Jamieson Papers*, LC, 101-2.

65. Receipted bill of sloop *Dreadnaught*, Norfolk, Sept. 8, 1761, 1 *Jamieson Papers*, LC, 109.

66. Account of ship *Hero* for sundry wages, Aug. 25, 1765, 5 *Jamieson* LC, 1116; Richard Norman *et al. vs.* the snow *Hobbestone*, Aug. 20, 1754, *Md. Vice-Admiralty Court Records, 1754-75*, ff. 4-5.

67. *VG(H)*, Oct. 20, 1752. 68. 5 *Jamieson Papers*, LC, 1116.

69. Richard Norman *et al. vs.* the snow *Hobbestone, Md. Vice-Admiralty Court Records, 1754-75,* ff. 4-5.
70. 1 *Jamieson Papers,* LC, 101-2. 71. *Jamieson Papers,* LC, 109.
72. Examples: George Plater, one of the greatest planters in Maryland and Collector of North Potomac, was counsel for the sailors that sued the ship Ann in 1692 for back wages: 8 *Md. Arch.,* 445-47; William Paca and Samuel Chase were counsel for mariners in Edwards *et al. vs.* snow Hannah, Sept. 19, 1763, *Md. Vice-Admiralty Court Records, 1754-75,* ff. 25-26.
73. Examples: 8 *Md. Arch.,* 334, 445; *MG(G),* June 17, 1746; *Md. Vice-Admiralty Court Records,* 1754-75, *passim.*
74. 4*H*109. 75. 5*H*36, 5*H*82; sailors were also excepted from the Virginia act of 1748, concerning the making of wills, 5*H*457.
76. 4*H*212. 77. 2 *Smith,* 803. 78. 2 *Smith,* 804.
79. Edwards *et al. vs.* snow Hannah, Sept. 19, 1763, *Maryland Vice-Admiralty Court Records,* 1754-75, ff. 25-26.
80. Petition of Shipmasters, 1*C*202.
81. For example: Walter King to Col. Thomas Jones, Sept. 8, 1744, 5 *Jones Papers,* LC, 706. In this case the crew deserted in a body and took with them all the boats, so the captain was marooned on his ship for two days.
82. Wertenbaker, *Norfolk,* 41. 83. 1 *APCC,* no. 473, pp. 299-300.
84. 4 *Beverley,* 60.
85. One ship, the *Liverpool Merchant,* while in the Choptank River, in 1746, had her entire crew fall ill. Five or six of the best hands were incapacitated, the gunner was dead, and the "deputy Captain" very ill. The factor in charge wrote "there's hardly a Man of them but has had fit of sickness." Henry Callister to Foster Cunliffe & Co., Sept. 28, 1746, *Callister Papers, 1741-80,* NYPL.
86. 1 *Bruce,* 444-45.
87. (Anon.) *A Letter from a Freeholder, to a Member of the Lower House of Assembly* (Annapolis, 1727).
88. *Ibid.,* 9. 89. *MG(P),* Apr. 15, 1729. 90. *Gould,* 143-44.
91. 4*H*247. This act directed that hogsheads were to be taken on vessels only "at the several warehouses."
92. Examples: 24*V*117; *MG(P),* June 10, July 1, 1729; *MG(G),* June 24, 1762.
93. *MG(P),* July 1, 1729; *VG(P&D),* Mar. 9, 1769; *VG(Pinckney),* July 20, 1775; *Freeman's Jour.,* 1781-83, no. 36 (December, 1781).
94. *CSPC,* 1710-11, no. 489, p. 262; no. 561, p. 325.
95. 3*H*72; 3*H*138; 3*H*170. 96. *MG(G),* July 26, 1753.
97. *Swain,* 11; 5 *Md. Arch.,* 31, 221-22.
98. 12*W(2)*43. Thomas P. Bagby, in 1888, said the inscription was wholly visible, and the stone was of seventeenth-century date.

## CHAPTER X

1. *Thomas,* 425; *CSPC, 1669-74,* no. 1159, p. 530.
2. 57 Mass. Hist. Soc., *Proceedings,* 396-414. 3. 1 Bruce, 385.
4. In 1665 five "rich and valuable" Bristol ships were taken on their homeward passage, "laden with Virginia tobacco." The same year several London ships were taken. The Bristolmen totalled 1,500 tons and carried 2,700 hhds. of tobacco. 1 *APCC,* no. 736, p. 449; *CSPC, 1661-68,* no. 930, p. 275.
5. 1 *APCC,* no. 642, p. 401.
6. *CSPC, 1661-68,* no. 1084, p. 329; 1 *Bruce,* 385.
7. 1 *APCC,* no. 642, p. 389. 8. *CSPC, 1661-68,* no. 1084, p. 329.
9. *CSPC, 1661-68,* no. 1145, p. 362. 10. 1 *APCC,* no. 690, p. 420.
11. 1 *APCC,* no. 690, p. 420. 12. *Tyack,* 20.
13. 1 *APCC,* no. 736, p. 449. 14. 1 *APCC,* no. 997, p. 607.
15. 1 *APCC,* no. 979, p. 598; no. 1002, p. 610.
16. 1 *APCC,* no. 1048, p. 639; no. 1055, p. 648. Upon his return, Cooke was given "a Chaine of Gould and a Medall of the usuall value in like Cases" by the lord chamberlain, "as of his Majesty's Royall Grace and Bounty for his service," and a month later was made captain of a 300-ton merchantman.
17. 1 *APCC,* no. 1092, p. 670.
18. 1 *APCC,* no. 659, p. 401; no. 1248, p. 809; 2 *APCC,* no. 331, p. 148; no. 471, p. 232.
19. 1 *APCC,* no. 1098, p. 675. 20. 1 *APCC,* no. 1098, p. 675 *n.*
21. *CSPC, 1689-92,* no. 579, p. 183. 22. *CSPC, 1689-92,* no. 596, p. 185.
23. *CSPC, 1689,* no. 1210, p. 612 Addenda.
24. *CSPC, 1689-92,* no. 787, p. 224; 8 *Md. Arch.,* p. 380; 23 *Md. Arch.,* p. 547.
25. 2 *APCC,* no. 331, p. 148; *CSPC, 1696-97,* no. 901, p. 438; *CSPC, 1702,* no. 793, p. 492.
26. *CSPC, 1702-1703,* no. 77, i, p. 59. 27. 2 *APCC,* no. 424, p. 201.
28. 2 *APCC,* no. 364, pp. 158-72; no. 859, p. 387; no. 861, pp. 394-96; *CSPC, 1706-1708,* Preface, p. xiv; no. 63, i, p. 28; no. 571, p. 228; no. 843, p. 416.
29. 2 *APCC,* no. 375, p. 177. 30. 32*V*25.
31. In 1690 William Byrd I declared "I was never So put to itt for fraight, in my life." He had no means of shipping his 200 hhds. to England: 26*V*132. For the freight rate of £17 per ton, see 27*V*285.
32. *CSPC, 1702-1703,* no. 450, i, p. 259. 33. 2 *APCC,* no. 891, p. 425.
34. *CSPC, 1702-1703,* no. 77, i, p. 59; no. 97, p. 76. 35. 2 *APCC,* no. 891, p. 425.
36. *CSPC, 1702-1703,* no. 763, i, p. 467.

37. *CSPC, 1704-1705*, no. 353, pp. 139-45. 38. 26*MHM*27.

39. *CSPC, 1706-1708*, no. 72, p. 33. 40. 2 *APCC*, no. 1016, p. 514.

41. 101 *CTP, 1702-1707*, no. 5, p. 483. 42. 26*MHM*27.

43. *VG(H)*, Oct. 24, 1754. 44. *MG(G)*, Aug. 10, 1748.

45. Francis Jerdone to Speirs and Brown, Aug. 19, 1757, *Jerdone Letterbook, 1756-63*, W&M.

46. Wright, *Carter Letters*, 94-95. 47. *Bassett*, 565.

48. Francis Jerdone to Neil Buchanan, May 20, 1742, *Jerdone Letterbook, 1736-44*, W&M.

49. 5 *Jones Papers*, LC, 692. 50. *MG(G)*, June 28, 1745.

51. *MG(G)*, July 26, 1745. 52. *MG(G)*, Aug. 16, 1745.

53. *MG(G)*, Oct. 25, 1745. 54. *MG(G)*, May 13, 1746.

55. *MG(G)*, May 18, 1748. 56. *MG(G)*, June 22, July 6, 20, 1748.

57. Samuel Hyde to John Eversfield, Jr., May 28, 1744, *MNPB, 1744-96*, B.

58. 5 *Jones Papers*, LC, 706.

59. Henry Callister to Ewan Callister, July 28, 1745, *Callister Papers, 1741-80*, NYPL.

60. Henry Callister to William Murray, Apr. 6, 1748, *Callister Papers, 1741-80*, NYPL.

61. Francis Jerdone to Neil Buchanan, Aug. 17, 1742; same to Buchanan & Hamilton, Dec. 25, 1744, *Jerdone Letterbook, 1736-44*, W&M.

62. Henry Callister to Anthony Bacon, Feb. 11, 1744/5, *Callister Papers, 1741-80*, NYPL; *VG(P)*, June 6, Sept. 12, 1745.

63. *MG(G)*, May 18, 1746. 64. Henry Callister to William Murray, Apr. 6, 1748, *Callister Papers*, 1741-80, NYPL.

65. Henry Callister to Foster Cunliffe & Sons, Oct. 5, 1748, *ibid.; MG(G)*, Oct. 19, 1748.

66. Francis Jerdone to Hugh Crawford, Dec. 10, 1757, also Apr. 20, 1759, *Jerdone Letterbook, 1756-63*, W&M; John Bland to William Allason, Dec. 4, 1760, *Allason Papers*, VSL; Thomas Ringgold to Samuel Galloway, Aug. 15, 1761, Ringgold Letters, 1760-70, *Galloway Papers*, NYPL: Receipt of Robert Cary & Co., Oct. 6, 1761, to Estate of John Parke Custis, *Custis Papers*, VHS.

67. Francis Jerdone to Hugh Crawford, Dec. 10, 1757, *Jerdone Letterbook, 1756-63*, W&M.

68. John Bland to William Allason, Dec. 4, 1760, *Allason Papers*, VSL.

69. Wertenbaker, *Norfolk*, 40. 70. *CSPC, 1702*, no. 390, p. 275-76.

71. *CSPC, 1730*, no. 348, i, p. 216.

72. William Johnston to Neil Buchanan, July 8, Aug. 25, 1740, *Jerdone Letterbook*, 1736-44 W&M. 73. 3*V*117.

74. James Hanrick to Samuel Galloway, Jan. 25, 1757, *Galloway Papers*, Box 1742-69, NYPL.

75. William Allason to Capt. James Chalmers, Aug. 12, 1757, *Allason Letterbook, 1757-70*, VSL.

76. 31 *Md. Arch.*, 145. 77. 32 *Md. Arch.*, 23. 78. 2*MHM*356.
79. Reese Meredith to Samuel Galloway, Mar. 21, 1764, *Galloway Papers,* Box 1742-69, NYPL.
80. Thomas Ringgold to Samuel Galloway, Jan. 26, 1763, Ringgold Letters, 1760-70, *Galloway Papers,* NYPL.
81. 4 *JEBH*, 89. 82. *CSPC, 1704-1705,* no. 353, p. 139.
83. *CSPC, 1702-1703,* no. 38, i, p. 45.
84. *CSPC, 1708-1709,* no. 253, p. 185; no. 322, p. 205; no. 131, p. 94; 2 *APCC,* no. 375, p. 177; 24*V*278.
85. *MG(G),* June 8, 1758. 86. *VG(P),* Oct. 24, 1745; *MG(G),* Aug. 10, 1748.
87. *Morriss,* 93.
88. "Sayling instructions for the Better Keeping Company with his Majesty Ship *Essex Prize*," James River, May 27, 1700, *C.O.* 5: 1311: no. 10(iv), pp. 403-5.
89. "A Line of Battle," [James River, June 5, 1700], *C.O.* 5: 1311: no. 10(v), p. 407.
90. "Fighting Instructions," James River, June 5, 1700, *C.O.* 5: 1311: no. 10(iv), p. 409.
91. 24*V*276. 92. 24*V*278. 93. 24*V*278. 94. 24*V*278. 95. 24*V*279.
96. 24*V*278.

## CHAPTER XI

1. Sir William Berkeley spoke of the enemy "whose swords are continually in our bowels or apprehensions." *Berkeley,* 12.
2. *CSPC, 1708-1709,* no. 421, p. 254. 3. *CSPC, 1700,* no. 501, p. 301.
4. See the interesting discussion of defense and the arguments advanced for moving the capital to Williamsburg where it would not "be open to the great Gunns and Bombs" of enemy warships, in a speech by a student of the College of William and Mary before the Virginia Assembly, May 1, 1699: 10*W(2)*330.
5. *Williams,* 4. 6. *CSPC, 1702, no. 210,* p. 142.
7. *Williams,* 5; *CSPC, 1702,* no. 210, p. 142. Colonel Quary in 1702 proposed stationing a squadron of five or six men-of-war in Chesapeake Bay. The attack he pictured came true in the Revolution and the War of 1812, except that he did not envision the Royal Navy as the attacker.
8. 1 *APCC,* no. 695, p. 422.
9. Wertenbaker, *Virginia,* 127; *CSPC, 1661-68,* no. 1545, p. 490.
10. Wertenbaker, *Virginia,* 129. 11. *Ibid.,* 129-30.
12. 1 *APCC,* no. 1183, p. 749. After the suppression of the rebellion, the owners of these vessels presented claims to the Admiralty for freight, wages, and victuals amounting to £2,564 10s. 6d.
13. Wertenbaker, *Virginia,* 174, 176-77. 14. *Ibid.,* 183.

15. *CSPC, 1681-85,* no. 260, p. 127.  16. *Williams,* 27.

17. *CSPC, 1681-85,* no. 1063, p. 425.  18. *Ibid.,* no. 1149, p. 454.

19. *Ibid.,* no. 1770, p. 660. The cost of the *Katherine* was assumed by the crown, and Culpeper received a royal warrant on the treasury for the sum of £1,086 13*s.* 4*d.* Captain Jones proved an unfortunate choice for commander of the *Katherine,* since in later years he was accused of deliberately undermanning the sloop in order to pocket the wages of the additional men. He was also charged with collaborating with the pirates, having "struck the King's colours" to them. When the pirates saw he "was one of themselves," they dismissed him with a present of French wines. *CSPC, 1689-92,* no. 2318, p. 665.

20. *CSPC, 1681-85,* no. 1273, p. 505; no. 1335, p. 529; no. 1342, p. 531; 2 *APCC,* no. 130, p. 54.

21. *Williams,* 5-6.  22. *Ibid.,* 6; 2 *Charnock,* 430.

23. *CSPC, 1697-98,* no. 281, p. 128.  24. *CSPC, 1685-88,* no. 608, p. 165.

25. 2 *Charnock,* 429, 435; *Williams,* 48.

26. *CSPC, 1693-96,* no. 1916, p. 518.

27. *CSPC, 1696-97,* no. 1257, p. 583.  28. *CSPC, 1700* no. 459, p. 263.

29. *CSPC, 1699,* no. 989, p. 539.

30. *CSPC, 1699,* no. 711, p. 390; no. 802, p. 444; *Williams,* 47-51.

31. *CSPC, 1699,* no. 705, p. 387; *Williams,* 50.

32. *CSPC, 1700,* no. 532, ii, p. 311; *Semmes,* 44-48; *Williams,* 57-62.

33. *CSPC, 1699,* no. 705, p. 387; *Williams,* 50-51.

34. *CSPC, 1701,* no. 228, p. 118; no. 423, p. 218.

35. *C.O.* 5: 1311: no. 10 (xiii), pp. 468-70; no. 10 (xv), pp. 510-11.

36. *CSPC, 1701,* no. 423, p. 217; *CSPC, 1702,* no. 911, p. 561; no. 1174, p. 734.

37. *CSPC, 1702,* no. 119, p. 80; no. 192, p. 129; for example, see *CSPC, 1702,* no. 474, p. 317; no. 1029, p. 653.

38. *CSPC, 1701,* no. 893, p. 539.  39. *CSPC, 1702,* no. 210, p. 140.

40. 2 *APCC,* no. 891, p. 425.  41. *CSPC, 1702-1703,* no. 171, p. 117.

42. *CSPC, 1702,* no. 1174, p. 734. E. P. Lull, *History of the Gosport Navy Yard* (Washington, 1874), 8, shows that the British finally established a navy yard at Gosport just prior to the Revolution.

43. *CSPC, 1706-1708,* no. 975, p. 472.  44. *CSPC, 1706-1708,* no. 1010, p. 486.

45. *CSPC, 1706-1708,* no. 1050, p. 505.  46. *JBT,* 1704-1708/9, p. 409.

47. *CSPC, 1706-1708,* no. 1573, p. 763.

48. *CSPC, 1706-1708,* Preface, p. xxviii.

49. *CSPC, 1706-1708,* no. 137, p. 96.

50. *CSPC, 1706-1708,* Preface, p. xxviii; *CSPC, 1706-1708,* no. 1570, p. 760.

51. *CSPC, 1708-1709,* no. 421, p. 254.

52. *CSPC, 1708-1709,* no. 137, p. 96. After the privateer entered the York, he withdrew to shoal water, thus escaping one of Commodore Hunting-

ton's men-of-war then taking on provisions in Virginia. This accounts for the Virginia Council's insistence upon a small armed vessel as well as a fourth-rate frigate.

53. *CSPC, 1708-1709,* Preface, p. xxviii; no. 254, p. 185.

54. *CSPC, 1708-1709,* no. 421, p. 255; no. 571, p. 343.

55. *CSPC, 1708-1709,* no. 765, p. 480.

56. *CSPC, 1708-1709,* no. 571, p. 343.

57. *CSPC, 1708-1709,* no. 765, p. 480.

58. *CSPC, 1710-11,* no. 21, p. 4.  59. *CSPC, 1701-11,* no. 208, p. 84.

60. *CSPC, 1710-11,* no. 263, p. 114.  61. *Ibid.*

62. *CSPC, 1710-11,* no. 349, p. 171.

63. *CSPC, 1710-11,* no. 363, p. 177; no. 449, p. 242.

64. *CSPC, 1711-12,* no. 42, p. 25.  65. *CSPC, 1711-12,* no. 120, p. 112.

66. 26V54.

67. *CSPC, 1711-12,* no. 301, p. 219. The whole expense for three months amounted to only £121.

68. *CSPC, 1711-12,* no. 418, p. 284.  69. *CSPC, 1712-14,* no. 375, p. 192.

70. 6 *APCC,* Unbound Papers, no. 251, p. 103; *CSPC, 1714-15,* no. 449, p. 199; no. 520, p. 232.

71. *CSPC, 1716-17,* Preface, p. xii.  72. *CSPC, 1720-21,* no. 513, p. 326.

73. *CSPC, 1716-17,* no. 595, p. 316.  74. *CSPC, 1720-21,* no. 513, p. 326.

75. *CSPC, 1717-18,* Preface, p. xv.  76. *CSPC, 1716-17,* no. 240, p. 139.

77. *CSPC, 1716-17,* no. 595, v, p. 316.

78. *CSPC, 1717-18,* Preface, p. xv; *Emmet Collection,* NYPL, no. EM 10661.

79. *CSPC, 1716-17,* no. 240, p. 139.  80. *CSPC, 1716-17,* no. 595, p. 316.

81. *CSPC, 1716-17,* no. 595, i, ii, p. 317.

82. *CSPC, 1717-18,* no. 800, p. 425; 3 *APCC,* no. 15, p. 23.

83. *CSPC, 1717-18,* no. 657, p. 332.

84. 3 *APCC,* no. 30, p. 36; 239 *CTP, 1720-28,* no. 54, p. 134; *CSPC, 1720-21,* no. 416, i, p. 272.

85. *CSPC, 1720-21,* no. 513, p. 326.  86. 32V25.

87. Wright, *Carter Letters,* 7, 96.  88. *CSPC, 1720-21,* no. 513, p. 326.

89. *CSPC, 1722-23,* no. 175, p. 85.

90. William Byrd II to John Custis, July 29, 1723, VHS.

91. Examples: 233 *CTP, 1720-28,* no. 22, p. 45; 242 *CTP,* no. 27, p. 186.

92. *CSPC, 1720-21,* no. 513, p. 326.  93. *CSPC, 1724-25,* no. 210, p. 112.

94. Except for a few cases of petty piracy: for example, *Williams,* 125-28; *MG(G),* Dec. 2, 1746; Mar. 28, 1754.

95. *CSPC, 1730,* no. 375, p. 229.  96. *CSPC, 1726-27,* no. 707, p. 353.

97. *CSPC, 1730,* no. 348, i, p. 217.  98. *CSPC, 1731,* no. 289, p. 169.

99. Francis Jerdone to Neil Buchanan, June 5, 1741, *Jerdone Letterbook, 1736-44,* W&M; same to same, Jan. 7, 1741/2, *ibid.*

100. Same to same, May 20, 1742, *ibid.*

101. 3 *APCC*, no. 590, p. 777. Peyton was court-martialed and dismissed from the Royal Navy in June, 1742, "for being negligent in the Execution of the Orders he was under while he was Stationed in Virginia."
102. *C.O.* 5: 1326: 11-12. 103. *C.O.* 5: 1326: 31-32; 1327: 173-4.
104. *VG(P)*, May 23, 1745. 105. *MG(G)*, July 12, 1745.
106. *MG(G)*, July 26, 1745. 107. *MG(G)*, June 22, 1748.
108. *MG(G)*, July 6, 1748. 109. *MG(G)*, July 6, 20, 1748.
110. *MG(G)*, July 20, 1748. 111. *MG(G)*, Aug. 10. 1748.
112. *C.O.* 5: 1327: 187, 242. The storm occurred in October, 1749.
113. *C.O.* 5: 1328: 330. The fort at Point Comfort never amounted to anything in colonial days after 1749. In 1763 Fauquier said it "serves now only as a signal house to give notice of what Ships enter the Capes." At that time it was manned by an officer and one man. *C.O.* 5: 1330: 548-49.
114. *C.O.* 5: 17: 1. 115. *C.O.* 5: 1329: 45. 116. *C.O.* 5: 18: 2.
117. *C.O.* 5: 18: 5-6. 118. *C.O.* 5: 8: 13-17.
119. John Glassford & Co. to Neil Jamieson, Aug. 10, 1761, 1 *Jamieson Papers, 1757-89*, LC, 74.
120. Depn. of Glassell and Mackie, Aug. 5, 1762, *MNPB, 1744-96*, B.

## CHAPTER XII

1. Chapin, *Privateer Ships*, 9.
2. 1*H*537; 2*H*512; see also the king's instructions to the sub-commissioner of prizes in Virginia, 1664, 15 *V*138.
3. 57 *Md. Arch.*, Introduction, lvii; 41 *Md. Arch.*, 302; 49 *Md. Arch.*, Introduction, ix, xv, xxi, xxiii, 23.
4. 12 *CTB*, Apr. 1697-Sept. 1697, 298, 312; 20 *Md. Arch.*, 72, 113, 165.
5. 25*V*378; 1 *EJC*, 379, 413. As for fees, the judge took 5% of the value of the prize, the register 2½%, and the marshal 2½%.
6. 5*W(1)*129; 20 *Md. Arch.*, 309; 2 *Channing*, 276.
7. 4 Andrews, *Col. Per.*, 236, asserts that probably more than a third of the American vice-admiralty court cases, 1702-63, were prize cases; the absence, or rarity, of privateers in Virginia can be seen in Governor Nicholson's report to the Board of Trade in 1704 that "no commission hath been granted here to any such Private Ship of war, nor is it like that any such will be fitted out from hence." 2 *EJC*, 378.
8. 25 *Md. Arch.*, 165-67; *CSPC, 1702-1703*, no. 1150, pp. 735-36.
9. 1 *EJC*, 367. 10. *CSPC, 1704-1705*, no. 104, p. 42.
11. 1*C*85. In August, 1704, William Byrd I presented his commission from the Commissioners of the Prize Office in England constituting him the Queen's Agent for Prizes in Virginia. 2 *EJC*, 378.
12. 25 *Md. Arch.*, 178, 183; *CSPC, 1704-1705*, Preface, xxviii, no. 583, p. 263; no. 605, p. 281; *CSPC, 1706-1708*, no. 160, p. 65; 2 *APCC*, no. 1028, p. 519.

13. *CSPC, 1706-1708,* no. 160, p. 65; no. 1570, p. 758.
14. 3 *EJC,* 69-70. Nott had been informed that the English Prize Office had appointed Harrison acting prize agent for Virginia, but the commission had not yet arrived. Nott therefore appointed Harrison acting prize agent and ordered him to proceed to Kiquotan (Hampton) and "do his duty in relation to the prize." However, Capt. Thompson refused to deliver the prize to Harrison because he did not hold a commission from the Prize Office in England. A compromise was effected whereby Harrison and Thompson disposed of the prize and handled the proceeds jointly. 3 *EJC,* 71.
15. 3 *EJC,* 186; 3 *Charnock,* 57.
16. 4 Andrews, *Col. Per.,* 236; 36*V*357. William Byrd II wrote Sir Robert Walpole in 1739 that the re-establishment of a Prize Office "will discourage and clog the affair [privateering] very much, as it did in the Reign of good King William. Besides paying a large share of what they took, I remember the captors were plagued with a vexatious attendance and most exorbitant Fees to the Vultures which hovered for prey about the Office. On complaint of these Grievances Queen Anne generously gave up her share of all Prizes to those Brave men that took them, and I hope the same will be done by his Present Majesty."
17. *CSPC, 1711-12,* no. 418, p. 284; 1 VHS *Collections,* new ser. (1882), 163.
18. *CSPC, 1716-17,* no. 595, p. 316; no. 595, iv, pp. 318-21; no. 240, p. 139; no. 240, iii, p. 142.
19. *CSPC, 1730,* no. 289, p. 149; 3 *EJC,* 506. In 1718 Anglo-Spanish relations reached the breaking point. In September, 1718, Great Britain declared war on Spain. In May, 1719, Gov. Spotswood ordered the declaration proclaimed "by Sound of Trumpett" in the Market Square, Williamsburg. Along with the declaration, Spotswood received a warrant from the Admiralty empowering the Virginia vice-admiralty court "to try and condemn Prizes taken . . . during the present Warr with Spaine in the same maner as such prizes were tryable during the late warr with France." Immediately thereafter Captain John Martin applied for and received a letter of marque for his privateer sloop *Ranger,* then fitting out.
20. In April, 1740, the Virginia governor received authority and instructions for the trial and condemnation of prizes. 5 *EJC,* 4.
21. 5 *EJC,* 57-59, 71. 22. 1*C*235.
23. 5 *Jones Papers,* LC, 699, 715. Walter King of Virginia, then in Bristol, observed that several of the privateers of that port were "as Compleat Ships as any of 40 Guns belonging to his Majesty's Navy." King owned an eighth part of the *Ranger.* After she was laid up, her prize, the *Rover,* was fitted out as a privateer at the cost of £5,000, and carried 20 carriage and 20 swivel guns and a crew of 200 men.
24. *C.O.* 5: 1326: 11-12. 25. 28 *Md. Arch.,* 324.

26. *MG(G)*, May 17, 1745.
27. *VG(P)*, June 20, July 4, 11, Sept. 12, Nov. 7, 1745. The vessel taken by the *William and Betty* was thought to be of New England construction and British-owned. The rum, sugar, and ginger were supposed to be the produce of Barbados.
28. *VG(P)*, Sept. 12, 1745; April 24, Aug. 28, Sept. 26, 1746; 5 *EJC*, 186. In the spring of 1746 Miller was reported to have taken a large French ship and carried her into Providence, where it was said to have been "the richest Prize carried into that Port this War." In the fall of 1746 the *Raleigh* was offered for sale at Norfolk "with all her Sails, Rigging, &c. as also her Guns, Powder, Shot, and other War-like Stores." In 1745 the Virginia Council urged that the "Rawleigh Privateer be immediately hired for the Service of the Government to cruize for two months."
29. *VG(P)*, July 3, 1746.
30. *MG(G)*, Jan. 20, Aug. 10, 1748. The two prizes retaken by the *Otter* and *Hector* were laden with West India rum and were consigned to Captain Hutchings of Norfolk. Chapin, *Privateering*, 202.
31. *VG(H)*, Aug. 27, 1756.
32. *MG(G)*, Dec. 1, 1757; May 11, 1758. The *Two Sisters* belonged to Samuel Galloway. She sailed for Barbados in December, 1757, and returned in May, 1758, after an eighteen-day passage from Barbados.
33. *VG(H)*, April 22, 1757. 34. 2 *Jamieson Papers*, LC, 430.
35. *C.O.* 5: 18: 213. 36. *Swain*, 10.
37. *MG(G)*, July 27, 1758.
38. Depn. of George Freebairn, Jan. 5, 1759, *MNPB, 1744-96*, B.
39. *C.O.* 5: 1315: no. 35, viii; 3 *EJC*, 558.

## CHAPTER XIII

1. 33*V*83.
2. Dr. Charles Carroll asserted that "by means of the great Bay of Chesapeak and the many Rivers falling therein and the many Creeks Coves and Branches thereof affords Carriage Commodious and Easie for Tobacco . . . were it not for this Convenience it would be impracticable or at least very Expensive to Carry on the making of Tobacco." 25*MHM*62.
3. By 1673 Virginia, in Sir John Knight's view, was "of as great importance to his Majesty as the Spanish Indies to Spain." *CSPC, 1669-74*, no. 1159, p. 530. In 1683 Lord Howard of Effingham asserted that "the revenue of Virginia exceeds that of all the other plantations put together." *CSPC*, 1681-85, no. 1273, p. 505. In 1775 Virginia and Maryland contained some 970,000 inhabitants, or nearly a third of the total population of the thirteen continental colonies soon to become the United States. 5 *Anderson*, 238.

4. 15*W(1)*147.

5. *Eddis,* 90-91, observed in 1771 that "in all probability, from the multitude of rivers, which with their branches, intersect this country in almost every direction, Maryland will never abound with ports . . . By the advantage of so many navigable waters, an opportunity is afforded to ship the produce of many extensive districts, even at the doors of the respective planters; who, consequently, have not that inducement, common to most countries, for establishing themselves in populous communities."

6. 33*V*83. Alexander Rose wrote in 1768 that the navigable waterways "will for ever occasion the People to live dispersed" in the tidewater. "We can expect to have great Towns at the Falls of the Rivers only, where the Commodities from the back Country must be brought for Exportation."

7. Lord Adam Gordon said in 1765 that the Virginians "have had always a much greater connection with, and dependance on the Mother Country, than any other Province," a fact which he rightly attributed to "the nature of their Situation being such from the Commodiousness and Number of Navigable rivers and Creeks, that they may Export to, and import from, home everything they raise or want, from within a few miles of their own houses, and cheaper than any neighbouring province can supply them." *Mereness,* 404.

8. For example, in 1701 the Virginia House of Burgesses resolved "that a Naval Force is the best way to secure this country from an enemy by water, and the charge of Maintaining it will be altogether insupportable to this country." *CSPC, 1701,* no. 893, p. 539.

9. The New England and Middle Colonies and the Carolinas and Georgia could defend themselves with forts or even batteries of 24-pounders, strategically placed at the mouths of rivers and the entrance of harbors. Virginia and Maryland alone of the continental colonies were unable to defend themselves in this manner.

10. 3 *Force,* no. 14, p. 7. See also *ibid.,* p. 22: Maryland is only separated or parted from Virginia, by a river . . . the commodities and manner of living as in Virginia."

11. 25*V*369. 12. 16*V*74. 13. 2 *Beverley,* 3. 14. 4 *Donnan,* 109.

15. Hall, *Plantations,* 73. 16. 2 *Douglass,* 361.

17. 3 *Force,* no. 14, p. 21.

18. 2 *Beverley,* 2; 1 *Oldmixon,* 404, said the same thing: Virginia and Maryland, "in common Discourse, are still called Virginia."

19. Mayne & Co. to Samuel Galloway, June 21, 1765, *Galloway Papers,* Box 1742-69, NYPL.

20. *Berkeley,* 6.

21. 1*Beverley,* 49.

# Bibliography

## MANUSCRIPT SOURCES

Although there are a few useful monographs that have a bearing on certain aspects of the subject, this work is based largely upon primary sources. All the principal manuscript collections pertaining to the colonial period of Virginia and Maryland at the institutions listed below were consulted. In addition, the voluminous records of some of the maritime counties of the Chesapeake Bay country have been dipped into, either at the county courthouses or in photostat at the Virginia State Library. Of the important collections, the following should be mentioned:

A. THE COLLEGE OF WILLIAM AND MARY, Williamsburg, Virginia.
   1. Carter Papers.
   2. Jerdone Papers, 1720-76. 5 vols.
   3. Philip Ludwell Letters, 1713-16.

B. THE COLONIAL NATIONAL HISTORICAL PARK, Yorktown, Virginia.
   1. William Nelson Letterbook, 1766-75, photostat.
   2. William Reynolds Letterbook, 1771-83, photostat. 2 vols.

3. COLONIAL WILLIAMSBURG, INC., Williamsburg, Virginia.
   1. Tucker-Coleman Papers.
   2. Norton Papers, 1750-95.
   3. Letters of Governor William Gooch to his brother Thomas, Bishop of Norwich, 1727-51, typescripts.
   4. York County Records, abstracts.

D. HALL OF RECORDS, Annapolis, Maryland.
   1. Notary Publick Record Book, Liber B, 1744-96.
   2. Port Books: Patuxent District, Ports of Annapolis and Oxford.
   3. Proprietary Papers, "Rainbow Series," Black Books. 11 vols.
   4. Record of Convicts, Anne Arundel County, 1771-75.

459

E. LIBRARY OF CONGRESS, Washington, D. C.[1]

  1. British Transcripts.[2]

    a. Colonial Office Papers, Public Record Office.
      Useful for documents not yet calendared in the *Calendar of State Papers, Colonial Series,* and for documents relating to shipping, exports and imports, illicit trade, and other matters relating to Virginia and Maryland.

    b. Treasury Papers.

    c. British Museum Additional Manuscripts.
      Especially nos. 15484, 15896, 18046, 27891, 29553, 29600, 30305, 30306.

    d. British Museum Miscellaneous Collections.
      Additional Charters, no. 26400.
      Sloane MSS, vol. 1426, ff. 73-125; vol. 2496, ff. 70-112.

    e. House of Lords Library.
      Committee Books 5, f. 608.
      Brickdale Notes, book 11, ff. 17-23.
      Photofilmed Series—containing documents relating to trade, customs, shipping, imports and exports, 1710-75.

    f. Library of the Royal Society.
      Especially MS Guardbook, vol. I, no. 1, 183; vol. L, no. 6, 44; vol. M, no. 1, 36a-37.

    g. Guildhall Library—Records Office.
      Bonds for transportation of felons, 1718-37.
      Certificates for landing felons at American Ports, 1718-36.

---

1. See *Handbook of Manuscripts in the Library of Congress.* Washington, 1918; supplemented by C. W. Garrison, *List of Manuscript Collections in the Library of Congress to July 1931.* Washington, 1932.
2. See Charles McLean Andrews and Francis Gardiner Davenport, *Guide to the Manuscript Materials for the History of the United States to 1783, in the British Museum, in Minor London Archives, and in the Libraries of Oxford and Cambridge* (Carnegie Institution of Washington). Washington, 1908; ................, *Guide to the Materials for American History to 1783, in the Public Record Office of Great Britain.* (Carnegie Institution of Washington). Vol. I, *The State Papers.* Washington, 1912. Vol. II, *Departmental and Miscellaneous Papers.* Washington, 1914.

2. Robert Beverley of Blandfield Letterbook, 1761-91.
3. Bozman Papers, 1730-1856.
4. Papers of Charles Carroll of Annapolis, 1661-1771.
5. Robert Carter of Nomini, Plantation and Business Accounts.
6. John Custis Letterbook, 1717-41.
7. John Digges Accountbook, 1720-49.
8. Edward Dixon Mercantile Papers, 1743-96.
9. Galloway Papers, 1718-1812. 37 portfolios and 75 vols.
10. Jamieson Papers, 1757-89. 23 vols.
11. Jones Papers.
12. Miscl. MSS of Lee Family.
13. Richard Bland Lee Papers.
14. Maryland—A Merchant's Accountbook, 1710-13.
15. Maryland and Virginia, Mercantile Accounts, 1753-1834. 181 vols.
16. Stone Papers.
17. Records of the Vice-Admiralty Court in Maryland, 1754-75.
18. George Washington Papers, Invoices and Letters, 1755-66.

F. MARYLAND HISTORICAL SOCIETY, Baltimore, Maryland.

1. Annapolis Port Records, 1756-75.
2. Bordley Papers, 1727-61. 6 vols.
3. Calvert Papers.
4. Dulany Papers, 3 boxes, and Daniel Dulany Letterbook, 1752-53.
5. Gilmor Papers. 3 vols.
6. Hamilton Papers, 1760-1800.
7. Hill Papers, 1685-1819. 4 vols.
8. Naval Officers' Reports, 1751-57.
9. Oxford Port Records, 1756-73.
10. Scharf Collection.
    Especially the Proceedings of the Directors and Miscellaneous Papers Connected with the Building of the Lighthouse at Cape Henry, 1773-75.
11. Ships: List of Ships and Shipping, 1753-76. (On cards in tin box.)
12. Sollers, Basil, Number of Ships Built in Maryland, 1746-75.

G. NEW YORK PUBLIC LIBRARY, New York.

1. William Beverley Papers, 1734-48.
2. Callister Papers, 1741-80, photostats of originals in the Easton Public Library, Easton, Maryland. 4 vols., 850 pieces.
3. Chalmers Papers, Virginia and Maryland, 1606-1775. 4 vols.
4. Dawson Papers.
5. Emmet Collection. 10,800 MSS in 94 vols. and 2,500 unbound pieces.
6. Galloway Papers, 1749-1803, including Ringgold Letters, 1760-70. 3 boxes.
7. Benjamin Mifflin Diary, July 26-Aug. 14, 1762.
8. Nathaniel Littleton Savage Accountbook, 1768-85.
9. George Washington Papers, Ledger A, 1750-74, photostat. 3 vols.

H. VIRGINIA HISTORICAL SOCIETY,[3] Richmond, Virginia.

1. William Beverley Accountbook, 1752.
2. Mrs. Browne's Journal of a Voyage from London to Virginia, 1754-55, photostat.
3. Letterbook of William Byrd 1, 1683-91.
4. Letters and Papers of William Byrd II, 1710-31.
5. Campbell Papers.
6. Carter Papers, 1705-85. 3 vols.
7. Custis Papers, 1740-48, 1758-59.
8. William Fitzhugh Letterbook, 1679-99.
9. Lee Papers.
10. Ludwell Papers.
11. Pendleton Papers.
12. Randolph Papers.
13. Washington Papers.
14. Miscellaneous Papers in Files 1-8.

I. VIRGINIA STATE LIBRARY, Richmond, Virginia.

1. Allason Papers, 1723-1818. 39 vols. and 6 boxes (to 1763).
2. Campbell Papers.
3. William Nelson Letterbook, 1766-75.

---

3. See *Catalogue of the Manuscripts in the Collection of the Virginia Historical Society.* Richmond, 1901.

4. County Records, photostats.

   a. Elizabeth City County, Order Book, 1731-47.

   b. Essex County, Order Book, 1745-47; Wills, Bonds, & Inventories, no. 4, 1722-30.

   c. Isle of Wight County, Deed Book 14, 1757-81; Order Book, 1755-57; Order Book, 1764-68.

J. OTHER COUNTY RECORDS.

   1. Accomack County Courthouse, Accomac, Virginia.

      Order Book, 1690-97.

      Will Book, 1737-43.

      Will Book, 1749-52.

      Order Book, 1764-65.

   2. Northampton County Courthouse, Eastville, Virginia.

      Order Book 14, 1698-1710.

      Order Book 16, 1716-18.

      Order Book 17, 1719-22.

      Order Book 20, 1732-42.

      Order Book 24, 1753-58.

      Wills, Deeds, etc., 19, 1740-50.

      Wills, Deeds, etc., 21, 1754-60.

      Wills, Deeds, etc., 22, 1760-63.

      Wills, Deeds, etc., 23, 1763-65.

   3. Prince George's County Courthouse, Upper Marlboro, Maryland.

      Records, Liber X.

# PUBLISHED PRIMARY SOURCES

A. OFFICIAL BRITISH RECORDS

   1. *Acts of the Privy Council, Colonial Series.* William L. Grant and James Munro, eds. 6 vols., Hereford, 1908-12.

   2. Andrews, Charles M., ed. "List of Reports and Representations of the Plantation Councils, 1660-1674, the Lords of Trade, 1675-96, and the Board of Trade, 1696-1782, in the

Public Records Office," American Historical Association, *Annual Report for 1913* (1914), I, appendix C, 321-406.

3. Brigham, Clarence S., ed. *British Royal Proclamations Relating to America, 1603-1783*, in American Antiquarian Society, *Transactions and Collections*, 12 (1911).

4. *Calendar of State Papers, Colonial Series, America and West Indies.* W. Noel Sainsbury (1860-93), J. W. Fortescue (1893-1905), Cecil Headlam (1905-37), Headlam and Arthur P. Newton (1938-............), eds. 40 vols., London, 1860-date.

5. *Calendar of Treasury Books,* 1660-March 1704/05. William A. Shaw, ed. 19 vols., London, 1904-34.

6. *Calendar of Treasury Books and Papers,* 1729-45. William A. Shaw, ed. 5 vols., London, 1897-1903.

7. *Calendar of Treasury Papers,* 1556/7-1728. Joseph Redington, ed. 6 vols., London, 1868-89.

8. Davenport, Francis G., ed. *European Treaties Bearing on the History of the United States.* 2 vols., Carnegie Institution of Washington, Washington, 1917-29.

9. *Journal of the Commissioners for Trade and Plantations,* April 1704-82. 14 vols., London, 1920-38.

10. Labaree, Leonard W., ed. *Royal Instructions to British Colonial Governors, 1670-1776.* 2 vols., American Historical Association, New York and London, 1935.

11. Stock, Leo F., ed. *Proceedings and Debates of the British Parliaments Respecting North America.* 2 vols., Carnegie Institution of Washington, Washington, 1924-27.

B. OFFICIAL COLONIAL RECORDS

1. *Archives of Maryland.* William H. Brown (1883-1912), Clayton C. Hall (1913-15), Bernard C. Steiner (1916-27), J. Hall Pleasants (1929............), eds. 59 vols., Baltimore, 1883-date.

2. Bond, Carroll T., and Richard B. Morris, eds. *Proceedings of the Maryland Court of Appeals, 1695-1729.* American Historical Association, *American Legal Records*, Washington, 1933.

3. *Calendar of Virginia State Papers.* William P. Palmer, ed. 11 vols., Richmond, 1875-93.

4. *Executive Journals of the Council of Colonial Virginia, 1680-1754.* Henry R. McIlwaine (1925-30) and Wilmer L. Hall (1945), eds. 5 vols., Richmond, 1925-45.

5. Hening, William Waller, ed. *The Statutes-at-Large, Being a Collection of All the Laws of Virginia.* 13 vols., Richmond, 1819-23.

6. *Journals of the House of Burgesses of Virginia, 1619-1776.* John P. Kennedy (1905-1907) and Henry R. McIlwaine (1908-15), eds. 13 vols., Richmond, 1905-15.

7. *Legislative Journals of the Council of Colonial Virginia.* Henry R. McIlwaine, ed. 3 vols., Richmond, 1918-19.

8. *Minutes of the Council and General Court of Colonial Virginia, 1622-1632, 1670-1676.* Henry R. McIlwaine, ed. Richmond, 1924.

c. OTHER PRIMARY MATERIAL

1. Allason, William. "The Letters of William Allason, Merchant, of Falmouth, Virginia," in Richmond College, *Historical Papers,* 2 (1916-17), 118-75.

2. Alsop, George. *A Character of the Province of Mary-Land.* London, 1666. (Also Newton D. Mereness, ed. Cleveland, 1902).

3. Anderson, Adam. *The Origin of Commerce.* 6 vols., Dublin, 1790.

4. Arber, Edward, ed. *Travels and Works of Captain John Smith.* 2 vols. Edinburgh, 1910.

5. Banning, Jeremiah. "Narrative of the Principal Incidents in the Life of Jeremiah Banning, Written by Himself, in 1793," in William F. Boogher, ed., *Miscellaneous Americana.* Philadelphia, 1883, 45-52.

6. Bell, Annie W. B., comp. *Abstracts of Wills in Charles and St. Mary's Counties, Maryland, 1744-1772.* Washington, 1937.

7. Berkeley, Sir William. *A Discourse and View of Virginia.* London, 1663. (Also reprinted by W. H. Smith, Jr., Norwalk, 1914).

8. Beverley, Robert. *The History and Present State of Virginia.* London, 1705 and 1722. (Also Louis B. Wright, ed. Chapel Hill, 1947).

9. Birket, James. Some Cursory Remarks . . . in His Voyage to North America, 1750-1751. *Yale Historical Publications, MSS and Edited Texts*, 4. New Haven, 1916.

10. Blanckley, Thomas R. *A Naval Expositor*. London, 1750.

11. Bland, John. "The Humble Remonstrance . . . on Behalf of the Inhabitants and Planters in Virginia and Maryland," *Virginia Magazine of History and Biography*, 1 (1893-94), 141-55.

12. *The Bland Papers, Being a Selection from the Manuscripts of Colonel Theodorick Bland, Jr., of Prince George County, Virginia*. Charles Campbell, ed. 2 vols., Petersburg, 1840.

13. Boucher, Jonathan. *Reminiscences of an American Loyalist, 1738-1789*. Boston and New York, 1925.

14. Brock, Robert A., ed. *The Official Records of Robert Dinwiddie, Lieutenant-Governor of the Colony of Virginia, 1751-1758* (2 vols.), Virginia Historical Society, Collections, new ser., 3 (1883) and 4 (1884).

15. Brock, Robert A., ed. *The Official Letters of Alexander Spotswood, Lieutenant-Governor of the Colony of Virginia, 1710-1722* (2 vols.), Virginia Historical Society, *Collections*, new ser., 1 (1882) and 2 (1885).

16. Brown, Alexander. *Genesis of the United States*. 2 vols., Boston and New York, 1890.

17. Brumbaugh, Gaius M., ed. *Maryland Records*. Baltimore, 1915.

18. Burnaby, Rev. Andrew. *Travels Through the Middle Settlements in North America, 1759 and 1760*. 3d edn., London, 1798.

19. Byrd, William. *History of the Dividing Line and Other Tracts*. T. H. Wynne, ed. 2 vols., Richmond, 1866.

20. Byrd, William. "Letters of Colonel William Byrd of Westover, 1736-1739," *American Historical Review*, 1 (1895-96), 88-90.

21. Byrd, William. *The Writings of Colonel William Byrd of Westover in Virginia Esquire*. John Spencer Bassett, ed. New York, 1901.

22. *Calvert Papers*. Maryland Historical Society, *Fund-Publications*, nos. 28, 34-35. 3 vols., Baltimore, 1889-99.

23. Carman, Harry J., ed. *American Husbandry*. Columbia University, *Studies in the History of Agriculture*, no. 6. New York, 1939.

24. *The Case of the Planters of Tobacco in Virginia, as Represented by Themselves; Signed by the President of the Council, and Speaker of the House of Burgesses.* London, 1733.

25. Chalkley, Thomas. *Journal of Life, Travels, and Christian Experiences of Thomas Chalkley.* 2d edn., London, 1751.

26. Chapman, Fredrik Henrik. *Architectura Navalis Mercatoria.* Holmiae (Stockholm), 1768.

27. Charnock, John. *History of Marine Architecture.* 3 vols., London, 1800-1802.

28. Clayton, Rev. John. *A Letter from Mr. John Clayton . . . May 12, 1688, Giving an Account of Several Observables in Virginia*, in Peter Force, ed., *Tracts and Other Papers.* Washington, 1836-46, III, no. 12.

29. Cook, Ebenezer. *The Sot-Weed Factor: or a Voyage to Maryland.* London, 1708. (Also in Maryland Historical Society, *Fund-Publications*, no. 36. Baltimore, 1900).

30. Cresswell, Nicholas. *The Journal of Nicholas Cresswell, 1774-1777.* New York, 1928.

31. Dampier, William. *A New Voyage Round the World.* London, 1697 and 1927.

32. Darnall, Henry. *A Just and Important Account of the Transactions of the Merchants in London for the Advancement of the Price of Tobacco.* Annapolis, 1728. (Photostat in Maryland Historical Society.)

33. De Vries, David P. *Voyages from Holland to America, 1632-1644.* New York, 1853.

34. Donnan, Elizabeth, ed. *Documents Illustrative of the History of the Slave Trade to America.* 4 vols., Carnegie Institution of Washington, Washington, 1930-35.

35. Douglass, William. *A Summary, Historical and Political, of the British Settlements in North America.* 2 vols., London, 1755.

36. (Durand of Dauphiné). *A Frenchman in Virginia; the Memoirs of a Huguenot Refugee in 1686.* Fairfax Harrison, trans. Richmond, 1923.

37. Eddis, William. *Letters from America, Historical and Descriptive; Comprising Occurrences from 1769, to 1777 Inclusive.* London, 1792.

38. Falconer, William. *An Universal Dictionary of the Marine.* London, 1769.

39. Farish, Hunter D., ed. *The Journals and Letters of Philip Vickers Fithian, 1773-1774. Williamsburg Restoration Historical Studies,* no. 3. Williamsburg, 1943.

40. Field, Thomas M., ed. *Unpublished Letters of Charles Carroll of Carrollton and His Father, Charles Carroll of Doughoregan.* New York, 1902.

41. Fisher, George. "Narrative of George Fisher, Commencing with a Voyage from London, May, 1750, for Yorktown in Virginia and ending in August, 1755, on his Return from Philadelphia to Williamsburg," *William and Mary Quarterly,* 1st ser., 17 (1908-1909), 100-139, 147-76.

42. Fitzpatrick, John C., ed. *The Diaries of George Washington, 1748-1799.* New York, 1925.

43. Force, Peter, ed. *Tracts and Other Papers Relating Principally to the Origin, Settlement, and Progress of the Colonies in North America.* 4 vols., Washington, 1836-46.

44. Furtenbach, Joseph. *Architectura Navalis.* Ulm, 1629.

45. (Gordon, Lord Adam). "Journal of an Officer who Travelled in America and the West Indies in 1764 and 1765," in Newton D. Mereness, ed., *Travels in the American Colonies.* New York, 1916, 367-453.

46. Hall, Clayton C., ed. *Narratives of Early Maryland, 1633-1684,* in J. Franklin Jameson, ed., *Original Narratives of Early American History.* New York, 1910.

47. Hall, F. *The Importance of the British Plantations in America to This Kingdom.* London, 1731.

48. Hammond, John. *Leah and Rachel, or the Two Fruitful Sisters: Virginia and Maryland* (1656), in Peter Force, ed. *Tracts and Other Papers,* Washington, 1836-46, III, no. 14.

49. Harker, Mrs. Edith, ed. *Seafaring Virginia; or a Table of Ship Entries and Clearances, Compiled from the Virginia Gazette 1736-1766.* Master's Thesis, Westhampton College, Richmond, Virginia.

50. Hartwell, Henry, James Blair, and Edward Chilton. *The Present State of Virginia, and the College* (1697). Hunter D. Farish, ed. *Williamsburg Restoration Historical Studies,* no. 1. Williamsburg, 1939.

51. James, Bartlett B. and J. Franklin Jameson, eds. *Journal of Jasper Danckaerts, 1679-1680,* in J. Franklin Jameson, ed., *Original Narratives of Early American History.* New York, 1913.

52. Jameson, J. Franklin, ed. *Privateering and Piracy in the Colonial Period: Illustrative Documents.* New York, 1923.

53. Jones, Rev. Hugh. *The Present State of Virginia.* London, 1724.

54. "Journal of a French Traveller in the Colonies, 1765," *American Historical Review,* 26 (1920-21), 726-47; 27 (1921-22), 70-89.

55. Keith, Sir William. *The History of the British Plantations in America,* pt. 1, *Containing the History of Virginia; With Remarks on the Trade and Commerce of That Colony.* London, 1738.

56. Kingsbury, Susan M., ed. *The Records of the Virginia Company of London.* 4 vols., Library of Congress, Washington, 1906-35.

57. Knowles, John. *Elements and Practices of Naval Architecture, or a Treatise on Shipbuilding in Great Britain.* 3d edn., London, 1822.

58. Le Froy, J. H., ed. *Memorials of the Discovery and Early Settlement of the Bermudas or Somers Island 1515-1685.* London, 1877.

59. *A Letter from a Freeholder, to a Member of the Lower House of Assembly.* Annapolis, 1727.

60. Mair, John. *Book-keeping Methodized.* 4th edn., Edinburgh, 1752. (The chapter from it concerning Virginia commerce appears in the *William and Mary Quarterly,* 1st ser., 14 (1905-1906), 87-93. A footnote incorrectly attributes it to a third edition in 1784.)

61. Makemie, Rev. Francis. "A Plain and Friendly Perswasive to the Inhabitants of Virginia and Maryland for Promoting Towns

and Cohabitation, London, 1705," *Virginia Magazine of History and Biography*, 4 (1896-97), 255-71.

62. Marestier, Jean-Baptiste. *Mémoire sur les Bateaux à vapeur des Etats-Unis d' Amérique.* Paris, 1824. (Includes lines of Baltimore clippers.)

63. Maryland Historical Society:
    *Fund-Publications.* 37 vols., Baltimore, 1867-1900.
    *Publications.* 3 vols., Baltimore, 1844-68.

64. Mason, Frances Norton, ed. *John Norton and Sons: Merchants of London and Virginia, Being the Papers from Their Counting House for the Years 1750-1795.* Richmond, 1937.

65. Massachusetts Historical Society, *Collections,* 4th ser., Boston, 1854-............

66. Mereness, Newton D., ed. *A Character of the Province of Maryland by George Alsop, reprinted from the original edition of 1666.* Cleveland, 1902.

67. Mereness, Newton D., ed. *Travels in the American Colonies.* New York, 1916.

68. Michel, Francis Louis. "The Journey of Francis Louis Michel from Berne, Switzerland, to Virginia, October 2, 1701-December 1, 1702," *Virginia Magazine of History and Biography*, 24 (1916), 1-43, 113-41, 275-303.

69. "Narrative of a Voyage to Maryland, 1705-1706," *American Historical Review,* 12 (1906-1907), 327-40.

70. Neill, Edward D. *History of the Virginia Company of London.* Albany, 1869.

71. Neill, Edward D. *Virginia Carolorum.* Albany, 1886.

72. Neill, Edward D. *Virginia Vetusta.* Albany, 1886.

73. Oldmixon, John. *The British Empire in America.* 2d edn., 2 vols., London, 1741.

74. Padelford, Philip, ed. *Colonial Panorama 1775; Dr. Robert Honyman's Journal.* San Marino, Cal., 1939.

75. Paltsits, Victor Hugo, ed. *Journal of Benjamin Mifflin; the Record of a Tour from Philadelphia to Delaware and Maryland, July 26 to August 14, 1762,* New York Public Library, *Bulletin,* 39 (1935).

76. Robertson, William. *History of Virginia and of New England.* Philadelphia, 1799.

# Bibliography

77. Sheffield, John Lord. *Observations on the Commerce of the American States.* 3d edn., London, 1784.

78. Stalkart, Marmaduke. *Naval Architecture.* London, 1781.

79. Steel, David. *The Elements and Practice of Rigging and Seamanship.* London, 1794. (Also Marine Research Society, Salem, 1925.)

80. Steiner, Bernard C., ed. *Early Maryland Poetry,* Maryland Historical Society, *Fund-Publications,* no. 36. Baltimore, 1900.

81. Sutherland, William. *The Prices of the Labour in Ship-Building Adjusted: or, The Mystery of Ship-Building Unveiled.* London, 1717.

82. Tatham, William. *Essay on the Culture and Commerce of Tobacco.* London, 1800.

83. Thomas, Sir Dalby. "An Historical Account of the Rise and Growth of the West-India Colonies, London, 1690," *Harleian Miscellany,* 9 (1810), 403-45.

84. Thompson, Henry F. "An Atlantic Voyage in the Seventeenth Century," *Maryland Historical Magazine,* 2 (1907), 319-26.

85. Tyler, Lyon G., ed. *Narratives of Early Virginia, 1606-1625,* in J. Franklin Jameson, ed., *Original Narratives of Early American History.* New York, 1907.

86. Virginia Historical Society, *Collections.*

87. White, Rev. Andrew. *Relatio Itineris in Marylandiam,* Maryland Historical Society, *Fund-Publications,* no. 7. Baltimore, 1874.

88. Winsor, Justin. *Narrative and Critical History of America.* Boston, 1884-89.

89. Wright, Louis B., ed. *Letters of Robert Carter 1720-1727, the Commercial Interests of a Virginia Gentleman.* San Marino, Cal., 1940.

D. NEWSPAPERS

1. *Maryland Gazette.* Annapolis, 1727-
   William Parks, 1727-34.
   Jonas Green, 1745-67.
   Anne Catherine Green, 1767-68, 1770-75.
   Frederick Green, 1775-77.

2. *Maryland Journal.* Baltimore, 1773-97.
   William Goddard, 1773-75.
   Mary K. Goddard, 1775-84.
3. *Virginia Gazette.* Williamsburg, 1736-
   William Parks, 1736-46.
   William Hunter, 1751-62.
   William Rind, 1766-74.
   Alexander Purdie and John Dixon, 1766-74.
   John Pinckney, 1775.

E. MAGAZINES

1. *Agricultural History.* Chicago, 1927-
2. *American Historical Review.* Lancaster, Pa., 1895-
3. *American Neptune.* Salem, Mass., 1941-
4. *Architectural Record.* New York, 1941-
5. *Gentleman's Magazine.* London, 1731-1907.
6. *Geographical Review.* New York, 1916-
7. *Journal of Economics and Business History.* Cambridge, Mass., 1928-32.
8. *Lower Norfolk County Virginia Antiquary,* Norfolk, 1895-1906.
9. *Mariner.* New York, 1927-36.
10. *Maryland Historical Magazine.* Baltimore, 1906-
11. *Old Time New England.* Boston, 1910-
12. *Patriotic Marylander.* Baltimore, 1914-17.
13. *Tyler's Quarterly Historical and Genealogical Magazine.* Richmond, 1919-1952.
14. *Virginia Magazine of History and Biography.* Richmond, 1893-
15. *William and Mary Quarterly.* 1st ser., July 1892-April 1919; 2d ser., January 1921-October 1943; 3d ser., January 1944-date.

F. CHARTS

1. Hoxton, Walter. *Mapp of the Bay of Chesapeack with the Rivers Potomack, Potapsco, North East, and part of Chester.* London, 1735.
2. Smith, Anthony. *A New and Accurate Chart of the Bay of Chesapeake as far as the Navigable Part of the Rivers Potowmack, Patapsco, and North-East, 1776,* in Thomas Jefferys, *The North American Pilot,* II, nos. 5 and 6. London, 1777.

# Bibliography

3. Thornton, John, and William Fisher. *Virginia, Maryland, Pensilvania, East and West Jarsey,* in *The English Pilot,* bk. 4 (no. 13), btw. 22 and 23. London, 1706.

4. van Keulen, Johannis. *Kaart van de Zee Kusten van Virginia.* Amsterdam, n.d. (*circa* 1700?), in Claas Jansszoon Voogt, *Le Nouveau et Grand Illuminant Flambeau de la Mer,* pt. 4, btw. pp. 42-43. Amsterdam, 1713.

## G. SECONDARY MATERIAL

1. Albion, Robert G. *Forests and Sea Power; the Timber Problem of the Royal Navy 1652-1862. Harvard Economic Studies,* 29. Cambridge, 1926.

2. Allen, Gardner W. "Naval Convoys," Massachusetts Historical Society, *Proceedings,* 57 (1924), 396-414.

3. Ames, Susie M. *Studies of the Virginia Eastern Shore in the Seventeenth Century.* Richmond, 1940.

4. Ames, Susie M. "A Typical Virginia Business Man of the Revolutionary Era: Nathaniel Littleton Savage and His Account Book," *Journal of Economic and Business History,* 3 (1930-31), 407-23.

5. Andrews, Charles M. *The Colonial Period of American History.* 4 vols., New Haven, 1934-38.

6. Andrews, Matthew P. *Virginia, the Old Dominion.* Garden City, 1937.

7. Barker, Charles A. *The Background of the Revolution in Maryland.* London and New Haven, 1940.

8. Bassett, John Spencer. "The Relation between the Virginia Planter and the London Merchant," American Historical Association, *Annual Report for 1901* (1902), I, 551-75.

9. Beer, George L. *The Origins of the British Colonial System, 1578-1660.* New York, 1908 and 1933.

10. Beer, George L. *The Old Colonial System, 1660-1754.* New York, 1912 and 1933.

11. Beer, George L. *British Colonial Policy, 1754-1765.* New York, 1907 and 1933.

12. Behrens, Kathryn L. *Paper Money in Maryland 1727-1789.* Johns Hopkins University, *Studies in Historical and Political Science,* 41, no. 1. Baltimore, 1923.

13. Berkley, Henry J. "Extinct River Towns of the Chesapeake Bay Region," *Maryland Historical Magazine,* 19 (1924), 125-34.

14. Berkley, Henry J., "Londontown on South River, Anne Arundel County, Maryland," *Maryland Historical Magazine,* 19 (1924), 134-43.

15. Beyer, Richard L. "American Colonial Commerce and British Protection," *Journal of American History,* 22 (1928), 265-69.

16. Bining, Arthur C. *British Regulation of the Colonial Iron Industry.* Philadelphia, 1933.

17. Bishop, James L. *A History of American Manufactures from 1608 to 1860.* 3 vols., Philadelphia, 1866.

18. Bourne, Ruth. *Queen Anne's Navy in the West Indies. Yale Historical Publications,* 33. New Haven, 1939.

19. Brewington, Marion V. *Chesapeake Bay Log Canoes.* The Mariners' Museum, *Publications,* no. 3. Newport News, 1937.

20. Bruce, Kathleen. *Virginia Iron Manufacture in the Slave Era.* New York, 1930.

21. Bruce, Philip Alexander. *Economic History of Virginia in the Seventeenth Century.* 2 vols., New York, 1895.

22. Butler, James D. "British Convicts Shipped to American Colonies," *American Historical Review,* 2 (1896-97), 12-33.

23. Cappon, Lester J. *Iron Works at Tuball: Terms and Conditions for Their Lease as Stated by Alexander Spotswood.* Charlottesville, 1945.

24. Carman, Harry J., ed. *American Husbandry.* Columbia University, *Studies in the History of Agriculture,* no. 6. New York, 1939.

25. Channing, Edward. *History of the United States.* New York, 1908.

26. Chapelle, Howard I. *American Sailing Craft.* New York, 1936.

27. Chapelle, Howard I. *The Baltimore Clipper.* Marine Research Society, Salem, 1930.

28. Chapelle, Howard I. *The History of American Sailing Ships.* New York, 1935.

29. Chapin, Howard M. *Privateer Ships and Sailors; the First Century of American Colonial Privateering, 1625-1725.* Toulon, 1926.

30. Chapin, Howard M. *Privateering in King George's War 1729-1748.* Providence, 1928.

31. Chatterton, E. Keble. *English Seamen and the Colonization of America.* London, 1930.

32. Chatterton, E. Keble. *Fore and Aft: the Story of the Fore and Aft Rig from the Earliest Times to the Present Day.* London, 1912.

33. Craven, Avery O. *Soil Exhaustion as a Factor in the Agricultural History of Virginia and Maryland, 1606-1680.* University of Illinois, *Studies in the Social Sciences,* 13. Urbana, 1925.

34. Craven, Wesley Frank. *Dissolution of the Virginia Company.* New York, 1932.

35. Crawford, Walter F. "The Commerce of Rhode Island with the Southern Colonies (Continental) in the Eighteenth Century," Rhode Island Historical Society, *Collections,* 14 (1921-22), 99-110, 124-30.

36. Crittenden, Charles Christopher. *The Commerce of North Carolina, 1763-1789.* New Haven, 1936.

37. Crittenden, Charles Christopher. "Ships and Shipping in North Carolina, 1763-1789," *North Carolina Historical Review,* 8 (1931), 1-13.

38. Crump, Helen J. *Colonial Admiralty Jurisdiction in the Seventeenth Century.* London, 1931.

39. Dielman, Louis H. "Transportation of Felons to the Colonies," *Maryland Historical Magazine,* 27 (1932), 263-74.

40. Dodson, Leonidas. *Alexander Spotswood, Governor of Colonial Virginia 1710-1722.* Philadelphia, 1932.

41. Donnan, Elizabeth. "Eighteenth-Century English Merchants: Micajah Perry," *Journal of Economic and Business History,* 4 (1931-32), 70-98.

42. Earle, Swepson. *The Chesapeake Bay Country.* 2d edn., Baltimore, 1938.

43. Earle, Swepson. *Maryland's Colonial Eastern Shore.* Baltimore, 1916.

44. Edgar, Matilda Ridout, Lady. *A Colonial Governor in Maryland: Horatio Sharpe and His Times, 1753-1773.* New York and London, 1912.

45. Fisher, Sidney G. *The Struggle for American Independence.* Philadelphia and London, 1908.

46. Flippin, Percy Scott. *The Financial Administration of the Colony of Virginia.* Johns Hopkins University, *Studies in Historical and Political Science,* 33, no. 2. Baltimore, 1915.
47. Flippin, Percy Scott. *The Royal Government in Virginia 1624-1775.* Columbia University, *Studies in History, Economics and Public Law,* 84, no. 1. New York, 1919.
48. Flippin, Percy Scott. "William Gooch: Successful Royal Governor of Virginia," *William and Mary Quarterly,* 2d ser., 5 (1925), 225-58; 6 (1926), 1-38.
49. Forrest, William S. *Historical and Descriptive Sketches of Norfolk and Vicinity.* Philadelphia, 1853.
50. Ford, Worthington C. "Captain John Smith's Map of Virginia, 1612," *Geographical Review,* 14 (1924-25), 433-43.
51. Ford, Worthington C. "Tyndall's Map of Virginia, 1608," Massachusetts Historical Society, *Proceedings,* 58 (1925), 244-47.
52. Gage, Charles E. "Historical Factors Affecting American Tobacco Types and Uses," *Agricultural History,* 11 (1936-37), 43-57.
53. Giddens, Paul H. "Trade and Industry in Colonial Maryland, 1753-1769," *Journal of Economic and Business History,* 4 (1931-32), 512-38.
54. Gipson, Lawrence H. *The British Empire Before the American Revolution,* II, *The Southern Plantations.* Caldwell, Idaho, 1936.
55. Gottschalk, L. C. "Effects of Soil Erosion on Navigation in Upper Chesapeake Bay," *Geographical Review,* 35 (1944-45), 219-38.
56. Gould, Clarence P. *Money and Transportation in Maryland, 1720-1765.* Johns Hopkins University, *Studies in Historical and Political Science,* 33, no. 1. Baltimore, 1915.
57. Gray, Lewis C. *History of Agriculture in the Southern United States to 1860.* 2 vols., Carnegie Institution of Washington, Washington, 1933.
58. Gray, Lewis C. "The Market Surplus Problems of Colonial Tobacco," *William and Mary Quarterly,* 2d ser., 7 (1927), 231-45; 8 (1928), 1-16.
59. Hall, Henry. *Report on the Ship-building Industry in the United States,* in United States Bureau of the Census, *Tenth Census, VIII.* Washington, 1884.

# Bibliography

60. Harker, Mrs. Edith, ed., *Seafaring Virginia; or a Table of Ship Entries and Clearances, Compiled from the Virginia Gazette 1736-1766,* Master's Thesis, Westhampton College, Richmond, 1941.

61. Harper, Lawrence A. *The English Navigation Laws.* New York, 1939.

62. Harrison, Fairfax. "When the Convicts Came; a Chapter from 'Land Marks of Old Prince William,'" *Virginia Magazine of History and Biography,* 30 (1922), 250-60.

63. Hayden, Ethel Roby. "Port Tobacco, Lost Town of Maryland," *Maryland Historical Magazine,* 40 (1945), 261-76.

64. Hoon, E. E. *The Organization of the English Customs Service, 1696-1786.* New York, 1938.

65. Jacobstein, Meyer. *The Tobacco Industry in the United States.* New York, 1907.

66. Jernegan, Marcus W. *Laboring and Dependent Classes in Colonial America 1607-1783: Studies in the Economic, Educational, and Social Significance of Slaves, Servants, Apprentices, and Poor Folk.* Chicago, 1931.

67. Jernegan, Marcus W. "Slavery and the Beginning of Industrialism in the American Colonies," *American Historical Review,* 25 (1919-20), 220-40.

68. Kelbaugh, Paul R. "Tobacco Trade in Maryland, 1700-1725," *Maryland Historical Magazine,* 26 (1931), 1-33.

69. Koontz, Louis Knott. *Robert Dinwiddie, His Career in American Colonial Government and Westward Expansion.* Glendale, Cal., 1941.

70. Lonn, Ella. *The Colonial Agents of the Southern Colonies.* Chapel Hill, 1945.

71. Lukens, R. R. "Captain John Smith's Map," *Military Engineer,* 23 (1931), 435-38.

72. MacInnes, Charles M. *The Early English Tobacco Trade.* London, 1926.

73. Maclay, Edgar S. *A History of American Privateers.* New York and London, 1924.

74. *Maryland, A Guide to the Old Line State,* Works Projects Administration, Writers' Program, American Guide Series, New York, 1940.

75. Mathews, Edward B. *The Maps and Map-Makers of Maryland,* Maryland Geological Survey, Special Publication, II. Baltimore, 1898.
76. McClellan, Williams S. *Smuggling in the American Colonies at the Outbreak of the Revolution, with Special Reference to the West Indies Trade.* New York, 1912.
77. Middleton, Arthur Pierce. "The Chesapeake Convoy System, 1662-1763," *William and Mary Quarterly,* 3d ser., 3(1946), 182-207.
78. Middleton, Arthur Pierce. "New Light on the Evolution of the Chesapeake Clipper-Schooner," *The American Neptune,* 9 (1949), 142-47.
79. Middleton, Arthur Pierce. "The Struggle for the Cape Henry Lighthouse," *The American Neptune,* 8 (1948), 26-36.
80. Middleton, Arthur Pierce. "Yachting in Chesapeake Bay, 1676-1783," *The American Neptune,* 9 (1949), 180-84.
81. Morris, Edward P. *The Fore-and-Aft Rig in America.* New Haven, 1927.
82. Morriss, Margaret Shove. *Colonial Trade of Maryland, 1689-1715.* Johns Hopkins University, *Studies in Historical and Political Science,* 32, no. 3. Baltimore, 1914.
83. Morton, Louis. *Robert Carter of Nomini Hall: A Virginia Tobacco Planter of the Eighteenth Century. Williamsburg Restoration Historical Studies,* no. 2. 2d edn., Williamsburg, 1945.
84. Nettels, Curtis P. *The Money Supply of the American Colonies before 1720.* Madison, 1934.
85. Nettles, Curtis P. *The Roots of American Civilization: A History of American Colonial Life.* New York, 1938.
86. Osgood, Herbert L. *The American Colonies in the Seventeenth Century.* 3 vols., New York, 1904-1907 and 1930.
87. Osgood, Herbert L. *The American Colonies in the Eighteenth Century.* 4 vols., New York, 1924-25.
88. Owen, John H. *War at Sea Under Queen Anne 1702-1708.* Cambridge and York, 1938.
89. Pares, Richard. *War and Trade in the West Indies, 1739-1763.* New York, 1936.
90. Phillips, P. Lee. "Some Early Maps of Virginia and the Makers, Including Plates Relating to the First Settlement of James-

town," *Virginia Magazine of History and Biography,* 15 (1907-1908), 71-81.

91. Phillips, P. Lee. *The Rare Map of Virginia and Maryland by Augustine Herrman, first Lord of Bohemia Manor, Maryland.* Washington, 1911.

92. Phillips, P. Lee. *Virginia Cartography; a Bibliographical Description,* Smithsonian Institution, *Miscellaneous Collection,* 37. Washington, 1896.

93. Pitman, Frank W. *The Development of the British West Indies 1700-1763.*

94. Richardson, Albert L. "Ships and their Masters of the Colonial Period," The Maryland Original Research Society, *Bulletin,* 3 (1912-13), 27-33.

95. Ripley, William Z. *The Financial History of Virginia, 1609-1776.* Columbia University, *Studies in History, Economics, and Public Law,* 4. New York, 1893-94.

96. Rive, Alfred. "A Brief History of the Regulation and Taxation of Tobacco in England," *William and Mary Quarterly,* 2d ser., 9 (1929), 1-12, 73-87.

97. Robinson, John. "Old-Time Nautical Instruments," *Old-Time New England,* 11 (1920-21), 147-59.

98. Schlesinger, Arthur M. *The Colonial Merchants and the American Revolution, 1763-1776.* 2d edn., New York, 1939.

99. Semmes, Raphael. *Captains and Mariners of Early Maryland.* Baltimore, 1937.

100. Sioussat, St. George L. *Economics and Politics in Maryland, 1720-1750.* Johns Hopkins University, *Studies in Historical and Political Science,* 21, no. 6. Baltimore, 1903.

101. Sioussat, St. George L. "Virginia and the English Commercial System, 1730-1733," American Historical Association, *Annual Report for 1905* (1906), I, 71-97.

102. Smith, Abbot Emerson. *Colonists in Bondage: White Servitude and Convict Labor in America 1607-1776.* Institute of Early American History and Culture. Chapel Hill, 1947.

103. Smith, Abbot Emerson. "Transportation of Convicts to American Colonies in the Seventeenth Century," *American Historical Review,* 39 (1933-34), 232-49.

104. Sollers, Basil. "The Acadians (French Neutrals) Transported to Maryland," *Maryland Historical Magazine,* 3 (1908), 1-21.

479

105. Sollers, Basil. "Transported Convict Laborers in Maryland during the Colonial Period," *Maryland Historical Magazine*, 2 (1907), 17-47.
106. Spruill, Julia C. *Women's Life and Work in the Southern Colonies*. Chapel Hill, 1938.
107. Steiner, Bernard C. "The Tobacco Stint," *Patriotic Marylander*, 1 (1914-15), 34-42.
108. Sutherland, Stella H. *Population Distribution in Colonial America*. New York, 1936.
109. Swain, Robert L., Jr. *Chestertown as a Colonial Port 1706-1775*. Chestertown, n.d.
110. Swem, Earl G. Maps Relating to Virginia, Virginia State Library, *Bulletin*, 7. Richmond, 1914.
111. Thomson, Edith E .B. "A Scottish Merchant in Falmouth in the Eighteenth Century," *Virginia Magazine of History and Biography*, 39 (1931), 108-17, 230-38.
112. Tyack, Norman C. P. *The Trade Relations of Bristol with Virginia during the Seventeenth Century*. Master's Thesis, Bristol University, Bristol, England, 1930, typescript in the William and Mary College Library.
113. Tyler, Lyon G. "William Howard, the Pirate," *Tyler's Quarterly Historical and Genealogical Magazine*, 1 (1919-20), 36-39.
114. Wertenbaker, Thomas J. *Norfolk, Historic Southern Port*. Durham, 1931.
115. Wertenbaker, Thomas J. *The Planters of Colonial Virginia*. Princeton, 1922.
116. Wertenbaker, Thomas J. *Virginia Under the Stuarts 1607-1688*. Princeton, 1914.
117. Williams, Lloyd H. *Pirates of Colonial Virginia*, Richmond, 1937.
118. Wroth, Lawrence C. "A Maryland Merchant and His Friends in 1750," *Maryland Historical Magazine*, 7 (1911), 213-40.
119. Wroth, Lawrence C. *The Way of a Ship: An Essay on the Literature of Navigation Science*. Portland, Me., 1937.
120. Wyckoff, Vertrees J. "Ships and Shipping of Seventeenth Century Maryland," *Maryland Historical Magazine*, 33 (1938), 334-42; 34 (1939), 46-63, 270-83, 349-61.
121. Wyckoff, Vertrees J. *Tobacco Regulation in Colonial Maryland*. Johns Hopkins University, *Studies in Historical and Political Science*, new ser., no. 22, extra vol., Baltimore, 1936.

*Appendices*

o    o    o

*Index*

*"How little I know after all my Studies. How dark, how intricate the Road that leads to intellectual Light.... Fancy tells me, that Angels and Spirits look down upon me with amazing Pity to see my Foolishness."*—JOHN LELAND, to ROBERT CARTER of Nomini, February 12, 1788.

# Appendices

## *Appendix A*
### POPULATION TABLES[1]

| YEAR | VIRGINIA | | | MARYLAND | | |
|------|-------|-------|-------|-------|-------|-------|
| | *White* | *Negro* | *Total* | *White* | *Negro* | *Total* |
| 1671 | | 2,000 | 40,000 | | | |
| 1676 | | | | | | 20,000 |
| 1701 | | | 54,934 | | | 32,258 |
| 1715 | 72,000 | 23,000 | 95,000 | 40,740 | 9,530 | 50,270 |
| 1730 | | | 114,000 | | | 80,000 |
| 1743 | 88,000 | 42,000 | 130,000 | | | |
| 1748 | | | | 94,000 | 36,000 | 130,000 |
| 1756 | 173,316 | 120,156 | 293,472 | 107,963 | 46,225 | 154,188 |
| 1770 | | 187,606 | 447,008 | | | 300,000 |
| 1774 | 300,000 | 200,000 | 500,000 | | | 320,000 |
| 1790 | 442,117 | 305,493 | 747,610 | 208,649 | 111,079 | 319,728 |

| YEAR | REGION | POPULATION[2] |
|------|--------|------------|
| 1688 | New England | 75,000 |
| | Middle Colonies | 42,000 |
| | Chesapeake Colonies | 75,000 |
| | Carolinas | 8,000 |
| | *Total* | 200,000 |
| 1715 | New England | 162,150 |
| | Middle Colonies | 99,300 |
| | Chesapeake Colonies | 145,200 |
| | Carolinas | 27,950 |
| | *Total* | 434,600 |
| 1765 | New England | 600,000 |
| | Middle Colonies | 580,000 |
| | Chesapeake Colonies | 720,000 |
| | Carolinas, Georgia, and the Floridas | 340,000 |
| | *Total* | 2,240,000 |

1. Evarts B. Greene and Virginia D. Harrington, *American Population Before the Federal Census of 1790*, 123-27, 134-42.
2. *Ibid.*, 3-7.

## *Appendix B*

### SCHEDULES OF RATES FOR PILOTAGE IN VIRGINIA, 1755 AND 1762

|  | Rate per Act of 1755[3] | 1762[4] |
|---|---|---|
| **JAMES RIVER, FOR ALL SHIPS, SNOWS, OR BRIGANTINES** | | |
| Cape Henry or Lynnhaven Roads to Hampton Roads or Sewell's Point | £1.0.0. | £1.0.0. |
| Norfolk, per foot* | 1.8. | 1.8. |
| Sleepy-hole, or Sack-Point, Nansemond, per foot | 2.0. | 2.0. |
| Pagan Creek, per foot | 1.6. | 1.6. |
| James-town, per foot | 4.6. | 4.6. |
| Martin's Brandon, per foot | 5.0. | 5.0. |
| Flower-de-Hundred, per foot | 5.6. | 5.6. |
| From Hampton Roads to: | | |
| Westover, per foot | 6.0. | 6.0. |
| City Point, or Bermuda Hundred, per foot | 7.0. | 7.0. |
| Four-Mile Creek, per foot | .......... | 9.0. |
| Osborne's Warehouse, per foot | .......... | 10.0. |
| Warwick, per foot | .......... | 11.0. |
| **YORK RIVER** | | |
| From the Cape or Lynnhaven to Yorktown | £2.0.0. | £2.0.0. |
| Back River, or Egg Island, to Yorktown | 1.0.0. | 1.0.0. |
| York to West Point, per foot | 3.0. | 3.0. |
| West Point to Holt's, or Dansie's Warehouse, per foot | 1.0. | 1.0. |
| West Point to Littlepage's, or to the highest landing ships can go on Pamunkey River, per foot | 1.6. | 1.6. |
| West Point to Shepherd's, per foot | 0.6. | 0.6. |
| West Point to Meredith's, Moore's or the highest landing on Mattapony River, per foot | 1.0. | 1.0. |
| The Cape, to any river, in Mobjack bay, the same pilotage as to Yorktown. | | |

---

*of draft.
3. 6*H*492. 4. 7*H*582.

| RAPPAHANNOCK RIVER | Rate per Act of 1755[3] | Rate per Act of 1762[4] |
|---|---|---|
| From the Cape to Urbanna | £3.0.0. | £3.0.0. |
| Urbanna to Hobb's Hole, per foot | 2.6. | 2.6. |
| Hobb's Hole, to Mulberry Island, or Naylor's Hole, per foot | 1.3. | 1.3. |
| Mulberry Island to Leeds, or Micou's, per foot | 1.3. | 1.3. |
| Leed's, or Micou's, to Port Royal, per foot | 2.0. | 2.0. |
| Port Royal to Morton's, per foot | .......... | 1.3. |

The Cape into Piankatank, to Kemp's warehouse, or any other place, the same pilotage as to Urbanna.

| POTOMAC RIVER | | |
|---|---|---|
| From Cape Henry to Smith's Point on South Potomac | £5.0.0. | £5.0.0. |
| Smith's Point to: | | |
| Coan, per foot | 1.6. | 1.8. |
| Yeocomico, per foot | 1.7. | 1.10. |
| Machodock, per foot | 1.8. | 2.0. |
| Nomini, per foot | 1.10. | 2.2. |
| Maddox, per foot | 2.0. | 2.6. |
| Upper Machodock, per foot | 2.3. | 3.0. |
| Nanjemoy, per foot | 3.6. | 4.0. |
| Boyd's Hole, per foot | 4.0. | 4.4. |
| Aquia, per foot | .......... | 4.9. |
| Quantico, per foot | 4.6. | 5.0. |
| Occoquan, per foot | .......... | 5.4. |
| Piscataway, per foot | .......... | 6.4. |
| Alexandria, per foot | 6.6. | 7.6. |
| Eastern Branch, per foot | .......... | 8.0. |

These rates are for ships, snows, and brigantines. All sloops and schooners pay two thirds of the rates for pilotage. Pilots are entitled to compensation at the rate of seven shillings six pence for every day they shall be detained by shipmasters.

## Appendix C

### FERRIAGE RATES, VIRGINIA, 1702, 1705, 1720[5]

| PLACE | Man | Man and Horse | Man | Man and Horse |
|---|---|---|---|---|
| **JAMES RIVER** | | | | |
| Varina | 6d | 1s | 3¾d | ...... |
| Bermuda Hundred | ...... | ...... | 6d | 1s |
| Westover | 1s | 1s6d | 7½d | 1s3d |
| Appomattox (Byrd's Store) | 3d | 6d | 3¾d | 7½d |
| Coggins Point | 1s | 1s6d | 3¾d | 7½d |
| Powhatan town to Swineherd's Landing | ...... | ...... | 7½d | 1s3d |
| Hog Island to Archer's Hope Creek | 1s | 2s6d | 1s3d | 2s6d |
| Upper Chippokes Creek to Martin's Brandon | 6d | 1s | 6d | 1s |
| Swann Point to Jamestown | 6d | 1s | 7½d | 1s3d |
| Crouches Creek to Jamestown | 9d | 1s6d | 1s | 2s |
| Princess Anne Port to Hog Island | ...... | ...... | 2s6d | 4s |
| Chickahominy (Freeman's Point) | 6d | 1s | 6d | 1s |
| John Goddale's to Williams or Drummond's Neck | ...... | ...... | 3¾d | 7½d |
| Cofield Point to Sleepy Hole Point (Nansemond River) | 6d | 1s | 6d | 1s |
| Hampton to Brooks Point | 3d | 6d | 3d | 6d |
| Hampton to Sewell Point | ...... | ...... | 3s | 6s |
| Norfolk to Sawyers Point | 6d | 1s | 6d | 1s |
| **YORK RIVER** | | | | |
| Brick House to Graves's | ...... | ...... | 1s | 1s10½d |
| Brick House to Gutteryes | 1s | 2s | ...... | ...... |
| Spencer's Ordinary to usual landing place | [6d] | 1s | 6d | 1s |
| Thomas Cranshaw's to usual landing place | ...... | ...... | 3d | 6d |
| Philip Williams to Robt Peasleys Point | 6d | 1s | 6d | 1s |

5. 3*H*218; 3*H*469; 4*H*45; 4*H*92; 4*H*438.

| PLACE | Man | Man and Horse | Man | Man and Horse |
|---|---|---|---|---|
| Abbot's landing over Mattaponi River | ...... | ...... | 3d | 6d |
| West Point to Brick House | 1s | 1s6d | 1s | 1s6d |
| West Point to Gutteryes | 6d | 1s | 3d | 6d |
| West Point to Graves's | ...... | ...... | 6d | 1s |
| Yorktown to Tindall's Point | 6d | 1s | 7½d | 1s3d |
| Queen Mary's Port (Williamsburg) to Claybank, Gloucester County | ...... | ...... | 2s6d | ...... |
| Bailey's over Piankatank River | 6d | 1s | 6d | 1s |
| Captain Mathew's on Scimmino Creek to Capahosic | ...... | ...... | 1s3d | 2s6d |
| Captain Walker's mill landing | ...... | ...... | 3d | 6d |
| Burfords to old Talbots | 6d | 1s | 6d | 1s |
| Piankatank Turks Ferry | 6d | 1s | 3d | 6d |

RAPPAHANNOCK RIVER

| | Man | Man and Horse | Man | Man and Horse |
|---|---|---|---|---|
| Dudley's to Chewning's (or Chowning's) Point | 1s3d | 2s6d | ...... | ...... |
| Dudley's to Wright's Plantation | 1s3d | 2s6d | ...... | ...... |
| Southing's Ferry | 6d | 1s | ...... | ...... |
| Bowlers to Suggetts Point | 1s | 2s | 1s3d | 2s6d |
| Shelton's to Mattrom Wright's | ...... | ...... | 2s | 4s |
| Brandon to Chowning's Point | ...... | ...... | 2s | 4s |
| Daniel Henry's to William Pannell's | ...... | ...... | 6d | 1s |
| Tappahannock over Rappahannock River to Webley Pavies or Rappahannock Creek | ...... | ...... | 1s3d | 2s6d |
| Henry Long's over Rappahannock River to the usual landing place | ...... | ...... | 6d | 1s |

ADDITIONAL

| | Man | Man and Horse | Man | Man and Horse |
|---|---|---|---|---|
| Col. William Fitzhugh's landing, Stafford County, over to Maryland | ...... | ...... | 2s6d | 5s |
| Port of Northampton to Port of York | ...... | ...... | 15s | 30s |
| Port of Northampton to Port of Hampton | ...... | ...... | 15s | 30s |

| | | 1720 | |
|---|---|---|---|
| PAMUNKEY RIVER | *Man* | *Horse* | *Hogshead of Tobacco* |
| Robert King's over said river | 3d | 3d | ...... |
| Sweet Hall over said river to mouth of Tank's Queen Creek | 6d | 6d | ...... |
| MATTAPONI RIVER | | | |
| Samuel Norment's over said river | 3d | 3d | 6d |
| William White's over said river | 3d | 3d | 6d |
| POTOMAC RIVER | | | |
| Col. Rice Hooe's to Cedar Point, Maryland | 2s | 2s | ...... |

The Act of 1720 extended all the provisions of the Act of 1705, encouraged ferry-keepers to provide "convenient boats, for the transportation of coaches, carts and waggons," and "other wheel-carriages," and enacted that "it shall and may be lawful for the keeper or keepers, of such ferries, to demand and take for the ferriage and transportation of such wheel-carriages, after the rates following, that is to say: For every coach, chariot, or chaise with four wheels, or waggon, the same rates as are by law established, at such ferries respectively, for the ferriage of six horses; and for every two-wheel chaise, or cart, the same rate as is by law established for the ferriage of four horses; and no more."

Between 1720 and 1776 some twenty-eight additional acts established new ferries, mostly in the Piedmont above the head of navigation of the Western Shore rivers. As the volume of wheeled vehicles grew, the rates were reduced. An act in 1734 provided that ferry-keepers might charge, "For every coach, chariot, or waggon, and for the driver thereof, the same as for the ferriage of six horses, according to the rates herein before settled at such ferries, respectively; and for every cart, or four-wheel chaise, and the driver of such four-wheel chaise, the same as for the ferriage of four horses; and for every two-wheel chaise, or chair, the same as for the ferriage of two horses, according to the said rates, and no more." This provision applied only to the new ferries established by this act, but another provision declared that "the rates heretofore settled by law, for the ferriage of wheel-carriages, at the several other public ferries in this dominion, are found to be too high," and modified them accordingly, so that "for the future, the said rates for the ferriage of wheel-carriages be lessened, and reduced to the same proportion as is herein before settled for the ferriage of such carriages, at the aforesaid three new erected ferries."

## Appendix D[1]

## IMPORTS AND EXPORTS BY GREAT BRITAIN FROM AND TO VIRGINIA AND MARYLAND, 1697-1773

| Year | Imports | | | Exports | | | Balance in favour of Imports | | | Balance in favour of Exports | | |
|---|---|---|---|---|---|---|---|---|---|---|---|---|
| | £. | s. | d. | £. | s. | d. | £. | s. | d. | £. | s. | d. |
| 1697 | 227756 | 11 | 4 | 58796 | 10 | 11 | 168960 | 0 | 5 | | | |
| 1698 | 174053 | 4 | 5 | 310135 | 0 | 0 | | | | 136081 | 15 | 7* |
| 1699 | 198115 | 16 | 10 | 205078 | 0 | 2½ | | | | 6962 | 3 | 4½ |
| 1700 | 317302 | 12 | 11¼ | 173481 | 10 | 4 | 143821 | 2 | 7¼ | | | |
| 1701 | 235738 | 18 | 4½ | 199683 | 2 | 3¼ | 36055 | 16 | 1¼ | | | |
| 1702 | 274782 | 14 | 9½ | 72391 | 13 | 11½ | 202391 | 0 | 10 | | | |
| 1703 | 144928 | 3 | 1¼ | 196713 | 9 | 8½ | | | | 51785 | 6 | 7¼ |
| 1704 | 264112 | 15 | 9¾ | 60458 | 11 | 1 | 203654 | 4 | 8¾ | | | |
| 1705 | 116768 | 17 | 8¼ | 174322 | 17 | 3¼ | | | | 57553 | 19 | 7 |
| 1706 | 149152 | 10 | 1 | 58015 | 12 | 1¾ | 91136 | 17 | 11¼ | | | |
| 1707 | 207625 | 8 | 5 | 237901 | 0 | 3¾ | | | | 30275 | 11 | 10¾ |
| 1708 | 213493 | 4 | 1¾ | 79061 | 1 | 1¼ | 134432 | 3 | 0½ | | | |
| 1709 | 261668 | 18 | 7¼ | 80268 | 15 | 9½ | 181400 | 2 | 9¾ | | | |
| 1710 | 188429 | 8 | 6 | 127639 | 0 | 5¾ | 60790 | 8 | 0¼ | | | |
| 1711 | 273181 | 4 | 1½ | 91535 | 11 | 3¾ | 181645 | 12 | 9¾ | | | |
| 1712 | 297941 | 9 | 4 | 134583 | 10 | 2¾ | 163357 | 19 | 1¼ | | | |
| 1713 | 206263 | 12 | 11½ | 76304 | 11 | 3¾ | 129959 | 1 | 7¾ | | | |
| 1714 | 280470 | 15 | 8¼ | 128873 | 10 | 10¾ | 151597 | 4 | 10 | | | |
| 1715 | 174756 | 4 | 6 | 199274 | 17 | 1 | | | | 24518 | 12 | 7 |
| 1716 | 281343 | 4 | 7 | 179599 | 17 | 7 | 101743 | 7 | 0 | | | |
| 1717 | 296884 | 2 | 7 | 215962 | 19 | 9 | 80921 | 2 | 10 | | | |
| 1718 | 316576 | 7 | 5 | 191925 | 0 | 7 | 124651 | 6 | 10 | | | |
| 1719 | 332069 | 14 | 1 | 164630 | 15 | 4 | 167438 | 18 | 9 | | | |
| 1720 | 331482 | 2 | 5 | 110717 | 17 | 10 | 220764 | 4 | 7 | | | |
| 1721 | 357812 | 0 | 11 | 127376 | 15 | 10 | 230435 | 5 | 1 | | | |
| 1722 | 283091 | 13 | 8 | 172754 | 10 | 5 | 110337 | 3 | 3 | | | |
| 1723 | 287997 | 6 | 8 | 123853 | 2 | 1 | 164144 | 4 | 7 | | | |
| 1724 | 277344 | 7 | 2 | 161894 | 6 | 2 | 115450 | 1 | 0 | | | |
| 1725 | 214730 | 2 | 2 | 195884 | 11 | 6 | 18845 | 10 | 8 | | | |
| 1726 | 324767 | 16 | 4 | 185981 | 18 | 8 | 138785 | 17 | | | | |
| 1727 | 421588 | 2 | 6 | 192965 | 6 | 10 | 228622 | 15 | 8 | | | |
| 1728 | 413089 | 9 | 9 | 171092 | 8 | 2 | 241997 | 1 | 7 | | | |
| 1729 | 386174 | 18 | 6 | 108931 | 0 | 7 | 277443 | 17 | 11 | | | |
| 1730 | 346823 | 2 | 3 | 150931 | 6 | 5 | 195891 | 15 | 10 | | | |
| 1731 | 408502 | 14 | 1 | 171278 | 1 | 5 | 237224 | 12 | 8 | | | |
| 1732 | 310799 | 11 | 6 | 148289 | 3 | 8 | 162510 | 7 | 10 | | | |

1. William Tatham, *Essay on Tobacco*, 284-85.
*Virginia only.

| Year | Imports £. s. d. | | | Exports £. s. d. | | | Balance in favour of Imports £. s. d. | | | Balance in favour of Exports £. s. d. | | |
|---|---|---|---|---|---|---|---|---|---|---|---|---|
| 1733 | 403198 | 18 | 10 | 186177 | 13 | 7 | 217021 | 5 | 3 | | | |
| 1734 | 373090 | 16 | 10 | 172086 | 8 | 9 | 201004 | 8 | 1 | | | |
| 1735 | 394995 | 12 | 5 | 220381 | 6 | 9 | 174614 | 5 | 8 | | | |
| 1736 | 380163 | 9 | 9 | 204794 | 12 | 8 | 175368 | 17 | 1 | | | |
| 1737 | 492246 | 9 | 10 | 211301 | 12 | 3 | 280944 | 17 | 7 | | | |
| 1738 | 391814 | 15 | 0 | 258860 | 8 | 0 | 132954 | 7 | 0 | | | |
| 1739 | 444654 | 10 | 2 | 217200 | 1 | 4 | 227454 | 8 | 10 | | | |
| 1740 | 341997 | 10 | 11 | 281428 | 10 | 11 | 60569 | 0 | 0 | | | |
| 1741 | 577109 | 1 | 4 | 248582 | 17 | 1 | 328526 | 4 | 3 | | | |
| 1742 | 427769 | 8 | 4 | 264186 | 2 | 5 | 163583 | 5 | 11 | | | |
| 1743 | 557821 | 0 | 10 | 328195 | 0 | 5 | 229626 | 0 | 5 | | | |
| 1744 | 402709 | 15 | 0 | 234855 | 18 | 4 | 167853 | 16 | 8 | | | |
| 1745 | 399423 | 6 | 3 | 197799 | 12 | 3 | 201623 | 14 | 0 | | | |
| 1746 | 419371 | 15 | 0 | 282545 | 8 | 7 | 136826 | 6 | 5 | | | |
| 1747 | 492619 | 6 | 7 | 200088 | 16 | 10 | 292530 | 9 | 9 | | | |
| 1748 | 494852 | 9 | 5 | 252624 | 16 | 3 | 242227 | 13 | 2 | | | |
| 1749 | 434618 | 15 | 8 | 323600 | 6 | 2 | 111018 | 9 | 6 | | | |
| 1750 | 508939 | 1 | 10 | 349419 | 18 | 3 | 159519 | 3 | 7 | | | |
| 1751 | 460085 | 16 | 9 | 347027 | 0 | 7 | 113058 | 16 | 2 | | | |
| 1752 | 569453 | 14 | 6 | 325151 | 13 | 2 | 244302 | 1 | 4 | | | |
| 1753 | 632574 | 4 | 8 | 356776 | 11 | 3 | 275797 | 13 | 5 | | | |
| 1754 | 573435 | 6 | 1 | 323513 | 19 | 2 | 249921 | 6 | 11 | | | |
| 1755 | 489668 | 17 | 10 | 285157 | 4 | 5 | 204511 | 13 | 5 | | | |
| 1756 | 337759 | 18 | 6 | 334897 | 8 | 6 | 2862 | 10 | 0 | | | |
| 1757 | 418881 | 12 | 3 | 426687 | 3 | 10 | | | | 7805 | 11 | 7 |
| 1758 | 454362 | 15 | 4 | 438471 | 17 | 8 | 15890 | 17 | 8 | | | |
| 1759 | 357228 | 7 | 4 | 459007 | 0 | 1 | | | | 101778 | 12 | 9 |
| 1760 | 504451 | 4 | 11 | 605882 | 19 | 5 | | | | 101431 | 14 | 6 |
| 1761 | 455083 | 0 | 2 | 545350 | 14 | 6 | | | | 90267 | 14 | 4 |
| 1762 | 415709 | 10 | 9 | 417599 | 15 | 6 | | | | 1890 | 4 | 9 |
| 1763 | 642294 | 2 | 9 | 555391 | 12 | 10 | 86902 | 9 | 11 | | | |
| 1764 | 559408 | 15 | 1 | 515192 | 10 | 6 | 44216 | 4 | 7 | | | |
| 1765 | 505671 | 9 | 9 | 383224 | 13 | 0 | 122446 | 16 | 9 | | | |
| 1766 | 461693 | 9 | 4 | 372548 | 16 | 1 | 89144 | 13 | 3 | | | |
| 1767 | 437926 | 15 | 0 | 437628 | 2 | 6 | 298 | 12 | 6 | | | |
| 1768 | 406048 | 13 | 11 | 475954 | 6 | 2 | | | | 69905 | 12 | 3 |
| 1769 | 361892 | 12 | 0 | 488362 | 15 | 1 | | | | 126470 | 3 | 1 |
| 1770 | 435094 | 9 | 7 | 717782 | 17 | 3 | | | | 282688 | 7 | 8 |
| 1771 | 577848 | 16 | 6 | 920326 | 3 | 8 | | | | 342477 | 7 | 8 |
| 1772 | 528404 | 10 | 6 | 793910 | 13 | 2 | | | | 265506 | 7 | 2 |
| 1773 | 589803 | 14 | 5 | 328904 | 15 | 8 | 260898 | 18 | 9 | | | |

## *Appendix E*

### A LIST OF THE FLEET FROM VIRGINIA ON THE 9TH JUNE, 1700, UNDER THE CONVOY OF H.M.S. *ESSEX PRIZE*[6]

| Ships and Commanders | Men | Guns | Of what place | Where bound |
|---|---|---|---|---|
| *Willm. & Ann* ..................19 Jno. Slap | | | Foye (Fowey) | Foye |
| *Loyallty*..................18 Hen. Brown | | 10 | Leverpool | Leverpool |
| *Jno. & Susana* ..................18 Tho. Cooper | | 04 | Bristow | Bristow |
| *Willm. & Oren* ..................10 Gafry Balye | | 02 | Do. | Do. |
| *Adventure*..................17 Tho. Oppiea | | 02 | Do. | Do. |
| *Expectation*..................12 Xpr. Scanderett | | | Do. | Do. |
| *Frind Ship* ..................11 Jno. Collewell | | | Bellfast | Leverpool |
| *Imployment* ..................16 Char. Cook | | 06 | London | London |
| *Sarah & Susana* ..................08 Nathanll. Davis | | 03 | Do. | Do. |
| *Danll. & Elizabeth* ..................11 Danll. Janurin | | | Jersey | Derttmouth |
| *Jno.* ..................09 Robt. Slowley | | 02 | Guernesey | Do. |
| *Ann & Mary* ..................22 Richd. Tibbots | | 12 | London | London |
| *Jno.* ..................20 Jno. Tanner | | 01 | Do. | Do. |
| *Geffrey* ..................32 Willm. Cooper | | 20 | Do. | Do. |
| *George*..................15 Jno. Kerne | | 08 | Plymouth | Plymouth |
| *Nicholson* ..................23 Robt. Lurty | | 16 | London | London |
| *Ann* ..................25 Benj. Dowlen | | 14 | Do. | Do. |

6. *C.O.* 5: 1311: no. 10 (iii), p. 400. This is one of the few complete, contemporary lists of ships in a convoy that the author has found.

491

| Ships and Commanders | Men | Guns | Of what place | Where bound |
|---|---|---|---|---|
| *Endian King* ............28 <br> Edwd. Weliker | 28 | o6 | Virginia | London |
| *Elizabeth & Mary* ..........20 <br> Jno. Burford | 20 | 10 | London | London |
| *Unety* ............................16 <br> Robt. Collebert | 16 | 10 | Lime | Lime |
| *Owners Adventure* ........18 <br> Jam. Michell | 18 | ...... | London | London |
| *Palmtree* ............................ 6 <br> Willm. Lewis | 6 | ...... | Plymouth | Plymouth |
| *America* ............................18 <br> Tho. Graves | 18 | o8 | London | London |
| *Dublin Mercht.* ................14 <br> Robt. Ross | 14 | 04 | Dublen | Dublen |
| *Reward* ............................ 7 <br> Jno. Pearce | 7 | ...... | London | London |
| *Lamb*............................ 9 <br> Richd. Murfey | 9 | ...... | Dublen | Leverpool |
| *Nicholas* ............................12 <br> Jno. Perkins | 12 | ...... | London | London |
| *Jno. Bablice* ............................11 <br> Nich. French | 11 | ...... | Leverpool | Leverpool |
| *Samll.* ............................07 <br> Tho. Canterell | 07 | o1 | Bedeford | Bedeford |
| *Loyallty* ............................o6 <br> Tho. Garrett | o6 | ...... | Ba[rn]stable | Ba[rn]stable |
| *Tho. & Ann* ............................09 <br> Jam. Renkins | 09 | 02 | London | London |
| *Industry* ............................12 <br> Tho. Latrop | 12 | ...... | Do. | Do. |
| *Thomas*............................12 <br> Geo. Gipson | 12 | ...... | Whitehaven | Whitehaven |
| *Harwich Prize* ............................10 <br> Jam. Jackson | 10 | ...... | Virginia | London |
| *Susana*............................16 <br> Jno. Coker | 16 | 10 | London | London |
| *Rogers* ............................10 <br> Jno. Sanders | 10 | 05 | Plymouth | Plymouth |
| *Bristow* ............................20 <br> Beling hamwest | 20 | 16 | London | London |
| *Hopewell*............................10 <br> Jam. White | 10 | 02 | Dublen | Buensores [Buenos Aires?] |

# Appendices

| Ships and Commanders | Men | Guns | Of what place | Where bound |
|---|---|---|---|---|
| *Jeane* | 11 | ...... | Do. | Do. |
| Will. Thornton | | | | |
| *Virginia Marchant* | 15 | 10 | Leverpool | Leverpool |
| Jam. Rotheram | | | | |
| *Jno.* | 14 | 01 | Bedeford | Bedeford |
| Tho. Leache | | | | |
| *Bird* | 15 | 08 | London | London |
| Jos. Peacock | | | | |
| *Hanapolis* | 10 | 02 | Bedeford | Bedeford |
| Tho. Marshall | | | | |
| *Hapy Success* | 05 | ...... | Do. | Do. |
| Anto. Pearce | | | | |
| *James* | 11 | ...... | Plymouth | Plymouth |
| Danll. Williams | | | | |
| *Abra.* | 21 | 14 | London | London |
| Josua Cook | | | | |
| *Comberland* | 23 | 04 | Whitehaven | Whitehaven |
| George Galle | | | | |
| *James & Elizabeth* | 20 | 16 | London | London |
| Tin Cook | | | | |
| *Speedwell* | 09 | ...... | Hull | Hull |
| Gerr. Bently | | | | |
| *Deptfford* | 16 | 08 | London | London |
| Richd. Sprackling | | | | |
| *Gloster* | 23 | 12 | Do. | Do. |
| Edwd. Elles | | | | |
| *Josia* | 17 | 02 | Do. | Do. |
| John Sowdon | | | | |
| *London Arms* | 20 | 06 | Do. | Do. |
| John Gallon | | | | |
| *Amyty* | 10 | ...... | Whitehaven | Whitehaven |
| John Ribton | | | | |
| *Nytengalle* | 09 | ...... | Do. | Do. |
| Abenezor Roberson | | | | |
| *Society* | 22 | 16 | London | London |
| Richd. Tregian | | | | |
| *Phoenix* | 30 | ...... | Bristoll | Bristoll |
| Wm. Jones | | | | |

Dated on board his Majtis. Ship *Essex Prize* this 9th. of June 1700.

## *Appendix F*
### SAYLING INSTRUCTIONS FOR THE BETTER KEEPING COMPANY WITH H.M.S. *ESSEX PRIZE*[1]

#### SIGNALLS BY DAY

1. When I would have the Fleet Unmore I will Loose my Maintops in the Top and Fire one Gun.
2. When I would have the Fleet to Weigh I will haule home my Maintops<sup>ll</sup> Sheets & Fire One Gun.
3. When I would have the Fleet to anch<sup>r</sup> I will hoist a white Ensigne in the mizon Shrouds and Fire One Gun.
4. When to more I will hoist My mizon Tops<sup>ll</sup> w<sup>th</sup> the Clulines hauled up and Fire One Gun.
5. Whoever Designes to Speak w<sup>th</sup> me must spread an English Ensigne from the head of his Main or Foretopm<sup>t</sup> Shrouds downwards Lowering his Main Or Foretops<sup>ll</sup> and Fire One Gun.
6. If any Should Loose Company & meet again in the Day Those to windward Shall Lower down their Tops<sup>ll</sup>s & those to Leeward Shall haule up their Courses.
7. If any Spring a Leak or any other Disaster hapens whereby y<sup>o</sup> are Disabled of Keeping Company y<sup>o</sup> are to make a Waft of y<sup>r</sup> Jack & Ensigne And haule up y<sup>r</sup> Low Sailes and Fire One Gun.
8. When I would speak w<sup>th</sup> all the Mast<sup>rs</sup> in the Fleet I will Spread an English Ensigne in the Mizon Shrouds & Fire one Gun.
9. He that First Discover Land shall hoist up his Ensigne.
10. When I would have all the Ships in the Fleet to bear Und<sup>r</sup> my Starn I will hoist a Pendent on Mizon Peak and Fire one Gun.
11. In the Evening all the Whatermost Ships are to bear up into My Weak the better to keep the Fleet togather.

#### SIGNALLS BY NIGHT

12. When I would have the fleet to unmore in the Night I will hang 3 Lights one over the other in the Maintopm<sup>t</sup> shrouds & Fire one Gun.
13. If to Weigh I will hang One Light on the Maintopm<sup>t</sup> shrouds & Fire one Gun.
14. If to Anch<sup>r</sup> I will Fire two Guns att a Small Space one from the other.

---

1. *C.O.* 5: 1311: no. 10 (iv), p. 403.

15. If to more I will Put a Light att Each Topm$^t$ head & Fire one Gun.

16. If I would have the Fleet to Make Saile after Lyeing by I will Put out 3 Lights one over the other in the Main shrouds & Fire two Guns.

17. When I would have the fleet To Tack I will hoist two Lights on the Ensigne Staf one over the other Above the Constant Light on the poop & fire one gun.

18. When I would have the fleet in blowing Whather to Ly by I will show Four Lights of Equall height & Fire two Guns.

19. He that Discover Land or Shoal watter Shall Put abroad two Lights on the Mizon Shrouds & bear away or Tack From it & Fire One Gun.

20. If any Spring A Leak or Any Other Disaster hapens whereby y$^o$ are Disabled of Keeping Company y$^o$ are to Fire Guns & Show Lights as many As y$^o$ Think Fitt & in the most Convenient Places to be Seen.

21. If any should Loose Company And meet Again in the Night he that first hales Shall ask w$^t$ Ships that & he that is haled Shall answer King William the other shall reply Great britain.

22. If it Blowes & be a very Darck Night in Case of Tacking Each Ship Is to Put out a Light to the end No Other May board him while he is goeing About.

23. If any should Meet Any Strange Ships in the Night y$^o$ are to Make Fals Fires and indeavour to Speak w$^{th}$ me.

24. That None Shall Presume to Goe a head to windward of the Light without orders.

### SIGNALLS IN A FOGG

25. If it Growes Thick & Foggy Whather I will Continue the Same Saile Sett that I had before it Grew foggy, & will Fire one Gun Every hour w$^{ch}$ is to be Answered by the fleet w$^{th}$ fireing Musquetts & ringing of bells & beating of drums.

26. If I would have All the Fleet to Tack I will Fire Four Guns then the Leeward Most & Sternmost Ships are to Tack First, & after they are about to goe w$^{th}$ the Same Saile they Tackt w$^{th}$, & Not to Ly by Expecting me to Com a head w$^{ch}$ is to Avoid the dang$^r$ of running aboard One Another.

27. If I Ly by I will Fire Three Guns.

28. If I Make Saile After Lyeing by I will Fire Five Guns.

29. If to Anch$^r$ I will Fire two Guns.

30. If to Weigh I will Fire Six Guns.

495

31. If any one Discover Any Dang[r] w[ch] he Can Avoyd by Tacking & Standing From it, he is to Make the Signall as for Tacking in a Fog, but if y[o] should Chance to Strick & Stick Fast y[o] are to Fire Gun after Gun tell y[o] beleve the Fleet have Avoyded the Dang[r] Either by Tacking bearing up or Anchoring.

Virginia

Dated on board his Maj[tes] Ship *Essex Prize* in James river
This 27th of May 1700

## *Appendix H*

### A LINE OF BATTLE[1]

To Lead w[th] the Starboard Tack Aboard

When I would Speak w[th] any Perticu[ll] Command[r] in the Line off battle I will put a w[te] pendent, as against their names, when w[th] all, a Pendent at the Mizon Peak & Fire A gun.

| Vice | Men | Guns | |
|---|---|---|---|
| Nicholson | 23 | 16 | Maintopmast head |
| Bristow | 20 | 16 | Starboard } Maine y[d] arme |
| Virginia Marchant | 15 | 10 | Larboard } |
| America | 18 | 08 | Starboard } Fore y[d] arme |
| Endian King | 28 | 06 | Larboard } |
| Deptford | 16 | 08 | Starboard } Sprits[ll] y[d] arme |
| Gloster | 23 | 12 | Larboard } |

| Cheiffe | | | |
|---|---|---|---|
| London Armes | 20 | 06 | Starboard } Foretops[ll] y[d] arme |
| Elizabeth & Mary | 20 | 10 | Larboard } |
| Anne & Mary | 22 | 12 | Mizon Topmast head |
| Essex Prize | 60 | 16 | |
| Ann | 25 | 14 | Starboard } Maintops[ll] y[d] arme |
| Susana | 16 | 10 | Larboard } |
| Abraham | 21 | 14 | Starboard Sprits[ll] tops[ll] y[d] arme |
| Society | 22 | 16 | Foretopmast Shrouds |

---

1. *C.O.* 5: 1311, no. 10 (v), 407.

Reare

| | | |
|---|---|---|
| James & Elizabeth ......20 | 16 | Larboard Sprits^ll Tops^ll y^d arme |
| Imployment ...............16 | 06 | Starboard ⎰ |
| George.......................15 | 08 | Larboard ⎱ Mizontops^ll y^d arme |
| Bird ........................15 | 08 | Starboard ⎰ |
| Unyty ......................16 | 10 | Larboard ⎱ Cros Jack y^d arme |
| Jeffrys ....................23 | 20 | Foretopmast head |

To Lead w^th the Larboard Tack aboard

All other ships that are Not in the Line Are To Keep to windward or Leeward of the Fleet as Shall find occasion.

Virginia [James River, June 6, 1700].

## *Appendix I*
### FIGHTING INSTRUCTION[1]

1. When I would have the Fleet to draw into a Line of battle one Ship a Head off a Nother I will hoist a Union Flag att the mizon Peak & Fire a Gun.

2. When I would have the Fleet draw into a Line of battle, a Brest one of a Nother, I will hoist an Union Flag, & Pendent at the Mizon Peak & Fire a Gun.

3. When I would have the Fleet to bear down into my weak, or graine,[2] I will hoist a white Flag at the Mizon Peak.

4. When I would have the Fleet to gaine the wind of the Enemies, I will Spread a white Flag att the Spritsaile topm^t head.

5. When I would have the Van to Tack First, I will Put abroad a w^te Flag att the Foretopm^t head, & Fire One Gun If the reare to Tack First, a w^te Flag att the Mizon topm^t head and Fire a Gun.

6. When I would have the Fleet Ly Their head Sailes to the Mast, I will hoist a w^te Flag att the Maintopm^t head & Fire a Gun then the reare to brace too First.

7. When I would have the Fleet to Fill Their head Sails, I will hoist an Ensigne att the Maintopm^t head & Fire a Gun then the van to Fill First.

---

1. *C.O.* 5: 1311, no. 10 (vi), p. 409.

2. For a discussion of the expression "wake or grain," meaning dead astern or dead ahead, *cf.* L. G. Carr Laughton, "Wake or Grain," *The Mariner's Mirror*, 26, (1940), 339-44.

8. When I would have the Van of the fleet, when in a Line of Battle to hoist, Lower, Sett or haule up any of his Sails, I will hoist a red Ensigne, att the Foretopm$^t$ head & Fireing a Gun use the Said Saile.

9. If I see the Enemies fleet Standing towards me, & I have the w$^d$ [windward] of them the van off the fleet is, to make Saile tell they have the Length of the Enemies reare, & our Reare to Come a brest of the Enemies Van, then he that is in the reare of our Fleet is to Tack First, & Every Ship one after Anoth$^r$, as Fast as they Can, throughout the Line, that may Ingage the Same Tack with the Enemie, but if the Enemies ships Tack in the Reare, our Fleet is to doe the Same with an Equall Nomb$^r$ of Ships.

10. If I have the wind of the Enemies & in a Line, the Van of our Fleet is to Stear with the Van of the Enemies, & to Ingage.

11. If any Ship be in Distress & make the Signall, w$^{ch}$ is a waft w$^{th}$ the Jack or Ensigne, the Next Ship to them is Strictly required to releive them.

12. In Case Any Ship in the Fleet Should be Forsed out of the Line to repaire Damages received in Battle the Next Ship to Cloze up the Line.

Virginia  Dated on board his Maj$^{tes}$ Ship *Essex Prize* in James river this 5th off June 1700.

498

# Index

# Index

# Index

# Index

CPSIA information can be obtained at www.ICGtesting.com
Printed in the USA
BVOW03s1053100514

352917BV00001B/1/A